Stockholm Arbitration Yearbook 2021

Stockholm Arbitration Yearbook

VOLUME 3

Editors

Axel Calissendorff is a partner in and founder of the law firm Calissendorff Advokatbyrå. Prior to that he was a partner in major Swedish law firms. He was the Solicitor to H.M. the King of Sweden and former President of the Swedish Bar Association. His focus is on Corporate and Public M&A. He often sits as an arbitrator. He has authored numerous articles.

Patrik Schöldström is a Judge of Appeal of the Svea Court of Appeal. He is also an Associate Professor of the Faculty of Law of Stockholm University. He has a doctorate in arbitration law and is a former member of the Swedish Bar. He regularly writes articles and case notes. He has extensive experience as an arbitrator – chairman, sole arbitrator, co-arbitrator and emergency arbitrator – in international and domestic disputes, ad hoc and institutional.

Introduction

The Yearbook is published under the auspices of the Stockholm Centre for Commercial Law, a part of the Stockholm University Faculty of Law. It is designed to meet the information needs of arbitration practitioners and parties from all over the world. The first volume was published in 2019.

Objective

The Yearbook is designed to meet the information needs of arbitration practitioners and parties from all over the world. It provides authoritative articles, some of them with a Swedish angle, that address current matters of global concern in arbitration. Each volume includes one or more chapters accounting for developments in Swedish case law and legislation since the previous volume.

Frequency

The publication is annual.

The titles published in this series are listed at the end of this volume.

Stockholm Arbitration Yearbook 2021

Edited by

Axel Calissendorff
Patrik Schöldström

Assistant Editor

Bruno Gustafsson

Editorial Committee

Christer Danielsson
James Hope
Kristin Campbell-Wilson
Niklas Berntorp

Stockholm Centre for Commercial Law
Faculty of Law

Stockholm University

Wolters Kluwer

Published by:
Kluwer Law International B.V.
PO Box 316
2400 AH Alphen aan den Rijn
The Netherlands
E-mail: international-sales@wolterskluwer.com
Website: lrus.wolterskluwer.com

Sold and distributed by:
Wolters Kluwer Legal & Regulatory U.S.
7201 McKinney Circle
Frederick, MD 21704
United States of America
E-mail: customer.service@wolterskluwer.com

ISBN 978-94-035-3524-1

e-Book: ISBN 978-94-035-3530-2
web-PDF: ISBN 978-94-035-3532-6

Editors

Axel Calissendorff is Partner in and founder of Calissendorff Advokatbyrå. Prior to that, he was at major law firms, Mannheimer Swartling (1981-2005) (Executive Partner 2003 and 2004) and Roschier (2005-2013), Senior Partner 2009-2012. He was the Solicitor to H.M. the King of Sweden (2009-2021) and President of the Swedish Bar Association (2001-2004). His focus is on corporate and M&A. He is a frequently appointed arbitrator. He has authored numerous articles.

Patrik Schöldström is a Judge of Appeal of the Svea Court of Appeal, and an Associate Professor of the Faculty of Law of Stockholm University. He has a doctorate in arbitration law and is a former member of the Swedish Bar. He regularly writes articles and case notes. He also sits as an arbitrator, and has participated in a number of domestic and international arbitrations (ad hoc and institutional) as chair of arbitral tribunal, sole arbitrator, emergency arbitrator, wing arbitrator, and counsel.

Contributors

Georges Affaki is Partner at AFFAKI, Professor of Law at the University of Paris, international arbitrator.

Christian Aschauer is Professor of Austrian Arbitration Law and International Arbitration at the University of Graz; Independent Arbitrator and Advocate based in Vienna; Member of the Council of the Milan Chamber of Arbitration.

Giuditta Cordero-Moss is Professor, University of Oslo.

Christer Danielsson is Advokat, Danielsson & Nyberg Advokatbyrå in Stockholm; Former President of the Swedish Bar Association (2017-2021); and Former President of the Swedish Arbitration Association.

James Hope is Partner and Head of Litigation and Arbitration at Advokatfirman Vinge, Stockholm; Advokat (Sweden) and Solicitor-Advocate (England & Wales).

Lisa Johansson is Senior Associate at Advokatfirman Vinge's dispute resolution practice group, Stockholm; Jur. Kand. (Sweden).

Anke Meier is Partner in the Frankfurt office of Noerr, co-heads the firm-wide litigation, arbitration & ADR practice. She is admitted to practise as an attorney in Germany and New York and has practised in the U.S., the Netherlands and Germany. She has broad experience in commercial and investment arbitration with a particular focus on disputes in the energy sector. Her practice comprises primarily large and complex international cases with a regional focus on the U.S.

Barbara Maucher, LLM (Tulane), FCIArb, is Counsel at Noerr Partnerschaftsgesellschaft mbB and admitted to practise as an attorney in Germany, New York and Washington, D.C. Barbara has practised in the US and Germany. She has broad experience in commercial and investment arbitration with a particular focus on disputes in the energy sector.

Fredrik Norburg is Swedish attorney and a founding partner of arbitration and litigation law firm Norburg & Scherp. He acts as counsel and arbitrator in Swedish and international arbitration, and as counsel in commercial litigation before Swedish courts of all types and instances. Fredrik Norburg's experience includes disputes concerning, e.g., construction, M&A, competition, banking and finance, professional liability, intellectual property, energy, insolvency, IT, and corporate investigations.

Viktor Saavola is Associate at Hannes Snellman's Dispute Resolution group in Helsinki, Finland.

Mika Savola is Finnish independent arbitrator based in Herzliya, Israel and specializes in resolving international commercial and investment disputes.

Matthias Scherer is Partner, LALIVE; ICSID Panel of Arbitrators; Council Member of the ICC Institute of World Business Law; Editor of the *ASA Bulletin*.

Christopher Spreigl is Associate at Roschier Attorneys Ltd. and specializes in dispute resolution.

Edward Jansson Stiernblad is Senior Managing Associate at Advokatfirman Vinge, Stockholm; Advokat (Sweden). He specializes in commercial arbitration and litigation and has acted as counsel in a large number of Swedish and international proceedings.

Anna-Maria Tamminen is Partner in Hannes Snellman's dispute resolution group working out of both Helsinki and Stockholm. Anna-Maria is specialized in international arbitration and acts as both counsel and arbitrator in both national and international cases.

Anna Tujakowska, LLM MIDS, is Senior Counsel at Sołtysiński Kawecki & Szlęzak, Poland.

Daniel Waerme is Partner at Gernandt & Danielsson Advokatbyrå KB in Stockholm and specializes in arbitration, commercial litigation, contentious regulatory matters, and other forms of dispute resolution. He is a board member of Young Arbitrators Sweden and regularly lectures on civil procedure law and arbitration law.

Louise Wendleby is a law clerk at Attunda District Court. She has previously worked for Gernandt & Danielsson Advokatbyrå KB as an associate in the firm's dispute resolution and financial regulation practice groups.

Rikard Wikström-Hermansen is Partner at Roschier Attorneys Ltd. He specializes in dispute resolution and has many years of experience with arbitration.

Roman Zykov is Secretary General of the Russian Arbitration Association and Managing Partner of the dispute resolution law firm Mansors in Moscow.

Summary of Contents

Table of Contents

Preface

Welcome to the third edition of the Stockholm Arbitration Yearbook!

You will find articles on arbitration law in general and Swedish arbitration law in particular. Some contributions are by senior and well-known authors, others by more junior ones.

We are happy to receive – at any time of the year – proposals for future contributions in the form of a short abstract.

Axel Calissendorff
Patrik Schöldström

CHAPTER 1

Swedish Arbitration-Related Case Law 2020-2021

Christer Danielsson

This chapter accounts for court cases relevant to arbitration law from Swedish courts for the period 1 May 2020-30 April 2021. The aim is to highlight cases that can be assumed to be of interest to a non-Swedish reader.

§1.01 INTRODUCTION

This chapter will account for court cases relevant to arbitration law from Swedish appellate courts for the period 1 May 2020-30 April 2021.[1] It does not purport to be exhaustive; the aim is to highlight cases that can be assumed to be of interest to a non-Swedish reader.

§1.02 BACKGROUND

The Swedish Arbitration Act of 1999[2] (the Act) applies to all arbitration proceedings seated in Sweden, whether the parties have any connection to Sweden or not.[3] The Act also sets out the requirements for foreign arbitral awards to be recognized and enforced in Sweden.[4]

Sweden has a three-tier court system: district courts, six regional appellate courts and the Supreme Court. However, district courts are only rarely involved in arbitration

1. The Supreme Court has not decided any arbitration-related cases in the period covered herein.
2. Lagen (1999:116) om skiljeförfarande.
3. The Act, section 46.
4. The Act, sections 52 et seq.

cases since the appellate courts are *Court of First Instance* for invalidity and set aside cases as well as for enforcement cases.

A Swedish arbitral award can be *declared invalid* if it determines an issue which under Swedish law cannot be decided by arbitrators, or if the award, or the manner in which it came about, is clearly incompatible with the basic principles of the Swedish legal system, i.e., *ordre public*.[5]

An arbitral award can be *set aside* at the request of a party, *inter alia*, when the arbitrators have exceeded their mandate and when, without fault of the party, an irregularity has occurred in the course of the proceedings which probably influenced the outcome of the case.[6]

An action to invalidate or set aside an arbitration award shall be considered by the Court of Appeal within whose district the arbitral proceedings were seated.[7] The Court of Appeal's permission is required in order to appeal its judgment.[8] Such leave to appeal is denied in the large majority of cases. For the case to be tried by the Supreme Court, leave is also required from that court.[9]

Historically, invalidity and set aside actions have very rarely been successful. A statistical survey for the period 1 January 2004-31 May 2014 shows that seven arbitral awards were set aside pursuant to section 34 of the Act while one award was declared invalid pursuant to section 33 of the Act, equal to 6% of all decided cases.[10]

In the period covered by this chapter, no award was declared invalid or set aside. Moreover, the number of such cases decided by the appellate courts were fewer than in recent years.

§1.03 *REPUBLIC OF POLAND V. PL HOLDINGS S.A.R.L.*

[A] Introduction

As reported in the 2019 and 2020 Stockholm Arbitration Yearbook,[11] the Svea Court of Appeal in February 2019 rendered a judgment in a case similar to *Achmea*,[12] the

5. The Act, section 33. In addition, under this provision an award is invalid if it does not fulfil the Act's requirements with regard to written form and signature.
6. The Act, section 34(1), items 3 and 7. Section 34 provides for five other grounds for setting aside an arbitral award but the two mentioned are those most frequently invoked in set aside proceedings.
7. The Act, section 43(1). The large majority of invalidity and set aside proceedings are brought before the Svea Court of Appeal. The reason for this is that most Swedish arbitrations are seated in Stockholm.
8. The Act, section 43(2), which provides that leave to appeal shall be granted 'where it is of importance, as a matter of precedent, that the appeal be considered by the Supreme Court'.
9. The Act, section 43(2). Such requirement was introduced in an amendment to the Act which entered into force on 1 March 2019.
10. Översyn av lagen om skiljeförfarande ('Review of the arbitration act'), SOU 2015:37, p. 79.
11. Pages 9 et seq. in the 2019 edition and pp. 2 et seq. in the 2020 edition.
12. Judgment by the European Court of Justice of 6 March 2018, *Slovak Republic v. Achmea BV*, Case No. C-284/16.

Republic of Poland v. PL Holdings S.a.r.l. (PL Holdings).[13] The Court of Appeal's judgment was appealed to the Supreme Court. The Supreme Court granted leave. On 4 February 2020, the Supreme Court decided to request a preliminary ruling from the Court of Justice of the European Union (CJEU). On 22 April 2021, Advocate General Kokott issued her opinion. The CJEU had not yet rendered its preliminary ruling when this article was written. However, since the case is of significant interest, the background of the case and the opinion of the Advocate General will be presented below as a part of this article.

[B] Facts

In 1987, Poland, on the one hand, and Luxembourg and Belgium, on the other hand, entered into an investment treaty (the Investment Treaty) with a dispute resolution clause (section 9) pursuant to which investors in any of the states party to the treaty have the right to initiate arbitration proceedings in accordance with three different options, one of which is the Arbitration Rules of the Stockholm Chamber of Commerce (the SCC Rules). Thus, the Investment Treaty is an intra-EU Bilateral Investment Treaty or BIT for short.

PL Holdings, a company registered in Luxemburg, initiated arbitration proceedings against Poland in accordance with the SCC Rules with Stockholm as the seat of arbitration. This was prior to the CJEU's judgment in *Achmea*. PL Holdings submitted that Poland had violated its obligations under the Investment Treaty by expropriating assets of PL Holding in Poland. PL Holdings claimed damages from Poland.

In June 2017, the arbitration tribunal rendered a partial arbitral award in which it found that Poland had violated its obligations under the Investment Treaty by expropriating PL Holdings' shareholding in a bank and that PL Holdings was entitled to damages. In the final award in September 2017, the arbitration tribunal ordered Poland to pay substantial damages (app. EUR 150 million).

[C] The Judgment by the Court of Appeal

Poland filed actions with the Svea Court of Appeal with regard to both the partial award and the final award. Poland requested that the awards be declared invalid (section 33 of the Act) or be set aside (section 34 of the Act) in light of *Achmea*. With regard to the set aside claim, Poland submitted that the awards should be set aside since they were not based on a valid arbitration agreement.

The Court of Appeal made the following statement with regard to the meaning of *Achmea*:

13. Judgment by the Svea Court of Appeal dated 22 February 2019 in Case Nos T 8538-17 and T 12033-7.

> The conclusion from the Achmea ruling is therefore that articles 267 and 344 TFEU[14] would not as such preclude Poland and PL Holdings from entering into an arbitration agreement and participating in arbitral proceedings regarding an investment-related dispute. What the TFEU precludes is that Member States conclude agreements with each other meaning that one Member State is obligated to accept subsequent arbitral proceeding with an investor and that the Member States thereby establish a system where they have excluded disputes from the possibility of requesting a preliminary ruling, even though the disputes may involve interpretation and application of EU law. Since the TFEU thus does not preclude arbitration agreements between a Member State and an investor in a particular case, a Member State is, based on party autonomy, free – even though the Member State is not bound by a standing offer as such as that in article 8 of the Achmea case or article 9 in this case – to enter into an arbitration agreement with an investor regarding the same dispute at a later stage, e.g. when the investor has initiated arbitral proceedings. An arbitration agreement and arbitral proceedings between, on the one hand, an investor from a Member State and, on the other hand, a Member State, is therefore as such not in violation of the TFEU.[15]

The Court of Appeal found that the awards should not be declared invalid pursuant to section 33 of the Act.

With regard to setting aside of the awards pursuant to section 34 of the Act, PL Holdings *inter alia* argued that Poland was precluded from invoking that the arbitral awards were not covered by a valid arbitration agreement since Poland had participated in the arbitral proceedings without raising this objection. Under the applicable rules for the proceedings, PL Holdings argued, Poland was obligated to raise an objection concerning the alleged invalidity of the arbitration agreement no later than in its statement of defence, which Poland had not done.

The Court of Appeal found that pursuant to the applicable SCC Rules the objection should have been made no later than in the statement of defence. Since it was not made until in the statement of rejoinder, the court concluded, with reference to section 34(2) of the Act, that Poland must be considered to have waived its right to raise the objection.

[D] The Supreme Court's Request for Preliminary Ruling

The judgment was appealed to the Supreme Court which, as noted, requested a preliminary ruling from the CJEU. In its decision, the Supreme Court stated the following under the heading 'The need for a preliminary ruling':[16]

> The question is what the implications of the principles elaborated by the CJEU in *Achmea* have for the outcome of the case before the Supreme Court.
>
> It is clear that the provision regarding dispute resolution in the investment agreement of relevance in this case before the Supreme Court is invalid. Thus, a possible conclusion is that the standing offer to initiate arbitration proceedings, which the state can be said to have extended to an investor through the dispute

14. The Treaty on the Functioning of the European Union.
15. Unofficial translation.
16. Decision by the Supreme Court 21 February 2020 in Case No. 1568-19 (unofficial translation).

resolution provision, is also invalid, considering that the offer is closely linked to the investment agreement.

In the case before the Supreme Court, it has also been argued that the situation is different in this case since it is the request for arbitration that constitutes an offer. The state would then, as a result of its freely expressed wishes, expressly or tacitly, be able to accept the jurisdiction of the arbitral tribunal, in accordance with the principles explained by the CJEU with regard to commercial arbitration.

The Supreme Courts does not consider it to be clear, or clarified, how EU law shall be interpreted with regard to the issues that arise in this case. Therefore, there are reasons for requesting a preliminary ruling from the CJEU in order to avoid the risk of an incorrect interpretation of EU law.

The Supreme Court formulated the question to the CJEU as follows:

Do Articles 267 and 344 TFEU, as interpreted in *Achmea*, mean that an arbitration agreement is invalid if it has been entered into by a member state and an investor – when there is an arbitration clause in an investment treaty which is invalid because the treaty was entered into by two member states – when the member State, after the investor having requested arbitration, as a result of the state's free will refrains from objecting to jurisdiction?

[E] Opinion by Advocate General Kokott

On 22 April 2021, Advocate General Kokott issued her opinion.[17] She proposed the following answer to the questions put by the Supreme Court:

Individual arbitration agreements between Member States and investors from other Member States concerning the sovereign application of EU law are compatible with the duty of sincere cooperation under Article 4(3) TFEU and the autonomy of EU law under Articles 267 and 344 TFEU only if courts of the Member States can comprehensively review the arbitration award for its compatibility with EU law, if necessary after requesting a preliminary ruling under Article 267 TFEU. Such arbitration agreements must furthermore be compatible with the principle of equal treatment under Article 20 of the Charter of Fundamental Rights of the European Union.

Set out below is a summary of the Advocate General's opinion.

In *Achmea*, the CJEU ruled that arbitration clauses in favour of investors in investment treaties between Member States are incompatible with Articles 267 and 344 TFEU and must therefore be disapplied. What are the consequences, however, she asked, if a Member State does not invoke the invalidity of the arbitration clause before the award is made? A Swedish court concluded from this, in the context of examining the validity of an arbitration award, that the Member State concerned had entered into an arbitration agreement for the dispute in question on an ad hoc basis by entering an appearance in the arbitration proceedings without raising an objection. However, the

17. CJEU case C-109/20.

Swedish Supreme Court has doubts as to whether this approach is compatible with *Achmea* and has therefore referred the matter to the CJEU.

In the case at hand, Poland brought an action against PL Holdings before the Swedish courts in which it sought to have both the separate and final award annulled. The Svea Court of Appeal dismissed Poland's action. According to the court, although the arbitration clause of the investment treaty is invalid in accordance with *Achmea*, that invalidity does not prevent a Member State and an investor from concluding an arbitration agreement in respect of the same dispute at a later stage. In such a case, that arbitration agreement is one which is based on the common intention of the parties and concluded in accordance with the same principles as commercial arbitration proceedings. However, the judgment in *Achmea* did not specifically preclude the permissibility of such agreements. In the present case, the agreement came about because Poland appeared in the proceedings without raising the objection that the arbitration clause was invalid in due time.

The Swedish Supreme Court wishes to ascertain whether the findings in *Achmea* also preclude an individual arbitration agreement.

Advocate General Kokott noted that *Achmea* concerned a general provision that permitted recourse to an arbitration tribunal in certain cases. In contrast, the question to be decided in the present case is whether Articles 267 and 344 TFEU preclude an individual arbitration agreement between a Member State and an investor.

In *Achmea*, the CJEU took objection to the agreement between two Member States that was the subject matter of those proceedings on the ground that, by virtue of that agreement, they agreed to remove from the system of judicial remedies, which the second subparagraph of Article 19(1) Treaty on European Union (TEU) requires them to establish in the fields covered by European Union (EU) law, disputes which may concern the application or interpretation of EU law. In so far as arbitration tribunals are not entitled to make a reference, they are not part of that system.

An individual arbitration agreement between a Member State and an investor can remove disputes concerning the application and interpretation of EU law from the EU judicial system in the same way as a general investment treaty between Member States that provides for the settlement of disputes between a Member State and an investor by way of arbitration. Whether an individual case is removed from the judicial system depends on the specific dispute and not on whether the dispute is brought before an arbitration tribunal under a general investment treaty between Member States or under an individual arbitration agreement between an investor and a Member State.

In the present case, the parties, according to their own submissions, are in dispute as to the application of banking supervision rules that arise from EU law, in particular from Article 21(2) of Directive 2006/48/EC of the European Parliament and of the Council of 14 June 2006 relating to the taking up and pursuit of the business of credit institutions. PL Holdings also invokes freedom of establishment. Although the Swedish courts would have to examine whether that plausible argument is well founded, it appears, at least according thereto, that the arbitration agreement did in fact concern an EU law dispute.

The arbitration award does not apply the provisions of EU law on banking supervision, but is based on the rules of the Investment Treaty. Nevertheless, it proceeds on the basis of standards which, in the view taken by the arbitration tribunal, Poland should have observed when exercising the banking supervision provided for under EU law, for example, with regard to proportionality or effective legal protection. While the arbitration tribunal assumes that those standards are in line with EU law, it does not comprehensively examine this question.

According to *Achmea*, the removal of such a dispute from the EU judicial system by means of an individual arbitration agreement between a Member State and an investor from another Member State would in fact be incompatible with Articles 267 and 344 TFEU. At the very least, it would constitute a circumvention of that judgment.

Advocate General Kokott went on to note that the arbitration tribunal in these proceedings is not part of the EU judicial system and, in particular, cannot refer doubts concerning EU law to the CJEU.

It is true, she noted, that the CJEU regularly derives a threat to the autonomy of EU law from situations in which a body outside the EU system interprets provisions of EU law. That risk would be low if the arbitration tribunal – as appears to be the case here – primarily applies the provisions of an investment protection agreement of Member States under international law. Moreover, despite the fundamental importance of the principle of proportionality in EU law, the arbitration tribunal also applied that principle not as part of EU law but because it also applies in other legal systems and in particular in the area of investment protection under international law.

Nevertheless, under the Investment Treaty, the arbitration tribunal was required to consider EU law as being, in principle, part of domestic law. In particular, however, there is a risk that the arbitration tribunal will take decisions that will *ultimately* result in an infringement of EU law.

Accordingly, in the present case, the Advocate General found, it cannot be ruled out that the arbitration tribunal misconceived the obligations of the Polish banking supervisory authority under the relevant directive. Moreover, there would be a risk that not only the Polish banking supervisory authority but also bodies of other Member States would take the decision of an arbitration tribunal into account in the future application of that EU legislation, especially if the CJEU has not yet taken a position on that question. This is because the arbitration award could set a precedent and lead to other investors in similar cases being awarded compensation.

It is true, Advocate General Kokott noted, that both the risk of an infringement of EU law and the risk of divergent interpretation could be limited or even eliminated if compliance with EU law by arbitration awards were comprehensively reviewed by the national courts – where appropriate, after having conducted a preliminary-ruling procedure.

She then referred to section 33 of the Act which provides that an arbitration award is void if it involves the examination of a question which under Swedish law may not be decided by arbitrators and void if the manner in which the award was arrived at is manifestly incompatible with the Swedish legal order. The court must raise the grounds of invalidity of its own motion. Only the Swedish courts can assess the extent to which those provisions allow for comprehensive enforcement of EU law. However, she noted, this prima facie constitutes only a very limited review in the sense of *ordre public*, which also corresponds to the standard of review applied by the Court of Appeal in the main proceedings.

The recognition of individual arbitration agreements between Member States and investors from other Member States would therefore, according to Advocate General Kokott, create the risk of an infringement of EU law by the arbitration tribunals in so far as the national courts could not ensure that arbitration awards comply with EU law.

However, she went on to note, the CJEU has at least implicitly recognized that the settlement of certain disputes by arbitration is permissible, and has thereby accepted a limited review of compliance with EU law. This related to what is referred to as commercial arbitration. Here, Advocate General Kokott discussed the *Nordsee* and *Eco Swiss* cases[18] and stated that both allow disputes to be referred to arbitration tribunals for a ruling, although they are unable to ensure the correct and uniform application of EU law through requests for a preliminary ruling under Article 267 TFEU. *Eco Swiss* even accepts an infringement of EU law by arbitration awards if the provisions concerned are not fundamental in nature.

The judgment in *Achmea* distinguishes commercial arbitration between private parties, which is permissible in accordance with that case law, from the impermissible arbitration between a private party and a Member State on the basis of investment treaties, in that the former originates in the freely expressed wishes of the parties, whereas the latter derives from a treaty between the Member States.

As stated by PL Holdings, Luxembourg, Finland and Sweden, an individual arbitration agreement between an investor and a Member State would be permissible on the basis of that distinction. This is because such an agreement also originates in the freely expressed wishes of the parties to the arbitration proceedings. In such a case, it would be permissible to limit the national courts' review of the arbitration award in cases concerning investment protection to compliance with the fundamental rules of EU law. However, she considered that Italy was to be agreed with in that the demarcation is not conclusively defined by merely referring to the will of the parties.

Advocate General Kokott noted that her colleague Advocate General Szpunar recently understood the distinction of commercial arbitration in the judgment in *Achmea* to mean that that judgment only precludes Member States from systematically removing EU law disputes from the EU judicial system by means of a prior obligation.[19] Such an understanding would also allow the present arbitration agreement.

Advocate General Kokott is not convinced by this view. Why, she asked, should Member States be allowed to remove EU law disputes from the EU judicial system in individual cases if they are not allowed to enter into a foreseeable general obligation of this kind? In addition to the risks to the uniform application of EU law, there would also be the risk of unequal treatment of different investors.

18. Judgment of 23 March 1982, *Nordsee* (102/81, EU:C:1982:107) and judgment of 1 June 1999, *Eco Swiss* (C-126/97, EU:C:1999:269).
19. Opinion in *Komstroy* (C-741/19, EU:C:2021:164, points 61 and 62).

It is expressly only in relation to *commercial arbitration* that the court has advanced the argument regarding the autonomy or freely expressed wishes of the parties. Such arbitration relates to disputes between parties operating on an equal footing. In such disputes, it is not only the arbitration agreement but also the disputed legal relationship itself that is based on the autonomous will of the parties.

However, the case in the main proceedings is not a commercial dispute between parties on an equal footing, but relates to the exercise of sovereign powers by Polish authorities. If a private party is subjected to a sovereign measure – *in casu*, banking supervision – there can be no question of free will, at least on the part of that party. For that reason alone, it seems unlikely that a Member State would subsequently enter into an arbitration agreement with the private party in relation to such a measure of its own free will. Above all, however, Member States may not remove disputes relating to the sovereign application of EU law from the EU judicial system.

This is because, in accordance with the principle of sincere cooperation enshrined in Article 4(3) TEU, it is the task of all bodies of the Member States to ensure compliance with EU law within the scope of their respective competences. Article 344 TFEU gives concrete expression to that obligation of the Member States. It is not limited to compliance with fundamental rules, but concerns *all* rules of EU law.

As a consequence, a structured network of principles, rules and mutually interdependent legal relations which justifies the autonomy of EU law with respect both to the law of the Member States and to international law binds the EU and its Member States reciprocally and binds its Member States to each other.

Private parties who freely submit to commercial arbitration are not subject to those obligations. In particular, Article 344 TFEU does not apply to disputes between private parties. Therefore, despite the risk of an infringement of EU law, it is consistent to permit arbitration proceedings concerning disputes between private parties.

In contrast, it is problematic when authorities of the Member States in EU law disputes use an arbitration tribunal which is neither part of the EU system nor subject to comprehensive review by national courts with regard to compliance with EU law. This is because it cannot be ruled out in such cases that the arbitration award will fail to have regard to EU law and will thereby impair its effectiveness.

The CJEU accepts the risk of an infringement of EU law if the arbitration is based on an agreement between the EU and non-Member States or on old agreements concluded by Member States with *non-Member States* before their accession to the Union, which continue to be effective under Article 351 TFEU. By contrast, EU law takes precedence over international agreements concluded between the Member States. Similarly, it is not compatible with the effectiveness of EU law for Member States to conclude with certain investors individual arbitration agreements in relation to sovereign measures for enforcing EU law, where such agreements create a risk that the arbitration award will infringe EU law.

However, the risk of an infringement of EU law can be countered if the courts of the Member States not only review the arbitration award with regard to whether it complies with fundamental provisions of EU law but also comprehensively verify compliance with EU law and refer the matter to the CJEU if necessary.

As already explained, it is doubtful whether Swedish law guarantees such verification. In any event, the Swedish Court of Appeal did *not* comprehensively examine the compatibility of the arbitration award with EU law, but only ruled out the existence of a breach of fundamental obligations. In so doing, it confined itself to the question of whether the arbitration agreement was compatible with EU law, without, however, taking a view on the relevant requirements of EU law for banking supervision.

Consequently, Advocate General Kokott concluded, individual arbitration agreements between Member States and investors from other Member States concerning the sovereign application of EU law are compatible with the duty of sincere cooperation under Article 4(3) TFEU and the autonomy of EU law under Articles 267 and 344 TFEU only if courts of the Member States can comprehensively review the arbitration award for its compatibility with EU law, if necessary after requesting a preliminary ruling under Article 267 TFEU.

After this main finding, Advocate General Kokott also briefly discussed equal treatment, the form of the arbitration agreement and possible limitations in time.

With regard to *equal treatment*, her opinion can be summarized as follows. The principle of equal treatment is a general principle of EU law which is enshrined in Article 20 of the Charter of Fundamental Rights of the European Union. If some investors were referred to national courts for disputes with the Member State, but others could have recourse to an arbitration tribunal, there would be unequal treatment. It is difficult to conceive of a legitimate objective with which a Member State could justify entering into an arbitration agreement with some investors in relation to a dispute that has already arisen while referring others to the national courts. It is ultimately for the national court to examine whether there is any such justification, however. For the purposes of the present proceedings, it is sufficient to note that individual arbitration agreements between Member States and investors from other Member States concerning the sovereign application of EU law must also be compatible with the principle of equal treatment under Article 20 of the Charter of Fundamental Rights of the European Union.

With regard to the *form of the agreement*, Advocate General Kokott stated, *inter alia*, the following. Based on the considerations made above, the incompatibility of the arbitration agreement with EU law does not depend upon whether it was concluded in the form of an entering of an appearance in the arbitration proceedings without raising an objection. Therefore the significance of that form is considered only for the event that the CJEU takes a different view on the points already examined.

The recognition of arbitration agreements concluded by way of an entering of an appearance without raising an objection would temporally limit the effectiveness of the judgment in *Achmea* to a certain extent, namely with regard to certain arbitration proceedings already pending at that time, even though the CJEU did not address such a limitation in that judgment. However, if the previous considerations do not convince the CJEU that the compatibility of the present arbitration agreement with EU law is doubtful, the effectiveness of the judgment in *Achmea* will also not be of any decisive importance for the assessment of the form of the arbitration agreement.

More generally, EU law does not contain any rule that would prohibit Member States from entering into an arbitration agreement in the form of an entering of an appearance without raising an objection. On the contrary, EU law recognizes the concept of an entering of an appearance without raising an objection in various rules that are not applicable in the present case.

Since EU law does not regulate this question in respect of the present case, the form of the arbitration agreement has no relevance for its compatibility with EU law.

Finally, PL Holdings has requested that the *temporal effect* of the judgment be limited in the event that the CJEU declares individual arbitration agreements to be incompatible with EU law. At the very least, arbitration proceedings that are already pending and thus, *a fortiori*, those that have been concluded should not be affected. However, Advocate General Kokott found that it is not possible to limit the temporal effect of the judgment to be delivered in the present proceedings.

The case before the CJEU is still pending. The CJEU's preliminary ruling and the Swedish Supreme Court's award will be discussed in SAY 2022 or later editions as the case may be.

§1.04 *GE POWER SWEDEN AB V. NATURA FURNITURE UAB*

In 2005 a construction contract was entered into between Swedish company Alstom Power Sweden AB and a state-owned Lithuanian company. Alstom Power, who was employed to rebuild a power plant outside Vilnius, hired a Lithuanian company (here referred to as Kruonio) as subcontractor. Kruonio performed construction work in the period 2006-2009. Following Kruonio's bankruptcy in 2010, Lithuanian company Natura Furniture UAB bought claims against Alstom Power from Kruonio's estate.

In 2016 Natura initiated arbitration under the ICC Rules against Alstom Power (now renamed GE Power Sweden AB after having been acquired by General Electric Company) seeking payment for claims bought from Kruonio's estate. The seat of the arbitration was Stockholm and the applicable law was Swedish law.

One objection made by GE Power in the arbitration proceedings was that it would be contrary to *ordre public* to issue an award in favour of Natura since the claim was based on an agreement that had come about as a result of bribes being paid. However, the sole arbitrator found that bribery had not been sufficiently proven. In the arbitration award rendered in late 2018, Natura was partially successful with its claim.

In 2019, GE Power requested that the Svea Court of Appeal invalidate the award pursuant to section 33 of the Act. GE Power alleged that: (i) the manner in which the award came about was clearly incompatible with the basic principles of the Swedish legal system, i.e., *ordre public*; and (ii) the award determined an issue which under Swedish law cannot be decided by arbitrators.

The factual basis for GE Power's request to invalidate the award was that bribes to Lithuanian politicians and civil servants had been channelled through Kruonio, that the bribes had been a prerequisite for Kruonio to be hired as subcontractor and that therefore the agreement had been tainted by corruption.

The Court of Appeal stated that agreements tainted by corruption are invalid under Swedish law and that such agreements are incompatible with the basic principles of the Swedish legal system. Accordingly, the court concluded, there is no doubt that arbitral awards involving corruption shall be declared invalid. However, the Court of Appeal found that GE Power had not proven the facts on which it based its request and therefore upheld the award. The Court of Appeal gave leave for GE Power to appeal to the Supreme Court which, as noted above, is rare.[20] GE Power has sought leave from the Supreme Court. Whether leave will be granted is not decided at the time of writing.

20. Judgment by the Svea Court of Appeal dated 22 April 2021 in Case No. T 603-19.

CHAPTER 2
Arbitration in Climate Change Finance

Georges Affaki

The exponential growth of climate change-related investments will prompt an increase in the relating disputes. Arbitration has the potential to become a favoured resolution mechanism for this type of disputes. The investment arbitration framework is particularly adapted for the expectation both of investors and of host States. International investment agreements include substantive protections that could provide a basis for investors to advance claims against States based on environmental and climate change-related losses. Likewise, the same framework could also provide for a defence, and potentially for grounds for a counterclaim, to respondent States which have adopted environmental regulations in compliance with climate change undertakings. Investors may find it difficult to argue that they had been unaware of the States' international obligations to take measures against climate change. Remarkably, out of the eleven investment arbitration cases where respondent States have raised counterclaims, the only two that were successful were based on environmental arguments.

This chapter makes the case for the suitability of the arbitral procedure for climate change disputes, with parties being able to choose experts in the field as arbitrators or possibly challenge arbitrators for their lack of specialist expertise. Transparency of the proceedings and public participation should be further encouraged by arbitral institutions in order for arbitration to gain legitimacy in resolving climate change disputes.

'I ask all of you to use the great power of arbitration to help the world overcome conflict and hatred and build a future of dignity for all on a healthy planet.' These powerful words closed former United Nations Secretary-General Ban Ki-Moon's address at the twenty-third Congress of the International Council for Commercial Arbitration.[1] Secretary-General Moon's words are undoubtedly the most inspiring message that the arbitration world could hope for, especially during this moment, in which the

1. Arbitration Institute of the Stockholm Chamber of Commerce, *Ban Ki-Moon Commends International Arbitration* (24 May 2016).

arbitration world must assume its responsibility to shape a better dispute resolution system for climate change disputes.

Arbitration has a key role to play in the resolution of climate change disputes. This is even more critical given that disputes are expected to multiply given the exponential increase of green investments. For instance, in 2018, climate-related investments – or 'climate finance' – amounted to USD 546 billion worldwide.[2] In Europe alone in the first quarter of 2020, inflows to sustainable funds represented EUR 30 billion.[3]

This chapter supports the case for arbitration as a preferred dispute resolution mechanism in climate change disputes, both as it now stands and as it should evolve. To that end, it will first address how the United Nations Framework Convention for Climate Change (UNFCCC) and the Paris Agreement's inducement for green investments will likely lead to a multiplication of disputes [§2.01].[4] It will then discuss the role of international arbitration in the resolution of climate change disputes, showing that the investment arbitration framework is particularly adapted for climate change-related disputes for both investors and host States [§2.02]. We close with a reflection on the procedural features of arbitration that particularly suit climate change disputes and the need for arbitral institutions to prepare to administer these disputes [§2.03].

§2.01 CLIMATE FINANCE: A CATALYST FOR CLIMATE CHANGE DISPUTES

Since the adoption of the UNFCCC in 1992, the world has witnessed a substantial increase in public and private funding of green investments and projects [A]. This increase in green finance and investments will inevitably lead to further climate change-related disputes [B].

[A] Financing a Green Transition

The current level of climate finance falls short of what is needed to comply with the commitments undertaken by the States Parties to the Paris Agreement,[5] as estimates of investment needed to reach the Paris Agreement's temperature reduction goals range between USD 1.6 trillion and USD 3.8 trillion annually from now to 2050.[6] To that end, Article 9(1) of the Paris Agreement imposes concrete obligations on developed

2. Climate Policy Initiative, *Global Landscape of Climate Finance*, Report, p. 2 (2019).
3. A. Mooney, P. Temple-West, *Climate Change: Asset Managers Join Forces with the Eco-Warriors*, Financial Times (26 July 2020).
4. United Nations Framework Convention for Climate Change (9 May 1992), T. S. No. 30822; Paris Agreement (12 December 2015), T. S. No. 54113.
5. Climate Policy Initiative, *Global Landscape of Climate Finance*, *supra* footnote 2, p. 3.
6. *Ibid.*

countries to increase their contributions to support developing countries' undertakings to mitigate climate change and to make a green energy transition.[7]

With massive investments needed, a number of climate change treaties have established dedicated public funds to stimulate climate finance.[8] The UNFCCC pioneered the use of financial mechanisms to combat climate change by creating two separate entities: the Global Environment Facility (GEF) and the Green Climate Fund (GCF). Since its creation in 1994, the GEF has financed over 4,800 projects in 170 countries by providing USD 20.5 billion in grants and USD 112 billion in co-financing.[9] The GCF, for its part, seeks to finance developing countries in their commitment to combat climate change and to promote private financing in these countries.[10]

Other United Nation (UN) entities encourage climate finance by providing grants and support mechanisms. The United Nations Development Programme (UNDP), for instance, has dedicated USD 2.3 billion for climate change-related projects.[11] Likewise, in 2008, the World Bank established two additional funds through the Climate Investment Funds, namely the Clean Technology Fund and the Strategic Climate Fund.[12] Overall, the World Bank dedicated over 30% of its financing to climate change-related projects in 2018 and 2019, reaching USD 20.5 billion in 2018 and USD 17.8 billion in 2019.[13] To ensure sustainability of public climate finance through these funds, and to stimulate green investments on a long-term basis, the UN bodies in charge – and particularly the UNDP – should endeavour to ensure the good governance of its climate funds. Allegations of fraud, such as those recently raised against the GEF, risk weakening this crucial system and slowing down public climate finance. Should the UNDP fail to react with the appropriate level of seriousness, these risks will be further heightened.[14]

According to the European Commission, the European Union (EU), its Member States and the European Investment Bank are the largest contributors of public climate financing in developing countries.[15] In 2019 alone, they injected up to EUR 23.2 billion

7. Wendy J. Miles, N. Swan, 'Climate Change Financing and Dispute Resolution', *Finances in International Arbitration*, p. 324 (Tung, Fortese et al., Kluwer Law International 2019): *Mitigation* investments aim at reducing or preventing greenhouse gas emissions, while investments for *adaptation* consist in the modification of existing infrastructures to minimise global warming and climate change.
8. *See* Article 9 paras 8 and 9 of the Paris Agreement.
9. Global Environment Facility, https://www.thegef.org/about-us (accessed 15 October 2020).
10. Green Climate Fund, https://www.greenclimate.fund/about (accessed 15 October 2020).
11. Wendy J. Miles, Nicolas Swan, 'Climate Change Financing and Dispute Resolution', *supra* footnote 7, p. 326.
12. Alexander Thompson, 'The Global Regime for Climate Finance: Political and Legal Challenges', *Oxford Handbook of International Climate Change Law*, p. 178 (Carlane et al., Oxford University Press 2016); Climate Investment Funds, *Timeline*, https://www.climateinvestmentfunds.org/timeline-cif (accessed 15 October 2020).
13. World Bank, *World Bank Group Exceeds its Climate Finance Target with Record Year*, 19 July 2018; World Bank, *Climate Finance*, https://www.worldbank.org/en/topic/climatefinance (updated 4 October 2019).
14. E. White, L. Hook, *UN Body Accused of Climate Project Fraud*, Financial Times (1 December 2020).
15. European Commission, *International Climate Finance*, https://ec.europa.eu/clima/policies/international/finance_en (accessed 15 October 2020).

in climate finance.[16] EU institutions also continue to pursue green finance efforts. For instance, in July 2020, the President of the European Central Bank (ECB), Christine Lagarde, announced that the EUR 2.8 trillion ECB asset purchase scheme will be used to promote green objectives more efficiently and to fight climate change.[17] The President of the Deutsche Bundesbank, Jens Weidmann, suggested that the ECB should only purchase securities or accept them as collateral for monetary policy purposes if their issuers meet certain climate-related reporting obligations.[18] A further step that could be taken would be for financial institutions and their regulators to use ratings only from credit rating agencies that include climate-related financial risks in their credit assessments.

However, the private sector remains the greatest contributor to climate finance. In 2017 and 2018, 56% of climate finance contributions came from the private sector, representing USD 326 billion per year on average.[19] Private climate finance has also been boosted by the green bond market. Bond financing and refinancing projects, along with business activities promoting efforts against climate change, are available on this expanding market which, according to the Organisation for Economic Co-operation and Development (OECD), has already exceeded USD 80 billion labelled green bonds in 2020.[20] This significant growth in the green bond market led to the creation of 'Green Bond Principles' by the International Capital Market Association,[21] the purpose of which is to provide relevant information to bond issuers, allowing their bonds to be labelled as a green bond, and to help investors assess the environmental impact of their investment.[22]

[B] Expecting the Increase in Climate Finance Disputes

This staggering growth in green investments will undoubtedly lead to a proportional increase in disputes. In its November 2019 report 'Resolving Climate Change Related Disputes Through Arbitration and ADR',[23] the International Chamber of Commerce (ICC) Arbitration Commission predicted that climate change disputes may arise in a broad variety of sectors, including energy, urban and infrastructure, land use systems, industry and new technologies, financing, and insurance.[24]

---

16. European Council and Council of the European Union, *Climate Finance: EU and Member States' Contributions Continued to Increase in 2019*, Press Release (29 October 2020).
17. R. Khalaf, M. Arnold, *Lagarde Puts Green Policy Top of Agenda in ECB Bond Buying*, Financial Times (7 July 2020).
18. J. Weidmann, *Central Banks Cannot Solve Climate Change on Their Own*, Financial Times (19 November 2020).
19. Climate Policy Initiative, *Global Landscape of Climate Finance*, *supra* footnote 2, p. 13.
20. Wendy J. Miles, Nicolas Swan, 'Climate Change Financing and Dispute Resolution', *supra* footnote 7, pp. 328-329; OECD, *Growing Momentum for Sovereign Green Bonds* (29 September 2020).
21. International Capital Market Association, *Green Bond Principles* (2018).
22. *Ibid.*
23. International Chamber of Commerce, *Resolving Climate Change Related Disputes Through Arbitration and ADR*, ICC Commission Report (2019).
24. *Id.*, p. 65, paras 25, 56, 63, 65, 67, 73.

Similarly, the Arbitration Institute of the Stockholm Chamber of Commerce (SCC) has identified three categories of potential climate change disputes (or 'green technology disputes'): those which arise directly or in connection with an international climate agreement or policy, disputes that are technical in nature, and non-technical disputes.[25]

According to the SCC, disputes directly related to international climate agreements and policies will increase, as States Parties to the Paris Agreement have enacted more than 1,500 national regulations relating to climate change.[26] To date, most of the disputes in this category relate to carbon emission trading schemes established under Article 17 of the Kyoto Protocol and Article 6 of the Paris Agreement. However, as the regulations promulgated to enact these were lacking, disputes relating to these programmes unsurprisingly arose, involving issues ranging from unit registration and issuance to the revocation of trading-related decisions.[27]

Arbitration has been used frequently to resolve carbon trading disputes. The Permanent Court of Arbitration (PCA) has administered nine contract-based cases relating to carbon emission trading.[28] Similarly, the SCC has administered a dispute pertaining to a party's failure to transfer emission rights on time within the EU emissions trading scheme, which resulted in the other party's payment of a penalty to the Environmental Protection Agency.[29] Recourse to arbitration in carbon trading disputes is not surprising, as carbon trading exchanges, such as the Intercontinental Exchange, sometimes impose dispute resolution through arbitration on their users.[30]

Regarding technical disputes, the SCC's docket includes cases involving software systems for the regulation of wind turbines, along with a case dealing with a partnership for the construction of a wind farm.[31]

Finally, with respect to non-technical disputes, the SCC provides the example of cases arising from the unpaid delivery of wind energy converters and from a distribution agreement providing for the exclusive distribution of bioenergy products.[32]

Alongside these green *technology* disputes, the number of green *investment* disputes is also on the rise, as revealed by institutions' own statistics. For instance, between 2012 and 2018, 28% of cases registered by the SCC fell within the category of

25. S. Dwi Andrina, *Green Technology Disputes in Stockholm*, Arbitration Institute of the Stockholm Chamber of Commerce (2019).
26. S. Field, H. Laufer, *Climate Change, the Environment and Commercial Arbitration*, Kluwer Arbitration Blog (9 March 2020).
27. Wendy J. Miles, Nicolas Swan, 'Climate Change Financing and Dispute Resolution', *supra* footnote 7, p. 339.
28. *Id.*, pp. 339-340; J. Levine, C. Pondel, *Updates on the Changing State of the Climate and International Arbitration*, 1 ACICA Rev. 35 (2019); ICC Commission Report, *Resolving Climate Change Related Disputes Through Arbitration and ADR, supra* footnote 23, p. 59, para. 44; R. Verheyen, C. Zengerling, 'International Dispute Settlement', *Oxford Handbook of International Climate Change Law*, p. 423 (Carlane et al., Oxford University Press 2016).
29. S. Dwi Andrina, *Green Technology Disputes in Stockholm, supra* footnote 25, p. 12.
30. Wendy J. Miles, Nicolas Swan, 'Climate Change Financing and Dispute Resolution', *supra* footnote 7, p. 339.
31. S. Dwi Andrina, *Green Technology Disputes in Stockholm, supra* footnote 25, p. 12.
32. *Id.*, p. 13.

green investment disputes.[33] All of these disputes were filed under the Energy Charter Treaty (ECT), confirming that the ECT promotes the use of arbitration in climate-related investment disputes.[34] The International Centre for Settlement of Investment Disputes (ICSID) has reported that, in 2020, it administered forty-eight energy cases either directly or indirectly related to climate change, 16% of that year's cases.[35] The PCA's 2019 caseload included twenty cases involving issues of environmental impact or climate change-related projects, accounting for 12% of disputes overall.[36]

Investment treaty-based disputes relating to climate finance are likely to further expand for two reasons. First, the European Commission has recently decided that the subsidies and exemptions for renewable energies should be progressively phased out from 2020 through 2030.[37] The early termination of these incentives could cause a loss for investors, who may initiate treaty-based arbitration proceedings in cases in which jurisdictional conditions are met.

Second, investment disputes relating to climate finance may proliferate following the recent decision on jurisdiction in the *Portigon v. Spain* ICSID arbitration, confirming that tribunals have jurisdiction over claims brought not only by equity investors but also by lenders to renewable energy projects under both the ICSID Convention and ECT.[38] In an earlier ICSID case, *Landesbank v. Spain*,[39] concerning a similar set of facts (the claimant financial institution had provided over 200 loans and financed dozens of renewable energy plants), the respondent did not even challenge that the financing of energy projects constitutes a protected investment under the ECT.[40] Cases such as *Portigon* and *Landesbank* may thus set the stage for the proliferation of ECT proceedings brought by lenders to renewable energy projects.

In addition to green technology and investment disputes, arbitration has also been used in inter-State arbitrations involving environmental issues. In three of these cases, tribunals have held that States have a 'duty to prevent, or at least mitigate, significant harm to the environment when pursuing large scale construction activities',[41] and applied the 'polluter pays' principle. According to this principle, first articulated by the OECD in 1972, the polluter bears the cost of the pollution or the

33. *Id.*, p. 18.
34. *Id.*, p. 19.
35. International Centre for Settlement of Investment Disputes, 2020 Annual Report, pp. 20, 22 (2020).
36. J. Levine, C. Pondel, *Updates on the Changing State of the Climate and International Arbitration*, *supra* footnote 28, p. 34.
37. European Commission, Communication, Guidelines on State Aid for Environment Protection and Energy 2014-2020, 2014/C 200/01, para. 108 (2014).
38. *Portigon AG v. Kingdom of Spain*, ICSID Case No. ARB/17/15, Decision on Jurisdiction, 20 August 2020 (decision not public).
39. *Landesbank Baden-Württemberg, HSH Nordbank AG, Landesbank Hessen-Thüringen Girozentrale and Norddeutsche Landesbank-Girozentrale v. Kingdom of Spain*, ICSID Case No. ARB/15/45.
40. D. Charlotin, *Greenwood-chaired Tribunal Offers up Decision Dismissing Intra-EU Objection in High-stakes 1.76 billion Dollar Energy Charter Treaty Claim*, IA Reporter (11 July 2019); L. Bohmer, *Majority Arbitrators Uphold Jurisdiction over Claims by Financial Institution Which Funded Renewable Energy Projects in Spain*, IA Reporter (21 August 2020).
41. *Iron Rhine Arbitration (Belgium v. The Netherlands)*, PCA Case No. 2003-02, Award, 24 May 2005, para. 59; *Indus Waters Kishenganga Arbitration (Pakistan v. India)*, PCA Case No.

environmental damage it caused.[42] Although the 'polluter pays' principle lacks normative value by itself, it has been enshrined in various environmental treaties, such as the Convention for the Protection of the Marine Environment of the North-East Atlantic and the Convention on the Protection and Use of Transboundary Watercourses and International Lakes, as well as in both general regional treaties, such as the Treaty on the Functioning of the European Union, and specialised regional treaties like as the Energy Charter Treaty.[43]

The first of these disputes articulating State responsibility to prevent or mitigate environmental harm is the 2005 *Iron Rhine Arbitration* between Belgium and the Netherlands, administered by the PCA.[44] The dispute concerned the Belgian reactivation of a railroad through Dutch territory, including a national park, under Belgium's transit rights over Dutch territory based on the 1839 Treaty of Separation. This reactivation, which gave rise to a disagreement on the allocation of costs and risks between the States related to the project's environmental impact.[45] Applying the 'polluter pays' principle, the tribunal concluded that Belgium was to bear the costs and financial risks of the reactivation of the railway for the segments that it used exclusively,[46] and costs and risks were allocated equally between the States for the segments of the railway used by both.[47]

Similar environmental issues arose in the *Indus Waters Kishenganga* arbitration between Pakistan and India in 2013, initiated under the 1960 Indus Waters Treaty.[48] In response to India's plan to build a hydroelectric plant on the Kishenganga River, Pakistan contended that the project violated India's obligation not to obstruct the flow of the natural channels of the river in a manner likely to cause material and environmental damage.[49] The tribunal ruled that the treaty authorised India's planned project,[50] but that, in application to the State's duty to mitigate environmental damages, India was required to guarantee that the project ensured a minimum flow of water downriver.[51]

The third of these cases was initiated by the Philippines against China in the *South China Sea* arbitration under the UN Convention on the Law of the Sea (UNCLOS).[52] These proceedings concerned, *inter alia*, whether Chinese construction of artificial islands in the South China Sea caused severe harm to the coral reef environment.[53] After an extensive review of the expert reports, the tribunal found that

2011-01, Partial Award, 18 February 2013, paras 451-452; *South China Sea Arbitration (The Republic of Philippines v. The People's Republic of China)*, PCA Case No. 2013-19, Award, 12 July 2016, para. 945.

42. A. Boyle, *Polluter Pays* (Max Planck Encyclopaedia of Public International Law 2009), para. 1.
43. *Ibid.*, paras 3, 6.
44. *Iron Rhine Arbitration*, Award, 24 May 2005, *supra* footnote 41.
45. *Id.*, paras 121, 206.
46. *Id.*, paras 226, 236.
47. *Id.*
48. *Indus Waters Kishenganga Arbitration*, Partial Award, 18 February 2013, *supra* footnote 41.
49. *Id.*, para. 256.
50. *Id.*, para. 510.
51. *Id.*, para. 451, p. 201.
52. *South China Sea Arbitration*, Award, 12 July 2016, *supra* footnote 41.
53. *South China Sea Arbitration*, Award, 12 July 2016, *supra* footnote 41, para. 22.

the Chinese artificial islands had caused devastating and long-lasting damage to the marine environment, amounting to a breach of its obligations under UNCLOS not to harm the marine environment.[54]

§2.02 THE ROLE OF ARBITRATION IN THE RESOLUTION OF CLIMATE CHANGE DISPUTES

States have consented to the jurisdiction of arbitral tribunals for the settlement of climate change-related disputes in numerous treaties. While arbitration is often included as an available dispute resolution mechanism for inter-State disputes, the implementation process has never been fully completed by State parties [A]. On the other hand, the use of investor-State arbitration for climate change-related disputes has expanded considerably [B].

[A] Inter-State Arbitration in Climate Change Disputes: A Missed Opportunity

Recourse to arbitration for inter-State disputes arising out of international environmental and climate change agreements once appeared promising. This began with the adoption of the Vienna Convention for the Protection of the Ozone Layer (VCPOL) in 1985,[55] Article 11(3) of which invites parties to make declarations on whether they consent to the jurisdiction of arbitral tribunals and/or of the International Court of Justice (ICJ) for disputes arising out of the Convention. The parties adopted an Annex to the Convention tailoring the arbitral procedure to the specificities of these disputes, demonstrating their awareness of the particularities of environmental disputes and their willingness to consider recourse to arbitration.[56] This Annex establishes an arbitral procedure under the supervision of the Secretariat of the VCPOL.[57] Notably, this arbitral procedure is tailored for environmental disputes, as it provides that Contracting Parties with an interest in the arbitral proceedings have the right to participate therein, explicitly grants the respondent State the right to file counterclaims, and it requires the tribunal to render its decision within a five-month period, renewable only once.[58]

In 1992, the parties to the UNFCCC followed the same path, as Article 14 of the Convention provides that disputes arising thereunder may be settled through arbitration. As with Article 11 of the VCPOL, Article 14 of the UNFCCC invites the parties to

54. *Id.*, para. 983.
55. Vienna Convention for the Protection of the Ozone Layer (22 March 1985), T. S. No. 26164.
56. W. Miles, M. Lawry-White, *Arbitral Institutions and the Enforcement of Climate Change Obligations for the Benefit of All Stakeholders: The Role of ICSID*, 24 ICSID Review 1, 11 (2019).
57. United Nations Environment Programme, *Handbook for the Vienna Convention for the Protection of the Ozone Layer*, 12th ed., pp. 60-61 (2019).
58. *Ibid.*

declare their acceptance of the compulsory jurisdiction of the ICJ and/or arbitral tribunals.[59]

The Kyoto Protocol and the Paris Agreement followed a similar route: Article 18 of the Kyoto Protocol and Article 24 of the Paris Agreement incorporate Article 14 of the UNFCCC by reference.[60] Although an annex on arbitration was supposed to complement these arbitration mechanisms, the parties to the UNFCCC, the Kyoto Protocol, and the Paris Agreement never adopted these additional instruments.[61]

This failure (or refusal) primarily reflects the Contracting Parties' unwillingness to consent to recourse to arbitration in environmental and climate change-related disputes. In 2020, only two (out of 197) Contracting Parties to the UNFCCC have made a declaration consenting to dispute settlement mechanisms (including arbitration) under Article 14.[62] With respect to the Kyoto Protocol, none of the 192 parties have made such declaration,[63] and the Netherlands is the sole State Party to have issued a declaration under Article 24 of the Paris Agreement consenting to the jurisdiction of the ICJ and arbitral tribunals.[64]

[B] The Suitability of Investment Treaty Arbitration to Deal with Climate Change Disputes

Recent investment treaty cases evince a trend of investors relying on the substantive protections provided under bilateral investment treaties (BITs), free trade agreements, and other multilateral investment treaties to seek recovery for climate change-related losses [1]. In parallel, recent investment treaty cases also indicate a new trend in which host States can avail themselves to climate change-based defences against investors who are non-compliant with environmental regulations [2].

[1] Investors' Climate Change-Related Arguments Falling under the Umbrella of the Substantive Protection of the Investment Treaty

The substantive protections offered to foreign investors under international investment agreements, including the Fair and Equitable Treatment (FET) and Full Protection and Security (FPS) standards, can provide a basis for investors to advance claims against States based on environmental and climate change-related losses.

59. Article 14 of the UNFCCC.
60. Article 18 of the Kyoto Protocol to the UNFCCC and Article 24 of the Paris Agreement both read that: 'The provisions of Article 14 of the [United Nations Framework Convention on Climate Change] on settlement of disputes shall apply mutatis mutandis to this Agreement.'
61. W. Miles, M. Lawry-White, *Arbitral Institutions and the Enforcement of Climate Change Obligations for the Benefit of All Stakeholders*, *supra* footnote 56, p. 10.
62. The Netherlands and the Solomon Islands made a declaration under Article 14 of the UNFCCC, consenting to the jurisdiction of arbitral tribunals; United Nations Framework Convention on Climate Change, *Declarations by Parties* (accessed 13 October 2020).
63. United Nations Treaty Collection, Kyoto Protocol, *Declarations and Reservations* (accessed 13 October 2020).
64. United Nations Treaty Collection, Paris Agreement, *Declarations and Reservations* (accessed 13 October 2020).

An example of the application of the FET standard in this context is the *Novenergia v. Spain* SCC case brought under the ECT.[65] The claimant had indirectly invested in photovoltaic plants in Spain following the adoption of Royal Decrees in 2000 and 2007, encouraging renewable energy production, resulting in the claimant's legitimate expectation that Spain would maintain this favourable regime.[66] However, following the late-2000s economic crisis, Spain issued a 2010 Royal Decree retroactively deleting feed-in tariff values for photovoltaic plants registered in 2007,[67] and subsequent regulations further altered the remuneration mechanism.[68] The tribunal agreed with the claimant and found that the investor had legitimate expectations arising out of Spain's initial Royal Decrees, which could not be radically or fundamentally altered,[69] and that this retroactive change of regulation required it to compensate the investor.[70]

The *Novenergia* award suggests that an investor may rely on its legitimate expectations under an investment treaty's FET provision that a State would continue to promote green energy investment and endeavour to ensure compliance with international environmental obligations.[71] Tribunals may indeed interpret the FET standard in light of the State's legitimate policy objective of complying with applicable international environmental law.[72] It will therefore come as no surprise that investors may rely on the FET standard moving forward as a basis for claims arising from a State's environmental and climate change action or inaction.

The 2018 *Zelena v. Serbia* ICSID case appears to confirm this trend.[73] In *Zelena*, the claimant, an operator of a plant using animal by-products to produce energy, asserted that Serbia's failure to enforce its environmental and veterinary laws

65. *Novenergia II – Energy & Environment (SCA), SICAR v. Kingdom of Spain*, SCC Case No. 063/2015, Final Award, 15 February 2018.
66. *Novenergia II v. Spain*, Final Award, 15 February 2018, *supra* footnote 65, para. 551.
67. *Novenergia II v. Spain*, Final Award, 15 February 2018, *supra* footnote 65, para. 121; Royal Decree 1565/2010, 'Regulating and Modifying Specific Aspects Related to Energy Production in the Special Regime', 19 November 2010.
68. *Novenergia II v. Spain*, Final Award, 15 February 2018, *supra* footnote 65, paras 132, 136, 139 and 145; G. Issac, *Luxembourg Fund Awarded EUR 53.3 Million for FET Breach Arising out of Spain's Curtailment of Renewable Energy Incentive Schemes*, International Institute for Sustainable Development (30 July 2018); Royal Decree-Law 2/2013 'Concerning Urgent Measures in the Electric System and Financial Sector', 1 February 2013 and Royal Decree-Law 9/2013 'Adopting Urgent Measures to Ensure the Financial Stability of the Electric System', 13 July 2013.
69. *Id.*, paras 666, 681.
70. *Id.*, para. 697.
71. Royal Decree 661/2007 'Regulating Electricity Production Under the Special Regime', 25 March 2007: The second paragraph of the Royal Decree Preamble provides that the energy policy should encourage renewable energies and decrease gas emissions, as committed in the Kyoto Protocol.
72. Annette Magnusson, 'New Arbitration Frontiers: Climate Change', *Evolution and Adaptation: The Future of International Arbitration*, p. 1020 (Kalicki, Abdel Raouf, Kluwer Law International 2019).
73. *Zelena N.V. and Energo-Zelena d.o.o Inđija v. Republic of Serbia*, ICSID Case No. ARB/14/27, Award, 9 November 2018 (unpublished).

amounted to a FET violation, as it favoured the claimant's non-compliant competitors.[74] The tribunal agreed, ordering Serbia to compensate the claimant for the FET violation.[75]

In addition to a host State's domestic law, the State's international obligations can also serve as a basis for an investor's claim. Broadly worded arbitration clauses (referring, e.g., to 'all disputes relating to an investment'), together with Article 31(3)(c) of the Vienna Convention on the Law of Treaties (VCLT), which provides for the applicability of 'any relevant rules of international law applicable in the relations between the parties', allow tribunals to apply other international conventions when faced with an investment claim.[76]

The ad hoc tribunal organised under the United Nations Commission on International Trade Law (UNCITRAL) Rules in the *S.D. Myers v. Canada* case relied on treaties ratified by Canada to determine whether that the State had breached its obligations to the US investor under the North American Free Trade Agreement (NAFTA). In that case, the claimant, a waste treatment company, brought a claim against Canada when the State issued an interim order prohibiting the export of the waste of a certain chemical compound.[77] In considering whether the order violated Canada's national treatment and minimum standard of treatment obligations under NAFTA, along with whether the order amounted to an expropriation, the tribunal considered the Canada-USA Transboundary Agreement on Hazardous Waste and the Basel Convention on the Control of Transboundary Movements of Hazardous Waste and Their Disposal.[78] In light of these treaty provisions, the tribunal held that, although a State may achieve its chosen level of environmental protection 'through a variety of equally effective and reasonable means', Canada was obliged to adopt the alternative 'that is most consistent with open trade'.[79]

The FPS standard, which protects the physical integrity and the legal security of the investment and imposes a due diligence obligation on the host State,[80] can also protect investors in situations in which the action or inaction of the State has degraded the environment and, consequently, the value of the investment.[81]

For example, the claimant in the PCA case *Allard v. Barbados* relied on the FPS standard after the Barbados Water Authority conducted an emergency discharge of raw

74. J. Hepburn, *Serbia Held Liable at ICSID in Case Alleging Failure to Enforce Environmental Regulations*, IA Reporter (10 November 2018).
75. *Ibid.*
76. R. de Paor, *Climate Change and Arbitration: Annex Time Before There Won't Be a Next Time*, 8 J. Int. Disput. Settl. 179, 209 (2017); Zachary Douglas, 'The Enforcement of Environmental Norms in Investment Treaty Arbitration', *Harnessing Foreign Investment to Promote Environmental Protection*, pp. 424-425 (Dupuy, Viñuales, Cambridge University Press 2013). In addition, Article 42(1) of the ICSID Convention allows tribunals to apply 'rules of international law as may be applicable' in the absence of an agreement on the applicable by the parties.
77. *Id.*, para. 128.
78. *Id.*, paras 220-221.
79. *Ibid.*
80. August Reinisch, Christopher Schreuer, *International Protection of Investments: The Substantive Standards*, pp. 558, 569, 580, paras 79, 129, 171 (Cambridge University Press 2020).
81. Annette Magnusson, 'New Arbitration Frontiers: Climate Change', *supra* footnote 72, p. 1021.

sewage in a nearby swamp,[82] degrading the claimant's ecotourism site.[83] The claimant contended that the FPS standard in the Barbados-Canada BIT included an obligation of due diligence, and that the State's failure to exercise such diligence resulted in an FPS violation.[84] Although the tribunal rejected the claimant's position, it nonetheless observed in obiter dictum that 'consideration of a host State's international obligations may well be relevant in the application of FPS standard to particular circumstances' and noted that Barbados had ratified the Convention on Biological Diversity and the Ramsar Convention on Wetlands of International Importance.[85]

Although the claimants were ultimately unsuccessful, the *obiter* in *Allard* opens the door to claims against States for violations of the FPS standard for their inappropriate actions or inactions on climate change.[86]

[2] Climate Change-Related Defences for Respondent States in Investment Arbitration

Not only does the investment arbitration framework allow investors to bring climate change-related arguments before arbitral tribunals but also this same framework provides a defence to respondent States.

Investment treaties, for example, do not restrict States from adopting environmental regulations.[87] As recalled by the *Invesmart v. Czech Republic* UNCITRAL tribunal, international investment agreements are not expected to prevent Contracting States from exercising their customary international law right to regulate.[88] Also known as the 'police powers' doctrine,[89] the right to regulate operates as a balance between the investor's private interests and the public purpose that the State pursues through action or abstention.[90] To that end, tribunals generally examine whether the State measure challenged by the claimant fulfils four criteria: whether the measure: (i) was adopted

82. *Id.*, paras 50, 43.
83. Flavia Marisi, *Environmental Interests in Investment Arbitration*, p. 23 (Kluwer Law International 2020).
84. *Peter A. Allard v. The Government of Barbados*, PCA Case No. 2012-06, Award, 27 June 2016, para. 249.
85. *Ibid.*, para. 244.
86. Annette Magnusson, 'New Arbitration Frontiers: Climate Change', *supra* footnote 72, p. 1021.
87. *Methanex Corporation v. United States of America*, UNCITRAL, Final Award, 3 August 2005, Part IV Ch. D paras 7, 9, 15; S. Schill, *Do Investment Treaties Chill Unilateral State Regulation to Mitigate Climate Change?*, 24 J. Int. Arbitr. 469, 470 (2007).
88. *Invesmart B.V. v. Czech Republic*, UNCITRAL, Award, 26 June 2009, para. 498. *See also SAUR International v. Argentine Republic*, ICSID Case No. ARB/04/4, Decision on Jurisdiction and Liability, 6 June 2012, para. 398.
89. Alain Pellet, 'Police Powers or the State's Right to Regulate', *Building International Investment Law: The First 50 Years of ICSID* (Fischer et al., Kluwer Law International 2015); Yulia Levashova, *The Right of States to Regulate in International Investment Law: The Search for Balance Between Public Interest and Fair and Equitable Treatment* (Kluwer Law International 2019); Catharine Titi, 'Police Powers Doctrine and International Investment Law', *General Principles of Law and International Investment Arbitration* (Gattini, Tanzi, Fontanelli, Brill Nijhoff 2018).
90. S. Schill, *Do Investment Treaties Chill Unilateral State Regulation to Mitigate Climate Change?*, *supra* footnote 87, p. 471.

in good faith, (ii) is for a public purpose, (iii) is proportional to this purpose, and (iv) is not discriminatory.[91] Environment protection has been routinely held by tribunals to be a public purpose on which police powers may be based.[92] As such, the State's right to regulate may constitute a successful defence against a claim regarding a polluting investment.

Likewise, just as a claimant may invoke its legitimate expectations under the FET standard to challenge a State environmental measure, the respondent State can equally invoke FET principles as a defence. Tribunals generally consider that investors' expectations are legitimate only when the investors exercised due diligence and carried out a risk assessment before investing.[93] This principle was articulated by the ad hoc tribunal established under the SCC Rules in the *Charanne v. Spain* case, stating 'the Claimants should have made a diligent analysis of the legal framework for the investment' in order to attract investment treaty protection.[94]

As climate change agreements are now part of the public debate, it would thus be difficult for any investor to successfully argue that it was, for example, unaware of the Paris Agreement and a host State's obligation to reduce greenhouse gas emissions thereunder. The enactment of a regulation by a State Party to the Paris Agreement implementing its commitments under this treaty is therefore likely to be held as reasonable on the State's part and foreseeable to any prudent investor.[95] An investor making an investment in a polluting industry after the adoption of the Paris Agreement would correspondingly have difficulty arguing that it could not have legitimately expected the State to take measures against climate change. As a result, the increase in the number of climate change treaties and increasing public knowledge thereof may well constitute a defence for States faced with investment claims.

States may also assert climate change-related arguments against claimants through counterclaims. Although whether States can bring counterclaims is still the

91. *See Saluka Investment BV v. Czech Republic*, UNCITRAL, Partial Award, 17 March 2006, para. 255; SAUR *International v. Argentine Republic*, ICSID Case No. ARB/04/4, Decision on Jurisdiction and Liability, 6 June 2012, para. 401; *Les Laboratoires Servier, S.A.S., Biofarma, S.A.S. and Arts et Techniques du Progrès S.A.S. v. Republic of Poland*, UNCITRAL, Award, 14 February 2012, para. 569.
92. *Magyar Farming Company Ltd, Kintyre Kft and Inicia Zrt v. Hungary*, ICSID Case No. ARB/17/27, Award, 13 November 2019, para. 366; *Crompton (Chemtura) Corporation v. Government of Canada*, UNCITRAL, Award, 2 August 2010, para. 266; *Marvin Roy Feldman Karpa v. United Mexican States*, ICSID Case No. ARB(AF)/99/1, Award, 16 December 2002, para. 103.
93. Yulia Levashova, *The Right of States to Regulate in International Investment Law, supra* footnote 89, pp. 163-164; *See Biwater v. Tanzania*, ICSID Case No. ARB/05/22 Final Award, 24 July 2008, para. 601; *Parkerings v. Lithuania*, ICSID Case No. ARB/05/8 Award, 11 September 2007, para. 335; *Mamidoil Jetoil Greek Petroleum Products Société S.A. v. Republic of Albania*, ICSID Case No. ARB/11/24, Award, 30 March 2015, para. 634; *Isolux Netherlands, BV v. Kingdom of Spain*, SCC Case V2013/153, Award, 17 July 2016, para. 781.
94. *Charanne Construction v. Spain*, SCC Case No. 062/2012, Award, 21 January 2016, para. 505 (unofficial translation).
95. M. Feria-Tinta, *The Role of International Law and Arbitration in Enforcing the Paris Agreement*, Kluwer Arbitration Blog (31 December 2016).

subject of debate,[96] and some commentators assert that States cannot file counterclaims when the obligation allegedly breached by the investor is not enshrined in the investment treaty,[97] eleven counterclaims have been filed by respondent States to date.[98] Out of these eleven counterclaims, tribunals have retained jurisdiction over only five, and only two of those counterclaims were ultimately successful.[99]

Notwithstanding the limited use of counterclaims in the past, no fewer than four separate legal bases exist for an investment tribunal's jurisdiction over a respondent State counterclaim, depending on the circumstances.[100] First, the investment treaty may expressly grant the contracting State the right to bring a claim or counterclaim, though only four do so and most are silent on this issue.[101] Second, the applicable arbitration rules may expressly authorise counterclaims, as is the case with most arbitration rules.[102] Third, the parties may agree to confer jurisdiction to the tribunal over counterclaims, as in the *Burlington v. Ecuador* ICSID case, discussed below.[103] Finally, a tribunal may base its jurisdiction over counterclaims on the applicable dispute resolution provision, in cases in which the provision is broadly worded, allowing the submission of 'all' or 'any' disputes related to investments.[104]

Interestingly, the two State counterclaims that, to date, were successful were both based on environmental arguments. Both were filed by Ecuador in the related *Burlington v. Ecuador* and *Perenco v. Ecuador* cases.[105] The claimants, Perenco and Burlington, formed a consortium and invested in two hydrocarbon blocks through ownership interests in Production Sharing Contracts (PSC) to operate in the Ecuadorian

---

96. Anne Hoffmann, 'Counterclaims', *Building International Investment Law: The First 50 Years of ICSID*, p. 510 (Fischer et al., Kluwer Law International 2015).
97. *Ibid.*
98. Flavia Marisi, *Environmental Interests in Investment Arbitration*, *supra* footnote 83, p. 238.
99. *Ibid.*; *Urbaser S.A. and Consorcio de Aguas Bilbao Bizkaia, Bilbao Biskaia Ur Partzuergoa v. Argentine Republic*, ICSID Case No. ARB/07/26, Award, 8 December 2016, para. 1155; *Hesham T. M. Al Warraq v. Republic of Indonesia*, UNCITRAL, Final Award, 15 December 2014, para. 664; *Perenco Ecuador Ltd. v. Republic of Ecuador*, ICSID Case No. ARB/08/6, Award, 27 September 2019, para. 1023(b); *Burlington Resources, Inc. v. Republic of Ecuador*, ICSID Case No. ARB/08/5, Decision on Counterclaims, 7 February 2017, para. 1099.
100. Flavia Marisi, *Environmental Interests in Investment Arbitration*, *supra* footnote 83, p. 239.
101. *See* Article 17 of the Slovak Republic–Iran BIT; Article 22 of the Slovak Republic–United Arab Emirates BIT; Article 28 of the Argentina–United Arab Emirates BIT; Article 9.19 of the Comprehensive and Progressive Agreement for Trans-Pacific Partnership.
102. *See* Article 46 of the ICSID Convention; Article 40(1) of the ICSID Arbitration Rules; Article 9 of the SCC Rules, Article 5 of the ICC Rules, Article 2(1)(iii) of the LCIA Rules, Articles 4(1)(b) and 25 of the SIAC Investment Rules; Article 21 of the 2010 UNCITRAL Arbitration Rules: Article 19(3) of the UNCITRAL Arbitration Rules originally authorised 'counter-claim[s] arising out of the same contract', but the reference to 'the same contract' was removed during the revision of the Rules in 2006 to leave no doubt on the permissibility of counterclaims in investment arbitration proceedings.
103. *Burlington Resources, Inc. v. Republic of Ecuador*, ICSID Case No. ARB/08/5, Decision on Counterclaims, 7 February 2017, para. 60.
104. Flavia Marisi, *Environmental Interests in Investment Arbitration*, *supra* footnote 83, p. 240; *See Urbaser S.A. and Consorcio de Aguas Bilbao Bizkaia, Bilbao Biskaia Ur Partzuergoa v. Argentine Republic*, ICSID Case No. ARB/07/26, Award, 8 December 2016, para. 1144.
105. *Burlington Resources Inc. v. Republic of Ecuador*, ICSID Case No. ARB/08/5; *Perenco Ecuador Ltd. v. Republic of Ecuador and Empresa Estatal Petróleos del Ecuador*, ICSID Case No. ARB/08/6.

forest.[106] The disputes arose out of a significant increase in windfall taxes imposed by Ecuador on the claimants, although the PSCs provided that the State-owned oil company would cover future tax increases.[107] Perenco and Burlington filed separate ICSID arbitration claims in April 2008.[108] In both cases, Ecuador filed a counterclaim alleging that the claimants were liable for environmental damage caused by soil and groundwater pollution in the two hydrocarbon blocks they operated.[109] Although differently constituted, both tribunals retained jurisdiction over the counterclaim, and both unanimously found that the claimants were liable for environmental damage and ordered compensation to Ecuador based on its counterclaims.[110]

The respondent State's climate change-related defence may also directly derive from the letter of the applicable investment treaty. Out of the 2,342 BITs currently in force,[111] approximately 10% include provisions addressing environmental issues.[112] More than sixty-six investment treaties refer to environmental matters in their preamble, including the recently ratified Agreement between the United States of America, the United Mexican States and Canada (USMCA), along with the ECT.[113] Some international investment agreements specify that non-discriminatory environmental measures do not amount to indirect expropriation,[114] and others encourage the Contracting Parties not to lower their environmental standards to attract investments.[115] Finally, some treaties deal with environmental issues directly in relation to investor-State dispute settlement. For instance, the Belgium/Luxembourg–Colombia

106. M. Levine, *ICSID Tribunal Renders Interim Decision on Ecuador's Environmental Counterclaim in Long-running Dispute*, International Institute for Sustainable Development (26 November 2015); J. Robalino Orellana, *Burlington Resources Inc v. Republic of Ecuador* (Decision on Ecuador's Counterclaims), ICSID Case No. ARB/08/5, 7 February 2017 (Contribution by ITA Board of Reporters, Kluwer Law International 2017).
107. *Perenco Ecuador Ltd. v. Republic of Ecuador and Empresa Estatal Petroleos del Ecuador (Petroecuador)*, ICSID Case No. ARB/08/6, Decision on Jurisdiction, 30 June 2011, paras 15-21; International Institute for Sustainable Development, *Burlington v. Ecuador*, Investment Treaty News (18 October 2018).
108. *Perenco v. Ecuador*, Decision on Jurisdiction, 30 June 2011, *supra* footnote 107, para. 21.
109. *Burlington v. Ecuador*, Decision on Counterclaims, 7 February 2017, *supra* footnote 103, para. 52(i); *Perenco Ecuador Ltd. v. Republic of Ecuador*, ICSID Case No. ARB/08/6, Interim Decision on the Environment Counterclaim, 11 August 2015, para. 36.
110. *Perenco Ecuador Ltd. v. Republic of Ecuador*, ICSID Case No. ARB/08/6, Award, 27 September 2019, para. 1023(b); *Burlington v. Ecuador*, Decision on Counterclaims, 7 February 2017, *supra* footnote 103, para. 1099.
111. Investment Policy Hub, *International Investment Agreements Navigator*, https://investmentpolicy.unctad.org/international-investment-agreements (accessed 7 December 2020).
112. K. Gordon, J. Pohl, *Environmental Concerns in International Investment Agreements: A Survey*, OECD Working Papers on International Investment 2011/01, p. 3 (2011).
113. *Id.*, pp. 11-13; The USMCA entered into force on 1 July 2020 and replaces NAFTA.
114. K. Gordon, J. Pohl, *Environmental Concerns in International Investment Agreements: A Survey*, OECD Working Papers on International Investment 2011/01, p. 11 (2011).
115. *Ibid.*

BIT excludes State environmental measures from the scope of the dispute settlement clause entirely.[116]

These treaties encourage arbitral tribunals to consider environmental issues when dealing with an investment dispute. On this basis, arbitral tribunals' interpretation of investment treaties in light of climate change matters could undoubtedly support a respondent states' defence based on their environmental regulations.

§2.03 THE SUITABILITY OF ARBITRATION PROCEEDINGS FOR THE RESOLUTION OF CLIMATE CHANGE DISPUTES

Arbitral institutions have increasingly acknowledged the role of arbitration in the resolution of climate change-related disputes. The PCA, for one, has been a pioneer, adopting in 2001 a special set of arbitration rules for environmental-related disputes.[117] Adapted to disputes involving 'a natural resources, conservation, or environmental protection component',[118] the PCA Environmental Rules are accompanied by the establishment of a list of arbitrators specialised in environmental matters and a list of scientific and technical experts.[119] In addition, the PCA Environmental Rules allow the arbitral tribunal to appoint experts and order interim measures to preserve the environment from serious harm within the subject matter of the dispute. These Rules have been applied in six contract-based disputes relating to carbon trading under the UNFCCC and the Kyoto Protocol.[120]

The ICC and the SCC have followed suit and taken initiatives to adapt arbitration proceedings administered under their rules to the specificities of disputes relating to climate change. These institutions highlighted, and sometimes improved, the advantages that arbitration offers to resolve these disputes, including tribunal expertise [A], transparency and public participation [B], and the expeditiousness of arbitral proceedings [C].[121]

116. Article VII(5) of the Belgium/Luxembourg-Colombia BIT deals with environment protection and policies, and provides that '[t]he dispute settlement mechanisms under Articles XII and XIII of this Agreement shall not apply to any obligation undertaken in accordance with this Article'.
117. PCA Optional Rules for Arbitration of Disputes Relating to Natural Resources and/or the Environment.
118. *Id.*, p. 183.
119. The Panel of arbitrators for environmental disputes was established under Article 8(3) of the PCA Environmental Rules and the Panel of experts was established under Article 27(5) of the Rules.
120. J. Levine, C. Pondel, *Updates on the Changing State of the Climate and International Arbitration*, *supra* footnote 28, p. 35.
121. ICC Commission Report, *Resolving Climate Change Related Disputes Through Arbitration and ADR*, *supra* footnote 23.

[A] Expertise on Climate Change Issues

Climate change disputes involve complex fields of law and require specific environmental and scientific knowledge.[122] As recalled by the ICC Arbitration Commission Report on Climate Change, it is essential to ensure that 'appropriate expertise is available to the parties and the tribunal' to facilitate the 'understanding of disputes and their resolution techniques'.[123] Since international lawyers are not usually equipped with the necessary skills to deal with these issues,[124] arbitration may respond to the demands of climate change-related disputes in terms of expertise in two ways: through the appointment of arbitrators specialised in environmental issues and/or the specific sector at hand, and through the designation of competent experts.

To select arbitrators capable of understanding the issues in dispute, the parties may, for example, request that arbitral institutions provide publicly available information on the arbitrators' expertise or present a list of arbitrators qualified to deal with these matters.[125] As noted above, the PCA Environmental Rules do just that by establishing a panel of arbitrators specialised in environmental issues. The SCC, for its part, has observed that arbitrators specialised in the energy or in the construction sector are appointed in most disputes involving climate change elements.[126]

Arbitrator expertise is of such importance that an arbitrator's lack of the necessary skills to understand and rule on the dispute could give rise to a challenge.[127] In support of this view, the ICC Arbitration Commission Report on Climate Change relies on Article 14(1) of the ICC Arbitration Rules, under which an arbitrator may be challenged 'whether for an alleged lack of impartiality or independence, *or otherwise*' (emphasis added), and considers that '[t]he language "or otherwise" is a catch-all phrase that could include lack of requisite qualifications'.[128] To avoid such a situation, the appointment of an arbitrator with the appropriate expertise may be included in the arbitration agreement as a condition for the valid constitution of the tribunal.[129]

122. D. Magraw, C. Giorgetti et al., *Model Green Investment Treaty: International Investment and Climate Change*, 36 J. Int. Arbitr. 95, 125 (2019); Wendy J. Miles, N. Swan, 'Climate Change Financing and Dispute Resolution', *supra* footnote 7, p. 342.
123. ICC Commission Report, *Resolving Climate Change Related Disputes Through Arbitration and ADR*, *supra* footnote 23, p. 19.
124. Joint dissenting opinion of Judges Al-Khasawneh and Simma, *Pulp Mills on the River Uruguay (Argentina v. Uruguay)*, International Court of Justice, Judgment, 20 April 2010, p. 109, para. 2: 'the Court has evaluated the scientific evidence brought before it by the Parties in ways that we consider flawed methodologically'.
125. ICC Commission Report, *Resolving Climate Change Related Disputes Through Arbitration and ADR*, *supra* footnote 23, p. 21.
126. S. Dwi Andrina, *Green Technology Disputes in Stockholm*, *supra* footnote 25, pp. 15, 23.
127. ICC Commission Report, *Resolving Climate Change Related Disputes Through Arbitration and ADR*, *supra* footnote 23, p. 23, para. 5.19.
128. *Ibid.*
129. *See, e.g.*, *Indus Waters Kishenganga Arbitration (Pakistan v. India)*, PCA Case No. 2011-01; Article IX(5)(4) of the 1960 Indus Waters Treaty requires that at least one highly qualified engineer composes the tribunal; J. Levine, 'Adopting and Adapting Arbitration for Climate Change-Related Disputes: The Experience of the Permanent Court of Arbitration', *Dispute Resolution and Climate Change: The Paris Agreement and Beyond*, p. 26 (Miles, ICC 2017), p. 29.

The arbitral tribunal may alternatively seek assistance on technical issues by designating experts.[130] For example, in the *Perenco v. Ecuador* case, the tribunal appointed its own independent expert, after it concluded that it was unable to determine which of the party-appointed experts was more reliable.[131] Similarly, in the *South China Sea* case, the tribunal appointed its own experts on coral reef environment to report and shed light on the potential consequences of the disputed construction activities.[132]

As climate change-related disputes encompass a wide range of issues that do not necessarily pertain to environmental science alone, the SCC correctly observes that other areas of expertise may also bring meaningful contributions to the resolution of these types of disputes. This is, for instance, the case of finance and taxation experts who can guide the tribunal in understanding the consequences of States incentive and support schemes in renewable energies, which are issues that appear increasingly in investment arbitration cases.[133]

[B] Transparency of the Arbitral Proceedings and Public Participation

Demand for transparency and public participation is growing in investment arbitration. This demand is particularly acute in climate change-related disputes, in light of actions initiated by citizen groups and non-governmental organisations (NGOs) against States and corporations for environmental inaction.[134]

In this context, the recent decision of the *Hoge Raad*, the Netherlands' Supreme Court, in *Urgenda Foundation v. Netherlands*, is particularly pertinent.[135] The Urgenda Foundation, together with a group of 900 Dutch citizens, initiated legal proceedings against the Dutch Government to compel it to reduce greenhouse gas emissions.[136] On 20 December 2019, the *Hoge Raad*, in consideration of the UNFCCC, ordered the State to reduce greenhouse gases by at least 25% compared to 1990 levels by the end of 2020.[137] This judgment inspired climate change cases in Europe, the Americas, Asia, and Oceania, demonstrating that civil society is willing and, in some cases, able to compel governments to comply with international climate obligations.[138] Enhanced transparency would therefore reconcile the arbitral process with civil society, allow

130. ICC Commission Report, *Resolving Climate Change Related Disputes Through Arbitration and ADR*, *supra* footnote 23, p. 24, paras 5.26-5.27.
131. *Perenco v. Ecuador*, Interim Decision on the Environment Counterclaim, 11 August 2015, *supra* footnote 109, paras 585, 587.
132. *South China Sea Arbitration (Philippines v. China)*, PCA Case No. 2013-19, Independent Expert Report on Coral Reef Environment, 26 April 2016.
133. S. Dwi Andrina, *Green Technology Disputes in Stockholm*, *supra* footnote 25, p. 23.
134. J. Setzer, R. Byrnes, *Global Trends in Climate Change Litigation: 2020 Snapshot*, Policy Report (2020).
135. *Urgenda Foundation v. The State of the Netherlands*, ECLI:NL:HR:2019:2007, 20 December 2019.
136. *Ibid.*
137. *Ibid.*
138. Urgenda, *Global Climate Litigation*, https://www.urgenda.nl/en/themas/climate-case/global-climate-litigation/ (accessed 30 November 2020); *See also* the case 'Commune de Grande-Synthe' brought before the *Conseil d'Etat* (French Supreme Administrative Court): the city of

arbitration to gain legitimacy, and ultimately facilitate public understanding of tribunal decisions.[139]

However, transparency may be subject to the consent of the parties to the dispute. Further, while transparency seems to be increasing in investment arbitration, it remains a rare feature in commercial arbitration, as confidentially remains one of the reasons why parties to commercial contracts choose arbitration over litigation.

Most rules used in investment arbitration proceedings nevertheless provide for some amount of transparency. For instance, the adoption of the UNCITRAL Rules on Transparency in Treaty-Based Investor-State Arbitration (UNCITRAL Transparency Rules) in 2013 is a step forward for transparency in investment arbitration. The Transparency Rules provide for the publication of certain documents from the arbitration proceedings, such as the parties' submissions, exhibit lists, expert reports, witness statements, and the tribunal's decisions.[140] The use of the UNCITRAL Transparency Rules is expected to increase along with an increase in the number of ratifications of the United Nations Convention on Transparency in Treaty-Based Investor-State Arbitration (Mauritius Convention). Importantly, Article 2(1) of the Mauritius Convention provides that '[t]he UNCITRAL Rules on Transparency shall apply to any investor-State arbitration, whether or not initiated under the UNCITRAL Arbitration Rules, in which the respondent is a Party that has not made a relevant reservation under article 3(1)(a)'.[141] In 2020, seven States had ratified the Mauritius Convention, and none had made a reservation under Article 3(1)(a), meaning that the UNCITRAL Transparency Rules will apply in investment arbitration proceedings in which these States will appear as respondents.[142]

Similarly, the ICSID Arbitration Rules provide for transparency under certain conditions. Rule 48(4) of the ICSID Arbitration Rules provides that, should the parties refuse to consent to the award being made public, ICSID may nevertheless publish excerpts of the tribunal's legal reasoning, and Rule 32(2) permits the tribunal, with the parties' consent, to hold the hearings in public. These efforts towards transparency in ICSID proceedings are confirmed by the review of the ICSID Arbitration Rules currently underway. To date, the latest proposals provide that the ICSID 'shall' publish any order or decision taken by the tribunal, with necessary redactions, within sixty days the

---

Grande-Synthe, later joined by other French cities and foundations, initiated judicial proceedings against the French government for refusing to take measures to comply with its obligation to reduce greenhouse gases under the UNFCCC and the Paris Agreement. In a decision dated 19 November 2020, the *Conseil d'Etat* ordered the French government to justify within three months the reasons why the government refuses to take additional steps to reduce emissions and to explain whether this refusal is compatible with the objectives set in the Paris Agreement.

139. ICC Commission Report, *Resolving Climate Change Related Disputes Through Arbitration and ADR, supra* footnote 23, p. 41, para. 5.69; W. Miles, M. Lawry-White, *Arbitral Institutions and the Enforcement of Climate Change Obligations for the Benefit of All Stakeholders, supra* footnote 56, p. 28.
140. ICC Commission Report, *Resolving Climate Change Related Disputes Through Arbitration and ADR, supra* footnote 23, p. 41, para. 5.68.
141. United Nations Convention on Transparency in Treaty-Based Investor-State Arbitration (18 October 2017), T. S. No. 54749.
142. To date, the Mauritius Convention has been ratified by Australia, Bolivia, Cameroon, Canada, Gambia, Mauritius and Switzerland.

issuance of an order or decision, and that the tribunal 'shall' authorise any third person to observe hearings, unless the parties otherwise agree.[143]

The recent increase in arbitral hearings being conducted remotely allows tribunals to manage the attendance of non-party observers more easily, when the rules allow it. The opportunity for non-parties to observe arbitral hearings will further legitimise arbitration as an effective means of resolving disputes in which the public has an interest, which is particularly the case for environmental disputes. Remote hearings offer the particular advantage of allowing tribunals to deactivate observers' video and audio connections for in camera sessions, thereby reducing the inefficiency of requiring the tribunal to ensure that only counsel and party representatives are physically present in a hearing room. The hearing of the ICSID *Vattenfall v. Germany* case,[144] for example, was recorded and made publicly available, which is particularly notable given the public interest in a case with environmental implications, as the *Vattenfall* claim was brought in response to Germany's decision to phase out nuclear power by 2022.[145]

The participation of non-parties in a dispute as amici curiae will also enhance transparency in the arbitral process.[146] Third-party participation is possible under most arbitration rules. Article 25 of the ICC Rules provides that the tribunal may hear 'any other person', and Article 4 of the UNCITRAL Transparency Rules and Article 4 of Appendix III to the 2017 SCC Rules authorise the tribunal to allow a non-disputing party to file written submissions. Similarly, ICSID Rule 37(2) states that the tribunal may authorise a non-disputing party to file a written submission to the tribunal, after considering whether the non-disputing party would assist the tribunal in determining a factual or legal issue related to the proceedings by bringing in a different perspective from that of the parties, whether the submission would address a matter within the scope of the dispute, and whether the non-disputing party has a significant interest in the proceedings. The proposals for amendments of the ICSID Rules reaffirm this possibility in proposed amended Rule 67.[147]

In the context of climate change-related disputes, amicus briefs from non-parties may offer the tribunal another perspective and additional expertise, as demonstrated in *Foresti v. South Africa*.[148] In that case, the claimant filed a claim for unlawful expropriation and the respondent State argued that the expropriation was lawful as it

143. International Centre for Settlement of Investment Disputes, *Proposals for Amendment of the ICSID Rules*, Working Paper 4, Vol. 1, pp. 65-66 (February 2020).
144. *Vattenfall AB and others v. Federal Republic of Germany*, ICSID Case No. ARB/12/12.
145. ICSID, *Vattenfall AB and others v. Federal Republic of Germany (ICSID Case No. ARB/12/12) – Public Hearing*, Press Release (29 September 2016); IA Reporter, *Germany is Sued at ICSID by Swedish Energy Company in Bid for Compensation for Losses Arising out of Nuclear Phase-Out* (1 June 2012).
146. ICC Commission Report, *Resolving Climate Change Related Disputes Through Arbitration and ADR*, *supra* footnote 23, p. 42, para. 5.70; W. Miles, M. Lawry-White, *Arbitral Institutions and the Enforcement of Climate Change Obligations for the Benefit of All Stakeholders*, *supra* footnote 56, pp. 28-29.
147. Proposals for Amendments of the ICSID Rules, *supra* footnote 143, p. 67.
148. ICC Commission Report, *Resolving Climate Change Related Disputes Through Arbitration and ADR*, *supra* footnote 23, pp. 44-45, para. 5.90; *Piero Foresti, Laura de Carli & Others v. Republic of South Africa*, ICSID Case No. ARB(AF)/07/01, Award, 4 August 2010.

pursued the public purpose of protecting the environment and communities in the area.[149] The arbitral tribunal allowed four NGOs to file submissions on the issues of substantive equality, human rights, sustainable development, and environmental protection in South Africa,[150] ordered the parties to give these non-disputing parties access to documents submitted to the tribunal, and invited the parties to comment on the amicus briefs.[151]

[C] Expeditiousness of Arbitral Proceedings

Climate change-related disputes often involve an element of urgency and require prompt resolution.[152] If not dealt with expeditiously, the environmental impact and the effect on populations in climate change-related disputes may be irreversible.[153] Parties may use various procedural options to expedite the resolution of the dispute. The ICC, for instance, recommends a host of measures to resolve a dispute efficiently, including the bifurcation of proceedings, deciding that some issues may be decided on a 'documents only' basis, and the limitation of submissions to key climate change-related issues.[154]

Arbitration presents the immense advantage of procedural rules that are adaptable to fit the needs of parties. To resolve a dispute quickly, parties may agree on the application of an expedited procedure when arbitral institutions, such as the ICC and the SCC, offer this possibility.[155] In 2019, out of 586 cases administered by the ICC, 146 cases had been or were being conducted under the ICC Expedited Procedure.[156] Similarly, the SCC states that 19% of the green technology disputes it administered between 2012 and 2018 were registered under the SCC Rules for Expedited Arbitrations and were terminated within a year, against an average of sixteen months for rendering an award in other proceedings.[157]

Should the circumstances of a climate change-related dispute require a decision prior to the constitution of the tribunal, the ICC Emergency Arbitrator Rules provide for the rendering of such a decision, but do not make it available in the case of treaty-based arbitration.[158] In such a situation, the President of the ICC Court will appoint an emergency arbitrator within no more than two days after the receipt of the application,

149. *Ibid.*; W. Miles, M. Lawry-White, *Arbitral Institutions and the Enforcement of Climate Change Obligations for the Benefit of All Stakeholders*, *supra* footnote 56, p. 30.
150. *Foresti v. South Africa*, Award, 4 August 2010, *supra* footnote 149, para. 27; *Foresti v. South Africa*, Petition for Limited Participation as non-Disputing Parties, 17 July 2009, para. 4.18.
151. *Id.*, paras 28-29.
152. *Ibid.*
153. ICC Commission Report, *Resolving Climate Change Related Disputes Through Arbitration and ADR*, *supra* footnote 23, p. 26, para. 5.34.
154. *Id.*, pp. 26-27, para. 5.35.
155. *Id.*, p. 27, para. 5.36; *See* Article 30 of the ICC Arbitration Rules and the SCC Rules for Expedited Arbitrations.
156. International Chamber of Commerce, ICC Dispute Resolution 2019 Statistics, p. 16 (2020).
157. S. Dwi Andrina, *Green Technology Disputes in Stockholm*, *supra* footnote 25, pp. 8, 10.
158. ICC Commission Report, *Resolving Climate Change Related Disputes Through Arbitration and ADR*, *supra* footnote 23, pp. 35-36, paras 5.54-5.55.

and the emergency arbitrator will issue an order within fifteen days after the receipt of the file.[159] In 2019, twenty-three emergency arbitrator applications were filed with the ICC, and half of them concerned disputes in the construction and the energy sectors, and two sectors particularly related to climate change.[160]

In contrast, the SCC Arbitration Rules extend emergency arbitration proceedings to investment treaty arbitration.[161] A party in SCC proceedings may apply for the appointment of an emergency arbitrator until the case has been referred to an arbitral tribunal. After the application has been received by the SCC Secretariat, and provided that the SCC does not manifestly lack jurisdiction, the SCC Board will proceed to the appointment of an emergency arbitration within twenty-four hours of the receipt of the application. Between 2014 and 2019, ten emergency arbitrator decisions have been rendered in investment treaty disputes under the SCC Rules, in six of which the emergency relief claimed was granted. Eight of these disputes were based on bilateral investment treaties. In all those cases, the emergency arbitrator was successfully appointed by the SCC Board in twenty-four hours, and the average term for rendering the emergency decision was five and half days.[162]

§2.04 CONCLUSION

As Wendy Miles QC correctly observes, arbitration may well become 'a tool of global climate governance',[163] as it offers the necessary mechanisms for the resolution of climate change disputes. With the number of climate change-related disputes being sure to increase, thanks to increase in green investments made each year, recourse to climate change-related arbitration should be further promoted. Arbitral institutions, for their part, are engaged and determined to welcome climate change-related disputes.

The potential for the increased use of arbitration in these matters now lies in the hands of the parties. Private and public entities, when concluding a contract related to energy, construction, or any other field in which climate or environmental issues may arise, should seriously consider including an arbitration clause. Likewise, States should complete the arbitration protocols in climate change treaties and incorporate climate change-related provisions in their investment promotion agreements.

The 'Model Green Investment Treaty' drafting competition launched by the SCC is an encouraging step towards incentivising States to ratify suitable investment agreements.[164] This Model Green Investment Treaty comprises express provisions promoting environmental actions and combating climate change. The first of these provisions pertains to States' rights to regulate generally, as well as to do so more

159. Appendix V, Articles 2(1) and 6(4) of the ICC Arbitration Rules.
160. ICC Dispute Resolution 2019 Statistics, *supra* footnote 156, p. 17.
161. A. Pirozhkin, *Emergency Arbitrator's Decisions in Investment Treaty Disputes at the SCC (2014-2019)*, May 2020.
162. *Ibid.*
163. Wendy J. Miles, Nicolas Swan, 'Climate Change Financing and Dispute Resolution', *supra* footnote 7, p. 342.
164. A. Havedal Ipp, *Stockholm Treaty Lab: Combating Climate Change Through Legal Crowdsourcing*, Kluwer Arbitration Blog (17 July 2020).

specifically in relation to climate change.[165] The treaty also requires investors to comply with local law and with the World Bank Environmental and Social Standards and the International Finance Corporation Performance Standards.[166] To that end, the Model Green Treaty explicitly grants the respondent State with the right to bring a counterclaim for a breach of international law and standards.[167] The Model Green Treaty also seeks to adapt arbitration proceedings to climate change-related disputes by requiring that arbitrators be familiar with the issues of climate change and sustainable development as well as with relevant laws and policies. Finally, the Model Green Treaty strengthens transparency by providing for public participation in the dispute resolution process and requiring reporting on the implementation of awards.[168]

In the same vein, the European Commission has proposed amendments to the ECT to introduce considerations of sustainable development and climate change.[169] In particular, the European Commission proposal seeks to reaffirm the Contracting Parties' right to regulate in environmental matters to fight climate change.[170]

Similarly, out of the twenty-six international investment agreements concluded since the beginning of 2019, at least seventeen include provisions addressing climate change issues. These agreements reaffirm the contracting State's right to regulate with respect to climate, include protection of the environment in the exception clause, provide that States should not lower environmental standards to promote investment, and address corporate social responsibility. These treaties thus require investors to comply with the host State's environmental regulations.[171] As recent developments show, despite the calls for the establishment of an international court of environment,[172] States are determined to ensure the viability of arbitration in climate change-related disputes, and the arbitration system is up to the challenge.

165. D. Magraw, C. Giorgetti et al., *Model Green Investment Treaty: International Investment and Climate Change*, 36 J. Int. Arbitr. 95, 99 (2019).
166. *Id.*, p. 118.
167. *Ibid.*
168. *Id.*, p. 96.
169. C. Sanderson, *EU Publishes Proposals for ECT Revamp*, Global Arbitration Review (28 May 2020).
170. *Ibid.*
171. *See* Belarus–Hungary BIT, Australia–Indonesia CEPA, Brazil–UAE BIT, CARIFORUM–UK FTA, Australia–Hong Kong BIT, Hungary–Cabo Verde BIT, Australia–Uruguay BIT, Burkina Faso–Turkey BIT, Uzbekistan–South Korea BIT, Morocco–Brazil BIT, Kyrgyz Republic–India BIT, Vietnam–EU FTA, Singapore–Myanmar BIT, Brazil–Ecuador BIT, Armenia–Singapore BIT, Morocco–Japan BIT, Brazil–India BIT.
172. International Bar Association, *Achieving Justice and Human Rights in an Era of Climate Disruption*, Report of the Climate Change Justice and Human Rights Task Force, p. 28 (2014).

CHAPTER 3

How Do Tribunals Deliberate? A Guide to Effective Arbitral Decision-Making in International Arbitration

Mika Savola

In any arbitration involving three arbitrators, deliberations between tribunal members are crucial to the outcome of a case. Yet deliberations do not always proceed smoothly. In cross-border disputes, differences in the arbitrators' cultural background, legal training, personalities and language skills will make it difficult for an ad hoc group of people who are not familiar with each other to work together efficiently. Some party-appointed arbitrators, while ostensibly independent and impartial, still exhibit inappropriate allegiance to the positions advocated by the party that appointed them.Even harmonious deliberations can pose challenges. Disputes submitted to international arbitration are often complex cases where clear answers are few and far between. Conscientious arbitrators may have legitimately different views on the correct outcome of the case. Not infrequently, those views are coloured by various psychological biases that are difficult to rein in.

The chapter discusses how arbitrators should approach their delicate duty to deliberate with a view to finding potential guidelines for effective arbitral decision-making. It focuses on issues such as rapport building, assigning duties among arbitrators, the role of administrative secretaries and tribunal-appointed experts, as well as on how to deal with bargaining, biases, dissents and 'difficult' tribunal members during deliberations. While realizing that each arbitration is unique, and what works well with one tribunal may not work well with another, the author suggests that there are some basic propositions which may help arbitrators to deal with the complexities of deliberations, especially in a multicultural setting.

§3.01 INTRODUCTION

In any arbitration involving three arbitrators, deliberations between tribunal members are crucial to the outcome of a case.[1] It is during the deliberation phase that arbitrators truly come together to form one unit to decide the dispute. Deliberations require cooperation among tribunal members at a level of intensity far exceeding that which prevails during the previous stages of the proceedings. The quality of deliberations has a direct bearing on – and is often determinative of – the quality of the tribunal's final award on the merits.[2]

Yet deliberations do not always proceed smoothly. There may be various reasons for that. In cross-border disputes, differences in the arbitrators' cultural background, legal training, personalities and language skills will make it difficult for an ad hoc group of people who are not familiar with each other to work together efficiently. Some party-appointed arbitrators, while ostensibly independent and impartial, still exhibit inappropriate allegiance to the positions advocated by the party that appointed them. In the worst-case scenario, a party-nominated arbitrator may act in an outright partisan manner, leak information of the tribunal's internal discussions or intentionally seek to derail the proceedings to block any decision against the appointing party.

Even harmonious deliberations can pose challenges. Disputes submitted to international arbitration are often complex cases where clear answers are few and far between. Conscientious arbitrators may have legitimately different views on the correct outcome of the case. Not infrequently, those views are coloured by various psychological biases that are difficult to rein in.

How should arbitrators then approach their delicate duty to deliberate? Relatively little has been written about the internal decision-making dynamics of a three-person tribunal, despite the importance of the subject. Indeed, for many arbitration practitioners, deliberations of an international arbitral tribunal remain *terra incognita*, something akin to a 'black box'.[3] This article seeks to shed light on the topic with a view to finding potential guidelines for effective arbitral decision-making. While realizing that each arbitration is unique, and what works well with one tribunal may not work well with another, I believe that there are some basic propositions which may help arbitrators to deal with the complexities of deliberations, especially in a multicultural setting.

---

1. This article is gender neutral. Wherever the author has used the masculine, this should be read as masculine or feminine.
2. L. Yves Fortier, *The Tribunal's Deliberations*, in Lawrence W. Newman and Richard D. Hill (eds), *The Leading Arbitrators' Guide to International Arbitration* (Third Edition, JurisNet, LLC, 2014), 831, 835-836.
3. Bernhard Berger, *The Legal Framework: Rights and Obligations of Arbitrators in the Deliberations*, in Bernhard Berger and Michael E. Schneider (eds), *Inside the Black Box: How Arbitral Tribunals Operate and Reach Their Decisions*, ASA Special Series No. 42 (JurisNet, LLC, 2014), 7; Ugo Draetta, *The Dark Side of Arbitration* (JurisNet, LLC, 2018), 147.

§3.02 DEFINING DELIBERATIONS

The term 'deliberations' is generally understood to refer to the tribunal's internal negotiations which take place after the evidentiary hearing and after the parties have exchanged their written submissions. During deliberations, the members of the tribunal consider and discuss the parties' arguments and evidence put to them and reach a decision on the disputed issues. Deliberations are considered confidential in the sense that only the arbitrators are entitled to be present[4] and receive information about the content of the deliberations, barring exceptional circumstances.[5] A breach of the duty to keep the deliberations confidential may result in a claim for damages against the arbitrator responsible.[6]

In some legal systems, the duty to deliberate is expressly provided for by law.[7] However, it is widely accepted that, even in the absence of clear statutory support, members of a three-person tribunal are required to deliberate in a collegial way before reaching any important substantive or procedural decision. This is both a duty and a right of each arbitrator: all tribunal members are expected, and should have an equal opportunity, to participate in any discussions that may have a bearing on the outcome of the tribunal's decisions.

The right of an arbitrator to take part in the deliberations is not unlimited, however. It suffices that each arbitrator is given a fair and equal opportunity to influence the tribunal's decision-making: if an arbitrator refuses to participate in the deliberations, or seeks to obstruct them unjustifiably, the majority may proceed to issue the final award despite the opposition of one tribunal member.[8] By the same token, when all three arbitrators have been given a reasonable opportunity to state their views and two of the arbitrators are in agreement on the outcome of the dispute,

4. Possibly with the exception of a tribunal-appointed secretary, if all arbitrators and the parties agree to that. On the role of tribunal secretaries, *see* further section §3.03[D].
5. An exception may apply if fundamental principles of due process are alleged to have been breached during deliberations. In some jurisdictions, including Sweden, arbitrators may even be called to testify in courts. *See* Finn Madsen, *Commercial Arbitration in Sweden* (Fourth edition, Jure Förlag AB, 2016), 324; and Patrik Schöldström, *The Arbitrators*, in Annette Magnusson, Jakob Ragnwaldh and Martin Wallin (eds), *International Arbitration in Sweden: A Practitioner's Guide* (Second Edition, Kluwer Law International B.V., 2021), 172-173. – For a critique of such approach, *see* Jean-François Poudret and Sébastien Besson, *Comparative Law of International Arbitration* (Second Edition, Sweet & Maxwell Ltd, 2007), 654.
6. The Chartered Institute of Arbitrators (CIArb) Guideline for Drafting Arbitral Awards, Part I – General, 14 (available at: guideline-10-drafting-arbitral-awards-part-i-general-2016.pdf (ciarb.org); accessed 23 March 2021).
7. This is the case, e.g., in France and Portugal. *See* José María Alonso, *Deliberation and Drafting Awards in International Arbitration*, in M. Á. Fernandéz-Ballesteros and David Arias (eds), *Liber Amicorum Bernardo Cremades* (La Ley, 2010), 133-134; Yves Derains, *La pratique du délibéré arbitral*, in Gerald Aksen, Karl-Heinz Böckstiegel, Michael J. Mustill, Paolo Michele Patocchi and Anne Marie Whitesell (eds), *Global Reflections on International Law, Commerce and Dispute Resolution: Liber Amicorum in honour of Robert Briner* (ICC Publishing, 2005), 222-223.
8. The problem with obstructionist or otherwise 'difficult' tribunal members is discussed in section §3.03[H].

the third arbitrator cannot prolong the deliberations by demanding continued discussions in an attempt to persuade the others to adopt his opinion.[9]

In the legal literature, the term 'deliberations' is sometimes understood more broadly, without connecting it to any specific phase of the proceedings or the tribunal's final decision on the merits of the dispute. Many commentators have noted that deliberations are necessary for all important decisions, not just for a final award. In fact, almost all decisions regarding the conduct of the arbitration require deliberation among the members of a tribunal: fixing of time limits, the manner in which submissions are to be filed and evidence is to be presented, document production requests, applications for interim relief, requests for the bifurcation of the proceedings, and so forth. It is a matter of definition whether the tribunal's internal discussions on such questions are considered part of 'deliberations' too.[10]

Additionally, it would be wrong to think that arbitrators refrain from forming any preliminary understanding on how the dispute might be resolved already prior to the conclusion of the evidentiary hearing and the exchange of the parties' written submissions. In many cases, the dialogue among arbitrators begins shortly before the hearing when they typically meet in person (or at least by videoconference), discuss the substance of the case and prepare questions for the witnesses and experts to be heard. Informal exchange of thoughts will then continue during the hearing breaks, which many arbitrators consider a useful opportunity to confer about the relevance and materiality of the most recent witness testimony and documentary evidence addressed. While striving to keep an open mind through the entire hearing, arbitrators tend to develop impressions and reach tentative conclusions with each witness presented, and although those conclusions may be refined and sometimes even changed significantly, psychological studies have shown that what is heard at an earlier point is of disproportionately greater persuasive value.[11]

Some practitioners claim that arbitrators should deliberate already *at the outset of a case*, and even before the first case management conference, in order to proactively manage the proceedings and adapt them to the characteristics of the case. For instance, it has been submitted that the tribunal should encourage the counsel to engage in an open 'without prejudice' discussion on the substance of each party's respective case already in connection with the first procedural meeting.[12] It has also been suggested that the tribunal could simultaneously convey its provisional opinion 'on what should

---

9. This is the essence of the Svea Court of Appeal's famous decision in *The Czech Republic v. CME Czech Republic BV*, 15 May 2003, Case No. T 8735-01.
10. *See, e.g.*, Yves Derains, *The Deliberations of the Arbitral Tribunal – 'retour au delibéré arbitral'*, in Markus Wirth (ed), *The Resolution of the Dispute – from the Hearing to the Award*, ASA Special Series No. 29 (September 2007), 16.
11. Fortier, *supra* n. 2, at 831-832; Paolo Michele Patocchi and Robert Briner, *The Role of the President of the Arbitral Tribunal*, in Newman and Hill, *supra* n. 2, at 301; Doak Bishop and James H. Carter, *The United States Perspective and Practice of Advocacy*, in Doak Bishop and Edward G. Kehoe (eds), *The Art of Advocacy in International Arbitration* (Second Edition, JurisNet, LLC, 2010), 543; Nicolas Ulmer, *Six Modest Proposals Before You Get to the Award*, in Berger and Schneider, *supra* n. 3, at 117. The effect of psychological biases on the arbitrators' deliberations and decision-making is discussed in further detail in section §3.03[F].
12. Derains, *supra* n. 10, at 16-17; Ulmer, *supra* n. 11, at 115.

be proved and how it should be done' which, however, is only possible if the arbitrators have deliberated prior to the case management conference.[13]

Others remain sceptical of the benefits of such guidance early on in the case, and for good reasons. For a start, any meaningful discussion on the merits will be difficult if the request for arbitration and the answer thereto are short on details (as is often the case). Second, many arbitrators are reluctant to openly debate about the burden of proof for fear of creating an impression of bias. Third, experience shows that counsel for the parties are uncomfortable with disclosing too much of their strategy at the outset, preferring instead to keep their options open. Against this backdrop, it may not be fruitful for the tribunal to engage in any in-depth deliberations on the substance of the dispute already before the first case management conference. In fact, there is an inherent risk that forming even preliminary opinions at an early stage of the proceedings may be counterproductive because initial views are more persistent than people tend to realize.[14]

In the following, I will use the term 'deliberations' in the narrower sense of the word to refer to the tribunal's internal negotiations that take place after the evidentiary hearing and the exchange of the parties' written submissions with a view to deciding on the disputed issues that need to be resolved for a tribunal to render its final award on the merits.

§3.03 ORGANIZING DELIBERATIONS

[A] Building Rapport

Effective deliberations require trust between the members of a tribunal. Trust, in turn, is predicated on mutual respect. An arbitrator should always show due respect to his fellow arbitrators, regardless of their cultural background, level of education, fields of expertise, arbitration experience, or the like. This is imperative as a tribunal simply cannot conduct productive deliberations in the absence of sufficient level of trust.[15]

It is difficult to trust people whom one does not know. Consequently, to ensure constructive deliberations, arbitrators should meet in person as early as possible and establish a bond between themselves. It falls primarily upon the chairperson to convene such a meeting, in a relaxed setting, and to clarify that 'the order of the day is getting to know one another, and not getting down to business'.[16] One cannot overestimate the importance of developing a positive personal relationship among the tribunal members from the outset, before they engage in any difficult negotiations regarding the merits of the case.

13. Derains, *supra* n. 10, at 17.
14. On the effect of biases in arbitral decision-making, *see* section §3.03[F].
15. Jingzhou Tao, *Deliberations of Arbitrators,* in Patricia Shaughnessy and Sherlin Tung (eds), *The Powers and Duties of an Arbitrator: Liber Amicorum Pierre Karrer* (Kluwer Law International B.V., 2017), 358.
16. Fortier, *supra* n. 2, at 832.

Occasionally two of the three arbitrators know each other well (from previous cases or some other professional context), but not the third arbitrator. This may create a perceived imbalance within the tribunal. It is vital that the tribunal cultivates a strong culture of inclusion so that the 'newcomer' feels welcome and on an equal footing with his fellow arbitrators. Failing this, the tribunal's decision-making dynamics may suffer.

Investing in building rapport, based on respect of those involved and a separation of the people from the problem, is crucial throughout the arbitration. The tribunal should seize any opportunity to foster the spirit of 'togetherness' at all stages of the proceedings. For example, during the hearing, arbitrators are encouraged to find ways to meet each other informally, wine and dine together, and take time for small talk before their negotiation session begins and as it ends. The better the arbitrators know one another, the better their deliberations will unfold, and the less room there will be for miscommunication or confrontation between tribunal members.[17]

All this will pay handsomely when the tribunal is finally faced with all the complex issues that need to be resolved in their deliberations. If the members of the tribunal have developed a good working relationship, they have a foundation of trust to build upon in a difficult negotiation. Knowing where the other arbitrators are coming from will help communication and defuse unnecessary tensions. It may even be possible to break the ice by a joke or informal aside.[18] A good working relationship is conducive to smooth deliberations and will pave the way to a high-quality award.

[B] General Format of Deliberations

Most national laws are silent on the question of how the arbitrators should arrange their deliberations.[19] The same is true for institutional arbitration rules. It follows that the tribunal has wide discretion to organize its internal decision-making procedures as it deems appropriate.

In practice, much will depend on case-specific circumstances and personal preferences of each individual arbitrator. The tribunal may choose to conduct the deliberations mainly in writing (e.g., by exchange of questionnaires, memoranda and email correspondence) or it may prefer to hold oral negotiations (in person or by videoconference). Very often, the deliberations will include both written and oral elements. The key is to allow each arbitrator an opportunity to express his views on the

17. *Ibid.*, at 832; Patocchi and Briner, *supra* n. 11, at 301; Pierre A. Karrer, *Introduction to International Arbitration Practice* (Kluwer Law International, 2014), 179-180. These tried and tested negotiation techniques are, of course, not unique to arbitral deliberations but apply more generally in any social interaction. For a particularly insightful presentation on the subject, *see* Roger Fisher, William Ury and Bruce Patton, *Getting to Yes: Negotiating Agreement Without Giving In* (Second Edition, Penguin Books USA Inc., 1991), passim.
18. Fisher, Ury and Patton, *supra* n. 17, at 37.
19. Some national legal systems, however, prescribe specific requirements for the process of arbitral deliberations, including establishing a date on which the deliberations will formally begin. France is one example. *See* Alonso, *supra* n. 7, at 133-134; Gary B. Born, *International Commercial Arbitration* (Third Edition, Kluwer Law International B.V., 2021), 2473, fn. 1061; Emmanuel Gaillard and John Savage (eds), *Fouchard Gaillard Goldman on International Commercial Arbitration* (Kluwer Law International B.V., 1999), 749.

issues to be determined and to stimulate a constructive dialogue among the tribunal members with the aim of reaching a well-reasoned decision. The format through which this takes place is less important.[20]

It is not unusual for the deliberations to proceed in a rather unstructured and ad hoc manner. However, to promote efficiency, the tribunal should plan and set up a procedure and timetable for its deliberations already at an early stage of the arbitration. This is typically done through informal discussions among tribunal members. In the relatively rare instances where the arbitrators disagree on the format of deliberations, they should decide by majority vote. Failing a majority, the procedure falls to be fixed by the chairperson.[21]

It is generally good practice to start deliberating immediately after the evidentiary hearing when the arbitrators are gathered together in the same place (assuming that the hearing has been conducted in person) and while the evidence and arguments are still fresh in their minds. This first round of formal deliberations will normally concentrate on the structure of the award and the way forward in the deliberations. It is also an opportune time to discuss on a general level whether a consensus seems likely to emerge on one or more of the issues to be decided or, conversely, which are the areas of disagreement where further deliberations should focus on. The chairperson should encourage all arbitrators to 'think out loud', clarifying where necessary that any opinions expressed will be considered tentative only. Also, the chairperson should see to it that no member of the tribunal will exert pressure on any of his colleagues and that the tribunal will not jump to conclusions on any of the issues to be decided.[22]

Occasionally, however, it may be best to defer the first formal deliberation meeting until after the tribunal has received the parties' post-hearing briefs and/or hearing transcripts (if any). This may be appropriate especially in heavily fact-driven cases with voluminous evidence. Some arbitrators are disinclined to enter into deliberations immediately after the hearing, fearing that this could overemphasize the weight of witness testimony recently heard as opposed to documentary evidence on the record. They may also wish to reflect on the arguments and evidence discussed at the

20. Alonso, *supra* n. 7, at 135; CIArb Guideline, *supra* n. 6, at 13; Gaillard and Savage, *supra* n. 19, at 749-750; Poudret and Besson, *supra* n. 5, at 650-652; Tao, *supra* n. 15, at 352; Richard M Mosk, *Deliberations of Arbitrators*, in David D. Caron, Stephan W. Schill, Abby Cohen Smutny and Epaminontas E. Triantafilou (eds), *Practising Virtue: Inside International Arbitration* (Oxford University Press, 2015), 487, 495.
21. Born, *supra* n. 19, at 2473-2474; Jeffrey Waincymer, *Procedure and Evidence in International Arbitration* (Kluwer Law International, 2012), 1292-1293; Jacques Werner, *The Arbitrator as Master of Time*, in Laurént Levy and Yves Derains (eds), *Liber Amicorum en l'honneur de Serge Lazareff* (Editions Pedone, 2011), 597.
22. Born, *supra* n. 19, at 2474; Fortier, *supra* n. 2, at 833; Karrer, *supra* n. 17, at 180; Mosk, *supra* n. 20, at 492; Patocchi and Briner, *supra* n. 11, at 301; Tao, *supra* n. 15, at 354-355; Ulmer, *supra* n. 11, at 118; Waincymer, *supra* n. 21, at 1292, 1295; Humphrey Lloyd, Marco Darmon, Jean-Pierre Ancel, Lord Dervaird, Christoph Liebscher and Herman Verbist, *Drafting Awards in ICC Arbitration*, 16 ICC International Court of Arbitration Bulletin, 19, 26 (2005); Robert Briner, *The Role of Chairman*, in Lawrence W. Newman and Richard D. Hill (eds), *The Leading Arbitrators' Guide to International Arbitration* (Second Edition, Juris Publishing, Inc., 2008), 63; Karl-Heinz Böckstiegel, *Case Management by Arbitrators: Experiences and Suggestions*, in Aksen et al., *supra* n. 7, at 125.

hearing in light, and with the benefit, of post-hearing briefs and transcripts. Some may even worry that starting deliberations straight after the hearing would not give the right impression to the parties, who may disapprove of the idea that the arbitrators proceed with their decision-making before the parties have filed their post-hearing submissions.[23]

The formal deliberations may proceed in different ways depending on the atmosphere and working relationship among the tribunal members. If the arbitrators have managed to establish smooth communication routines and a high level of trust, the deliberation procedures may be quite informal. By contrast, in the absence of trust, procedures are necessarily more formal and the deliberations may drag on at a slow pace.[24] Particularly if the chairperson has a reason to suspect the impartiality of one (or both) of the party-appointed arbitrators, he should tread cautiously when conducting the deliberations in order to avoid any breach of due process.[25]

Before the first deliberation meeting takes place, the chairperson should circulate a sufficiently detailed meeting agenda so that the deliberations can be conducted in an orderly fashion. At the same time, the chairperson may wish to draw up and send out a tentative list of issues to be determined by the tribunal and invite his fellow arbitrators to add to the list any items they may consider important. Depending on the circumstances, the chairperson may also invite the co-arbitrators to prepare and exchange short memoranda setting out their preliminary views on one or more of the issues to be resolved. In all cases, however, the members of the tribunal should abstain from taking any definitive positions on the questions at stake at this early stage of the deliberations. Experienced arbitrators will know that if they espouse certain views prematurely, relations among the tribunal may go sour. [26]

Some commentators have suggested that, whenever possible, the chairperson should produce a 'decision tree' before the deliberation meeting. This is a schematic outline which identifies, in logical sequence, the decisions to be taken on the merits of the case, starting with those of a preliminary nature; each decision is then followed by a binary list of consequences, depending on whether the decision is positive or negative, and so on for all the sub-decisions.[27] However, while a 'decision tree' approach may work well in some cases, it may not be appropriate in all circumstances. Critics have noted that an overly detailed agenda may operate like a 'straitjacket' and will often prove to be impractical as 'each arbitrator may wish to give his or her own

23. *See* Alonso, *supra* n. 7, at 135; and the discussion at the ASA Annual Full Day Conference of 1 February 2013 on the topic of *Inside the Black Box: How Arbitral Tribunals Operate and Reach Their Decisions* as recorded in Berger and Schneider, *supra* n. 3, at 35-39 (especially the comments made by Andreas Reiner, Kirstin Dodge, David W. Rivkin and Matthias Scherer).
24. Alonso, *supra* n. 7, at 137; Born, *supra* n. 19, at 2473; Böckstiegel, *supra* n. 22, at 126; Mosk, *supra* n. 20, at 488.
25. *See* in more detail the discussion in section §3.03[H].
26. Alonso, *supra* n. 7, at 137; Mosk, *supra* n. 20, at 489; Patocchi and Briner, *supra* n. 11, at 301; Waincymer, *supra* n. 21, at 1293; Nigel Blackaby, Constantine Partasides, Alan Redfern and J Martin Hunter, *Redfern and Hunter on International Arbitration* (Sixth Edition, Oxford University Press, 2015), 9.110; Karl-Heinz Böckstiegel, *Notes and Samples on Tribunal Deliberations*, in Berger and Schneider, *supra* n. 3, at 129-130.
27. Draetta, *supra* n. 3, at 154-155.

views on certain general aspects of the case and there should be time for an exchange of views on some general aspects whenever one of the arbitrators wishes to do so'.[28]

Even if a tribunal chooses to dispense with a 'decision tree' approach, the first thing it should do when commencing deliberations is to clarify the issues that need to be decided in order for the tribunal to deliver the final award on the merits. This is not necessarily an easy task as the parties' submissions are frequently unclear, with claims and defences sometimes hidden in footnotes or expressed in equivocal terms. Generally speaking, the parties should bear in mind that the quality of the award will often be heavily affected by the quality of their own submissions. If the prayers for relief are not carefully thought out, or the parties leave gaps in their evidence or arguments, there is only so much a tribunal can do by way of proactive case management when striving to produce a well-reasoned award.[29]

Once the stage is set for the deliberation meeting, the question arises as to 'who goes first', meaning the order in which the members of the tribunal should express their preliminary opinions on all the different issues being discussed. Views differ on this question. Many commentators seem to favour a procedure where the chairperson speaks last, allowing his fellow arbitrators to convey their opinions first.[30] But others think the opposite, arguing that the chairperson should express his view first and then ask for the co-arbitrators' input. For example, Yves Derains submits that this method is to be recommended because 'to do the contrary makes the task of reaching unanimity more difficult' for the reason that 'when a co-arbitrator has expressed an opinion, there is a danger that such opinion be crystallized and this co-arbitrator will be less easily convinced that he or she may accept a different opinion at the end of a discussion'.[31]

There is probably no one-size-fits-all answer to the question of which method is the better one. Both have certain advantages and disadvantages. To illustrate: Having the chairperson convey his opinion first will give the co-arbitrators a framework they can address and may have the positive effect that the co-arbitrators can focus on those points where they disagree with the chairperson, which can reduce the length of the discussion.[32] On the other hand, it will run the risk that the co-arbitrators' debate will be confined to less important aspects, or even become meaningless, with each

28. Patocchi and Briner, *supra* n. 11, at 301.
29. To ensure due process, tribunals should be cautious not to 'enrich' the parties' argumentation with aspects that were not clearly invoked during the proceedings. This is sometimes difficult. Particularly if counsel for a party is not qualified in the law applicable to the dispute, the legal argumentation may be deficient to such an extent that the tribunal will be hard-pressed to draft persuasive reasoning. *See* Matthias Scherer, *Drafting the Award*, in Berger and Schneider, *supra* n. 3, at 28-29; Petri Taivalkoski, *Ensuring Enforceability of the Award Against Challenges Based on Alleged Violation of Due Process*, 35 Revista del Club Espanõl del Arbitraje 59, 67 (2019).
30. Alonso, *supra* n. 7, at 137; Briner, *supra* n. 22, at 63; Patocchi and Briner, *supra* n. 11, at 301; Piero Bernardini, *Organisation of Deliberations*, in Berger and Schneider, *supra* n. 3, at 18.
31. Derains, *supra* n. 10, at 23. The author notes, however, that this recommendation only works if the deliberations are 'harmonious'. If they are 'pathological' – meaning that one or both of the co-arbitrators are not fully impartial or independent – the chairperson should refrain from disclosing his thoughts at the early stage of the deliberations to eliminate the risk that the partisan arbitrator may derail the proceedings, leak information to his appointing party or even resign from the tribunal. *Id.*, at 23-24.
32. Briner, *supra* n. 22, at 63; Mosk, *supra* n. 20, at 489.

co-arbitrator promptly joining the chairperson's position whenever the views coincide, thus forming a majority.[33] Added to that, weak or inexperienced co-arbitrators may have a tendency to join the opinion of a strong or eminent chairperson for a misguided sense of loyalty or professional admiration, irrespective of their true views.

But having the co-arbitrators speak first is not without its problems either. While ideally promoting an open and unconstrained exchange of thoughts within a tribunal permeated by a strong sense of collegiality, it may also have the downside of locking the co-arbitrators into their mental positions. Apart from that, if the tribunal's working relations are less than optimal – and particularly if the party-appointed arbitrators are not truly impartial – it may also result in an unnecessarily antagonistic debate between the two co-arbitrators, with each advocating the positions of the party that appointed them. In the end, the chairperson may realize that his fellow arbitrators are simply continuing the parties' 'war' by other means inside the tribunal.

How should the tribunal then go about managing this issue? My suggestion is that, rather than electing either method as inherently superior to the other one, the tribunal should decide the manner in which to proceed based on the case-specific circumstances.[34] The chairperson may explicitly invite his fellow arbitrators to express their preferences, if any, as to the question of 'who goes first'. This may pre-empt unpleasant surprises and reduce tensions between the co-arbitrators.

In all cases, it is paramount that decisions will actually be reached at the deliberations. It is not unusual for the arbitrators to have constructive discussions, especially over a good lunch or dinner, but stop short of reaching ultimate findings in respect of all the issues that need to be resolved. Subsequently, when the award is being drafted, it may transpire that critical issues are still open and need to be further negotiated among the arbitrators. To avoid unnecessary prolongation of the deliberations, it will often be useful for the chairperson to confirm the outcome of the tribunal's discussions in writing, possibly indicating the points on which no full agreement has yet been reached, and communicate this as soon as possible to the co-arbitrators, noting that their agreement will be assumed if they do not raise objections by a set time limit.[35]

---

33. Bernardini, *supra* n. 30, at 18.
34. Some experienced arbitrators have voiced similar ideas. By way of example, Karl-Heinz Böckstiegel writes that 'it will depend on circumstances whether it is more advisable for the party-appointed co-arbitrators to express their opinions first – in that case probably starting with the arbitrator appointed by the claimant – or for the chairman's inclinations to be disclosed first so that the discussion can concentrate on issues where the co-arbitrators disagree'; Böckstiegel, *supra* n. 22, at 126. In the same vein, *see* Draetta, *supra* n. 3, at 155; Mosk, *supra* n. 20, at 488-489; and Waincymer, *supra* n. 21, at 1293, who also observes that 'psychological studies show that the last person in a group who has a different view to preceding speakers will often feel intimidated and reluctant to speak out about their honest belief. Shifting the order so that they can sometimes speak first ensures that tribunal members feel that their views are equally important'.
35. Briner, *supra* n. 22, at 63; Patocchi and Briner, *supra* n. 11, at 301; Scherer, *supra* n. 29, at 27. Ugo Draetta also suggests that 'it is a good idea to document [the tribunal's] decisions immediately, for example, by marking them on a whiteboard or by using some other device, immediately followed by the minutes of the meeting drawn up by the President and setting out the conclusions reached'. The author warns that a failure to do so increases 'the risk of the

Equally important, to avoid any undue delay in the rendering of a final award, the tribunal should set aside sufficient time for the deliberations from the outset. International arbitrators are invariably busy people who may find it difficult to schedule deliberation meetings at short notice. All too often the tribunal has blocked out time for the hearing but is then immediately immersed in wholly unrelated matters once the hearing is finished, desperately seeking to fit deliberations into whatever slots the arbitrators may find in their calendars. On a related note, it is probably not an overstatement to say that too many arbitrators consider deliberations to be a low-priority exercise, although in actual fact it should be on the very top of their agenda. It falls primarily upon the chairperson to proactively manage the tribunal's decision-making procedures, which includes establishing a well-planned process and timetable for the deliberation, reaching-a-decision and drafting-the-award phases with a view to promoting efficiency and ensuring that the final award can be issued swiftly.[36]

One final point merits mentioning. During the deliberations, the tribunal should avoid any communications between the chairperson and only one of the co-arbitrators. Put differently, all deliberations on the substance of the dispute should be conducted between all three arbitrators so as to avoid any suspicions or later allegations by a party (or an arbitrator) that one of the arbitrators did not have an opportunity to fully participate in the deliberations and influence the tribunal's decision-making on a particular point. A limited exception to this general rule may, however, arise in cases where one co-arbitrator intentionally refuses to participate in the deliberations or seeks to obstruct them. Such exceptional situations are discussed later in this article.[37]

[C] Assigning Duties Among Arbitrators

The end product of an arbitration is the final award on the merits. Arbitrators should start preparing the first draft of it early on. They should also consider whether the work might be split between the members of the tribunal, with each contributing specific parts of the draft.

In many cases, the chairperson is responsible for the drafting of the entire award, while the co-arbitrators' role is limited to commenting on the draft(s) prepared by the chairperson. Ideally, the latter should begin to prepare the narrative section (the so-called recital) already soon after the first case management conference. The draft

deliberation being reopened later "on paper"' and may also have the effect that 'when the President produces the draft award, at least one of the co-arbitrators is likely to be taken by surprise, which surely will be immediately followed by criticism and arguments, which will provoke in turn a similar reaction from the other co-arbitrator. Sometimes the entire deliberation must be repeated'. *See* Draetta, *supra* n. 3, at 158-159.

36. Böckstiegel, *supra* n. 26, at 129; Ulmer, *supra* n. 11, at 118-119; Werner, *supra* n. 21, at 597. Jeffrey Waincymer aptly notes that 'the chair should manage the stages of deliberation, preparation of drafts, reviewing drafts, revisions, finalisation, signature and service' and that 'it makes sense to allocate time periods where all tribunal members are needed for any of these steps at the same time as designating hearing times [as] otherwise delays are only to be anticipated for busy arbitrators trying to coordinate their spare time'. *See* Waincymer, *supra* n. 21, at 1292-1293.
37. *See* section §3.03[H].

recital should then be updated throughout the proceedings by including information on the parties and their counsel, the arbitral tribunal and administrative secretary (if any), the procedural history of the case, the relief sought by the parties and their main factual and legal arguments, as well as other non-contentious matters. The chairperson will typically circulate the first draft award before, or shortly after, the evidentiary hearing for any technical comments by the co-arbitrators. No member of the tribunal should include his views on any substantive issues in this first draft.[38]

It is not unusual, however, for a chairperson to suggest that his fellow arbitrators produce the first draft of certain parts of the award for comment by the other tribunal members. For example, it may be agreed that one co-arbitrator will draft the procedural history section and the other one the section dealing with the costs of the arbitration. Other arrangements are possible too. Not infrequently, if only one of the arbitrators is qualified in the law applicable to the contract in dispute, the other tribunal members may expect specific contributions from him. According to one prominent practitioner, such an arbitrator may be 'invited to study complex legal issues and to submit memoranda on them' and even 'draft the parts of the award on these legal issues, in particular if the conclusion in this respect is against the party by which he or she was nominated'.[39]

Tribunals should think carefully though before agreeing on any division of work among their members. 'Collective drafting' may not be advisable if the arbitrators come from vastly different legal cultures, or if their linguistic skills differ greatly.[40] In any event, the chairperson ought to be responsible for the coordination of the work and the consistency of the tribunal's reasoning. Further, in all cases, the chairperson should maintain the overall editorial control in order to ensure consistency in the use of terms and in style.[41]

[D] Role of Administrative Secretaries and Tribunal-Appointed Experts

Different arbitrators take different views on the use of tribunal secretaries. Some consider them useful, especially in document-heavy cases where an administrative secretary can arguably add efficiency to the arbitral process; others resist delegating any part of the arbitrators' duties to any third person, irrespective of the nature of the dispute.

The process of appointing an administrative secretary will depend on the applicable rules. Some rules leave the decision to the tribunal itself, whereas others

38. Born, *supra* n. 19, at 2475; Böckstiegel, *supra* n. 26, at 129-130; Draetta, *supra* n. 3, at 151-152; Fortier, *supra* n. 2, at 833-834; Lloyd et al., *supra* n. 22, at 25; Patocchi and Briner, *supra* n. 11, at 303; Waincymer, *supra* n. 21, at 1313; Albert Jan van den Berg, *Organizing an International Arbitration: Practice Pointers*, in Newman and Hill, *supra* n. 2, at 418.
39. Derains, *supra* n. 10, at 20. The author also states that 'this is advisable as, provided that co-arbitrator is really convinced of the correctness of the solution, he or she will know how to express it in a way which may convince the losing party that it could not win'.
40. Michael Black, *A Short Note on the Decision-making Process*, in Berger and Schneider, *supra* n. 3, at 121; Scherer, *supra* n. 29, at 27.
41. Black, *supra* n. 40, at 121; Lloyd et al., *supra* n. 22, at 25.

require the acceptance of the parties and/or the institute concerned. Even where not mandated to do so by the applicable rules, it is good practice for a tribunal to consult the parties before proceeding with the appointment. If any party objects to the use of a secretary, the arbitrators should generally refrain from appointing one.[42]

The duties of an administrative secretary have been the subject of much debate in recent years. There is a general consensus that the arbitrator's mandate is fundamentally personal and non-delegable in the sense that the tribunal is not permitted to delegate its essential decision-making functions to anyone else, including a tribunal secretary. But apart from that, the question of whether particular tasks may be entrusted with an administrative secretary – especially in the context of deliberations – provides a fertile ground for disagreement. For instance, views diverge among arbitration practitioners as to whether it is appropriate to allow a secretary to:

- summarize the parties' written submissions, evidence or legal positions for the benefit of the tribunal;
- be present at the deliberations for the purpose of subsequently drafting (parts of) the final award for the tribunal's review; or
- discuss any part of the merits of the case with the arbitrators, possibly voicing the secretary's own opinion during the deliberations.[43]

While some practitioners think that there is nothing wrong in allowing a secretary to do any of these things so long as the tribunal retains its decision-making control, others fear that relying too much on the assistance of an administrative secretary may discourage the arbitrators from acquiring intimate knowledge of the complete case file or put a damper on their direct personal communications. It has also been said that the act of writing is the ultimate safeguard of intellectual control over the decision-making process,[44] which is why the tribunal should never let a secretary to draft any part of the tribunal's reasoning or the dispositive section of the award.

Various arbitration institutes have published guidance notes providing specific examples of apparently non-controversial tasks that may be safely delegated to an administrative secretary in arbitration proceedings governed by the rules of the institute in question.[45] In the absence of such guidance, a tribunal should consult the

42. Some arbitration institutes expressly forbid the appointment of a secretary over the objection of a party; *see, e.g.*, the ICC Note to Parties and Arbitral Tribunals on the Conduct of the Arbitration (effective as of 1 January 2021), para. 221. Other institutes, however, cater for the eventuality that one party may raise a purely dilatory objection which should not necessarily exclude the appointment where considered appropriate. For example, the Finland Arbitration Institute (FAI) Note on the Use of a Secretary (2020) provides that 'if any party objects to the use of a secretary, the arbitral tribunal may proceed with the appointment only where the tribunal is convinced that this will benefit all parties by saving time and costs' (para. 2.3).
43. For these and other examples, *see* J. Ole Jensen, *Aligning Arbitrator Assistance with the Parties' Legitimate Expectations: Proposal of a 'Traffic Light Scale of Permissible Tribunal Secretary Tasks'*, 38 ASA Bulletin, 375, 390-394 (2020).
44. Zachary Douglas, *The Secretary to the Arbitral Tribunal*, in Berger and Schneider, *supra* n. 3, at 89.
45. *See, e.g.*, the list of 'organisational and administrative tasks' set out in para. 224 of the ICC Note, *supra* n. 42.

parties regarding the tasks of a secretary.[46] This is prudent to avoid later allegations that the arbitrators have exceeded their mandate, or violated due process, by allowing an administrative secretary to influence the tribunal's decision-making in an improper manner.

The use of *tribunal-appointed experts* is relatively rare in international arbitration; it is much more common for each party to rely on its own party-appointed experts.[47] Sometimes a tribunal-appointed expert is needed though. There are a number of practical issues that a tribunal has to consider and agree with the parties when engaging a tribunal expert.[48] In addition, as with the administrative secretary, the tribunal must be careful not to delegate its decision-making function to the expert, and to avoid any impression of doing so. To that effect, arbitrators should resist the idea of having private meetings with the expert, without the presence of counsel for each party. Ignoring this advice can have costly consequences. I concur with the view that 'if a tribunal were to listen to additional input from the expert during a meeting or deliberations without giving the parties the opportunity to comment on that input before taking it into account, this would undoubtedly breach rules of natural justice. While the tribunal may want the expert present to walk them through the available evidence, it would be very easy for the line between explanation and comment to be crossed'.[49]

[E] About Bargaining

The decision-making dynamics within a three-person tribunal may be greatly influenced by the applicable arbitration regime, particularly the question of how the arbitrators will reach a decision if they are not unanimous. Laws and rules differ on this point, with some requiring a majority decision and others allowing the chairperson to decide alone where a majority cannot be obtained. In the former system (in the following, 'system A'), the chairperson must 'win' the vote of at least one of the co-arbitrators (assuming that the co-arbitrators disagree with each other) for a tribunal to be able to render an award. In the latter system (in the following, 'system B'), however, the chairperson may act more independently, and his role and influence in the deliberations may therefore be much more substantial.[50]

---

46. A few arbitration rules expressly provide for such consultation. *See, e.g.*, the Arbitration Rules of the Arbitration Institute of the Stockholm Chamber of Commerce (the SCC Rules) of 2017, Article 24(2).
47. Nathan D. O'Malley, *Rules of Evidence in International Arbitration: An Annotated Guide* (Second Edition, Informa Law from Routledge, 2019), 5.03.
48. For an informative overview of such issues and how they may be dealt with, *see* O'Malley, *supra* n. 47, at 6.19-6.22, 6.39-6.43; and Roman Khodykin and Carol Mulcahy (Consultant Editor Nicholas Fletcher QC), *A Guide to the IBA Rules on the Taking of Evidence in International Arbitration* (Oxford University Press, 2019), 9.30-9.37, 10.20-10.47 and a separate checklist in Appendix 11.
49. Khodykin and Mulcahy, *supra* n. 48, at 9.121. The authors go on to note that 'unsurprisingly, there have been instances where national courts have found that *ex parte* meetings between a tribunal and a tribunal-appointed expert amount to an irregularity'. *Id.*, at 9.122.
50. Born, *supra* n. 19, at 2474, 3302; Gaillard and Savage, *supra* n. 19, at 747-748.

The far-reaching consequences of this difference may be illustrated with the following example: Company X has commenced arbitration proceedings against company Z, claiming damages for breach of contract in the amount of EUR 50 million. The arbitrator nominated by the claimant finds that Z has breached the contract but that it should (for whatever reason) be ordered to pay only half of the damages claimed by X, i.e., EUR 25 million. On the other hand, the arbitrator nominated by the respondent holds that Z is not liable at all and that X's claim against Z should be rejected entirely. Under system B, if the chairperson is of the opinion that Z has breached the contract but that the amount of damages to be awarded to X should not exceed EUR 10 million, then the chairperson can impose his view and the award will be made accordingly. By contrast, under system A – which requires a majority decision – the chairperson would have needed to reach a compromise with one of the co-arbitrators in order to issue an award.

There is much to commend in system B, with the possibility of a chairman-alone award, as it will avoid a deadlock where the arbitrators are unable to agree on the outcome of a case. While it may be expected that the chairperson is normally able to work out a compromise with one of the co-arbitrators and to reach a majority decision, there may be situations where he finds *both* co-arbitrators' positions unreasonable. The prospect of a chairman-alone award will prove valuable in such circumstances as the presiding arbitrator – presumptively the most neutral member of the panel – need not compromise his views and join with the least unreasonable of the co-arbitrators in order to form a majority. Moreover, that possibility may have a preventive effect in and of itself, as knowledge that unreasonable positions can yield no tactical benefit dissuades partisan conduct on the part of the co-arbitrators.[51]

It goes without saying that no member of a tribunal should enter into deliberations with the aim of bulldozing his way through the fellow arbitrators' arguments, convinced that only he holds all the right answers. Quite the contrary: it is the hallmark of a good arbitrator to be open-minded, always prepared to listen and willing to be persuaded. A diligent arbitrator should not hesitate to modify his views if it becomes apparent, in the course of the deliberations, that his initial position was untenable.[52]

In practice, most arbitrators are reasonable people able to negotiate and compromise in order to reach a unanimous decision. Occasionally this tendency to concede and abandon initial negotiation positions may go so far that arbitrators are accused of falling victim to the 'splitting the baby syndrome', delivering an uneasy compromise award rather than deciding the dispute strictly according to the applicable legal rules and the merits of the case.[53] For example, in a case concerning damages for an early

51. Jan Paulsson and Georgios Petrochilos, *Revision of the UNCITRAL Arbitration Rules* (2006), 126 at para. 235 (available at: http://uncitral.un.org/sites/uncitral.un.org/files/media-documents/uncitral/en/arbrules_report.pdf; accessed 26 March 2021).
52. Fortier, *supra* n. 2, at 834; Tao, *supra* n. 15, at 356; Yves Derains and Laurent Lévy, *Introduction*, in Yves Derains and Laurent Lévy (eds), *Is Arbitration Only As Good As the Arbitrator? Status, Powers and Role of the Arbitrator* (ICC Publication No. 714E, 2011), 9.
53. Gary Born remarks that 'in some deliberations, there is a substantial amount of what might look like "negotiation," in which different issues are resolved through give-and-take. This give-and-take sometimes derives from purely-objective assessment of the merits of different issues and

termination of a business contract where the respondent disputes that the termination was unlawful, one co-arbitrator (typically the one appointed by the respondent) may agree to find liability for damages if the other co-arbitrator (typically the one appointed by the claimant) is willing to compromise on the amount of damages to be awarded to the claimant.[54] Further, it sometimes happens that the co-arbitrator who is left in the minority in the tribunal's deliberations on the substance of the dispute indicates, more or less directly, that he might be willing to accept the majority's reasoning and outcome provided that the tribunal will adjust its decision on the allocation of costs, for example, by not awarding full costs to the claimant although it prevailed on the merits in full.[55]

Are arbitrators within their rights when engaging in such give-and-take? Should the chairperson allow such 'bargaining' when necessary to reach a unanimous award? Anecdotal evidence suggests that many chairpersons are willing to go to great lengths to secure unanimity, feeling that they have failed to manage the deliberations if all arbitrators are not able to agree on the outcome. However, there are also many practitioners who frown upon the kind of quid pro quo setting, where one arbitrator is amenable to concurring with another one only if the latter concedes a particular point. The critics of 'bargaining' underscore that the chairperson should not be overzealous about achieving unanimity because the tribunal's ultimate goal is to reach a correct decision, even if it results in one co-arbitrator issuing a dissenting opinion. If the chairperson agrees with one co-arbitrator that X is right, it is not legitimate to 'bargain' with the minority arbitrator and compromise the correct outcome, so the argument goes.[56]

Whatever the rights and wrongs of this debate, arbitrators should be candid about its existence and prepared to deal with any 'bargaining attempts' if and when they arise in actual deliberations. It is then primarily the chairperson's task to accommodate the different approaches that individual tribunal members may have to the negotiation process and to ultimately strike a balance between the quest for the accurate outcome, on the one hand, and the quest for a unanimous award, on the other hand.[57]

---

sometimes from other factors (including personal egos, general adjudicative philosophies, non-neutral co-arbitrators and the like)'. *See* Born, *supra* n. 19, at 2474. Ugo Draetta proposes various reasons for 'split the baby' decisions, such as the tribunal's lack of 'courage to decide', 'a distorted sense of "equity"', or simply 'the kind of laziness on the part of the arbitrators, in particular the President, in addressing the merits of the claims and counterclaims'. *See* Draetta, *supra* n. 3, at 164-165. *See* also Derains and Lévy, *supra* n. 52, at 8 (explaining brilliantly why 'the worst arbitrator' is 'the one who hates to displease the parties').

54. This example was specifically discussed at the ASA Conference of 1 February 2013, *supra* n. 23. The discussion is recorded in Bernhard F. Meyer, *Structuring a Bargaining Process*, in Berger and Schneider, *supra* n. 3, at 59-66.
55. Bernard Hanotiau, *The Parties' Costs of Arbitration*, in Yves Derains and Richard H. Kreindler (eds), *Evaluation of Damages in International Arbitration* (ICC Publication No. 668, 2006), 221.
56. *See* the discussion at the ASA Conference of 1 February 2013, *supra* n. 23, as recorded in Berger and Schneider, *supra* n. 3, at 65-66, 70 (especially the comments made by Paolo Michele Patocchi and Andreas Reiner).
57. Further on dissenting opinions, *see* section §3.03[G].

The question of 'bargaining' should be separated from the formal *voting rules* that the arbitrators need to comply with under the *lex arbitri*. As an alternative to the chairperson's casting vote, some arbitration laws have introduced a so-called co-adjustment rule which is applicable when the arbitrators are to award a sum of money, and cannot obtain a majority for any particular sum. In such event, the votes in favour of the highest amount are counted with the votes in favour of the next highest amount until a majority is reached.[58] The difference between these two methods may be illustrated with the following example: All three arbitrators grant a claim for damages and vote that the respondent shall pay EUR 1 million, EUR 2 million and EUR 10 million (the chairperson). According to the co-adjustment rule, the amount of the award will be EUR 2 million, whereas under the model based on the chairperson's casting vote, the amount will be EUR 10 million.[59]

How the arbitrators arrange their voting procedures can be decisive to the outcome of the case in other circumstances as well. By way of illustration, imagine that the co-arbitrators are in agreement that liability in damages exists but disagree as to the quantum of the damages. The chairperson, on the other hand, wishes to dismiss the case on the grounds that there is no liability in damages at all. Should the co-arbitrators be in agreement on all issues in order to avoid the outcome being decided by the chairperson? Or is the voting to be divided into different votes so that each question is decided independently?

Arbitration laws are generally silent on this question, and commentators have proposed conflicting solutions. For instance, Redfern and Hunter submit that 'if there is lack of unanimity in relation to one of many issues, the award as a whole will usually be issued by a majority. If there is no majority in relation to a number of issues, the award as a whole should be that of the presiding arbitrator if the relevant rules permit; otherwise, the arbitrators will have to continue, in one way or another, to try and reach a majority decision'.[60] By contrast, Poudret and Besson assert that the chairman should not 'necessarily make use of his casting vote and decide alone on all the issues when a majority is reached on some points only but not on others. Unless such questions are necessarily linked, we feel that it is preferable to vote on each of them and only allow the chairman's casting vote where this is indispensable'.[61]

As evident from the above discussion, arbitrators enjoy certain discretion when fixing their internal voting procedures. They should exercise that discretion prudently in light of the importance that specific voting arrangements may have on the final outcome of the case.

58. *See, e.g.*, section 32(1) of the Finnish Arbitration Act (967/1992, as amended). *See* also Article 22(3) of the 1966 European Convention providing a Uniform Law on Arbitration (known as the 'Strasbourg Uniform Law'; available at https://rm.coe.int/CoERMPublicCommonSearchServices/DisplayDCTMContent?documentId=090000168006ff61; accessed 26 March 2021).
59. Madsen, *supra* n. 5, at 319-320.
60. Redfern and Hunter, *supra* n. 26, at 9.118.
61. Poudret and Besson, *supra* n. 5, at 661. Madsen appears to be of the same opinion; *see supra* n. 5, at 320-322.

[F] Dealing with Biases

It is common knowledge that arbitrators with different cultural background view arguments and evidence in a different light. By way of example, the evidentiary weight of oral versus documentary evidence may be considered differently depending on the nationality and legal training of the tribunal members. Similarly, what strikes one arbitrator as a credible witness testimony may appear as evasive and untrustworthy to another one, simply because of cultural predispositions.

In recent years, psychologists and other students of human behaviour have also investigated how various psychological biases affect legal decision-making, including during the deliberations of an arbitral tribunal. In remarkable studies, researchers have determined that a sizable percentage of arbitrators have established a clear leaning in the case by the end of the opening statement (prior to any exposure to witness evidence). Moreover, with each arbitrator being uniquely influenced by his lifetime experiences, they construct different assessments of cases even when exposed to the very same facts, evidence and arguments. This process of creating a narrative for the case is central to the arbitrator's ultimate findings on the substance of the dispute: once a narrative has become firmly visualized, arbitrators will rarely change their opinions about what happened, although they will occasionally change their minds about how the events should be legally classified.[62]

Researchers have labelled this tendency as 'confirmation bias' (sometimes also referred to as 'belief bias effect'). Essentially, it stands for the proposition that the evaluation of evidence is influenced by prior beliefs such that people are inclined to selectively use the information to arrive at conclusions that justify their prior beliefs. Additionally, when confronted with information that contradicts their existing views, people evaluate it with greater scepticism.[63] This tendency is closely related to another phenomenon known as the pre-decisional distortion of information, which posits that once initially neutral decision-makers identify a leading alternative based on the evaluation of the first evidence they encounter, they then have a tendency to bias their evaluation of subsequently encountered information towards supporting the leading alternative.[64]

'Anchoring' is another well-documented bias. Study after study has shown that when people make numerical estimates, they commonly rely on the *initial value* available to them (irrespective of their expertise). That initial value tends to 'anchor'

62. Richard C. Waites and James E. Lawrence, *Psychological Dynamics in International Arbitration Advocacy*, in Bishop and Kehoe, *supra* n. 11, at 109-110, 114; Edna Sussman, *Biases and Heuristics in Arbitrator Decision-Making: Reflections on How to Counteract or Play to Them*, in Tony Cole (ed), *The Roles of Psychology in International Arbitration* (Kluwer Law International B.V., 2017), 64.
63. Peter Ayton and Geneviève Helleringer, *Bias, Vested Interests and Self-Deception in Judgment and Decision-Making: Challenges to Arbitrator Impartiality*, in Cole, *supra* n. 62, at 38. American judge and legal scholar Richard Posner has summarized the idea concisely: 'people hate being in a state of doubt and will do whatever is necessary to move from doubt to belief'. *See* Richard Posner, *The Jurisprudence of Skepticism*, 86 Michigan Law Review 827, 873 (1988).
64. Ayton and Helleringer, *supra* n. 63, at 39-40.

their final estimates even if the anchor provides no useful information.[65] In other words, even completely irrelevant numbers unconsciously move the decision-maker's thinking in the direction of that number. The 'anchoring bias' may be pernicious especially in the tribunal's assessment of the parties' conflicting damages calculations.[66]

The difficulty with biases lies in the fact that they are largely subconscious. People are oblivious to the contaminating effect that biases have on their judgment, labouring instead under the illusion of objectivity. Worse still, studies have concluded that simply understanding the need to avoid biases, and the desire to overcome them, is not sufficient to cure the problem: awareness of the mental contaminant and motivation to correct it is unlikely to lead to full control.[67]

All this paints a rather grim picture of the hurdles that arbitrators will face when endeavouring to conduct their deliberations impartially and with an open mind. While not a fail-safe procedure to counter the harmful effects of biases, arbitrators may find it useful to consider the following list of actions in order to mitigate the problem:

- Create a checklist with columns for each party, listing the facts that favour the party in question. Then do the same for legal arguments.
- Reduce your reliance on memory. Look for record citations for all of the important facts for both sides to ensure that you have recalled them correctly.
- Consult your fellow arbitrators closely. Review all aspects of the facts and law with them. Elicit independent thinking of each member of the tribunal.
- Identify why you may be wrong, what are the important pieces of evidence that go the other way and why are they not reliable or credible.
- Replay how you reached your conclusion. Think about what evidence you rejected, and why, in reaching that conclusion.
- Ask yourself what the losing party would feel that you overlooked in your analysis.[68]

65. Mark A. Cymrot and Paul Levine, *Going First Makes a Difference: Decision-Making Dynamics in Arbitration*, in Cole, *supra* n. 62, at 180-182; Sussman, *supra* n. 62, at 55.
66. Sussman, *supra* n. 62, at 55-56. *See* also US District Judge Mark W. Bennett (as quoted in Cymrot and Levine, *supra* n. 65, at 184): 'anchoring bias suggests that the first items of information are likely to receive more consideration than information that appears later. Although the order in which information is received should be irrelevant to decisions that rely on that information, the mind does not work this way. First impressions are powerful influences on judgment and seem to provide the prism through which subsequent information is filtered. Even when first impressions are erroneous, they continue to affect judgment long after they have been discredited'.
67. Ayton and Helleringer, *supra* n. 63, at 41-43; Sussman, *supra* n. 62, at 65-66. As eloquently explained by the late, great Lord Goff in *R v. Gough* [1993] 2 All ER 724: 'bias is such an insidious thing that, even though a person may in good faith believe that he was acting impartially, his mind may unconsciously be affected by bias'.
68. The above list is inspired by, and partly quoted from, Sussman, *supra* n. 62, at 67-68.

[G] Dealing with Dissents

Harmonious deliberations do not necessarily imply unanimity on all issues to be decided. Even tribunals permeated by a strong spirit of collegiality and mutual respect may disagree on complex substantive or procedural matters.[69] The question then arises whether, and how, a dissenting arbitrator may voice his dissent where necessary.

Most arbitration laws and rules do not mention dissenting opinions. Under such systems, dissenting opinions are generally permitted (although not encouraged). In practice, however, many arbitrators (especially chairpersons) feel that they should do their utmost to produce a unanimous award and avoid dissents. There are many reasons for that: unanimous awards have a greater legitimacy in the eyes of the parties and may encourage voluntary compliance, whereas a majority award may engender doubts about the outcome and invite unmeritorious challenges; allowing arbitrators to dissent 'too easily' can dissuade them from seeking a unanimous solution; in some legal systems, dissents may be seen as impinging upon the secrecy of the tribunal's deliberations; and last but not least, in commercial arbitration, dissenting opinions rarely serve any meaningful purpose as there is no 'auditorio' except for the parties, who need a decision, not an opinion. Besides, it is beyond question that dissenting opinions should not be issued merely in order to 'provide therapy' for the losing party (who nominated the dissenting co-arbitrator) or for the dissenter himself (who may feel marginalized for not being able to persuade his co-arbitrators to agree with him).[70] If party-appointed arbitrators show their allegiance through a dissent, they undermine the authority and perceived neutrality and independence of the arbitral tribunal.[71]

There is undoubtedly force in the arguments against dissenting opinions in commercial cases.[72] To add one consideration to the list, arbitrators – and the parties

69. Derains explains this well: 'L'harmonie ne se confond pas avec l'unisson. En matière internationale, les arbitres appartiennent souvent à des traditions juridiques différentes. Il en résulte des conceptions opposées non seulement quant à la conduite de la procédure mais aussi quant à l'analyse des dispositions contractuelles et la perceptions des relations d'affaires, voire des relations humaines plus généralement. ... Un délibéré harmonieux n'est pas un délibéré dominé par une unanimité permanente. Il connaît des confrontations d'idées, des débats parfois difficiles. Mais il se distingue du délibéré pathologique, en ce que les divergences d'opinions entre les arbitres résultent de convictions personnelles de chacun d'entre eux et ne sont pas le simple reflet des positions contradictoires des parties.' *See* Derains, *supra* n. 7, at 231.
70. C Mark Baker and Lucy Greenwood, *Dissent – But Only If You REALLY Feel You Must: Why Dissenting Opinions in International Commercial Arbitration Should Only Appear in Exceptional Circumstances*, 7 Dispute Resolution International, 31, 39 (2013).
71. For a concise summary of arguments for and against dissents, *see* Manuel Arroyo, *Dealing with Dissenting Opinions in the Award: Some Options for the Tribunal*, 26 ASA Bulletin 437, 457-459 (2008); and Audley Sheppard and Daphna Kapeliuk, *Dissents in International Arbitration*, in Cole, *supra* n. 62, at 324-328, 332-336.
72. Investment arbitration is a slightly different animal. While reliable statistics are hard to find, dissenting opinions seem to be more common in investor-state cases than in commercial arbitration. Some see them as contributing to the development of investment law, especially as most treaty-based awards are publicly available. However, a few renowned practitioners have criticized dissenting opinions in investment cases too for the reason that nearly 100% of them are in favour of the party that appointed the dissenting arbitrator, which raises concerns about neutrality. On this debate, *see* Jan Paulsson, *Moral Hazard in International Dispute Resolution*, 25 ICSID Rev – FILJ 339, 339-355 (2010); Albert Jan van den Berg, *Dissenting Opinions by*

themselves - should realize that an arbitrator is not expected to issue a dissent even though he would disagree on some aspect of the tribunal's decision. Indeed, there is no duty to dissent, except perhaps in the very rare case of breach of due process during deliberations.[73] Still, in the end, intellectual honesty and rigour must rule the day, and in certain cases dissents may be appropriate. I personally subscribe to the view that if an arbitrator strongly believes that the majority is taking such a seriously wrong decision that his conscience does not allow him to remain silent - and the minority arbitrator fails to convince his fellow arbitrators to change their mind - there is nothing wrong in penning a dissent. But such circumstances probably do not arise very often.

There are many different ways in which an arbitrator may express his dissent: decline to sign the award at all; sign the award noting his dissent next to his signature; sign the award, but request that his dissent be expressly mentioned in the reasoning of the award, in more or less detail, for example, next to the portions of the award to which the dissent relates (or even just in a footnote); or write a separate dissenting opinion to be appended to the award.[74] As a practical matter, the tribunal will need to discuss internally how the dissent should be technically dealt with. If the majority arbitrators agree on the incorporation of the dissenting opinion in the award, they could include it in full; include a summary of the dissenter's views; or intersperse particular aspects of the dissent throughout the majority reasoning. Where reference is made to the dissent, the majority arbitrators can then decide whether or not to give reasons as to why they disagree with the dissenter.[75]

An arbitrator who wishes to issue a dissenting opinion should exercise that right with due respect for the integrity of the process and his duty of collegiality to fellow arbitrators. The dissenting opinion should not disclose any details of the deliberations; it should be clearly identified as the personal opinion of its author; it should be limited to explaining the basis of the opinion, rather than criticizing and thereby undermining the majority reasoning; it should not raise any new arguments that the arbitrator failed to raise at the deliberations; and it should not unduly assist the losing party in asserting

Party-Appointed Arbitrators in Investment Arbitration, in Mahnoush H Arsanjani, Jacob Katz Cogan, Robert D Sloane and Siegfried Wiessner (eds), *Looking to the Future: Essays on International Law in Honor of W Michael Reisman* (Martinus Nijhoff, 2011), 821-843; Charles N. Brower and Charles B. Rosenberg, *The Death of the Two-Headed Nightingale: Why the Paulsson–van den Berg Presumption That Party-Appointed Arbitrators are Untrustworthy is Wrongheaded*, 29 Arbitration International 7, 7-44 (2013); Albert Jan van den Berg, *Charles Brower's Problem with 100%–Dissenting Opinions by Party-Appointed Arbitrators in Investment Arbitration*, in Caron et al., *supra* n. 20, 504-513; Born, *supra* n. 19, at 3313.

73. Waincymer, *supra* n. 21, at 1299; Antonias Dimolitsa, *Are Genuine Dissenting Opinions of Any Real Use?*, in Andrea Carlevaris, Laurent Lévy, Alexis Mourre and Eric A. Schwartz (eds), *International Arbitration Under Review: Essays in Honour of John Beechey* (ICC Publication No. 772E, 2015), 139; Bernhard Berger, *Rights and Obligations of Arbitrators in the Deliberations*, 31 ASA Bulletin 244, 260 (2013). Berger refers approvingly to Article 9 of the IBA Rules of Ethics for International Arbitrators (1987), which provides that an exemption from the general confidentiality of deliberations may have to be made if the minority arbitrator 'considers it his duty to disclose any material misconduct or fraud on the part of his fellow arbitrators'.
74. Draetta, *supra* n. 3, at 168-169; Sheppard and Kapeliuk, *supra* n. 71, at 313.
75. Arroyo, *supra* n. 71, at 459-461; Waincymer, *supra* n. 21, at 1307.

grounds for annulment or challenges to enforcement.[76] Also, the minority arbitrator should produce a written draft of the dissenting opinion for consideration by the other arbitrators so as not to take them by surprise, and to give the majority arbitrators an additional chance to reconsider and improve their reasoning.[77]

It is primarily the chairperson's responsibility to organize the deliberations smoothly in the face of dissenting opinion(s). Unperturbed by the prospect of dissent, the chairperson should make the arrangements required in order for the dissent to be received, considered and incorporated into the award. As a general rule, no extension of time to complete the deliberations should be granted merely on the grounds that the minority arbitrator wishes to formulate a dissenting opinion.[78] The chairperson should also ensure that the rendering of the award will not be delayed because of a dilatory dissenting arbitrator.[79]

[H] Dealing with Partisan Arbitrators and Other Difficult Tribunal Members

It is often said that party-appointed arbitrators have a special role in ensuring that their appointing party's case is properly understood by the tribunal. However, there is a fine line between fulfilling that role and sacrificing one's integrity. Experience tells that some co-arbitrators have difficulties being fully impartial, and they may express a tendency to discount the more complex or weaker aspects of the nominating party's case.[80] Occasionally a party-appointed arbitrator may act in a completely partisan manner. Examples include: explicitly advocating the nominating party's positions during the deliberations; threatening to resign if the majority will not agree to rule in

76. Arroyo, *supra* n. 71, at 456; CIArb Guideline, *supra* n. 6, at 14-15; Draetta, *supra* n. 3, at 171-172; Waincymer, *supra* n. 21, at 1311-1312; James H. Carter, *The Rights and Duties of the Arbitrator: Six Aspects of the Rule of Reasonableness*, in Jean-François Bourque (ed), *The Status of the Arbitrator, ICC International Court of Arbitration Bulletin: 1995 Special Supplement* (ICC Publishing S.A., 1995), 33; Alan Redfern, *The 2003 Freshfields Lecture – Dissenting Opinions in International Arbitration: The Good, the Bad and the Ugly*, 20 Arbitration International 223, 226 (2004). Redfern submits that 'the "good" dissent may be short, polite and above all restrained, so that the dissenter says: "It is with regret that I must dissent from the views of my learned colleagues", followed perhaps by a few short, sharp sentences' (*id.*, at 226).
77. CIArb Guideline, *supra* n. 6, at 14; Fortier, *supra* n. 2, at 835; Lloyd et al., *supra* n. 22, at 33; Draetta, *supra* n. 3, at 172-173. Draetta notes, however, that 'often dissenting opinions are issued only at the last minute and unexpectedly by the other arbitrators', with the result that they fail to 'give any time to the other co-arbitrators to possibly change their mind' (*id.*, at 173).
78. Arroyo, *supra* n. 71, at 461-462; Patocchi and Briner, *supra* n. 11, at 302; Waincymer, *supra* n. 21, at 1308.
79. Arroyo, *supra* n. 71, at 461-462; Sheppard and Kapeliuk, *supra* n. 71, at 334; Dominique Hascher, *Collection of Procedural Decisions in ICC Arbitration 1993–1996* (ICC Publishing S.A. – Kluwer Law International, 1998), 70.
80. Sophie Nappert and Dieter Flader, *Psychological Factors in the Arbitral Process*, in Bishop and Kehoe, *supra* n. 11, at 126. The authors put forth various possible explanations for 'partisan' behaviour: 'arbitrators are free agents. Unlike judges, they have no tenure, and operate in a competitive market for services. The quest for future appointments may colour the arbitrators' behaviour, and impact on their decision-making. They may be reticent to render difficult, or unpopular, decisions and prefer to split cases down the middle. In a three-member tribunal, they may tend to rely on dissents rather than look for consensus in deliberations, which could imply

favour of the party in question; secretly informing the appointing party of the views of the other tribunal members so that it could anticipate the tribunal's decisions; or refusing to participate in the deliberations so as to derail the proceedings and delay the rendering of an award.[81]

While such conduct is obviously improper, it is not unheard of in practice. Partisan arbitrators present a real threat to the legitimacy of international arbitration. Apart from that, they pose difficult questions to the fellow arbitrators, and particularly the chairperson, as to how to conduct the deliberations and award drafting. Below are some suggestions that conscientious arbitrators may find useful in the event that the deliberations turn out to be 'pathological' because of one arbitrator's objectionable tactics:

- If the relationship between the tribunal members is suboptimal, a chairperson might best conduct deliberations in a formal manner with written records.[82] He should also be careful not to disclose his preliminary views on the merits of the case too early in order to avoid any attempt by a partisan co-arbitrator to disrupt the proceedings by dilatory manoeuvres, such as untimely resignation or leakage of information of the tribunal's internal discussions to the appointing party.[83]
- As soon as one of the co-arbitrators starts dissenting on procedural or substantive issues, every effort should be made by the majority to continue keeping that arbitrator fully informed, invited to and involved in the tribunal's deliberations and decision-making.[84] However, if one arbitrator refuses to participate in the deliberations without good reason, the other arbitrators may proceed in the arbitrator's absence after giving appropriate notice of the meeting(s) and offering an opportunity to submit comments on the issues to be decided.[85]
- Where the majority arbitrators proceed with the deliberations, they should draft the award and then ask the non-participating arbitrator to review the draft and submit any comments he may have. It is a good precaution to send the draft by registered mail with notice of receipt or by any equivalent means allowing proof of delivery.[86]
- As long as the non-participating arbitrator has not resigned, such arbitrator should be treated as if he is still willing to participate in any deliberation

a degree of compromise that they consider would affect their eligibility for reappointment'. *Id.*, at 126. *See* also Derains and Lévy, *supra* n. 52, at 8; and Sheppard and Kapeliuk, *supra* n. 71, at 331, 333.

81. Alonso, *supra* n. 7, at 143-144; Born, *supra* n. 19, at 2473; Briner, *supra* n. 22, at 64; Derains, *supra* n. 10, at 23-24; Marc J. Goldstein, *Living (or Not) with the Partisan Arbitrator: Are There Limits to Deliberations Secrecy?*, 32 Arbitration International 589, 595-596 (2016).
82. Böckstiegel, *supra* n. 22, at 126; Waincymer, *supra* n. 21, at 1294.
83. Derains, *supra* n. 10, at 23-24.
84. Böckstiegel, *supra* n. 22, at 121.
85. CIArb Guideline, *supra* n. 6, at 13.
86. Briner, *supra* n. 22, at 65; CIArb Guideline, *supra* n. 6, at 13; Patocchi and Briner, *supra* n. 11, at 303.

meeting and available to comment on a draft award. Even if he has made it clear that he will not participate, he should continue to receive the drafts and be given adequate time to present his comments.[87]

- The majority is well advised to record in the final award all of its efforts to engage the minority arbitrator in the tribunal's deliberations. This serves to minimize the risk of later allegations that the arbitrator was improperly excluded from the tribunal's decision-making and/or did not have a reasonable opportunity of submitting his views and influencing the content of the award. The best protection against ill-conceived setting aside actions is to demonstrably offer every opportunity for the minority arbitrator to take part in the tribunal's deliberations and decision-making.[88]
- Once the chairperson is satisfied that the necessary opportunity has been given to both co-arbitrators to express their views, he should fix a date at which deliberations will be closed and the award will be issued. The chairperson should simultaneously note that all questions have been discussed and decided and indicate whether certain (or all) decisions will be taken by majority (or possibly by the chairperson alone, if permitted under the applicable rules).[89]

Behaviour does not have to be criminal to be obnoxious.[90] Rather than being outright partisan, some arbitrators display other unwelcome personality traits. There are arbitrators who are simply lazy, or too busy with other cases; they may show up in hearings and deliberations unprepared and without proper knowledge of the case file. Equally difficult are those tribunal members who are 'a law unto themselves', too intransigent to even consider revaluation of their position.[91] There is not much that even the most experienced chairperson can do to effectively manage arbitrators with flawed personalities. The only advice is for the parties (and the arbitral institutions, as the case may be) to avoid reappointing incompetent or unprincipled arbitrators in future cases.

One should not, however, overstate the problem with the partisan arbitrators. In practice, the problem is often resolved by the other two tribunal members adopting a suspicious attitude towards the biased arbitrator so that he will end up in the minority and have no influence on the outcome.[92] The point has also been made that, although there will inevitably always be some arbitrators who deviate from duty, for most people, the incentive to maintain a reputation for independent judgment trumps any temptation to inappropriate behaviour. A strong incentive to good conduct derives

87. Patocchi and Briner, *supra* n. 11, at 303.
88. Briner, *supra* n. 22, at 64; CIArb Guideline, *supra* n. 6, at 12; Taivalkoski, *supra* n. 29, at 67.
89. Briner, *supra* n. 22, at 65.
90. William G. Bassler, *An Essay on the Challenges to Collegiality*, in Berger and Schneider, *supra* n. 3, at 112.
91. Bassler, *supra* n. 90, at 112-114; Born, *supra* n. 19, at 2474, fn. 1063 (quoting Pierre-Yves Tschanz); Phillip Capper, *Dealing with Bias and Obstruction*, in Berger and Schneider, *supra* n. 3, at 46-47; Draetta, *supra* n. 3, at 150; Tao, *supra* n. 15, at 358.
92. Goldstein, *supra* n. 81, at 598; Julian D M Lew, Loukas A Mistelis and Stefan M Kröll, *Comparative International Commercial Arbitration* (Kluwer Law International, 2003), 316.

from the shame of appearing as biased, lazy or incompetent in the eyes of fellow arbitrators.[93]

[I] Final Considerations

Deliberations is a broad and many-faceted topic. This article has touched on only some of the key aspects. Other important issues, which can only be listed briefly here, include the following:

- Arbitrators may sometimes realize, during deliberations and after the proceedings have already been closed, that there are points not adequately addressed by the parties that may be decisive to the outcome of the case. The question arises as to whether the parties should be given the opportunity to address such points.[94] As a rule, the tribunal's reasoning and findings should not extend to matters that the parties have not had a chance to comment upon in their submissions, as the award may otherwise become vulnerable to attack. The tribunal may therefore need to consider reopening the proceedings on a particular point.
- When contemplating whether to reopen the proceedings, the tribunal should be careful to avoid any appearance of bias. This may be difficult as the reopening of the case on a given point sua sponte may well give the parties a clear indication as to what direction the tribunal seems to be going in the resolution of the merits of the dispute. In such circumstances, the tribunal must seek to reconcile its desire to do justice with the need to maintain its impartiality and neutral image in the eyes of the parties. A decision to reopen the proceedings should never be made lightly; rather, it should be reserved to situations where it is necessary in order to secure due process.[95]
- An arbitration is only as good as the final award. While efficiency, expeditiousness and procedural fairness are important, it is the award that is the true measure of quality in an arbitration.[96] In drafting the award, the tribunal needs to have in mind first and foremost the parties: the award is intended for them. The tribunal should facilitate voluntary compliance by producing an award which explains clearly and persuasively how and why it has arrived at its conclusions. Additionally, the tribunal must resist the temptation to express opinions on matters of fact or law which do not need to be determined in order to decide the case. The cardinal principle of judicial restraint – if it is not

93. William W. (Rusty) Park, *Rules and Reliability: How Arbitrators Decide*, in Cole, *supra* n. 62, at 17.
94. Mosk, *supra* n. 20, at 497.
95. Mika Savola, *Guide to the Finnish Arbitration Rules* (Lakimiesliiton Kustannus, 2015), 355-356.
96. Anja Ipp, *Show, Don't Tell: Creative Writing for Arbitrators*, in Antonio Crivellaro and Mélida N. Hodgson (eds), *Explaining Why You Lost – Reasoning in Arbitration* (ICC Publication No.: 810E, 2020), 68.

necessary to decide more, it is necessary not to decide more – ought to guide the award drafting.[97]

- The drafting process should be organized efficiently and conducted in a collegial manner. When submitting their comments on the chairperson's draft, usually in a marked-up form, the co-arbitrators should focus not only on the substantive questions but also on typographical errors and potential inconsistencies or gaps in the chairperson's reasoning. At the same time, the co-arbitrators should bear in mind that everyone has his own 'style' and that the purpose of the cooperation is not to rewrite the draft out of a misplaced pride of authorship. This also means that, in the event of disagreement over some of the amendments suggested by a co-arbitrator, the chairperson has the final say.[98]
- There are often issues related to the arbitrators' tax liabilities, or social security payments, that need to be considered before the final award is made. The chairperson should see to it that these are properly taken care of.[99]
- An award has to be signed by all arbitrators. Real signatures are required; electronic signatures will not suffice. The process for gathering signatures has to be planned and organized sufficiently early on to accommodate the busy calendars of all three tribunal members and to avoid any unnecessary delay in the rendering of an award because of the unavailability of the arbitrator(s) to sign the award at a given point in time.[100]
- Finally, the award must be properly distributed to the parties and/or the arbitration institute concerned.[101] The lex *arbitri* will determine whether the parties are entitled to have an original of the award or only a copy thereof. Differences exist across jurisdictions also when it comes to the question of whether the award can be validly delivered to counsel for the parties or whether it has to be delivered to the party itself. The tribunal should investigate these issues before making the award to ensure its valid service to the parties.[102]

97. Lloyd et al., *supra* n. 22, at 27. Böckstiegel advises as follows: 'Decide the case, no more! The award is not the place for the arbitrators' missionary feelings or academic ambitions.' *See* Böckstiegel, *supra* n. 22, at 126. In a similar fashion, van den Berg reminds that 'arbitration is not about academic hobby-horsing; rather, it is a service industry. This means in particular that the tribunal has to aim at a result where both parties have the feeling that (a) their case has been carefully considered, and (b) that they have been treated fairly'. *See* van den Berg, *supra* n. 38, at 418.
98. Draetta, *supra* n. 3, at 159.
99. Scherer, *supra* n. 29, at 29.
100. Scherer, *supra* n. 29, at 28.
101. In some jurisdictions, a copy of the award may also have to be deposited at the state court's register. *See* Hans van Houtte, *The Delivery of Awards to the Parties*, 21 Arbitration International 177, 179 (2005).
102. van Houtte, *supra* n. 101, at 181.

§3.04 CONCLUDING REMARKS

Tant vaut l'arbitre, tant vaut l'arbitrage. This old adage is particularly true for deliberations. In the words of one prominent arbitrator, deliberations can be 'a stimulating exercise' when all members of the tribunal have the 'moral and intellectual qualities required' and 'a nightmare' when one co-arbitrator (or, occasionally, both) have 'no other purpose than to continue the parties' war inside the tribunal'.[103] Even when the arbitrators have cultivated good working relations, managing deliberations is an art which requires prudence, skill and firmness.[104] It does not come naturally to everyone, but like any other skill, it can be learned through experience.

In this article, I have tried to outline some practices that international arbitrators may wish to apply in their deliberations. I readily admit that a degree of humility is in order when approaching the subject: as each arbitration is a world of its own,[105] all generalizations are difficult and potentially dangerous. Still, I believe that following the advice and guidelines discussed above will generally be conducive to successful deliberations. And the better the deliberations, the greater the likelihood of the tribunal producing a high-quality award – which is what matters most at the end of the day.

103. Derains, *supra* n. 10, at 24.
104. Alonso, *supra* n. 7, at 132; Poudret and Besson, *supra* n. 5, at 652.
105. Alonso, *supra* n. 7, at 136; Tao, *supra* n. 15, at 353.

CHAPTER 4

Comments on the Use of Dissenting Opinions

*Christian Aschauer**

The author describes the different types of dissenting opinions and the different approaches towards the issuing of dissenting opinions in different jurisdictions, with a particular emphasis on Sweden, Italy, Austria and Germany. Subsequently, the author analyses the differences between deliberations of state court judges and deliberations by arbitral tribunals. On this basis, characteristic features of arbitrators' deliberations are identified. Lastly, the author sets out parameters that may serve as guidelines for expressions of arbitrator's dissent.

§4.01 INTRODUCTION

It will happen in the practice of every arbitrator that a co arbitrator is not very happy with a part of the reasoning, or not satisfied with the outcome of the proceedings. Usually, this will lead to further discussions among the arbitrators who will use their best efforts to achieve unanimity. The president bears much of the responsibility for achieving this goal. First and foremost, however, the arbitral tribunal must deliver justice rather than unanimity, and there may be situations where the majority of the tribunal, even with the best of intentions, will be unable to follow the views of the minority. In such cases, it is not uncommon for the minority arbitrator to issue a dissenting opinion. This may help to unblock protracted deliberations and is an accepted practice in domestic as well as international cases.

The purpose of this chapter is to consider the use of dissenting opinions in domestic and international cases. To this end, the author will set out the different types of dissent (section II) and different approaches towards dissent in different jurisdictions (section III). Subsequently, the author will undertake a comparative analysis of

* The author is indebted to Ms Elisabeth Painsi for her diligent assistance with research.

deliberations by state court judges and arbitral tribunals (section IV). In section V, four characteristic features of arbitrators' deliberations will be identified, namely collegiality, confidentiality, the *intuitu personae* character of the work of arbitrators, as well as the principle of independence and impartiality. Lastly, section VI contains a list of parameters that may serve as guidelines for the drafting of dissenting opinions by arbitrators.

§4.02 DIFFERENT TYPES OF DISSENTING OPINIONS IN THE PRACTICE OF ARBITRAL TRIBUNALS

An arbitrator can express his or her dissent (or a lack of consent) in different forms, which may be indicative of the vehemence of the dissent.[1] The rather common form is to insert the dissenting opinion into the body of the award's reasoning, where the issues that give rise to the dissent are discussed. This may make the award less readable but it will usually be the most appropriate form. As a variation of this type that is perhaps less useful, the arbitral tribunal may merely state in the award that one of its members dissented, without identifying the dissenter and without giving any reasons.

Another, louder but still rather common form of non-agreement is to create a separate document that is attached to the award, with a reference to the attached dissent beneath the signature of the dissenting arbitrator. The loudest (but perhaps least convincing) form of dissent is where the dissenter refuses to sign the award altogether. In this case, the applicable *lex arbitri* usually provides that the two remaining arbitrators may make the award alone.[2]

Even where an arbitrator does not express any dissenting opinion at all, this does not imply that he or she is in full agreement with every comma in the award, or even with the outcome of the proceedings. If an arbitrator fails to sway his or her fellow arbitrators, the arbitrator may have to concede that another opinion is possible and accept that the majority view takes precedence.[3] The opinion of a panel of three arbitrators should never be mistaken for the personal opinion of any of its members, nor even for the opinion of the president of the tribunal. It lies within the nature of collegial decision-making that the outcome of the arbitration cannot be imputed to any of the members of the tribunal individually.

1. Regarding the different types of dissent, *see* in particular Ugo Draetta, *Cooperation Among Arbitrators in International Arbitration*, Indian Journal of Arbitration Law 2015, p. 107 (pp. 139ff.).
2. For example, section 31 Swedish Arbitration Act; Article 823(7) Italian civil procedure code; § 606(1) Austrian civil procedure code; § 1054(1) German civil procedure code.
3. Antonias Dimolitsa, *Are Genuine Dissenting Opinions of Any Real Use?* Essays in Honour of John Beechey 2015, p. 137 (p. 139).

§4.03 DIFFERENT APPROACHES TOWARDS DISSENTING OPINIONS IN DIFFERENT JURISDICTIONS

The Swedish Arbitration Act of 1999 is silent on the question of whether an arbitrator may issue a dissenting opinion.[4] It is nevertheless acknowledged that arbitrators are allowed (but not obliged) to disclose a dissenting opinion, provided that they respect the confidentiality of the deliberations.[5] Article 32(4) of the 1999 edition of the Stockholm Chamber of Commerce (SCC) Rules expressly stated that '[a]n arbitrator may attach a dissenting opinion to the Award'. That provision was deleted in the subsequent 2007 edition of the Arbitration Rules of the Arbitration Institute of the Stockholm Chamber of Commerce (SCC Rules).[6] The current 2017 edition of the SCC Rules does not deal with dissent either. Dissenting opinions nevertheless continue to be allowed in arbitrations under the SCC Rules. If a dissent is expressed, it is common to make a note next to the signature of the dissenter which refers to an annex of the award that contains the dissent.[7] Hence, if anything can be concluded from the deletion of Article 32(4) of the 1999 edition of the SCC Rules, it is only that arbitrators are not encouraged to issue dissenting opinions.

In Italy, the legal framework is very similar. Dissenting opinions are allowed.[8] In arbitrations under the Rules of the Milan Chamber, the dissent, which is 'not infrequent', is attached to the award, but still not considered part of the award, and not endorsed by the institution. Furthermore, the institution does not communicate the dissenting opinion if the dissenter reveals information about the internal deliberation process.[9]

Austrian authors have shown more reluctance in accepting dissents, pointing out in particular that there is no 'obligation' on the part of the majority to include the dissent in the body of the award. It has also been noted in Austria that dissenting opinions may be frequent in common law jurisdictions, before both courts and arbitral tribunals, but that this practice has not established itself in continental European jurisdictions.[10] In the practice of the Vienna International Arbitral Center (VIAC), the dissent is sent to the parties as a separate document together with the award, provided

4. According to a survey conducted in 2008, 24 out of 107 national arbitration laws dealt with the issue by expressly allowing dissenting opinions: *see* Manuel Arroyo, *Dealing with Dissenting Opinions in the Award: Some Options for the Tribunal*, ASA Bulletin 2008, p. 437 (pp. 440ff.).
5. Kristoffer Löf, Aron Skogman and Sara Johnsson, in Magnusson, Ragnwaldh and Wallin (eds.), *International Arbitration in Sweden: A Practitioners' Guide*, 2nd ed., 2021, p. 313; Robin Oldenstam, Kristoffer Löf, Alexander Förster et al., *Mannheimer Swartling's Concise Guide to Arbitration in Sweden*, 2nd ed., 2019, p. 80.
6. Article 36 SCC Rules 2007.
7. Kristoffer Löf, Aron Skogman and Sara Johnsson, in Magnusson, Ragnwaldh and Wallin (eds.), *International Arbitration in Sweden: A Practitioners' Guide*, 2nd ed., 2021, p. 313.
8. Massimo Benedettelli, *International Arbitration in Italy*, 2020, p. 370.
9. Antonia Crivellaro, in Ugo Draetta and Riccardo Luzzato (eds.), *The Chamber of Arbitration of Milan Rules*, 2012, pp. 518-519.
10. Christian Hausmaninger in Hans W. Fasching and Andreas Konecny, *Kommentar zu den Zivilprozessgesetzen*, vol. IV/2, 3rd ed., 2016, § 606 ZPO, ¶¶ 75-76; Eliane Fischer and Günther Horvath, in Czernich, Deixler-Hübner and Schauer, *Handbuch Schiedsrecht*, 2018, ¶ 15.10.

that this entails no prejudice to the confidentiality of the deliberation process or the enforceability of the award.[11]

The aversion to dissenting opinions, if one can call it that, seems to be even more widely held in Germany. This is illustrated by the mere titles of academic articles, where authors speak about a betrayal of secrets ('*Geheimnisverrat*')[12] and a nuisance ('*Ärgernis*').[13] It is suggested in Germany that a dissenting opinion may only be expressed: (a) with the consent of the parties, or (b) with the consent of the majority of the tribunal, or (c) with the consent both of the parties and of the majority.[14] According to one view, permission of the majority of the tribunal is needed even if the dissent does not violate the secrecy of the deliberations.[15]

In the wake of this approach, the Frankfurt Court of Appeal recently observed, *obiter*, that an arbitrator is not allowed to express his or her dissent in German domestic arbitration proceedings on the ground that this violates the secrecy of deliberations. Furthermore, according to the Frankfurt Court of Appeal, the secrecy of deliberations, which protects the independence and impartiality of the members of the tribunal, pertains to (procedural) *ordre public* and cannot be waived, either by the parties or by the arbitrators.[16]

Eminent authors have already come forward in support of the Frankfurt Court of Appeal.[17] They emphasise in particular that arbitrators' deliberations deserve the same protections as those of judges[18] and that the dissenting opinion, if published, inevitably violates the secrecy of the arbitrators' deliberations, as it discloses how an arbitrator has cast his or her vote.[19] In this context, one must know that (with the prominent exception of the German Constitutional Court)[20] German state court judges never issue

11. Wulf Gordian Hauser, in VIAC (ed.), *Handbook Rules of Arbitration and Mediation*, 2019, Article 36, ¶¶ 13-15.
12. Axel Bartels, *Geheimnisverrat des Dissenters im schiedsrichterlichen Verfahren?* SchiedsVZ 2014, p. 133; Axel Bartels, however, holds the view that dissenting opinions are allowed in principle.
13. Anke Sessler and Christine Ruß, *Dissenting Opinions – Aufhebungsgrund oder bloßes Ärgernis?* SchiedsVZ 2020, p. 210; as for the relative infrequency of dissenting opinions in Germany, *see* a survey published by Mirjam Escher, *Die Dissenting Opinion im deutschen Handelsschiedsverfahren – Fear of the Unknown*, SchiedsVZ 2018, p. 219.
14. A comprehensive overview of the various positions is offered by Heiner Nedden and Johanna Büstgens, *Die Beratung des Schiedsgerichts – Konfliktpotential und Lösungswege*, SchiedsVZ 2015, p. 169 (p. 178) with further references, as well as by Axel Bartels, *Geheimnisverrat des Dissenters im schiedsrichterlichen Verfahren?* SchiedsVZ 2014, p. 133 (p. 133).
15. Peter Schlosser in Stein and Jonas (eds.), Kommentar zur Zivilprozessordnung, 23rd ed., 2014, § 1054 ZPO, ¶¶ 20.
16. OLG Frankfurt 16 January 2020, 26 Sch. 14/18, published on the website www.rv.hessenrecht .hessen.de/bshe/search, rv.Hessenrecht.hessen.de, last accessed on 1 April 2021.
17. Rolf A. Schütze, *Beratungsgeheimnis v. Dissenting Opinion*, RIW 11/2020, p. 1; Anke Sessler and Christine Ruß, *Dissenting Opinion – Aufhebungsgrund oder bloßes Ärgernis?* SchiedsVZ 2020, p. 210. The German Supreme Court rejected an appeal against the decision of the Frankfurt Court of Appeal, but expressly declined to comment on the *obiter*: BGH 26.11.2020, I ZB 11/20, margin no. 41, published on the website of the BGH under https://juris.bundesgerichtshof.de/cgi-bin /rechtsprechung/, last accessed on 21 June 2021.
18. Rolf A. Schütze, *Beratungsgeheimnis v. Dissenting Opinion*, RIW 11/2020, p. 1.
19. Anke Sessler and Christine Ruß, *Dissenting Opinion – Aufhebungsgrund oder bloßes Ärgernis?* SchiedsVZ 2020, p. 200 (p. 203).
20. § 30(2) Act on the German Constitutional Court ('Bundesverfassungsgerichtsgesetz').

dissenting opinions, considering that a state court judge must keep the history of the deliberations and the voting confidential pursuant to § 43 of the German Act on Judges.[21] This comports with the legal tradition in many continental European jurisdictions.[22]

If the reasoning of the Frankfurt Court of Appeal is accepted, it applies also to international arbitrations because the 'monistic' German arbitration law does not distinguish between domestic and international arbitrations.[23] It is therefore an urgent matter for German and non-German arbitrators alike to consider whether the *obiter* comment expressed by the Frankfurt Court of Appeal should be adhered to. In this context, it is appropriate to consider, as an initial matter, the differences between the deliberations of state court judges and those of arbitral tribunals.

§4.04 DELIBERATIONS OF STATE COURT JUDGES VERSUS DELIBERATIONS BY ARBITRAL TRIBUNALS

At present, but with the prominent exceptions of supranational or international courts such as the European Court of Justice (ECJ), the European Court of Human Rights (ECHR) or the International Criminal Court, state court judges are almost always of the same nationality. In many cases, they have the same or a very similar legal education and very similar legal careers. When they have been sitting together on the same appellate court panel over the course of many years, they will even know the legal thinking of their colleagues on the panel.

The situation of arbitrators is very different. In international arbitrations, the members of the arbitral tribunal usually do not share the same nationality, and they come from very diverse legal and professional backgrounds.[24] Sometimes, they are not even professional lawyers. Arbitrators may have different perceptions not only of the law and how it should be applied but also of the way business relations should be conducted or how society as a whole should be organised.[25] In most cases, they do not share one and the same native language and are formed by different civilisations. More often than not, they do not know each other from prior appointments and cannot rely on any pre-existing experience with each other.[26] While this diversity is one of the assets of the system, it comes with the challenge that different personalities must find common ground. It is natural that there will be a greater potential for disagreement. For

21. § 43 Act on Judges ('Richtergesetz'): 'Der Richter hat über den Hergang bei der Beratung und Abstimmung auch nach Beendigung seines Dienstverhältnisses zu schweigen.'
22. As for a comparative analysis between the practice of dissenting opinions in common and civil law traditions, *see* Lord Mance, *In a Manner of Speaking: How Do Common, Civil and European Law Compare?* RabelsZ 78 (2014), p. 231.
23. However, different rules apply in regard to the enforcement of domestic and foreign awards according to § 1060 and § 1061 German civil procedure code.
24. *See* Audley William Sheppard and Daphne Kapeliuk-Klinger, *Dissents in International Arbitration*, in Cole (ed.), *The Roles of Psychology in International Arbitration*, 2017, p. 313 (p. 329).
25. Yves Derains, *La pratique du délibéré arbitral*, in Liber Amicorum in honour of Robert Briner, 2005, p. 221 (p. 230).
26. *See* Bernhard Berger, *Rights and Obligations of Arbitrators in Deliberations*, ASA Bulletin 2013, p. 244 (p. 245).

these reasons alone, arbitrators' deliberations will necessarily take a different form and can have a wider outreach than those of state court judges.

Arbitrators' deliberations must also be more extensive because state court judges are usually bound by a procedural code that dictates almost every procedural step. By contrast, arbitral tribunals have broad discretion to design the procedure that will then be best suited for the needs of the particular case. To achieve this goal, it will be necessary to consult with the parties, and importantly, to have ample discussions among the members of the tribunal not only about the substance of the case but also about procedure.[27] The deliberative process of the arbitral tribunal continues throughout the whole arbitration from the drafting of the first 'welcome' letter up to the signing of the final award.

If we consider these differences, then it does not really seem helpful to equate arbitrators' deliberations with those of state court judges. It seems much less appropriate to apply the prohibition on dissenting opinions by judges, which exists in many continental European jurisdictions, in relation to arbitrators. It would seem that the better approach is to consider the characteristic features of the deliberative process within arbitral tribunals and to assess whether and to which extent those features are compatible with the delivery of a dissenting opinion.

§4.05 CHARACTERISTIC FEATURES OF ARBITRATORS' DELIBERATIONS

As stated, the arbitral tribunal's deliberations are an ongoing process which covers the arbitral process from the start up to the signing of the final award. They can take place orally or in writing, and they may be conducted by telephone or videoconference.[28] Even sole arbitrators go through a deliberative process before they decide, but they do so in complete solitude, which perhaps makes their task even more difficult.[29]

In the course of deliberations, the arbitrators may use written notes, chronologies, memoranda and other documents they have drafted as by-products while studying the case. The secretary of the arbitral tribunal, if any, is allowed to provide assistance, e.g., by locating specific documents, but there are different views as to whether the secretary should be allowed to remain in the room while the arbitrators are discussing and voting.[30]

While discussing the case with a plurality of arbitrator colleagues, every arbitrator must be able to freely share his or her thoughts. This includes, for example, a right

27. Yves Derains, *La pratique du délibéré arbitral*, in Liber Amicorum in honour of Robert Briner, 2005, p. 221 (p. 222); Heiner Nedden and Johanna Büstgens, *Die Beratung des Schiedsgerichts – Konfliktpotential und Lösungswege*, SchiedsVZ 2015, p. 169 (pp. 169ff.).
28. Bernhard Berger, *Rights and Obligations of Arbitrators in Deliberations*, ASA Bulletin 2013, p. 244 (p. 250).
29. Yves Derains, *La pratique du délibéré arbitral*, in Liber Amicorum in honour of Robert Briner, 2005, p. 221 (p. 232).
30. Bernhard Berger, *Rights and Obligations of Arbitrators in Deliberations*, ASA Bulletin 2013, p. 244 (p. 256). According to the LCIA Notes for Arbitrators, ¶ 71, the arbitral tribunal should inform the parties of its intention to allow the tribunal secretary to attend the deliberations.

to communicate first impressions after a hearing, or to perform a comprehensive (written or oral) analysis of any factual and legal issue, as well as a right to correct one's own opinion. All of this would be impossible without the protections offered by the secrecy of deliberations. Legal writers have rightly pointed out that the secrecy of arbitrators' deliberations is designed to protect the arbitrators,[31] but not exclusively. The secrecy of deliberations should also ensure that no party becomes aware of the contents of the arbitrators' discussions. If those contents were leaked, they might give one side an undue advantage and violate the equality of the parties.[32] The secrecy of deliberations is therefore not only a duty that binds the arbitrators in their internal relations but also a duty owed by the arbitrators to the parties. This is reflected in Article 9 of the International Bar Association (IBA) Rules of Ethics for International Arbitrators (1987), which states that the tribunal's deliberations remain confidential in perpetuity unless the parties release the arbitrators from this obligation. Furthermore, according to this rule, an arbitrator should not disclose any information about the deliberations for the purpose of giving assistance in proceedings to review the award unless, exceptionally, the arbitrator considers it his or her duty to disclose material misconduct or fraud on the part of the fellow arbitrators. The secrecy of deliberations is thus a widely acknowledged characteristic feature of the deliberative process of arbitrators.

However, arbitrators' deliberations must be distinguished from the reasoning of the award, which is the outcome of the process. The situation is similar to that of a team of three architects who are commissioned to jointly design a bridge, for example. While they will have ample discussions among themselves about the design of the bridge and exchange their statics calculations, the product of their work will be the one plan for the one bridge that must be submitted to the principal.

If an arbitrator accepts a mandate to serve on a tribunal, it is implied that he or she is agreeing to work with the co-arbitrators that have already been appointed or will be appointed in accordance with the appointment process agreed by the parties. According to this principle, which one may call the collegiality-principle, the arbitrator agrees in advance to form one opinion with the other members of the arbitral tribunal on all relevant issues of fact and of law. In this vein, the arbitrators not only have a right but also have a duty to participate in the deliberations.[33] Importantly, they must also listen to one another. The Code of Ethics of Arbitrators of the Milan Chamber of Arbitration (which is binding on every arbitrator who accepts a mandate in arbitrations administered by the Milan Chamber) makes this duty of collegiality and cooperation clear when it states in Article 11(3) that arbitrators shall promptly participate in the deliberations.

31. Anke Sessler and Christine Ruß, *Dissenting Opinion – Aufhebungsgrund oder bloßes Ärgernis?* SchiedsVZ 2020, p. 200 (p. 203); *see also* Christian Hausmaninger in Fasching and Konecny, *Kommentar zu den Zivilprozessgesetzen*, vol. IV/2, 3rd ed., 2016, § 604 ZPO, ¶ 41.
32. Bernhard Berger, *Rights and Obligations of Arbitrators in Deliberations*, ASA Bulletin 2013, p. 244 (p. 258).
33. *Supra* n. 32 (p. 252).

While the three architects mentioned above may or may not delegate their work, depending on their contract with the principal or the applicable statutory law, the work of the arbitrators is always *intuitu personae* in nature and must not be delegated to anybody, not even the president of the tribunal.[34] The parties have selected the individual members of the tribunal, or they have been appointed by the institution, because of their specific knowledge and understanding, which they must apply throughout the whole deliberative process.

The *intuitu personae* character of the deliberative process comes with another characteristic feature of the work of arbitrators, namely their independence and impartiality. This also includes a position of independence and impartiality in relation to the other members of the arbitral tribunal, as is illustrated by IBA Guidelines on Conflict of Interest which refer to relationships between an arbitrator and another arbitrator on the orange list of conflicts. A conflict subject to disclosure will be present if two arbitrators are lawyers in the same law firm, the same barristers' chambers, if an arbitrator has been a partner of, or otherwise affiliated with another arbitrator within the past three years, or even if a lawyer in the arbitrator's firm is an arbitrator in another dispute involving the same party or parties, or affiliates thereof.[35] All these circumstances may prevent an arbitrator from forming his or her opinion freely and without *undue*[36] influence by other arbitrators.

More importantly still, an arbitrator cannot be compelled to sign the award. Neither the president nor the majority of the tribunal has any coercive power over the minority. This is spelled out in Article 11(3) of the Code of Ethics of Arbitrators of the Milan Chamber of Arbitration which states that the arbitrator shall remain 'free' to refuse his or her signature where the decision was taken by majority vote. This also allows an arbitrator to remain independent and impartial in the deliberative process. The ability to issue a dissenting opinion is only one part of this independence and impartiality.

§4.06 PARAMETERS FOR AN ARBITRATOR'S DISSENTING OPINION

Having considered the characteristic features of arbitrators' deliberations (collegiality, confidentiality, *intuitu personae* character as well as independence and impartiality), it should now be possible to define parameters which may serve as guidelines for expressions of an arbitrator's dissent.

34. *Supra* n. 32 (p. 255).
35. Guideline 3.3, 'Relationships between an arbitrator and another arbitrator or counsel'.
36. Naturally, an arbitrator is allowed to persuade the other arbitrators through his or her arguments.

[A] The Dissent Must Be Limited to the Reasoning of the Award, Without Disclosing the Contents of Prior Deliberations

Legal writers in Germany rightly emphasise that the dissent must be limited to the reasoning of the award and thus refer to issues that are dealt with in the reasoning.[37] It must not reveal the positions taken by the fellow arbitrators during the deliberation process or in prior drafts of the award.[38] Hence, the minority may state the reasons why it is declining to follow the majority. However, the minority is not allowed to disclose the reasons for which the majority refused to follow the minority unless these reasons are already set out in the award.[39]

Provided that the relevant issues are reflected in the reasoning, the dissent may refer not only to legal issues but also to the facts of the case.[40] Furthermore, not only the award but also procedural orders may be subject to dissent, provided that the dissent is limited to the reasoning of the procedural order. The parameters set out for dissent in respect of awards apply *mutatis mutandis* to procedural orders.

If a certain issue was submitted by (one of) the parties, but found to be irrelevant by the majority, then the dissenting arbitrator may also refer to it in the dissent. In this case, while the dissent does not refer to the reasoning, it identifies an issue that, in the dissenter's view, should be contained in the reasoning. However, in such a situation, the dissenter must have drawn the attention of his or her colleagues to the specific issue while the deliberations were ongoing (*see* the following point).

There can be no suggestion that dissenting opinions should only be issued if the dissenter fears a breach of public policy or other potentially serious defects. A statement of dissent does not imply, by any means, that the award will have to be set aside. It is completely within the discretion of the dissenting arbitrator to decide whether the issue at stake is such that it warrants a dissent. The dissenter is the master of his or her diverging view.[41] At the end of the day, the dissenting opinion is worth what it is worth, no more and no less.

The dissenter must also know that a dissent is not necessary merely to demonstrate that he or she would have decided otherwise because it lies within the nature of collegial decision-making, as stated,[42] that the decision cannot be imputed to any member individually.

---

37. Axel Bartels, *Geheimnisverrat des Dissenters im schiedsrichterlichen Verfahren?* SchiedsVZ 2014, p. 133 (p. 135 and p. 137).
38. Ugo Draetta, *Cooperation Among Arbitrators in International Arbitration*, Indian Journal of Arbitration Law, 2016, p. 107 (p. 141).
39. Heiner Nedden and Johanna Büstgens, *Die Beratung des Schiedsgerichts – Konfliktpotential und Lösungswege*, SchiedsVZ 2015, p. 169 (p. 178).
40. Antonias Dimolitsa, *Are Genuine Dissenting Opinions of Any Real Use?* Essays in Honour of John Beechey 2015, p. 137; even though dissent on legal issues will be more frequent, there seems to be no reason why dissent should be limited to issues of law, which is submitted by Manuel Arroyo, *Dealing with Dissenting Opinion in the Award: Some Options for the Tribunal*, ASA Bulletin 2008, p. 437 (p. 456).
41. Manuel Arroyo, *Dealing with Dissenting Opinion in the Award: Some Options for the Tribunal*, ASA Bulletin 2008, p. 437 (p. 452).
42. *See supra*, section II.

In exceptional circumstances, a dissenting opinion may also be necessary and allowed where the collegial principle of deliberations or the parties' right to be heard was breached.[43] This would constitute circumstances of material misconduct or fraud within the meaning of Article 9 of the IBA Rules of Ethics for International Arbitrators (1987). However, if an arbitrator refers to such issues only in a dissenting opinion, the parties may ask why he or she did not raise red flags earlier.

There should be no concern that, by issuing a dissenting opinion, the dissenter might disclose how the arbitrators cast their votes[44] because it may already be noted in the award that the award was made by a majority. This information is not a breach of confidentiality because an arbitrator is also entitled to refuse to sign the award.[45] Furthermore, there should be no concern that the publication of dissenting opinions undermines the independence and impartiality of arbitrators. The independence and impartiality of arbitrators are already protected by the provisions dealing with arbitrators' challenges, which allow a removal only under rather limited circumstances.[46]

[B] A Dissenting Opinion Should Not Contain any Arguments Which the Dissenter Did Not Previously Bring into the Deliberations with the Other Arbitrators

This rule[47] follows from the principle of collegial decision-making. If the issue referred to in the dissent is new, the dissenting arbitrator has failed in his or her duty to actively participate in the deliberations.

[C] The Dissent Should Not Be Made in Order to Assist One Side in Actions to Challenge the Award in Setting Aside or Enforcement Proceedings

The dissent should not be instrumental in creating the basis for setting aside proceedings, or facilitating the possible refusal by a national court to enforce the award.[48] If that was the goal of the dissent, then the dissenter has breached his or her duty of independence and impartiality. Be this as it may, experienced state courts will be able to sense whether the dissent was driven by illicit motives and will attach no weight to it if this was the case.

---

43. Antonias Dimolitsa, *Are Genuine Dissenting Opinions of Any Real Use?* Essays in Honour of John Beechey 2015, p. 139.
44. This concern is emphasised by Anke Sessler and Christine Ruß, *Dissenting Opinion – Aufhebungsgrund oder bloßes Ärgernis?* SchiedsVZ 2020, p. 200 (p. 204).
45. As the Austrian Supreme Court stated in its decision OGH 13 April 2011, 3 Ob 154/10h, the signature of two arbitrators is sufficient to form a valid award not only in cases where the third arbitrator is prevented from signing due to reasons of incapacity (illness) but also where he or she is simply unwilling to sign.
46. For example, section 8 Swedish Arbitration Act; Article 19(1) SCC Rules (2017).
47. Also expressed by Manuel Arroyo, *Dealing with Dissenting Opinion in the Award: Some Options for the Tribunal*, ASA Bulletin 2008, p. 437 (p. 456).
48. Ugo Draetta, *Cooperation Among Arbitrators in International Arbitration*, Indian Law Journal 2016, p. 107 (p. 141).

[D] The Dissenter Must Express Himself or Herself in Impartial and Tactful Terms

The dissenting arbitrator remains subject to a duty of independence and impartiality vis-à-vis the parties. The dissent does not exempt the dissenting arbitrator from this duty. [49] Therefore, the dissenter must express himself or herself in impartial and tactful terms, not only vis-à-vis his or her co-arbitrators but also vis-à-vis the parties. Anecdotal evidence seen by the author suggests that, when there have been respectful deliberations, any dissent will also be respectful.

[E] The Majority Must Be Given an Opportunity to Learn about the Dissent Before It Is Communicated to the Parties

The dissenting opinion can be issued without the approval of the parties. This is so because the dissent must refer to the reasoning of the award, and the reasoning is not subject to the parties' agreement.[50] Furthermore, on the basis of his or her independence vis-à-vis the co-arbitrators, the dissenting arbitrator does not require the consent of the other members of the tribunal and, of course, the dissenter is not allowed to disclose anything about their deliberations.[51]

However, the dissenter must give the other arbitrators an opportunity to learn of the dissent. He or she is not allowed to take the other members of the tribunal by surprise. This would be a breach of the requirement of collegial decision-making.[52] Thus, the other members of the tribunal must have an opportunity to disclose in the reasoning of the award why they did not follow the view of the dissenter.[53] They must also be given an opportunity to raise flags where, in their opinion, the dissenter would breach the secrecy of the deliberations. To achieve this goal, it is within the power of the president (or the secretariat of the institution, as the case may be) to fix an appropriate deadline for submission of the dissent.[54]

It is improper for the dissenter to notify the parties directly of the dissenting opinion, as this would be an ex parte communication.[55] Only under very exceptional circumstances (which will hopefully never arise), where the majority (or the arbitral

49. Ugo Draetta, *Cooperation Among Arbitrators in International Arbitration*, Indian Law Journal 2016, p. 107 (p. 141).
50. Axel Bartels, *Geheimnisverrat des Dissenters im schiedsrichterlichen Verfahren?* SchiedsVZ 2014, p. 133 (p. 135).
51. In this sense Ugo Draetta, *Cooperation Among Arbitrators in International Arbitration*, Indian Law Journal 2016, p. 107 (p. 140); Axel Bartels, *Geheimnisverrat des Dissenters im schiedsrichterlichen Verfahren?* SchiedsVZ 2014, p. 133 (p. 135).
52. Manuel Arroyo, *Dealing with Dissenting Opinion in the Award: Some Options for the Tribunal*, ASA Bulletin 2008, p. 437 (p. 456).
53. Harm Peter Westermann, *Das dissenting vote im Schiedsgerichtverfahren*, SchiedsVZ 2009, p. 102 (p. 108).
54. Manuel Arroyo, *Dealing with Dissenting Opinions in the Award: Some Options for the Tribunal*, ASA Bulletin 2008, p. 437 (pp. 461f).
55. Ugo Draetta, *Cooperation Among Arbitrators in International Arbitration*, Indian Law Journal 2016, p. 107 (p. 141).

institution) unreasonably declines to communicate the dissent to the parties, may the dissenter write to the parties directly, assuming the full risk of being seen as lacking impartiality and breaching the confidentiality of the deliberations.

[F] The Dissent Is or Is Not Part of the Award

It is commonly stated that the dissent does not form part of the award.[56] However, this depends on the circumstances in which it was made. If the dissenting opinion is inserted into the body of the award, it naturally forms part of the award and it will be impossible to submit the award to state courts without the accompanying dissent.

If the dissenting opinion is contained in a separate document, one must assess whether the award contains a reference such that the separate document is incorporated. If there is only a reference beneath the signature of the dissenter stating that the arbitrator in question is signing 'by reference to the attached consent', or the like, this will *not* be the case, because in that case, only the dissenter refers to the attachment and the dissent is not covered by the signatures of all three arbitrators.

Depending on the question of whether or not the dissent forms part of the award, it must be subject to scrutiny by the arbitral institution if such scrutiny is prescribed. Furthermore, a dissent that is not part of the award does not have to be submitted to the court where enforcement is sought, as has been recognised by the enforcement courts in Austria.[57]

§4.07 CONCLUSION

In the opinion of the author, we have nothing to fear from the practice of civilised dissent. This is also more in line with modern societies that have learned to live with a plurality of opinions, even where it is difficult at times to do so. As was beautifully stated by Lord Mance,[58] we should not accept a system that resembles the rood screen in mediaeval cathedrals, which stood between the ordinary faithful and the high priests who administered their religion. Arbitration is becoming more open and accessible in many respects, with the possibility of civilised dissent being only one aspect of this.

56. Manuel Arroyo, *Dealing with Dissenting Opinions in the Award: Some Options for the Tribunal*, ASA Bulletin 2008, p. 437 (p. 453); Ugo Draetta, *Cooperation Among Arbitrators in International Arbitration*, Indian Law Journal 2016, p. 107 (p. 141); *see also* OGH 13 April 2011, 3 Ob 154/10h.
57. OGH 26 April 2006, 3 Ob 211/05h and 13 April 2011, 3 Ob 154/10h; *see also* the comments on OGH 13 April 2011, 3 Ob 154/10 by Veit Öhlberger, ecolex 2011, p. 1016.
58. Lord Mance, *In a Manner of Speaking: How Do Common, Civil and European Law Compare*, RabelsZ 78 (2014), p. 231 (p. 250).

CHAPTER 5

Calling Uncooperative Witnesses With or Without the Arbitral Tribunal's Assistance

Matthias Scherer

Matthias Scherer touches on a problem frequently encountered in international arbitration, that of recalcitrant or otherwise unavailable witnesses and their forced production. His chapter illustrates practical and legal issues and how an arbitral tribunal might determine them. The chapter reports orders issued in international arbitration proceedings as well as a recent decision of the Swiss Federal Supreme Court (4A_36/2020) reviewing an arbitral award rendered in Switzerland under the SCC Rules. Production of witnesses is ordered only exceptionally, in particular if it involves request to state courts to compel a witness.

A 2020 decision of the Swiss Federal Supreme Court (the 'Federal Tribunal') brought to light a matter that could not be more suited for a Swiss author's publication in the Stockholm Arbitration Yearbook: An arbitration with its seat in Switzerland, but governed by the Stockholm Chamber of Commerce (SCC) Rules.[1]

The case touched on a problem frequently encountered in international arbitration, that of recalcitrant or otherwise unavailable witnesses. This chapter illustrates, through the 'Swiss SCC' case and a few other examples, how an arbitral tribunal might determine such issues.

The plaintiff in *Federal Tribunal case no. 4A_36/2020*, a German pasta manufacturer, had been the unsuccessful respondent in the underlying arbitration initiated by its former United States (US) distributor. The arbitral tribunal had granted damages to the distributor (claimant in the arbitration) among others based on a sales contract between the distributor and a US customer which the distributor was unable to perform as a result of the German company's termination of the exclusive importation and sales

1. Swiss Federal Tribunal Decision 4A_36/2020 of 27 August 2020 based on an arbitral award rendered in SCC arbitration V 2017/164. The matter was reported in Global Arbitration Review, 13 October 2020, Sebastian Perry, Pasta Maker can't rehear fraud claim, https://globalarbitrationreview.com/pasta-maker-cant-reheat-fraud-claim

agreement. In the arbitration, the German company contended that the sales contract and the subsequent out-of-court settlement between the US distributor and its alleged US customer were a sham. The arbitral tribunal did not accept the argument.

After the award had been issued, the German company conducted discovery proceedings in the US. It obtained the deposition of the daughter of the US distributor's founder as well as documents in discovery proceedings before the United States District Court of the Eastern District of New York. The daughter, a lawyer, testified that she had not drawn up or negotiated the settlement. This and the metadata of emails found appeared to show that the contract and the settlement had been drawn up later than the distributor had stated before the arbitral tribunal. The German company considered that this was proof that the contract and the settlement had been created only for the purpose of artificially creating a damage claim in the arbitration.

The German company requested the Swiss Federal Tribunal to review the award. It is indeed possible under Swiss law to seek to revise an arbitral award based on decisive evidence that could have been introduced in the arbitration had it been discovered previously. A strict test applies to determine whether the party seeking revision was diligent in seeking the evidence it now pretends to be new.

The Federal Tribunal rejected the revision request on the grounds of both relevancy and diligence. The new evidence was neither decisive nor had the respondent been unable to procure it during the arbitration. True, the distributor had stated that the daughter had drawn up the settlement, which the arbitral tribunal had accepted as a possibility. True also that the arbitrators had assumed that the contract and the settlement had been established earlier than what seemed to flow from the newly found evidence. However, neither element had been decisive for the arbitral tribunal in rejecting the respondent's fraud defence. The evidence on which the arbitrators relied primarily was the testimony of an officer of the customer company which it found credible. The officer had testified to the genuine nature of the sales contract and the settlement.

The German party had apparently argued before the Federal Tribunal that it was de facto impossible to obtain evidence through discovery proceedings during the arbitration.[2] The Federal Tribunal noted that it did not have to engage with this issue since the new evidence (testimony from deposition) stemmed from steps that could and should have been undertaken during the arbitration. In the Federal Tribunal's

2. Depending on the location of the court, it would have been possible to commence proceedings under 28 USC 1782 while the arbitration was under way. There is currently a circuit split as to whether the statute, which allows discovery in the United States in aid of a foreign or international tribunal, is available in matters involving international commercial arbitration. The more important question is whether discovery would have yielded evidence in time for it to be used in arbitration, including any possible stay or extension ordered by the arbitral tribunal to account for such discovery proceedings. A similar possibility exists in the English courts. *See A, B v. C, D and E* [2020] EWCA Civ 409 where the Court of Appeal held that section 44(2)(a) of the Arbitration Act 1996 empowered the English courts to compel a witness, present in England and Wales, who was not a party to the arbitration agreement, to give evidence for use in arbitration proceedings seated not only in England and Wales but also in other jurisdictions (James Freeman, Karolina Latasz, *Non-identical twins: judicial assistance for obtaining evidence under sections 43 and 44 of the English Arbitration Act,* ASA Bulletin 1 (2021), 61.

view, the German party had not been diligent. It had argued in the arbitration that the settlement was a fraud and would have had every reason to call the alleged author and negotiator of the settlement to testify (the daughter of the distributor's founder). The German company argued that the applicable arbitration rules (the Arbitration Rules of the Arbitration Institute of the Stockholm Chamber of Commerce – SCC Rules) did not provide for the possibility of calling witnesses. As the Federal Tribunal pointed out, this was wrong since the SCC Rules provide that 'In advance of any hearing, the Arbitral Tribunal may order the parties to identify each witness or expert they intend to call and specify the circumstances intended to be proven by each testimony.' [3]

The Federal Tribunal could also have referred to Article 184(2) of the Swiss Federal Act on Private International Law (Swiss PIL Act).[4] The place of arbitration was in Geneva/Switzerland. Therefore, the Swiss international arbitration law (Chapter 12 of the PIL Act) applied to the proceedings, in addition to any specific institutional rules the parties had agreed upon (the SCC Rules in the present case). At the relevant time Article 184(2) of the Swiss PIL Act provided that:

> 2 If the assistance of state judiciary authorities is necessary for the taking of evidence, the arbitral tribunal or a party with the consent of the arbitral tribunal may request the assistance of the state judge at the seat of the arbitral tribunal; the judge shall apply his own law.[5]

Article 184(2) PIL Act does not create a monopoly. A party is not obliged to seek the assistance of the Swiss *juge d'appui*, with or without the arbitral tribunal's consent, but can directly apply to any foreign judge willing to assist with the taking of evidence in support of the arbitration seated in Switzerland. Regardless of Article 184(2) PIL Act, it would thus have been open to the German party to apply to a US court under 28 USC 1782.

A further example of a belated application to hear witnesses who are not under the applying party's control is provided in a procedural order in *ICC Case No. 20441 of 2016*. In that case, the claimant had called several individuals under the respondent's control. It had done so during the arbitration, and before the hearing, but only on the deadline when the parties were to call their witnesses as per the procedural timetable. In the prevailing circumstances, the arbitral tribunal found this to be late. The deadline by which the parties had to identify the witnesses which were to attend the hearing was not meant to provide an opportunity to call new witnesses who had not previously been identified in the parties' pleadings submitted in accordance with the procedural timetable:

> The Respondent objects to the Claimant's application, considering that it is untimely and unwarranted. The Respondent relies on 4.10 of the IBA Rules. This provision states that a party who is ordered to provide for the appearance of a

3. The Federal Tribunal referred to Article 33 of the SCC Rules.
4. *See* Michael E Schneider, Matthias Scherer, Basler Kommentar zum IPRG, 4th edition 2020, n 70 ff ad Article 184.
5. In its current version (since 1 January 2021) Article 184 provides that the judge can also apply or consider other laws. The Swiss judge could thus take depositions or other forms of evidence unknown in Swiss law.

person whose testimony has not yet been offered, may object for any reasons set forth in Article 9.2 of the IBA Rules. According to the Respondent, several of the grounds of Article 9.2 apply, in particular that the request is overly burdensome and not material.

It is the Claimant's position that its application was made timely, namely on the date provided for pursuant to the Procedural Timetable, i.e. the date for the identification of witnesses and experts to be cross-examined (8 April 2016). However, the milestone for the identification of witnesses of 8 April 2016, in accordance with the Procedural Timetable, concerns only witnesses who have provided a witness statement. It serves merely the organisation of the hearing (which starts on 22 May), not as an opportunity for the parties to make applications for new evidence. The timeliness of the Claimant's request therefore needs to be assessed on its own strength.

The Tribunal accepts that a party may seek the assistance of the Tribunal for the production or evidence, be it documentary or witness evidence. However, this is not an unfettered right. It has to be exercised in keeping with the overall procedural timetable. The parties were to establish their case in fact and law in their written submissions, including all witness statements, or at least identification of witnesses not under a party's control for which no witness statement could be adduced. The Claimant has not identified the prospective witnesses in its submissions. Nor does the Claimant state that it has approached the prospective witnesses directly with a view to obtain a witness statement from them.

It would not be appropriate for the Tribunal to order either party to procure the attendance of a witness, unless the party who wanted to rely on that witness had demonstrated reasonable efforts to obtain his attendance at the hearing, and that the other party was likely to be able to do so. The Tribunal is not satisfied that either of these matters has been demonstrated by the Claimant.

The reason why the Claimant did not approach the prospective witnesses may have been that the Claimant expected the Respondent to produce witness statements by these individuals. However, it has been clear since the exchange of the witness statements on 1 March 2016 (or in any event, since the exchange of the rebuttal witness statements on 25 March 2016) that the Respondent will not adduce witness statements. The Claimant was therefore in a position to make its request earlier, and should have done so given the close hearing dates, and the ongoing organisation of the hearing. The Claimant did not mention that there could be additional witnesses when the hearing schedule was discussed with the Tribunal. The Tribunal would then have been in a position to assess the relevance and materiality of any evidentiary application at this stage, as it did with regard to the document production requests on 27 January 2015.

There may be situations where witnesses can be called by a Tribunal even closer to the hearing than would be the case in the present arbitration. In its letter, the Claimant referred to such examples which it summarizes as follows: In *Rumeli and Telsim v. Kazakhstan*, ICSID Case No. ARB/05/06, Award dated July 29, 2008, where Claimant requested, on September 19, 2007, the Tribunal to order Respondent to cause the production of two witnesses, which the Tribunal chaired by Prof. Bernard Hanotiau granted on September 24, 2007, with the Hearing scheduled to take place less than four weeks thereafter, on October 19, 2007. Similarly and most recently, in *Caratube International Oil Company and Mr. Devincci Hourani v. Kazakhstan*, ICSID Case No. ARB/13/13, the Tribunal chaired by Prof. Laurent Levy granted, a mere two weeks before the Hearing (i.e. on October 13, 2015, the Hearing being scheduled to begin on November 2, 2015), the Claimant's request made on September 28, 2015, to order the Respondent to cause the production of two witnesses.

> Request for production of witnesses are necessarily fact specific. The Tribunal finds that in light of the above circumstances the Claimant's request for the production of witnesses is belated and therefore dismissed.
>
> The Tribunal also, and in any event, has doubts about the relevancy of the testimony which the Claimant hoped to obtain from them.

In another illustrative case, *ICC Case No. 13706* seated in Geneva/Switzerland, the claimant informed the arbitral tribunal that one of its witnesses could not attend the hearing for medical reasons. He would be available by video link, or alternatively a hearing could be arranged in his hometown. The respondent questioned the alleged health issues and objected to an examination in a separate hearing or by video link. Extracts of the arbitral tribunal's directions (of 2008) are reproduced below:

> 2. The seat of the arbitration is Geneva, Switzerland. Therefore the arbitration proceedings are governed by the Swiss arbitration law (chapter 12 of the PIL Act) and by the ICC Rules of Arbitration that the parties have selected as they are authorized to do under Swiss law.
> 3. The Tribunal issued Procedural Order no. 1 on 21 September 2005 which addressed the issue of witness hearings. According to Section 3 of this Order, the Tribunal may refer to the IBA Rules on the Taking of Evidence in International Commercial Arbitration ('IBA Rules') without being bound by them.
>
> **A. The examination of Mr XX**
>
> 4. The Claimant argued that it has no control over Mr XX. However, Mr XX has signed a witness statement at a time where he was already retired. With respect to the Claimant's control, or absence of control, no change has occurred since that time. It is the Claimant's responsibility to summon Mr XX and make him available at the hearing (Article 4.7 of the IBA Rules).
> 5. If a witness who has submitted a witness statement does not appear without a valid reason for testimony at the hearing, the Tribunal shall disregard the witness statement except in exceptional circumstances, where the Tribunal may determine otherwise (IBA Rules, Article 4.8).
> 6. While medical reasons can certainly constitute an exceptional circumstance preventing a witness from attending a hearing, the Claimant has not demonstrated the existence of such medical reasons, although they have allegedly existed since at least August 2007. Moreover, Mr XX's purported medical condition is apparently not the only reason for Mr XX's unavailability. He seems to be generally unwilling to be involved in the arbitration.
> 7. Thus, the Claimant has no valid excuse for not making Mr XX available at the hearing at the very least through a video link, a possibility which Article 4.7 of the IBA Rules does not exclude. Consequently, the Tribunal will grant a short time limit to the Claimant to confirm that Mr XX will either be available for examination by video link on 17 March 2008 or be present in person on that date in the hearing room in London. Should Mr XX fail to be available for examination by either of these two methods, the Tribunal will disregard his witness statement.
>
> As to the alleged practical difficulties regarding examination by video link, the Tribunal considers that in spite of presenting certain unavoidable disadvantages compared to in-person hearings, video examination is a valid alternative to the latter. If the cross-examiners' ability to examine the witness were indeed substantially hampered, as the Respondent maintains, video link hearings would not have become as widespread as they have.

> In any event, it is in the Tribunal's sole discretion to weigh up the evidence tendered by the Parties in light of all circumstances, which includes the nature of the facts on which testimony is offered, and the refusal of a witness to avail himself for an in-person hearing.
>
> As to the suggestion of the Claimant to hold a hearing in Kiev to examine Mr XX after the hearing in London, there is no justification for splitting the hearing merely for the convenience of a witness alleged by the party who produced him. Moreover, as the Claimant pointed out in its letter, it would be disproportionate for the hearing to be held in Ukraine, in whole or in part.
>
> **IN LIGHT OF THE ABOVE THE TRIBUNAL ISSUES THE FOLLOWING ORDER**
>
> 1. The hearing will take place in London on 17 March 2008
> 2. […]
> 3. The Claimant shall inform the Tribunal and the Respondent on 22 February 2008, 5 p.m. London time at the latest whether Mr XX will be physically present at the hearing on 17 March 2008, or if he will be available by video link, or if he will not be available during the hearing in person or through video link.
> 4. If Mr XX is neither present at the hearing nor available by video link, his witness testimony shall be disregarded.

In 2021 it has become common place to conduct entire hearings virtually, as a result of the COVID-19 pandemic. As the above procedural order of 2008 recalls, examinations by video are no novelty:

> As to the alleged practical difficulties regarding examination by video link, the Tribunal considers that in spite of presenting certain unavoidable disadvantages compared to in-person hearings, video examination is a valid alternative to the latter. If the cross-examiners' ability to examine the witness were indeed substantially hampered, as the Respondent maintains, video link hearings would not have become as wide spread as they have.

In an *ICC arbitration reported in Swiss Federal Tribunal Decision 4A_539/2008,*[6] the tribunal upheld an arbitral award that had been challenged on the ground of a violation of the right to be heard. The plaintiff (in the annulment proceedings before the Federal Tribunal) complained that the arbitral tribunal sitting in Geneva had refused to order the examination of two of its witnesses by letter rogatory in Milan. The facts were as follows:

The plaintiff had filed two unsigned witness statements from two former employees. When several weeks after the production the other party called the two witnesses for cross examination at the hearing, the plaintiff informed the tribunal that the two witnesses were unwilling to attend the hearing in Switzerland. The plaintiff then sought the tribunal's assistance under paragraph 10 of procedural order no 1.

Procedural order no. 1 of the arbitral tribunal laid out ground rules for the arbitration proceedings. The procedural order addressed the issue of recalcitrant witnesses as follows:

6. Swiss Federal Tribunal, Decision 4A_539/2008 of 19 February 2009, ASA Bulletin 4 (2009), 801.

8.

Each party shall name the witnesses upon whom it intends to rely and, to the extent possible, it shall file written witness statements of each such witness. The Arbitral Tribunal will decide issues such as possible filing of rebuttal witness statements or the refusal of witnesses to cooperate. If it proves impossible for a party to obtain a written witness statement from a witness (who is not under the control of such party), the party shall at least specify, when it provides the name of the witness, on what issues this witness will have to testify at the witness hearing.

10.

Where a witness should ultimately not be able to attend even for a valid reason, the Arbitral Tribunal shall in principle not be entitled to consider his written statement, except if extraordinary circumstances so warrant. In such event the Arbitral Tribunal shall hear the parties and decide by taking, however, into account all relevant circumstances, including the parties' legitimate interests.

...

The parties shall be responsible for ensuring the presence of the witnesses at the hearing. Upon request, the Arbitral Tribunal will assist the parties with respect to witnesses not under their control.

The arbitral tribunal wrote immediately to the two witnesses inviting them to attend the hearing the following week. Both responded that they had already provided the plaintiff's counsel with a jointly signed statement to which the plaintiff could refer. The tribunal convened a telephone hearing with counsel during which it was averred that the witnesses refused to sign their statements. At the telephone hearing, the plaintiff requested that the two former employees were heard in Milan by letter rogatory. The tribunal did not accede to the request. Instead, it proceeded with the hearing and invited the parties to address the witness issue after the hearing. In these post hearing submissions, the plaintiff produced the witnesses' signed joint declaration and explained that this joint declaration had not been considered satisfactory. The plaintiff had instructed its counsel to draw up proper witness statements based on notes and internal memos from the two former employees. Counsel had sent them to the witnesses and allegedly received assurances that they would be signed. Based on such assurances, counsel filed the unsigned witness statements rather than their signed joint declaration. For unknown reasons, the witnesses did not agree to sign the statements after all.

In a procedural order issued after the hearing, the tribunal found that the witness statements were inadmissible, and that the plaintiff had foregone its right to seek the tribunal's assistance calling the witnesses. It was noted that rather than seeking such assistance immediately when it became clear that the witnesses would not sign the statement drawn up by counsel, the plaintiff had waited until a few days before the hearing.

The arbitral tribunal's award was challenged by the plaintiff among others on the ground that the tribunal's handling of the witness issue offended due process. The plaintiff noted that the procedural rules did not impose any deadline for seeking the tribunal's assistance. It was therefore wrong for the arbitral tribunal to find that plaintiff had forfeited its right to such assistance. Furthermore, the plaintiff observed that the arbitrators' position was contradictory. At first, they had granted assistance and invited the witnesses to attend. However, in their procedural order after the hearing, they declined to assist.

The Federal Tribunal found no inconsistency. The arbitral tribunal had actually noted in its procedural order that when it first granted assistance it was on the basis of an incomplete account of the relevant circumstances. At that time it had not known that the two witnesses were not merely unwilling to attend the hearing but actually unwilling to sign the witness statements they had allegedly authored. As to the question of forfeiture, the Federal Tribunal could simply have approved the arbitral tribunal' conclusion for want of the plaintiff's good faith procedural conduct. Ultimately, the tribunal stopped short of this and merely noted that the plaintiff's annulment request did not engage with the issues raised by the plaintiff's procedural conduct. Regardless of the characterisation of the plaintiff's conduct, the right to seek assistance had not been exercised in compliance with the procedural rules. Consequently, the arbitral tribunal had not violated the plaintiff's procedural rights.

What **conclusions**, if any can be drawn from these few cases?

First, it is clear that there is a right to obtain the arbitral tribunal's assistance to try to compel witnesses to give testimony. However, the right must be exercised timely and the witnesses whose testimony is sought need to be relevant. A prudent party will request the arbitral tribunal's assistance early and not leave such a request until the moment when it has to call witnesses under the applicable procedural rules.

In many instances, a party will not call witnesses over which it has no control. Indeed, it would be naïve to think that recalcitrant witnesses are necessarily helpful to the party forcing them to appear. Another downside of forced appearance is the possible disruption of the arbitration timetable. The delays which these procedural incidents inevitably entail may not be worth the effort. The risk of disruption of the arbitration is also why arbitrators will think twice before compelling witnesses or suspending the arbitration during evidentiary proceedings in state courts. Arbitrators are rather liberal in writing to a called witnesses upon request of a party, but will only in very special circumstances allow a party to put a hearing date at risk by compelling witnesses through court proceedings. Ultimately, however, every case will have to be assessed on its own specificities.

CHAPTER 6

United States Case Law Developments under 28 U.S.C. §1782 with Regard to International Arbitration Proceedings

Barbara Maucher & Anke Meier

One of the most significant and well-known differences between litigation and arbitration proceedings in the United States (U.S.) and the same proceedings in many civil law traditions is discovery. With regard to its scope and methods, it is very unique. It may, however, be used by foreign litigants, outside the U.S. as well. When an arbitration proceeding abroad involves a connection to the U.S., an application for seeking evidence in the U.S. under 28 U.S.C. §1782 can be made to benefit from U.S. style discovery. 28 U.S.C. §1782 permits any party or other "interested person" involved in proceedings before a "foreign or international tribunal" to make a request to a U.S. federal district court for an order compelling discovery from a person or entity that resides or is found in the district in which the U.S. court sits. There have been two recent notable lower court developments redefining the scope of 28 U.S.C. §1782. First, the applicability of 28 U.S.C. §1782 was clarified with regard to evidence located outside the U.S., i.e., extraterritorial discovery. Then, several U.S. Courts of Appeals have rendered decisions regarding the applicability of 28 U.S.C. §1782 in private international arbitration proceedings, i.e., arbitration proceedings conducted outside of arbitration institutions, resulting in a veritable circuit split. The chapter explains the different approaches taken with regard to an interpretation of 28 U.S.C. §1782, including the filing of a writ of certiorari with the U.S. Supreme Court.

§6.01 INTRODUCTION

Undoubtedly, the most significant and well-known difference between litigation and arbitration proceedings in the United States and the same proceedings in many civil law traditions is discovery. Discovery is the procedure parties to a lawsuit, and their attorneys utilize to obtain information from each other before trial. Specifically, discovery occurs through demands for production of documents, depositions of parties and potential witnesses, written interrogatories (questions and answers written under oath), written requests for admissions of fact, examination of the scene and the petitions and motions employed to enforce discovery rights. Parties can file requests for discovery for the preparation of a claim even before they initiate the proceedings in court. While common law practitioners consider discovery requests to be an "indispensable tool for determining the truth,"[1] discovery requests by one of the parties are often denounced as overly expensive "fishing expeditions"[2] and rejected as inadmissible in many civil law jurisdictions.[3]

In international arbitration, however, the Anglo-American approach has caught on in general, even though it is less extensive than the traditional U.S.-style discovery process. Requests for document production are common in most present-day international commercial and investment arbitrations despite considerable cost implications.[4] The legal basis for document production or other discovery requests during an ongoing arbitration proceeding is usually an agreement between the parties to the arbitration. Many arbitration rules also provide for the arbitral tribunal to order document production, e.g., Article 34(2)(a) of the International Centre for Settlement of Investment Disputes (ICSID) Arbitration Rules, Article 27(3) UNCITRAL Arbitration Rules 2010, Article 28(2) DIS Arbitration Rules 2018, but they never take on the broad and expansive approach U.S. law does.

§6.02 GATHERING EVIDENCE FOR PROCEEDINGS WITH A UNITED STATES ELEMENT

When arbitration involves a connection to the United States, even if it appears to be remote at first glance, one should consider one very unique tool for obtaining discovery—an application for seeking evidence in the United States under 28 U.S.C. §1782 ("§1782"), a U.S. federal statute.

The tool of §1782 generally extends to proceedings abroad, as it is an expression of Congress' intention for the judiciary branch to cooperate internationally. Accordingly, the wording is quite broad. §1782 permits any party or other "interested person" involved in proceedings before a "foreign or international tribunal," or the tribunal

1. Klaus Sachs, *Use of Documents and Document Discovery: "Fishing expeditions" Versus Transparency and Burden of Proof*, SchiedsVZ 2003, p. 193-194.
2. *Ibid.*
3. Civil law jurisdictions, if at all, usually provide for merely rudimentary discovery procedures: For example, according to sections 422, 423 of the German Code of Civil Procedure (*Zivilprozessordnung*), a party to a court proceeding can only claim production of documents by other parties if it is entitled to do so under substantive law or if the other party itself referred to these documents. Also, in accordance with section 142 para. 1 of the German Code of Civil Procedure, the court may direct one of the parties or a third party to produce records or documents, as well as any other material, that are in its possession, but only if one of the parties has made reference to such records, materials or documents.
4. Akram Mirza, *28 U. S. Code § 1782—Overview and latest Developments*, GRUR Int. 2019, pp. 781 et seq.

itself, to make a request to a U.S. district court for an order compelling discovery from a person or entity that resides or is found in the district in which the U.S. court sits.

28 U.S.C. §1782 reads:

> (a) The district court of the district in which a person resides or is found may order him to give his testimony or statement or to produce a document or other thing for use in a proceeding in a foreign or international tribunal, including criminal investigations conducted before formal accusation. The order may be made pursuant to a letter rogatory issued, or request made, by a foreign or international tribunal or upon the application of any interested person and may direct that the testimony or statement be given, or the document or other thing be produced, before a person appointed by the court.

The requirements for a successful discovery request under §1782, therefore, are that:

(i) the request seeks testimony or statement of a person or production of a document or "other thing";
(ii) the addressee of the discovery resides or is found in the district of the court before which the application is made;
(iii) the discovery is for use in a proceeding in a "foreign or international tribunal"; and
(iv) the petitioner is a "foreign or international tribunal" or "any interested person."

If these requirements are met, the court has broad discretion to grant discovery.[5]

Apart from requesting discovery for ongoing litigation or arbitration proceedings from the opposing party, §1782 also allows for ex parte requests. Since the parties are not limited to requesting discovery only from the opposing party, the petitioner of a successful request made under §1782 therefore gains access to documents and witnesses that might have nothing to do with the actual litigation proceedings. According to the wording, the documents to be produced need not be located in the United States.

Discovery pursuant to §1782 thus affords litigants an attractive alternative to the limited discovery procedures available under the procedural rules in their respective home countries. Thanks to the broad wording of the legal provision, the requirements for a successful request made under §1782 are quite easy to satisfy.

A petitioner can obtain discovery for use in either civil or criminal proceedings and from either a party to the foreign litigation or a third party. The statute does not even impose a requirement that a petitioner first seeks the requested discovery from the foreign tribunal. Nor must an applicant demonstrate that the discovery it seeks is admissible in the foreign proceedings.[6]

5. "The district court '*may* order'" (emphasis added).
6. United States Court of Appeals: *John Deere Ltd v. Sperry Corp*, 754 F.2d 132, 136 (3d Cir. 1985).

In addition, according to the wording, a request under §1782 can also in general be made by the tribunal itself—which is one of the biggest differences to most discovery procedures in other countries.

Given the broad discretion U.S. district courts have in granting requests under §1782, it is hard to reverse any order. Basically, such order will only be reversed upon a finding that the court abused its discretion. The argument of foreign judicial considerations, such as that discovery is not known in the jurisdiction in question, alone will likely not suffice. The U.S. district court is not required to determine whether the evidence will be admissible. It is not necessary to obtain the foreign tribunal's permission first, either.

As the wording shows, the scope of discovery available under §1782 is potentially very broad. Any U.S. district court deciding on a request made under §1782 has the authority to direct that discovery under §1782 takes place in accordance with U.S. discovery procedures. U.S. discovery is recognized as among the most extensive and costly in the world. Specifically, a person from whom discovery is sought can be ordered to produce documents directly to the petitioner or even to sit for a deposition conducted by the petitioner. U.S. district courts also have the authority to accommodate requests for foreign discovery procedures, even if those are not identical to the ones under the Federal Rules of Civil Procedure.[7]

Compliance with such a request can be exceptionally expensive, require disclosure of sensitive or private information, and possibly expose an entity to future liability. In view of these serious consequences of having to comply with a potential order under §1782, opposition to such requests must be carefully crafted.

§1782 has long been an untapped resource for obtaining access to documents and electronic data. In the last ten years, requests through §1782 have become more popular, as they have proven to be a powerful and increasingly successful tool for litigants involved in foreign proceedings, including more recently international arbitration proceedings.

Especially in arbitration, where litigating parties are more in control of the rules and procedures to be followed, this tool could be of great importance. The tool could especially be of great importance as document production has become a prominent fixture in most arbitral proceedings anyways and often features in the procedural timetable from the start.

However, while the tool of §1782 gained more and more attention over the last years, there are still unresolved issues that arbitrators and counsel should have in their mind before considering using it. The terms of §1782 have been subject to interpretation by different courts of different instances in the United States, especially with regard to its applicability in international arbitration proceedings.

7. For instance, in *In re Application of Merck & Co., Inc.*, 197 FRD 267 (NDNC 2000), the district court issued an order deciding that the discovery should follow the U.S. Federal Rules of Civil Procedure, but that in accordance with U.K. law, written summaries of the witness were to be given to the opposing party in appropriate time prior to the depositions.

So, in order to decide whether §1782 is the right tool to use in an arbitration proceeding, and how to handle a discussion about it, it is necessary to take a closer look at the judicial developments in the United States with regard to this provision.

§6.03 THE INTEL DECISION BY THE UNITED STATES SUPREME COURT

In the leading §1782 case, *Intel Corp. v. Advanced Micro Devices* (2004), the U.S. Supreme Court addressed several inconsistencies of the provision.[8]

The first inconsistency, which was raised by *Intel*, concerns the meaning of the word "tribunal" in the statute. The U.S. Supreme Court cited an article written by Professor Hans Smit from Columbia Law School in 1965, which suggested that the term "tribunal," in §1782 covers, *inter alia*, "administrative judges, arbitral tribunals and other adjudicative bodies."[9] The court then laid out a test to answer the question of whether an adjudicative institution abroad can be considered a "tribunal" in accordance with §1782.

The Supreme Court held that aside from ensuring that the statutory requirements are satisfied, a judge must also undertake a secondary four-step analysis:

(i) Whether the person from whom discovery is sought is not a participant in the foreign proceeding and is therefore outside the foreign tribunal's jurisdictional reach.
(ii) The nature of the foreign tribunal and its receptivity to judicial assistance by U.S. federal courts.
(iii) Whether the request conceals an attempt to circumvent foreign evidence-gathering rules.
(iv) Whether the request is unduly intrusive or burdensome.

What is more, the court held that if the foreign institution considers evidence in order to decide a dispute, it can be considered a "tribunal" in accordance with §1782.[10]

§6.04 TWO UNRESOLVED ISSUES WITH 28 U.S.C. §1782: EXTRATERRITORIALITY AND FOREIGN PRIVATE ARBITRATION

While *Intel* clarified some aspects of §1782, it still left much for the lower courts' interpretation.

There have been two recent lower court developments redefining the scope of §1782. First, the applicability of §1782 was clarified with regard to evidence located outside the United States, i.e., extraterritorial discovery (V). Then, several U.S. Courts of Appeals have rendered decisions regarding the applicability of §1782 in private

8. United States Supreme Court: *Intel Corp. v. Advanced Micro Devices, Inc.* 542 U.S. 241 (2004).
9. Hans Smit, *International Litigation Under the United States Code,* 65 Colum. L. Rev. 1015, 1026 n. 71 (1965).
10. United States Supreme Court: *Intel Corp. v. Advanced Micro Devices, Inc.* 542 U.S. 241, at 264 (2004).

international arbitration proceedings per se, i.e., arbitration proceedings conducted outside of arbitration institutions, such as ICSID or International Chamber of Commerce (ICC) (VI).

§6.05 EXTRATERRITORIAL DISCOVERY IS PERMITTED UNDER 28 U.S.C. §1782

Regarding applicability of §1782 to evidence located outside the United States, the U.S. Court of Appeals for the Second Circuit on October 7, 2019, issued a decision significantly broadening the scope of discovery available to foreign litigants seeking evidence from persons or entities with contacts to the U.S. in the *In re Application of Antonio del Valle Ruiz* decision.[11]

[A] The Second Circuit *In re del Valle Ruiz* Decision

In *In re Application of Antonio del Valle Ruiz*, the Second Circuit held that petitioners could, in principle, file an application under §1782 to obtain documents held outside the U.S. if and to the extent the entity from which the documents were sought had sufficient links to the forum state so as to satisfy the requirements of constitutional due process.

[1] The Facts in In re del Valle Ruiz

The facts in *In re del Valle Ruiz* were quite complex. In 2017, Banco Popular Español, S. A. (BPE), a Spanish bank, underwent a forced sale by the Spanish government. After a short due diligence phase, Banco Santander S. A. (Santander), another Spanish bank, purchased BPE for only EUR 1.00, even though BPE had previously been valued at almost EUR 160 billion. Pacific Investment Management Company LLC and Anchorage Capital Group, LLC (the "Petitioners") were two former investors in BPE that claimed to have lost over EUR 1 billion as a result of the forced sale. Faced with such a significant financial loss, the Petitioners challenged the sale before the Court of Justice of the European Union, initiated an international arbitration against the Government of Spain, and sought to intervene in Spanish criminal proceedings against BPE. In support of the proceedings, all of which were pending outside the United States, the Petitioners filed an application in the Southern District of New York under §1782 seeking discovery from Santander and three of its affiliates for use in those foreign proceedings.

In the application, Petitioners requested documents regarding the financial state of BPE at the time of its forced sale from: (1) Santander itself and (2) Santander's New York-based affiliate, Santander Investment Securities Inc. (SIS). The district court granted the application in part, rejecting the application as to Santander itself but ordering SIS to produce documents, including those not located in the United States.

11. United States Court of Appeals: *In re del Valle Ruiz* 939 F.3d 520 (2nd Cir. 2019).

On appeal, the Second Circuit affirmed the district court's decision, thereby departing from earlier jurisprudence.[12] Explicitly joining the U.S. Court of Appeals for the Eleventh Circuit,[13] the Second Circuit found that "a district court is not categorically barred from allowing discovery under §1782 of evidence located abroad."

Indeed, the Second Circuit held that discovery was possible where a court had personal jurisdiction over the party from which the evidence was requested. The Second Circuit further held that discovery of documents located outside the United States may be sought under §1782, thereby affirming an extraterritorial application of §1782.

[2] The Test Devised by the Second Circuit in **In re del Valle Ruiz**

In its reasoning, the Second Circuit first found that the presumption against extraterritorial application of laws was not applicable to strictly jurisdictional statutes such as §1782. While the Second Circuit noted that previous commentators had argued that §1782 only applies to companies over which the court has general jurisdiction and therefore, only U. S. companies within the court's district could be subject to the broad discovery under §1782, the Second Circuit extended the scope of applicability of §1782 by referring to the broad language of the provision. Particularly, the Second Circuit reasoned that Congress intended the scope of discovery under §1782 to be similar to the scope of discovery available in an ordinary domestic lawsuit.[14] In an ordinary domestic lawsuit, discovery that is conducted in accordance with the Federal Rules of Civil Procedure permits extraterritorial discovery so long as the *evidence sought is within the subpoenaed party's* "possession, custody, or control." The Second Circuit did caution,

---

12. *See* United States Court of Appeals: *In re Sarrio*, 119 F.3d 143, 147 (2nd Cir. 1997); United States District Court: *Purolite Corp. v. Hitachi America, Ltd.*, 2017 WL 1906905 (S.D.N.Y 2017); United States District Court: *In re Application of Gorsoan Ltd. and Gazprombank OJSC*, 2014 WL 7232262 (S.D.N.Y. 2014); United States District Court: *In re Fuhr*, 2014 WL 11460502 (S.D.N.Y. 2014); United States District Court: *In re Godfrey*, 526 F.Supp.2d 417, 423-424 (S.D.N.Y.2007) ("The bulk of authority in this Circuit, with which this Court agrees, holds that, for purposes of §1782(a), a witness cannot be compelled to produce documents located outside of the United States").
13. The U.S. Court of Appeals for the Eleventh Circuit had been the first U. S. Circuit Court to recognize that §1782 could apply to documents held outside the United States, see United States Court of Appeals: *Sergeeva v. Tripleton*, 834 F.3 d 1194 (11th Cir. 2016). The Eleventh Circuit reasoned that the text of §1782 authorizes discovery pursuant to the Federal Rules of Civil Procedure. The Federal Rules of Civil Procedure in turn authorize extraterritorial discovery so long as the documents to be produced are within the subpoenaed party's possession, custody, or control.
14. United States Court of Appeals: *In re Valle Ruiz*, 939 F.3d at 529 (2nd Cir. 2019) citing to United States Court of Appeals: *In re Edelman*, 295 F.3d at 177 (2nd Cir. 2002): "Given this, and legislative history expressing Congress's 'aim that the statute be interpreted broadly and that courts exercise discretion in deciding whether, and in what manner, to order discovery in particular cases,' we concluded that tag jurisdiction was sufficient to satisfy §1782's 'found' requirement. Id. at 179–80." And: "Indeed, we have repeatedly recognized Congress's intent that §1782 be 'interpreted broadly,' especially given the district court's ability 'to exercise discretion in deciding whether, and in what manner, to order discovery in particular cases'." Referring as well to, *inter alia*, United States Court of Appeals: *Brandi-Dohrn v. IKB Deutsche Industriebank AG*, 673 F.3d 76, 80 (2nd Cir. 2012).

however, that an order compelling production of documents was not automatic if such request was filed.

Instead, the Second Circuit devised a framework in which the court must: (i) "'first assess the connection between the nonparty's contacts with the forum and the order at issue' and *[(ii)]* 'then decide whether exercising jurisdiction for the purposes of the order would comport with fair play and substantial justice.'"[15]

According to the Second Circuit, courts are still obligated to consider a number of factors in determining whether to actually exercise their discretion. In particular, the Second Circuit noted that "*a court may properly, and in fact should, consider the location of documents and other* evidence when deciding whether to exercise its discretion to authorize such discovery (emphasis added)."[16]

The Second Circuit explicitly relied on the four-factor test the U.S. Supreme Court had developed in *Intel Corp. v. Advanced Micro Devices, Inc.*[17] In applying the *Intel* factors, the Second Circuit found that the district court had not abused its discretion in ordering SIS to produce documents held abroad and that, therefore, the district court order of discovery as to SIS had been proper. However, the Second Circuit also found that it did not have personal jurisdiction with regard to Santander and that, consequently, production of documents could not be ordered.

[B] United States District Courts Have Started Applying and Following *In re del Valle Ruiz*

The *In re del Valle Ruiz* decision opened the doors for extending the reach of §1782 to the multitude of international companies doing business with and in the United States. Indeed, several district courts in the Second Circuit have already issued decisions referring to *In re del Valle Ruiz,* related to both, litigation and arbitration proceedings abroad.[18]

15. United States Court of Appeals: *In re del Valle Ruiz*, 939 F.3d at 529 (2nd Cir. 2019).
16. *Ibid., at 533.*
17. In its *Intel* decision, the U.S. Supreme Court had held that aside from checking whether the statutory requirements are satisfied, a court must undertake a secondary four-step analysis to determine whether and how it should exercise its discretion. The steps in the analysis are: "(1) whether the person from whom discovery is sought is a participant in the foreign proceeding, 'in which event' the need for § 1782(a) aid generally is not as apparent as it ordinarily is when evidence is sought from a nonparticipant in the matter arising abroad; (2) the nature of the foreign tribunal, the character of the proceedings underway abroad, and the receptivity of the foreign government or the court or agency abroad to U.S. federal- court assistance; (3) whether the § 1782(a) request conceals an attempt to circumvent foreign proof-gathering restrictions or other policies of a foreign country or the United States; and (4) whether the request is 'unduly intrusive or burdensome'," United States Supreme Court: *Intel Corp. v. Advanced Micro Devices,* 542 U.S. at 264, 265.
18. The following decision shall serve as an example for the applicability of *In re del Valle Ruiz* to discovery requests made with regard to litigation proceedings pending abroad: in 2020, the United States District Court for the Southern District of New York granted a §1782 application filed by a German national, but only in part. After the respective petitioner's investment in certain silver certificate options derivative securities had been rendered worthless due to the allegedly illegal activities of Deutsche Bank AG and DZ Bank AG, Deutsche Zentral-Genossenschaftsbank and their coconspirators, petitioner had filed a claim for damages in a

For instance, the United States District Court for the Eastern District of New York in 2020 granted the §1782 application of German pasta manufacturer ALB-GOLD that sought discovery in aid of a proceeding before the Federal Supreme Court of Switzerland to overturn an arbitral award rendered against ALB-GOLD. The individual from whom discovery was sought disputed that he "*resided*" or was "*found*" in the district, but the district court held that *In re del Valle Rui* foreclosed any further inquiry into his geographical whereabouts since the district court had personal jurisdiction over him. The district court held that it had specific personal jurisdiction over the individual based on the fact "*that he engaged in all of the transactions and occurrences that are the subject of ALB-GOLD's application while in this District.*" Accordingly, the district court concluded that the individual "*resided or is found*" in the Eastern District of New York.

Likewise, also in 2020, the United States District Court for the Southern District of New York granted a §1782 application made by petitioner Union Fenosa Gas, S.A. (*UFG*) as an ex parte petition for judicial assistance.[19] UFG had obtained a USD 2 billion arbitral award against Egypt from a tribunal constituted under the Agreement on the Reciprocal Promotion and Protection of Investments between the Kingdom of Spain and the Arab Republic of Egypt and the ICSID Convention for impairment of investments made by UFG in Egypt. Egypt had refused to voluntarily comply with the award.

UFG filed a petition under §1782 against an agent in the payment chain between Egypt and the holders of notes issued by Egypt under a sovereign bond program. UFG hoped to execute funds belonging to Egypt that would be sued to service and/or redeem the notes. After confirming that the statutory requirements of §1782 were met, the district court explicitly referred to the *Intel* test. Again, the fourth factor, whether a request is unduly intrusive or burdensome, was considered the most important.

The district court explicitly relied on *In re del Valle Ruiz* to hold that the location of documents and other evidence is important when considering the burden or appropriateness of a request for documents located outside the United States.[20] In

German court. During the proceedings, petitioner then filed for an order permitting him to take discovery from respondents Deutsche Bank AG, DZ Bank AG Deutsche Zentral-Genossenschaftsbank, and Commodity Exchange Inc., for use in the proceedings pending in Germany. The court applied the test devised by the Second Circuit, making reference to *In re del Valle Ruiz* throughout its decision. Since the banks had "purposeful[ly] and regular[ly] use[d] the precious metals markets in New York to conduct" their business, especially by trading through COMEX, which operates in New York, New York, the court found that there were sufficient contacts and consequently, a sufficient basis for the court to exercise specific personal jurisdiction over the banks. Next, the court applied the *Intel* test. While affirming the presence of the three first factors of the *Intel* test, the court found that the fourth factor, i.e., whether the discovery sought would be unduly intrusive or burdensome, stood in fact in the way of granting the request in its entirety, since the discovery requests made were too broad. However, quoting to the Second Circuit and its instruction that "it is far preferable for a district court to reconcile whatever misgivings it may have about the impact of its participation in the foreign litigation by issuing a closely tailored discovery order rather than by simply denying relief outright," the court granted the request in part. *See*, United States District Court: *Pfaff v. Deutsche Bank AG*, 2020 WL 3994824 (S.D.N.Y. 2020).

19. United States District Court: *Unión Fenosa Gas, S.A. v. Depository Trust Co.*, 2020 WL 2793055 (S.D.N.Y. 2020).
20. United States District Court: *Unión Fenosa Gas, S.A. v. Depository Trust Co*, 2020 WL 2793055 (S.D.N.Y. 2020), at 24.

conclusion, the mere fact that the documents were located abroad did not hinder the district court from granting the request, although it did limit its breadth.

[C] Impact on Multinational Companies in the District of the Second Circuit

The Second Circuit's reasoning was largely the result of a textual and literal reading of the statute. The Second Circuit determined that the language did not create a per se bar on extraterritorial application. Under this interpretation, companies—regardless of whether they are incorporated or have their principal place of business within the court's district—are subject to §1782 if they have minimum contacts with the United States and those contacts relate to the discovery sought.

The *In re del Valle Ruiz* decision by the Second Circuit could have significant consequences for all financial institutions or other multinational corporations that fall under the jurisdiction of the Second Circuit and have documents or other evidence in another country. The broadening in scope is likely to result in an increase in the potential burden domestic entities must bear when responding to discovery requests in aid of foreign proceedings. Entities may assert that the request is overly burdensome or unduly intrusive to correct this course. They can also argue that the respective court dealing with the request does not have personal jurisdiction for lack of a sufficient nexus between the target's contact with the forum and the actual discovery sought. The mere maintaining of an office and conducting a business in the district of the Second Circuit will not be enough for a request for discovery under §1782 to be successful.

Therefore, even for arbitration proceedings held abroad, discovery under §1782 could provide a useful tool to obtain evidence located in another third country. That only is the case, however, if private international arbitration proceedings were to be considered as proceedings before a foreign tribunal within the meaning of §1782.

The question of the applicability of §1782 to private international arbitration proceedings is different, but not less important than the question of the extraterritorial reach of a U.S. court's §1782 order. This question has become a hotly debated issue, with an interesting recent development of note that will be discussed hereafter and which is of relevance for every arbitrator and litigant involved in private arbitration proceedings held abroad.

§6.06 THE APPLICABILITY OF 28 U.S.C. §1782 IN PRIVATE INTERNATIONAL ARBITRATION PROCEEDINGS

Over the past two years, the issue of whether §1782 assistance may extend to private arbitral tribunals has become the subject of a cascade of federal circuit court decisions, actually creating a deep circuit split among the courts.

While it is undisputed that state courts and arbitral tribunals established by public entities (e.g., ICSID arbitrations) constitute "tribunals,"[21] there has long been a difference in opinion among U.S. district courts as to whether §1782 also allows for obtaining information for use in private arbitration proceedings.

[A] The Circuit Split: Different Decisions by the United States Courts of Appeals

Following the U.S. Supreme Court's *Intel* decision, more courts seemed to adopt the opinion that the term "tribunal" in §1782 comprises arbitral tribunals as well.[22] For example, the Sixth Circuit in 2019 decided in *Abdul Latif Jameel Transportation Company Ltd. v. FedEx Corporation* that requests for discovery under §1782 may be filed by parties to international private arbitration proceedings.[23]

Other U.S. Court of Appeals, however, denied the application of §1782 for international private arbitration proceedings. For instance, in *Republic of Kazakhstan v. Biedermann International* in 1999, the Fifth Circuit denied the request for discovery under §1782, citing the legislative history of the legal provision.[24] Again, in 2009, in *El Paso Corp. v. La Comision Ejecutiva Hidroelectrica Del Rio Lempa*, the Fifth Circuit decided against the petitioner, arguing that a private arbitration tribunal in Switzerland was not a tribunal within the meaning of §1782.[25]

The split among the Circuit Courts seeped through to the lower courts, creating all-around uncertainty. Referring to the dicta of the U.S. Supreme Court's *Intel* decision, a number of district courts granted applications filed by foreign individuals under §1782 for international private arbitral proceedings,[26] even within the Second

21. *Jane Wessel & Peter J. Eyre, U. S. Discovery in Aid of Foreign or International Proceedings. The Rise of 28 U.S.C. Sec. 1782*, TDM 2007 Vol. 4/5, 8; *David Zaslowsky & Kristina Fridman, Use of Section 1782 in Aid of Arbitration*, in Edward M. Mullins & Lawrence W. Newman (eds.), *Obtaining Evidence for Use in International Tribunals under 28 U.S.C. § 1782, 2020*, pp. 173 et seq.
22. For instance, in 2012, the U.S. Court of Appeals for the Eleventh Circuit was open to the idea that §1782 could be invoked in international private arbitration proceedings: In *Consorcio Ecuatoriano de Telecomunicaciones S.A.*, 685 F.3d 987 (11th Cir. 2012), the U.S. Court of Appeals for the Eleventh Circuit cited the U.S. Supreme Court's *Intel* decision and found the *Intel* decision to have good arguments to include private arbitration tribunals in the term "*tribunal*" of §1782. However, later, the Eleventh Circuit reversed its decision sua sponte in 2012 and issued a decision with a much narrower reading, leaving open the question of the scope of application but allowing discovery in the specific case at hand, *see* United States Court of Appeals: *In Re Consorcio Ecuatoriano de Telecomunicaciones S.A.*, 2014 WL 104132 (11th Cir. 2014).
23. United States Court of Appeals: *Abdul Latif Jameel Transportation Company Ltd. v. FedEx Corporation,* 2019 WL 4509287 (6th Cir. 2019).
24. United States Court of Appeals: *Republic of Kazakhstan v. Biedermann International,* 168 F.3d 880 (5th Cir. 1999).
25. United States Court of Appeals: *El Paso Corp. v. La Comision Ejecutiva Hidroelectrica Del Rio Lempa,* 341 Fed. Appx. 31 (5th Cir. 2009).
26. Cases allowing application of §1782 for private international arbitrations are, e.g., United States District Court: *In re Roz Trading Ltd., 469 F.Supp.2d 1221 (N.D. Ga. 2006);* United States District Court: *In re Hallmark Capital Corp., 534 F.Supp.2d 951 (D. Minn. 2007);* United States District Court: *Ukrnafta v. Carpatsky Petroleum Corp., 2009 WL 2877156 (D. Conn.)*; United States District Court: *In re Winning (HK) Shipping Co. Ltd.*, 2010 WL 1796579 (S.D. Fla. 2010). In these

Circuit.[27] Other district courts denied such requests. For instance, in *EWG Gasspeicher GMBH v. Halliburton Co.* in 2020, the United States District Circuit in Delaware held that the term "tribunal" in §1782 does not cover private commercial arbitrations.[28] In that case, the arbitration proceedings were in accordance with the rules of the German Arbitration Institute (DIS). The district court held, however, that the arbitration proceeding arising from a private commercial contract was not one before a foreign court or a quasi-judicial agency and that the merits of an award were not subject to judicial review before a public body.[29]

In 2020 alone, three different circuit courts issued three different decisions with regard to arbitration proceedings pending abroad, thus deepening the circuit split and adding to the confusion.

On May 10, 2021, the U.S. District Court for the District of Columbia granted a request for discovery under §1782, ordering a law firm that was a third party to arbitration proceedings pending before the Dubai International Finance Centre–London Court of International Arbitration (DIFC-LCIA) to produce certain nonprivileged documents and a detailed privilege log of any privileged documents. In its opinion, the court noted the circuit split, but noted it did not have to take sides, as the DIFC-LCIA even passed the narrower standard of a state-sponsored tribunal, as followed by the Second, Fifth and Seventh Circuits. The court considered the DIFC-LCIA to be sanctioned, regulated, and overseen by the UAE government, and hence a state-sponsored arbitral tribunal, for the following reasons: The DIFC-LCIA is a joint venture between the DIFC and the LCIA. The DIFC itself was established by a United Arab Emirates decree, as was the DIFC Arbitration Centre. The Arbitration Centre is funded by the Dubai government and governed by a board of trustees appointed by a dispute resolution authority within the DIFC. The DIFC Arbitration Institute also staffs the DIFC-LCIA, including legal counsel, case work managers and administrators.[30]

---

cases, the courts in general held that the Supreme Court's *Intel* decision, with its reference to the Smit article and the famous footnote, meant that private international arbitral tribunals were indeed "tribunals" within the §1782 definition of "*foreign and International tribunals.*" A majority of district courts addressing the issue, however, followed the rationale of the *NBC and Biedermann* decisions and did not allow for an application of §1782 for private international arbitrations: e.g., United States District Court: *In re Operadora DB Mexico, S.A. De C.V., 2009 WL 2423138 (M.D. Fla.);* United States District Court: *In re Norfolk Southern Corp., 626 F.Supp.2d 882 (N.D. Ill. 2009);* United States District Court: *In re Dubey, 949 F. Supp.2d 990 (C.D.Cal. 2013)*; and United States District Court: *In re Grupo Unidos Por Canal S.A., 2015 WL 1810135 (D.Colo.)*.

27. United States District Court: *In re Children's Inv. Fund Found. (UK), 363 F. Supp. 3d 361, 370 (S.D.N.Y. 2019);* United States District Court: *In re Ex Parte Application of Kleimar N.V., 220 F. Supp. 3d 517, 521 (S.D.N.Y. 2016)* ("[w]hile the Second Circuit has previously excluded private foreign arbitrations from the scope of qualifying Section 1782 proceedings, dictum of the Supreme Court in [Intel], suggests the Supreme Court may consider private foreign arbitrations, in fact, within the scope of Section 1782").
28. United States District Court: *EWG Gasspeicher GMBH v. Halliburton Co., Case No. 20-*1830 (D Del. 2020).
29. This decision has since been appealed with the Third Circuit in April 2020.
30. United States District Court: *In re Application of Food Delivery Holding S.A.R.L v. DeWitty and Associates CHTD*, Case No. 1:21-mc-0005 (GMH), available at https://ecf.dcd.uscourts.gov/cgi-bin/show_public_doc?2021mc0005-20.

[B] The Fourth Circuit's *Servotronics* Decision

On March 30, 2020, the Fourth Circuit joined the Sixth Circuit in allowing the use of §1782 in the context of private arbitration in the *Servotronics, Inc. v. The Boeing Company and Rolls-Royce PLC* case.[31] The *Servotronics* case involved a private arbitration between Servotronics, Inc. and Rolls-Royce PLC under the rules of the Chartered Institute of Arbitrators (CIArb). After the engine of the new Boeing 787 Dreamliner aircraft caught fire, causing significant damage to the aircraft itself, Rolls-Royce settled Boeing's claim for damages. Rolls-Royce thereafter alleged that Servotronics had supplied it with defective engine valves that Rolls-Royce used when building the engine for the Boeing 787 Dreamliner, seeking indemnification from Servotronics. Servotronics rejected Boeing's indemnification claim, and Rolls-Royce commenced the arbitration in the United Kingdom (U.K.) pursuant to the parties' contract.

During the arbitration, Servotronics argued it had not received critical documents from Rolls-Royce and Boeing. To resolve these discovery issues, Servotronics brought an ex parte application pursuant to §1782 in the United States District Court for the District of South Carolina to obtain testimony of South Carolina residents, i.e., the chair of Boeing's Incident Review Board, which had investigated the fire, as well as two other Boeing employees involved in troubleshooting the engine issues for use in the U.K. arbitration. The South Carolina Federal District Court, however, declined to apply §1782, finding the CIArb was not a "tribunal" under the statute.

On appeal, the Fourth Circuit reversed the decision, holding that §1782 can be used in a private "foreign or international" arbitration. The Fourth Circuit refused to follow *NBS* and *Biedermann*. Instead, the Fourth Circuit found that the 1964 change of wording from "in any judicial proceeding pending in any court in a foreign country" to the current phrase, "in a proceeding in a foreign or international tribunal," reflected Congress' policy to increase international cooperation "by providing U.S. assistance in resolving disputes before not only foreign courts but before all foreign and international tribunals."[32] Thus, according to the Fourth Circuit, the term *"tribunal"* in §1782 includes arbitral tribunals.

Lastly, the Fourth Circuit held that even if following *NBS* and *Biedermann*, the outcome would not have been different, as CIArb was "acting within the authority of the state" because the arbitration is subject to the U.K. government's sanctions, regulations, and oversight.[33]

[C] The Ninth Circuit Has Been Asked for a Decision, but Is Still in the Determination Stage

Less than a week after the Fourth Circuit's *Servotronics* decision, appellants in *HRC-Hainan Holding Co., et al. v. Yihan Hu et al.* asked the Ninth Circuit to reverse the

31. United States Court of Appeals: *Servotronics, Inc. v. The Boeing Company and Rolls-Royce PLC*, 954 F.3d 209, 212 (4th Cir. 2020).
32. *Ibid*, at 213.
33. *Ibid*, at 213-214.

Northern District of California's decision to allow discovery pursuant to §1782 for use in an arbitration before the China International Economic and Trade Arbitration Commission (CIETAC).[34]

In *HRC-Hainan Holding Co., LLC v. Yihan Hu*, a group of Delaware and Chinese companies initiated ex parte §1782 proceedings in the Northern District of California seeking leave to serve document and deposition subpoenas on nonparties to a CIETAC arbitration residing within the court's jurisdiction. The district court granted the applications.[35] With regard to the question of whether the language used in §1782, i.e., "foreign or international tribunal," covers a private arbitral tribunal, such as the one in the CIETAC proceedings, the Northern District of California followed the Sixth Circuit's approach in light of *Intel*. Specifically, it found that: (a) the ordinary meaning of "tribunal" is unambiguous; (b) the legislative history does not indicate Congress' intent to exclude private arbitral tribunals; and (c) policy concerns raised by the Second Circuit such as the popularity of arbitration based on its asserted efficiency and cost-effectiveness being "at odds with the broad-ranging discovery" that is possible under the Federal Rules of Civil Procedure (FRCP) were unpersuasive. Accordingly, the Northern District of California largely compelled respondents to provide the requisite documents and deposition testimony. Respondents filed an appeal with the Ninth Circuit, and the Ninth Circuit heard the case in September 2020 but has yet to render a decision.

[D] The Second Circuit's Decision in *In Re Application and Petition of Hanwei Guo*

On July 8, 2020, the Second Circuit decided in *In Re Application and Petition of Hanwei Guo* that §1782 is applicable to arbitration proceedings before private international tribunals.[36]

The petitioner, a Chinese businessman named Hanwei Guo, filed a request for discovery against several banks (such as Deutsche Bank, JPMorgan Chase, Bank of America Corp, and Morgan Stanley) pursuant to §1782 in the U.S. District Court for the Southern District of New York. Hanwei Guo intended to use the requested documents in the arbitral proceedings with the Chinese music streaming company *Tencent Music Entertainment* (at the time known as *Ocean Music*) pending before CIETAC. The district court denied the petition, and Hanwei Guo filed an appeal in the Second Circuit Court of Appeals.

The question of §1782's applicability arose against the background of the Second Circuit's decision *NBC v. Bear Stearns & Co.* issued in 1999, which dealt with

34. United States Court of Appeals: *HRC-Hainan Holding Co., et al. v. Yihan Hu, et al.*, No. 20-15371 (9th Cir. 2020).
35. United States District Court: *HRC-Hainan Holding Co., LLC v. Yihan Hu*, No. 19-MC-80277-TSH, 2020 WL 906719 (N.D. Cal. 2020).
36. United States Court of Appeals: *Hanwei Guo v. Deutsche Bank Securities Inc., J.P. Morgan Securities LLC, Merrill Lynch, Pierce, Fenner & Smith Incorporated, Morgan Stanley & Co. LLC.*, 965 F.3d 96 (2nd Cir. 2020).

commercial arbitration.[37] In *NBC v. Bear Stearns & Co.*, the Second Circuit decided that the term "tribunal" did not extend to private arbitration tribunals, but only covered "state sponsored adjudicatory bodies," i.e., tribunals acting as state instrumentalities or with the authority of the state. In reaching this conclusion, the Second Circuit mainly relied on legislative history.[38]

In *Hanwei Guo*, the Second Circuit confirmed its *NBC v. Bear Stearns & Co.* decision and held that *NBC v. Bear Stearns & Co.* was not overruled by the U.S. Supreme Court's *Intel* decision.[39] In the view of the Second Circuit, the U.S. Supreme Court had not decided the question of whether the term "tribunal" covered private arbitral tribunals as well. Since private arbitral tribunals were only mentioned in passing via dictum, it could not have the effect of abrogating the Second Circuit's *NBC v. Bear Stearns & Co.* precedent.[40] *NBC v. Bear Stearns & Co.* therefore remains good law in the Second Circuit, and the term "tribunal" covers "state-sponsored arbitral bodies," but not private arbitral tribunals.[41]

Consequently, the Second Circuit analyzed and developed a test for whether CIETAC qualified as a private international arbitral tribunal or a state-sponsored arbitral body. The test included factors such as the degree of state affiliation and functional independence from the state possessed by the entity as well as the degree to which the parties' arbitration clause controls the panel's jurisdiction.[42]

After applying these factors to CIETAC, the Second Circuit concluded that any CIETAC arbitration proceedings were private arbitration proceedings, despite CIETAC having been originally created through state action. According to the Second Circuit, the Arbitration Center operated independently of the Chinese government in the administration of its arbitration cases and the arbitrators were not affiliated with the Chinese government but, rather, independent from the state.[43] The Chinese government is unable to influence the outcome of the proceedings and, pursuant to Chinese law, is unable to set aside an arbitration award except on grounds that "overlap extensively" with the grounds under U.S. law.[44] Lastly, the Second Circuit found that CIETAC derives its jurisdiction exclusively from the parties' arbitration agreement.[45]

37. United States Court of Appeals: *National Broadcasting Co. v. Bear Stearns & Co.* 165 F.3d 184 (2nd Cir. 1999).
38. *Ibid*, at. 189: "In sum, the legislative history reveals that when Congress in 1964 enacted the modern version of § 1782, it intended to cover governmental or intergovernmental arbitral tribunals and conventional courts and other state-sponsored adjudicatory bodies. The legislative history's silence with respect to private tribunals is especially telling because we are confident that a significant congressional expansion of American judicial assistance to international arbitral panels created exclusively by private parties would not have been lightly undertaken by Congress without at least a mention of this legislative intention."
39. United States Court of Appeals: *Hanwei Guo v. Deutsche Bank Securities Inc., J.P. Morgan Securities LLC, Merrill Lynch, Pierce, Fenner & Smith Incorporated, Morgan Stanley & Co. LLC.*, 965 F.3d 96 (2nd Cir. 2020), at 105: "(...) we conclude that NBC's holding remains good law."
40. *Ibid.*, at 105.
41. *Ibid.*, at 107.
42. *Ibid.*
43. *Ibid.*
44. *Ibid.*
45. *Ibid.*, at 108.

Thus, the Second Circuit concluded that CIETAC is a private arbitral tribunal and denied the application under §1782.

[E] The Seventh Circuit's *Servotronics* Decision

On September 22, 2020, the Seventh Circuit unanimously ruled in *Servotronics, Inc. v. Rolls-Royce PLC, et al.* that §1782 cannot be invoked in aid of foreign private commercial arbitrations.[46] This decision marks the first time the Seventh Circuit has spoken on the issue of whether §1782 authorizes a district court to provide discovery assistance to foreign arbitral tribunals. Since the Seventh Circuit directly contradicted its colleagues from the Fourth Circuit in the same arbitration, thus involving the same parties, its decision dramatically further deepened the circuit split on the issue.

The basic facts of the Seventh Circuit's *Servotronics* decision are the same as in the case before the Fourth Circuit. After filing the aforementioned ex parte application in South Carolina, Servotronics filed an application in the U.S. District Court for the Northern District of Illinois asking the court to issue a subpoena compelling Boeing to produce documents for use in the CIArb arbitration proceedings pending in the U.K.

The U.S. District Court for the Northern District of Illinois denied the ex parte application and held that §1782 cannot be used in aid of private commercial arbitrations. Servotronics appealed.

In its decision, the Seventh Circuit aligned with the Second and Fifth Circuits, upholding the U.S. District Court's decision and finding that §1782 does not authorize a U.S. District Court to compel discovery for use in private foreign arbitration. First, the Seventh Circuit observed that the term "tribunal" is not defined in the statute. Turning to statutory interpretation, the Seventh Circuit then held that even considering dictionary definitions does not resolve the issue of whether or not the term "tribunal" covers private commercial arbitration panels—notwithstanding the fact that some dictionary definitions are "more expansive, leaving room for both competing interpretations." Due to the plausibility of both interpretations, the Seventh Circuit found this approach to be inconclusive.

The Seventh Circuit then assessed §1782 in its statutory context. To this end, the Seventh Circuit compared §1782's use of the phrase "foreign and international tribunal" to the phrase's use in 28 U.S.C. §1696 (assistance regarding service-of-process) and §1781 (letters rogatory). The Seventh Circuit concluded that the phrase "foreign or international tribunal" in these statutes undoubtedly refers to state-sponsored tribunals only—not private commercial arbitration tribunals. As a result, the Seventh Circuit considered a more expansive reading of the term "tribunal" in 28 U.S.C. §1782 even "*far less plausible.*"[47]

Furthermore, the Seventh Circuit also cautioned against an interpretation of §1782 that would provide more than what is permitted under the Federal Arbitration

46. United States Court of Appeals: *Servotronics, Inc. v. Rolls-Royce PLC, et al.*, 975 F.3d 689 (7th Cir. 2020).
47. *Ibid.*, at 694.

Act (FAA).[48] Section 7 of the FAA only permits the arbitration panel, but not the litigating parties, to summon witnesses before the panel to testify at arbitration hearings and to petition district courts to enforce those summonses. 28 U.S.C. §1782 does not have such a limitation, but allows both the panel and the litigating parties to obtain discovery orders from U.S. district courts. The Seventh Circuit considers this to be a distinction without any good rationale. According to the Seventh Circuit, it is untenable that a broad application of. §1782 could result in litigating parties in foreign arbitrations having "access to much more expansive discovery than litigants in domestic arbitrations." Moreover, because the FAA applies to some foreign arbitrations, the Seventh Circuit concluded that there would be a potential conflict between a broad interpretation of §1782 and the FAA.[49] Thus, the Seventh Circuit supports a more narrow reading of the term "tribunal" and consequently a narrower scope of application of §1782.

Finally, the Seventh Circuit analyzed the Supreme Court's analysis of §1782 in *Intel Corp. v. Advanced Micro Devices, Inc.* The Seventh Circuit found that, in the absence of any explicit indication that the term "tribunals" was meant to include private arbitral tribunals, there was "no reason to believe" that the U.S. Supreme Court by quoting a law-review article in a passing intended to broaden the scope of application of §1732 to provide discovery assistance in private foreign arbitrations. The Seventh Circuit found that the quote had "taken on outsized significance" as a mere "part of an explanatory parenthetical" and thus should not be used to justify discovery assistance for private foreign arbitration proceedings.[50]

[F] Servotronics' Petition for a Writ of Certiorari with the U.S. Supreme Court

On December 7, 2020, Servotronics appealed the Seventh Circuit's decision to the Supreme Court, filing a petition for a writ of certiorari. In its petition, Servotronics cited the Fourth and Seventh Circuit decisions and pointed to other circuit court decisions exacerbating the inconsistent application of §1782. Warning that the "*3 2 circuit split*" may only deepen and with appeals pending in other circuit courts on the same issue, Servotronics asked the U.S. Supreme Court to "remove uncertainty" over the issue and provide a "uniform standard" on whether the discretion granted to district courts under 28 U.S.C. §1782 includes evidence gathering for "private commercial arbitral tribunals." On March 22, 2021, the U.S. Supreme Court agreed to hear the appeal filed by Servotronics. Both the petition and the U.S. Supreme Court's decision to agree to hear the appeal were met with great interest in the litigation and arbitration community, as a decision by the U.S. Supreme Court promised to do away with the topic once and for all. In fact, several amicus curiae briefs were filed, some in favor of one of the parties,

48. *Ibid.*, at 695.
49. *Ibid.*, at 695.
50. *Ibid.*, at 696.

some neutral.[51] However, for reasons unknown, in the first week of September 2021, Servotronics unexpectedly filed a motion to dismiss with the U.S. Supreme Court, effectively withdrawing its petition. Consequently, the U.S. Supreme Court dropped the case from its calendar.

[G] The Impact of an Enduring Circuit Split: An Outlook

From an arbitration standpoint, the motion to dismiss filed by Servotronics resulting in the U.S. Supreme Court no longer deciding this case can only be considered regrettable. Instead of providing clarity, the insecurity with regard to what constitutes a tribunal under §1782 now continues. There is a risk that this issue will never be settled by the U.S. Supreme Court at all, as proceedings require a litigant willing to see their dispute all the way through to the U.S. Supreme Court.

But the missed opportunity is also felt by the Circuit Courts themselves, which had been waiting for the U.S. Supreme Court to clarify the matter. Indeed, as laid out above, both the Third and Ninth Circuit have pending cases on this very issue. In March 2021, the Ninth Circuit even explicitly stated that in view of Servotronic's petition for a writ of certiorari, it was holding off on a decision regarding the issue of §1782 until the U.S. Supreme Court had provided guidance on this matter. Both Circuit Courts will now decide the cases on their own, potentially deepening the Circuit split. An enduring and deepened Circuit split, however, cannot be in anyone's interest.

51. For instance, the Federal Arbitration, a U.S.-based alternative dispute resolution provider, filed an amicus curia brief, arguing that the petitioner's appeal should be upheld and that private arbitral bodies should qualify for discovery. The amicus curiae brief is available at https://www.supremecourt.gov/DocketPDF/20/20-794/179032/20210512164053430_20-794_Amicus%20Brief.pdf. Likewise, Prof. George Bermann filed an amicus curiae brief in support of the petitioner, arguing that the "plain meaning of Section 1782 compels the conclusion that the statute applies to proceedings before international commercial arbitral tribunal," and thus a broad application of the provision was warranted. According to Prof. Bermann, the term "tribunals" used in §1782 is a term used to identify the bodies that conduct international arbitral proceedings. The distinction between state-sponsored and private tribunals does not find any backing in neither the wording nor the history of the legal provision. The amicus curiae brief is available at https://www.supremecourt.gov/DocketPDF/20/20-794/179133/20210513153854699_20-794tsacProfessorGeorgeA.Bermann.pdf. In a separate amicus curiae brief, the ICC focused on the relationship between the arbitral tribunal and the U.S. court and whether the opinion of the arbitral tribunal regarding discovery should be taken into account by the U.S. court faced with a petition under §1728. In the ICC's view, the U.S. court "should afford a very high degree of deference to the arbitral tribunal's view on the discovery sought" for the following reason: "Affording a very high degree of deference to the tribunal would also be in line with the fundamental principle in private international commercial arbitrations that the arbitral tribunal has the primary authority and control over the proceedings, including discovery matters. As a result of this authority and an arbitral tribunal's familiarity with the governing arbitration rules and the underlying dispute, the arbitral tribunal constituted for a particular dispute is best placed to assess the propriety and utility of evidence that may result from a Section 1782 application." The amicus curiae brief is available at https://www.supremecourt.gov/DocketPDF/20/20-794/179108/20210513141908841_2021.05.13%20ICC%20Amicus%-20Brief.pdf.

In any event, the enduring Circuit split will have a huge impact on litigants' approach to discovery in international arbitration and their strategy with regard to obtaining evidence in the United States and actually might lead to an increase in evidentiary forum shopping.

CHAPTER 7

Arbitral Jurisdiction in Respect of Claims Based on Fraud and Other Non-contractual Grounds

Fredrik Norburg

In commercial arbitration, it is relatively common that some claims or part of claims are based on tortious or criminal liability. This chapter examines the issue of whether an arbitral tribunal in commercial arbitration is authorized to try claims based on tort, fraud, bribery and other non-contractual grounds, assuming that the arbitration agreement is worded in accordance with the commonly used model arbitration clauses. The focus is on the position taken under Swedish and other Nordic laws.

The legal development both in Sweden and in other Nordic jurisdictions referred to in the chapter shows an increased focus on the interpretation of the arbitration clause and the reasonable expectations of the parties to the agreement, rather than on limiting the scope of the matters to be resolved by arbitration due to a narrow interpretation of the concept of 'legal relationship' found in the New York Convention and in national legislation. Thus, it appears from case law that claims based on non-contractual liability are generally accepted in arbitrations seated in the Nordics, provided that the arbitration clause, interpreted according to general contract interpretation principles, is deemed to cover the disputed facts in question.

§7.01 INTRODUCTION

In commercial arbitration it is relatively common that some claims or part of claims are based on tortious or criminal liability. The claimant may argue that certain actions of the respondents constituted, e.g., fraud, not only breach of contract. The aim of such claims may be, e.g., to avoid the application of a limitation of liability clause. Criminal liability may also be invoked as an entirely independent ground, or as the sole basis for the claim in the arbitration.

The purpose of this chapter is to examine the issue of whether an arbitral tribunal in commercial arbitration is authorized to try claims based on tort, fraud, bribery and other non-contractual grounds, assuming that the arbitration agreement is worded in accordance with one of the model clauses connected to the most commonly used arbitration rules set out below. The focus of this article is on the position taken under Swedish and other Nordic laws.

According to the model clause of the Arbitration Institute of the Stockholm Chamber of Commerce (SCC), 'Any dispute, controversy or claim arising out of or in connection with this contract, or the breach, termination or invalidity thereof, shall be finally settled by arbitration.' The United Nations Commission on International Trade Law (UNCITRAL) model clause refers to 'Any dispute, controversy or claim arising out of or relating to this contract, or the breach, termination or invalidity thereof', whereas the International Chamber of Commerce (ICC) model arbitration clause refers to 'disputes arising out of or in connection with the present contract'. Both the London Court of International Arbitration (LCIA) and the Singapore International Arbitration Centre (SIAC) model clauses refer to 'Any dispute arising out of or in connection with this contract'.

The wordings of these model clauses do not expressly exclude non-contractual disputes if they 'arise out of' or are 'connected with' or 'relate to' the contract in which the clause is included. Moreover, the clauses do not state that the dispute's connection with the main contract must be close or strong.

Historically, the predominant view was that claims relating, e.g., to corruption and bribery should not be tried by arbitrators. In an ICC arbitration award of 1963, the sole arbitrator Gunnar Lagergren, a Swedish judge, decided that a dispute relating to a contract concerning payments to Argentine officials was not arbitrable because it concerned payment of bribes.[1] Judge Lagergren refused to try the matter because, as he stated in the award, 'corruption is an international evil; it is contrary to good morals and to an international public policy common to the community of nations'.[2] However, this view has developed and today such disputes are commonly deemed arbitrable, but the claims may of course be dismissed on the merits, e.g., under the principle of *pactum turpe*.[3] The question remains, however, whether such disputes are covered by the relevant arbitration agreement invoked as the basis for the jurisdiction of the arbitral tribunal.

§7.02 THE NEW YORK CONVENTION

According to Article II(1) of the New York Convention, the contracting states must recognize arbitration agreements covering legal relationships 'whether contractual or not'. Thus, the wording of the convention supports the proposition that also non-contractual claims could be tried in arbitration.

1. ICC Case No. 1110.
2. *See* para. 20 of the award.
3. *See* Kaj Hobér, *International Commercial Arbitration in Sweden*, 2nd ed. p. 109.

However, Article II(1) of the New York Convention also states that the arbitration agreements to be recognized under the convention are agreements under which the parties undertake to submit to arbitration differences which have arisen, or which may arise between them in respect of a 'defined legal relationship', concerning a subject matter capable of settlement by arbitration. Is a possible future right to damages based on criminal liability a 'defined legal relationship' under this provision?

The term 'legal relationship' is not defined in the New York Convention. Nor is the word 'defined' in 'defined legal relationship' further clarified in the convention. However, according to case law that has developed in several contracting states, this wording should be given a broad and pro-arbitration meaning; see further below, e.g., concerning the Swedish case of *Belgor*.[4]

§7.03 SWEDEN

[A] Introduction

Under Swedish law, arbitration agreements covering existing disputes based on non-contractual grounds are valid and enforceable if the dispute is capable of settlement by agreement. Claim for damages based on fraud or other non-contractual grounds are capable of settlement, and, thus, if the arbitration agreement refers to such a dispute existing at the time of entering the arbitration agreement, the arbitrators would clearly have jurisdiction.

However, most arbitration agreements are made to cover potential future and yet unknown disputes, and the question is then whether this could include future disputes based on non-contractual grounds.

Under section 1 of the Swedish Arbitration Act, an arbitration agreement 'may relate to future disputes pertaining to a legal relationship specified' in the arbitration agreement.[5] As a starting point, this may include both contractual and non-contractual legal relationships. The Arbitration Act does not state how the legal relationship should be specified and whether a reference to one legal relationship may infer a reference to another legal relationship. The reason for the requirement to specify the legal relationship in the arbitration agreement is that the parties should be able to oversee the consequences of the arbitration agreement.[6] Thus, there is an element of foreseeability and party autonomy to consider when analysing the issue. The requirement is also based on the fundamental right to a fair trial and the right to go to court as protected under Article 6 of the European Convention on Human Rights.

According to the traditional view, a consequence of the requirement that the legal relationship must be specified in the arbitration agreement is that an arbitration agreement in respect of future disputes does not cover non-contractual claims. This may appear logical because the future then-unknown non-contractual dispute is

4. NJA 2017 p. 171 (Belgor).
5. *See also* Government Bill 1998/99:35 p. 212.
6. *See* NJA 2019 p. 171 (Belgor), para. 12 of the judgment.

strictly speaking another legal relationship than the one normally identified in the arbitration agreement (e.g., 'this contract' and 'the present contract' in the model arbitration clauses quoted above).[7]

However, Swedish case law developed since 2007 suggests that an arbitration clause concerning future disputes may also cover then-unknown non-contractual claims.

NJA 2007 p. 475 (Vägmaterialet)

In *NJA 2007 p. 475* (*Vägmaterialet*), the claimant had initiated court proceedings and claimed damages on three grounds, of which two were contractual or semi-contractual and one was based on an alleged crime, dishonest conduct,[8] by an employee of the defendant. Under Swedish tort law, a party who has suffered financial loss resulting from a crime is entitled to damages, and an employer is liable for such damages if an employee has committed the crime while on duty.[9] The parties had an agreement which included an arbitration clause merely stating that 'possible disputes should be resolved in accordance with the arbitration act'. Notably, the arbitration clause did not include a wording relating to disputes 'in connection with the contract' as found in model clauses. The district court and the Svea Court of Appeal dismissed the claim for lack of jurisdiction with reference to the wording of the arbitration agreement. The Supreme Court granted leave to appeal in respect of the issue of whether third ground, i.e., damages on the basis of the alleged crime, was covered by the arbitration agreement.

The Supreme Court found, first, that the arbitration clause should be interpreted to include all disputes in connection with the contract, although this was not expressly stated in the clause. Second, the court found that the factual circumstances invoked as a basis for the alleged crime had a direct connection with the contract. Third and finally, the court concluded that, because the two other grounds for the claim were covered by the arbitration clause, also the third ground should be deemed covered by the clause. Thus, the Supreme Court agreed with the lower courts essentially because of the alleged crime's connection with the legal relationship specified in the arbitration clause, and for reasons of procedural efficiency.

NJA 2008 p. 120 (Ystad Hamn)

In *NJA 2008 p. 120 (Ystad Hamn)*, the Supreme Court tried the question, whether certain claims based on infringement of competition law (abuse of dominant position) and violation of administrative legislation governing municipalities were covered by an arbitration agreement in a contract between *BornholmsTrafikken*, a ferry company owned by the Danish state, and *Ystad Hamn Logistik AB*, a company operating the

7. *See* Stefan Lindskog, *Skiljeförfarande*, Juno Version 3, section I:0:5.2.1.
8. Chapter 9, section 8 of the Swedish Criminal Code states that 'A person who ... acts dishonestly by inducing someone by deception into an action or omission, thereby harming the person deceived or someone in whose place they are, is guilty of dishonest conduct.'
9. Chapter 2, section 2 and Chapter 3, section 1 of the Swedish Tort Liability Act.

Ystad port and owned by the Swedish municipality of Ystad, a place well known for readers of Henning Mankell's crime novels about Inspector Kurt Wallander.

Under the contract, *Ystad Hamn Logistik AB* had charged fees for its port services, and *BornholmsTrafikken* claimed that certain of these fees were excessive and constituted a violation both of competition law and of administrative law. The contract included an arbitration clause merely stating that possible disputes should be resolved by arbitration according to Swedish law. Thus, in this contract, there was no 'in connection with' wording in the arbitration clause.[10] *Ystad Hamn Logistik AB* requested that the court should dismiss the claim for repayment of fees due to the arbitration clause.

The Supreme Court agreed with this argument and dismissed the repayment claim for lack of jurisdiction. First, it stated that, according to an express provision in section 1 of the Arbitration Act, arbitrators may rule on the civil law effects of competition law as between the parties. In this part, the Supreme Court also referred to the judgment of the European Court of Justice in *Eco-Swiss v. Benneton*.[11] Second, the court stated that the claim had a strong connection to the contract and, therefore, that it was covered by the arbitration clause. Although *BornholmsTrafikken* did not base its claim directly on the contract, the claim concerned the fees charged under the contract.

NJA 2010 p. 734 (Tupperware)

In *NJA 2010 p. 734 (Tupperware)*, the bankruptcy estate of *Facht Distribution AB* initiated court proceedings against *Tupperware Nordic A/S*, a Danish company, and claimed that certain goods should be returned to the estate or, alternatively, that an amount equivalent to the value of the goods should be paid. The parties had a franchise agreement which had been terminated by *Tupperware Nordic A/S*. The franchise agreement included a dispute resolution clause stating that disputes should be resolved by the court at the seat of *Facht Distribution AB*. Therefore, the estate filed its claim with a district court south of Stockholm. *Tupperware Nordic A/S* objected to Swedish jurisdiction and stated that it is a company seated in Denmark.

Although the case was not about an arbitration clause, the Supreme Court refers to arbitration law and compares the requirement for a defined legal relationship in section 1 of the Arbitration Act to the requirements for a defined legal relationship in prorogation clauses. The Supreme Court stated, obiter dictum as regards arbitration clauses, that the existence between a legal relationship, covered by a prorogation clause or an arbitration clause, and another legal relationship only in certain cases and in very special circumstances may extend the clause to cover such other legal relationship. The court also stated that the above-referenced judgment in *Vägmaterialet* of 2007 constituted such an exception to the main rule. Notably, none of the justices

10. *See* further Daniel Waerme, *Behörighetsproblematiken i tvister som endast delvis omfattas av skiljeavtal*, SvJT 2010 pp. 714-725; Finn Madsen, *Kompetenz-Kompetenz in Swedish Arbitration Law is being recast, how should it be done?*, SvJT 2016 pp. 653-673.
11. ECJ Case No. C-126/1997.

involved in the ruling of 2007 were involved in this ruling of 2010.[12] Eventually, the Supreme Court stated that, although it did not have jurisdiction because of the prorogation clause, it confirmed Swedish jurisdiction because *Tupperware Nordic A/S* had assets in Sweden in the form of a claim against the estate to be handled in the bankruptcy proceedings.

NJA 2017 p. 226 (Avräkningsavtalet)

In *NJA 2017 p. 226 (Avräkningsavtalet)*,[13] the Supreme Court continued in the line of reasoning found in *NJA 2010 p. 734 (Tupperware)*. The parties to the latter dispute were former shareholders in a limited liability company, *Arvika Gjuteri Holding AB*, which had been sold to a third party. When the company was sold, one of the shareholders, *Kemisten AB*, undertook the task of administering the sale on behalf of all shareholders, including receiving the purchase price and distributing the money to the sellers. For this purpose, the sellers concluded a contract with an arbitration clause. According to the wording of the clause, disputes relating to the interpretation or implementation of the contract was to be settled by arbitration under the SCC Rules. Thus, there was no wording to the effect that disputes 'in connection with' the contract.

After the transaction was completed, *Kemisten AB* paid a part of the purchase price to a third party, in breach of the parties' contract. Therefore, three of the sellers filed claims with a district court against *Kemisten AB* and its managing director and claimed damages on the grounds that the managing director had committed criminal offences by paying funds to a third party, and that *Kemisten AB* had vicarious liability for the actions of the managing director.

The defendants requested dismissal of the case with reference to the arbitration agreement. The district court allowed for court proceedings, but the Court of Appeal dismissed the claim due to the arbitration clause.

The Supreme Court agreed with the district court and concluded that the claims were not covered by the arbitration clause. The court referred to *Tupperware* and stated that it is only in certain cases and in very special circumstances that the arbitration clause may extend to cover another legal relationship than the one referred to in the arbitration clause. Thus, according to the reasoning in *Avräkningsavtalet*, an arbitration clause in a contract basically only covers the legal relationship or relationships regulated in the contract and no other legal relationships.

As regards non-contractual grounds, the Supreme Court stated that, if a breach of contract also constitutes tortious or criminal liability, then the tortious or criminal liability may in some cases be covered by an arbitration clause. However, the Supreme Court stated that this requires that the facts invoked as a legal basis for the non-contractual liability in all material aspects correspond to facts that could have constituted contractual liability.

12. *See* further Finn Madsen, *Kompetenz-Kompetenz in Swedish Arbitration Law is being recast, how should it be done?*, SvJT 2016 p. 662.
13. *See* further Fredrik Norburg and Erika Finn, *Supreme Court clarifies doctrine of connection*, International Law Office, 11 May 2017.

In the case at hand, the Supreme Court determined that the claims were based on also other facts than a possible claim for payment under the contract, including issues concerning the alleged criminal actions of the managing director and *Kemisten AB's* responsibility for such actions.

NJA 2019 p. 171 (Belgor)

After *Tupperware* of 2010 and *Avräkningsavtalet* of 2017, one could have concluded that the ruling of *Vägmaterialet* of 2007 had a very limited application. However, this may have changed through the landmark ruling of *NJA 2019 p. 171 (Belgor)*.[14]

The SCC arbitration between the Turkish company *Koca Inşaat Sanayi Ihracat Anonim Şirketi* and the Belarusian *Joint Stock Company Belgorkhimprom* (Belgor), concerning a construction project in Turkmenistan, was initiated on the basis of an SCC clause covering disputes 'emerged because of or in connection with' the construction contract.

There were several claims made in the arbitration, including claims relating to additional works governed by five separate service agreements. The service agreement did not include an SCC arbitration clause, but a clause stating that, if the parties failed to resolve the dispute through negotiations, 'each of the Parties has the right to petition Minsk economic court and the laws and regulations of the Republic of Belarus shall apply to such disputes'.

The arbitral tribunal found that the claims for additional works did not arise out of the construction contract containing the SCC arbitration clause and that it was 'undisputed that the Additional Works were performed on the basis of five separate contracts, which did not have arbitration clauses, but which stipulated that the Parties had the right to refer disputes to the Economic Court in Minsk'.[15]

However, the arbitral tribunal also found that the additional works in relation to these claims were performed in connection with the construction contract and, therefore, as such covered by the wording of the arbitration clause in the construction contract. Moreover, the arbitral tribunal decided that the dispute resolution clause in the service agreements only gave the parties a right but not an obligation to refer their disputes to the court in Minsk.

In a judgment dated 31 October 2017, the Svea Court of Appeal set aside the award partially, including on the ground that the arbitral tribunal lacked jurisdiction to rule on the claims relating to the additional service agreements.[16] In its judgment, the Svea Court of Appeal quoted the reasoning of the Supreme Court in *Avräkningsavtalet*. At the same time, however, the Svea Court of Appeal expressed a subtle uncertainty as to the issue of when legal relationships connected with the main contract should be deemed covered by an arbitration clause when it stated that 'at least nowadays' it is only in exceptional cases possible to extend the scope of an arbitration clause based on a connection with the legal relationship covered by the arbitration clause. This

14. The author acted as counsel in the challenge proceedings.
15. Paragraph 84 of the arbitration award.
16. An English translation of the Svea Court of Appeal judgment is available online at the Swedish Arbitration Portal.

statement of uncertainty was possibly a reference to the Supreme Court judgment in *Vägmaterialet*.

The Supreme Court reversed the Svea Court of Appeal judgment and clarified, or perhaps changed, Swedish arbitration law in certain aspects, including in relation to jurisdiction.[17]

First, the Supreme Court stated that the scope of an arbitration agreement is determined under customary principles for contract interpretation. It referred to the ruling in *NJA 2015 p. 741 (Partneravtalet)* concerning general contract interpretation and concluded that it is natural to assume that the arbitration agreement should fulfil a sensible function and serve as a reasonable set of rules for the parties' respective interests. Therefore, it may be assumed that the parties intended that disputes should be resolved swiftly and in one comprehensive proceeding before an arbitral tribunal appointed by the parties.

Moreover, the court stated that, when interpreting arbitration agreements and the term 'legal relationship', the principles of the New York Convention should be considered. It noted that the principles of the convention have in foreign case law and international jurisprudence been taken to justify an expansive interpretation of both the arbitration agreement and the concept of a 'legal relationship'.[18]

As regards its previous ruling in *Avräkningsavtalet*, it repeated a statement in this judgment that the term 'legal relationship' does cover not only those rights and obligations that have been set forth in an original agreement but also subsequent legally relevant circumstances, which alter the content of the agreement, fall within the scope of the term and thereby within the applicable scope of an arbitration clause in the original agreement. As regards *Vägmaterialet*, the Supreme Court stated that 'a ground outside the contractual relationship could be deemed to fall inside the applicable scope of the arbitration clause' and noted that in *Vägmaterialet* the non-contractual ground for the claim was deemed so closely related to the other grounds that also the non-contractual ground was deemed covered by the arbitration clause. Notably, in *Belgor*, the Supreme Court did not repeat the statements made in *Avräkningsavtalet* that the arbitration clause may extend to cover another legal relationship than the one referred to in the arbitration clause only in certain cases and in very special circumstances.

To bridge a possible conflict between the rulings in *Avräkningsavtalet*, on the one hand, and *Vägmaterialet* and *Belgor*, on the other hand, the difference in the wordings of the arbitration clauses should be noted. In *Avräkningsavtalet*, the clause only

17. The Supreme Court's judgment, NJA 2019 p. 171 (Belgor), has been discussed in several articles, including Patrik Schöldström, *Har Belgor förändrat prövningen av en skiljenämnds behörighet och handläggningsfel?*, Juridisk Tidsskrift Nr 1 2019/20, p. 243; Christer Danielsson, *Swedish Arbitration-Related Case Law 2017–2019*, Stockholm Arbitration Yearbook 2019; Lars Heuman, *Har det skett en omsvängning eller omläggning av praxis från restriktiv till extensiv tillämpning av skiljeavtal?*, SvJT 2019 p. 534. An English translation of the Supreme Court judgment is available online at the Swedish Arbitration Portal.
18. Here the Supreme Court also referred to Gary B. Born, *International Commercial Arbitration*, 2nd ed. 2014, pp. 1317 ff., and Howard M. Holtzmann and Joseph E. Neuhaus, *A Guide to the UNCITRAL Model Law on International Commercial Arbitration*, 1994, p. 259.

referred to interpretation or implementation of the contract, not disputes 'in connection with' the contract. In *Belgor*, the arbitration clause expressly included disputes in connection with the contract, whereas in *Vägmaterialet* this was how the Supreme Court interpreted the clause, although there was no express wording to this effect.

Since the Supreme Court accepted the reasoning of the arbitral tribunal in *Belgor*, a model arbitration clause, including the wording 'arising out of or in connection with the contract', should arguably be interpreted to include disputes concerning legal relationships connected with the contract, or at least closely connected with the contract. Although *Belgor* concerned contractual relationships, the judgment does not exclude that the same reasoning is applied in respect of claims based on tortious or criminal liability. Examples of such claims in connection with a contract could be non-contractual claims based on circumstances that presuppose the existence of the contract, or non-contractual claims that, alternatively, could have been formulated as a contractual claim. Claims based on non-contractual legal relationships only loosely connected with the contract would then, arguably, fall outside of the scope of the arbitration clause. Potentially, a very expansive interpretation and application of an arbitration clause could violate the parties' reasonable expectations in respect of the foreseeable effects of the arbitration clause.

A similar view was expressed by the arbitral tribunal in an unpublished SCC arbitration award rendered in 2021.[19] The arbitration, seated in Stockholm, was initiated on the basis of an SCC model arbitration clause, and included negative declaratory claims covering claims based on allegations of fraud and bribery. However, all circumstances invoked as a basis for the claims presupposed the existence of the contract, i.e., without the contract the alleged criminal liability as a basis for damages would not have been possible. Moreover, it would likely have been possible to formulate the claims as arising directly under the contract instead of as non-contractual claims. Therefore, with reference to the Supreme Court's rulings in both *Avraknungsavtalet* and *Belgor*, the arbitral tribunal accepted jurisdiction and tried the claims based on criminal liability.

§7.04 NORWAY

Sweden is not regarded as a UNCITRAL Model Law jurisdiction. Therefore, it may be of interest to see if the issues discussed in this article have been dealt with differently in its neighbouring Model Law jurisdictions Norway and Denmark.

As regards Norway, its Supreme Court came to similar conclusions as *Vägmaterialet* and *Belgor* in the case of *I.M. Skaugen Marine Service v. MAN Diesel* of 2017.[20]

This case included claims that respondents requested the court to dismiss with reference to an arbitration clause stating that '[a]ny dispute arising out of or relating to

19. The author acted as counsel in the SCC arbitration.
20. HR-2017-1932, *IM Skaugen Marine Service Pte Ltd v. MAN Diesel & Turbo SE, Man Diesel & Turbo Norge AS. See also* comments concerning another part of the judgment by Carl E Roberts and Norman Hansen Meyer, *International Arbitration Review*, 11th ed. 2020, pp. 327-329.

this Contract shall be finally settled by arbitration in accordance with the Rules of Procedure of the Copenhagen Court of Arbitration'.

The Supreme Court first stated that it should not only consider how the claimant has formulated its case, and quoted a statement by Gary B. Born that '... it is frequently said that a party may not defeat an arbitration clause by casting its claim in tort, rather than contract'.[21] Therefore, the Supreme Court concluded that whether or not the claim is subject to arbitration 'must consequently be decided based on an interpretation of the arbitration agreement'.[22]

The Supreme Court continued and noted that the wording of the arbitration clause is general, and that it does not give room for reading limitations into it. Moreover, the Supreme Court referred to a previous case between *SAS* and *Icelandair* where it was held that it must be assessed whether there is a connection between the claim and the contract, irrespective of whether the claim is non-contractual or contractual.[23] The Norwegian Supreme Court referred to international case law and literature[24] and stated that '[i]rrespective of the fact that the alleged legal basis for Skaugen's claim for damages is non-contractual liability, this claim and the claims arising from the contract are closely connected'.

The Supreme Court also noted that several claims for damages relating to the alleged fraud had been submitted for arbitration by Skaugen as reflected in an arbitral award previously rendered in Stockholm. Thus, also Skaugen appeared to have shared the view that these types of claims were covered by the arbitration clause.

Finally, the Supreme Court stated that policy considerations suggest that various disputes arisen in connection with the contract should be heard as one. The court assumed that this had been the purpose of the general wording of the arbitration clause.[25]

§7.05 DENMARK

In Danish law, it is also held that a broadly worded arbitration clause may comprise claims for damages based on non-contractual grounds, including claims based on criminal liability.[26]

In case *U2013.2338H*, the Danish Supreme Court found that an arbitration clause covered non-contractual claims concerning, *inter alia*, a violation of the financial business act.

Some of the defendants in the case, including former management of *Ebh Bank*, had reached severance agreements following the termination of their contracts with the

21. Gary B. Born, *International Commercial Arbitration*, 2nd ed. p. 1359.
22. In this connection the court also referred to Norwegian Official Report 2001:33 p. 39.
23. Case Rt-1993-777.
24. Gary B. Born, *International Commercial Arbitration*, 2nd ed. p. 1359, and the House of Lords' decision of 17 October 2007 in *Premium Nafta Products Limited and others v. Fili Shipping Company Limited and others.*
25. Here the court also referred to the Supreme Court decision in case Rt-1994-1489.
26. Jakob Juul and Peter Fauerholdt Thommesen, *Voldgiftsret*, 3rd ed. p. 120; Niels Schiersing, *Voldgiftsloven med kommentarer*, 2016, pp. 110-113.

bank. The severance agreements included an arbitration agreement that referred the parties to resolve disputes concerning the interpretation of the severance agreements by arbitration under the Rules of the Danish Arbitration Institute.

Following the collapse of *Ebh Bank* in 2008, claims for damages were initiated in court against the former directors, management and auditors of the bank, including some of the parties to the severance agreements. According to the Western High Court, the action was outside of the prerequisites of the severance agreements. After appeal, however, the Supreme Court found that the wording of the arbitration agreement covered the dispute in question and dismissed the case.[27]

§7.06 FINLAND

Finland is not a Model Law jurisdiction, but it is currently exploring whether it should adopt the Model Law. Whether or not a future reform will affect the issues discussed in this article remains to be seen. As regards the present law on the topic of non-contractual claims in arbitration, the Finnish Supreme Court rendered a judgment in 2008 in which it confirmed that also non-contractual claims connected to a contract with an arbitration clause may be tried in arbitration.[28]

In this case, two parties to a shareholders' agreement brought a claim for damages against the third party to the agreement. However, the claim was filed in criminal proceedings where the third party was prosecuted for fraud. The shareholders' agreement included an arbitration clause stating that disputes arising out of the agreement shall be settled by arbitration. The question then arose whether the claim for damages brought in the criminal proceedings should be dismissed because of the arbitration clause.

Essentially, the facts invoked as a basis for the claim for damages were related to certain terms in the shareholders' agreement and a supplement to this agreement concerning the duty of a party to inform the other parties on the intention to sell the shares in a company, and on how the purchase price should be divided. According to the claimants, the breach of these terms constituted a criminal offence.

The Supreme Court found that the parties had agreed to having all claims arising out of the shareholders' agreement settled by arbitration. The court also found that, even when a breach of contract is also a criminal offence, a claim for damages based on such facts can be settled by arbitration. A claim which is covered by the arbitration agreement cannot be tried by a general court just because the claim is based on a criminal offence.[29] According to the court, the claims were, therefore, covered by the arbitration clause and should be dismissed for lack of jurisdiction, even if the claimants invoked the alleged criminal offence as a ground for the claim.

27. *See also* the Supreme Court cases 217/2013 and U2014.2042H where the claims were dismissed with reference to the arbitration clause in the General Conditions for Consulting Services (ABR 89), even if non-contractual grounds were included.
28. Case KKO:2008:102, commented by Marko Hentunen, *Supreme Court: Arbitration Clause is Obstacle to Claiming Damages in Criminal Trial,* International Law Office, 12 February 2009.
29. Case KKO 2008:102, p. 6.

§7.07 CONCLUDING REMARKS

The legal development both in Sweden and in other Nordic jurisdictions referred to in this article shows an increased focus on the interpretation of the arbitration clause in accordance with general contract interpretation principles and on the reasonable expectations of the parties to the agreement, rather than on limiting the scope of the matters to be resolved by arbitration due to a narrow interpretation of the concept of 'legal relationship'.

This also corresponds to a legal trend where arbitration agreements are treated and interpreted as any other commercial contract, rather than being restrictively interpreted and applied because arbitration agreements exclude the important right to go to court. In many jurisdictions, the current position is rather that arbitration agreements should be interpreted expansively.[30]

As regards wordings such as 'relating to' and 'in connection with', there is support for a broad application in the case law of many jurisdictions, including England, USA, France, Switzerland, and other major arbitration jurisdictions.[31] This international practice is now established also in Sweden through the ruling of *Belgor*.

In a number of jurisdictions, there have been attempts to define what is required to determine the sufficient 'connection' between the non-contractual claim and the contract containing the arbitration clause, including 'go to the core of the parties' contractual relationship', are 'intertwined factually and legally' and 'greatly overlap'. Gary B. Born has stated that these attempts 'usefully capture the core concept that the focus of analysis should be on the underlying factual setting and actions, as well as on the parties' presumed desire for efficient, centralized and fair proceedings'.[32]

In any event, it appears from the case law discussed in this article that damage claims based on non-contractual liability are generally accepted in arbitrations seated in the Nordics, provided that the arbitration clause, interpreted according to general contract interpretation principles, is deemed to cover the disputed facts in question. This arbitration-friendly interpretation is also consistent with the case law developed in many other important arbitration jurisdictions.[33]

If a broad or liberal approach to the scope of the arbitration agreement is taken very far, this may of course surprise the parties to the arbitration agreement and violate their reasonable expectations as regards what dispute resolution method they have chosen and what they have decided not to choose. This may, e.g., be the case when the facts indicate that the parties indeed intended to resolve their various disputes in separate fora, even if such disputes are related.[34]

However, it is likely that reasonable businesspersons expect that the model arbitration clauses referring to disputes 'arising out of or in connection with the

30. Gary B. Born, *International Commercial Arbitration*, 3rd ed. p. 1432.
31. Gary B. Born, *International Commercial Arbitration*, 3rd ed. pp. 1455-1459.
32. Gary B. Born, *International Commercial Arbitration*, 3rd ed. p. 1471.
33. Gary B. Born, *International Commercial Arbitration*, 3rd ed. pp. 1465-1471.
34. *Cf.* the reasoning in *Belgor* in relation to the dispute resolution clause referring to a court in Minsk.

contract' should be interpreted and applied to give full effect rather than adding implied limitations to the scope through the concept of the legal relationship. This expectation includes that non-contractual claims based on fraud and other criminal or tortious liabilities should be deemed covered by the arbitration clause if they have arisen in connection with the contract. Arguably, this should at least be the case for non-contractual claims that presuppose the existence of the contract, and non-contractual claims that could have been brought as a claim under the contract.

CHAPTER 8

The Impact of Unilateral Sanctions on Institutional Arbitration

Roman Zykov

Unilateral restrictive measures (URM) are economic measures that are imposed by one sovereign state or a group of sovereign states against another state and/or its national(s), to achieve a specific foreign policy or national security objective. Commonly, URM have the express purpose of changing the policy of a foreign state by making it difficult for a specially designated national of that state (SDN) to trade with the nationals of the state which imposed URM.

An avalanche of national URM programs introduced by some states against the nationals of other states as well as counter-URM laws negatively affect global trade, and consequently, international commercial arbitration. Accordingly, to pursue its case in an international arbitration, an SDN must master an ultimate obstacle course of legal restrictions and commercial limitations, which quite often become an insurmountable impediment to "having one's day in court."

Difficulties may arise at each stage when an SDN:

(a) instructs the service providers (legal counsel, expert witness, support services);
(b) initiates arbitration proceedings and pays arbitration fees;
(c) constitutes an arbitral tribunal;
(d) deals with the effect of URM on an underlying commercial contract;
(e) deals with the setting aside of an arbitral award;
(f) pursues the recognition and enforcement of the arbitral award.

Although this list is not exhaustive, the above are probably quite common for most SDNs, irrespective of which national URM program they are designated by.

§8.01 INTRODUCTION

The twentieth century brought unprecedented growth in global trade and investments. To facilitate global trade, the international community deployed an array of legal and institutional instruments, such as free trade agreements, bilateral and multilateral investment treaties, customs unions, world and regional trade organizations, international commercial and investment arbitration and others. The main objective of all these was to ensure a free flow of goods and services at a global level. To enable global trade, the states consented to delegate part of their judiciary powers to private parties, who have been at liberty to decide how to resolve their commercial disputes. One obvious advantage of international commercial arbitration is a possibility to ensure that parties, be it the state, legal or natural person, enjoy equal and unbiased legal treatment irrespectively of their size, ownership, and nationality.

The growing importance of global trade made it an important instrument of foreign policy in some states, which strived to leverage their economic powers over others. In such circumstance, unilateral restrictive measures (URM) became a tool for projecting national foreign state policy internationally, in other words, a tool of strategic communication of national interests. While the global economy was on the rise, URM were imposed mainly in response to political events abroad.

However, together with global economic decline in recent years, international trade competition has intensified. Arguably, now URM are also used as an instrument for projecting national economic interests outward.

Indeed, in the past two decades, the use of URM increased exponentially. For example, from 2014 to date, around five hundred Russian companies have been designated by the U.S. alone under various national sanctions programs. Although it was said to be done in response to certain political events, one could notice that many designated companies are visible international competitors in research and engineering, biotech, aerospace, military, manufacturing and production, construction, agriculture, banking, energy, mining and other sectors. A similar situation concerns some of the leading Chinese companies, the number of which has also grown in the past years.

Today, the body of different national URM programs has become the Great Barrier Reef of global trade, with its dangerous currents, sharp reefs, and deceptively beautiful predators. To be able to navigate in these dangerous waters, a diligent person needs to employ a sophisticated compliance apparatus. The current situation harms global trade and consequently international arbitration. This chapter discusses the impact of URM on arbitration as a global system for the resolution of commercial disputes, and possible ways for mitigating URM-related risks.

§8.02 INTERNATIONAL CRITICISM OF UNILATERAL RESTRICTIVE MEASURES

URM are economic measures that are imposed by one sovereign state or a group of sovereign states against another state and/or its national(s), to achieve a specific foreign policy or national security objective. Commonly, URM have the express purpose of changing the policy of a foreign state by making it difficult for a specially designated national of that state (SDN) to trade with the nationals of the state which imposed URM.

URM emanate from national foreign policy or national security objectives of an individual state, and therefore they are not based on international consensus. Consequently, URM lack international (universal) legitimacy because they do not pass a so-called *shared-values-test* which would make them shared and accepted universally:

> [a] common feature of sanctions is the label of "unfriendliness". Most of them will be issued in breach of rules of international law and in violation of the notion of free trade between states and individuals. The issue therefore does arise as to their justification in law.[1]

URM are issued not only in breach of rules of international law but also without meeting the basic standards of proof. A lot has been said about the decision-making process for including a person in an SDN list, which is often arbitrary and has a considerable degree of subjectivity and politization in the standards of proof. Indeed, when a state designates a foreign national under its URM program, it usually does so without providing any compelling evidence:

> what amount of evidence is required in order for a designation under a U.S. economic sanction program to occur? For example, there is no statute or regulation that states, OFAC will only designate individuals based on clear and convincing evidence. That means that OFAC may designate an individual or entity at their discretion. In theory, although unlikely, so much as a rumor or an anonymous tip could lead to a designation.[2]

Insofar as no evidence is required, the URM designations essentially employ the same standard of proof as the Salem witch trials:

> Hearsay is not, however, the only category of evidence that we now generally ban but that found a welcoming home at the Salem witch trials. The court also accepted evidence about the bad or suspicious character of the defendant. The evidence came in all forms (reputation, opinion, and allegations of specific acts) and recounted everything from unpleasant personal interactions to vicious rumors.[3]

Regretfully, it is a return to the Dark Age of the law.

Furthermore, the URM regulations are usually worded in a vague language which not only makes it difficult to establish the true meaning and effect of URM but also undermines the principle of legal certainty, which is one of the fundamental pillars of law. Uncertainty in the wording of URM regulations complicates the compliance process. In such circumstance, many avoid transactions with SDNs to eliminate said

---

1. Marc Blessing, Impact of the Extraterritorial Application of Mandatory Rules of Law on International Contracts (Helbing & Lichtenhahn 1999), p. 19.
2. Erich Ferrari, OFAC Director Offers Distinctions If Not Evidence. https://sanctionlaw.com/ofac-director-offers-distinctions-if-not-evidence/#.XXVx9RheOT9.
3. Len Niehoff, Proof at the Salem Witch Trials. https://www.americanbar.org/groups/litigation/publications/litigation_journal/2020-21/fall/proof-salem-witch-trials/.

risk, even if a proposed transaction is in fact permitted. This is a common issue with commercial banks, which may refuse money transfers just because a payor is designated under a URM program albeit not being binding on the bank. In such circumstances, banks usually do not burden themselves with an in-depth legal analysis of URM regulations and simply decline transactions.

Precisely because URM are unilateral, lack objectivity, and are often unclear, they receive criticism from international community. Several United Nations (UN) reports have emphasized that URM are impermissible under international law; they are:

> "considered to be violations of the principles of the Charter of the United Nations, the norms of international law and the rules-based multilateral trading system"[4] and that "the international community views as unlawful those unilateral coercive measures the extraterritorial effects of which affect the sovereignty of other States, the legitimate interests of entities or persons under their jurisdiction and the freedom of trade and navigation."[5]

URM are also under heavy criticism by the UN General Assembly,[6] the UN Human Rights Council[7] and other international organizations.

Finally, URM are commonly criticized by states. For example, when the U.S. imposed URM against Russian nationals, the members of the UN refuted the imposition of the unilateral economic sanctions. Among others, China stated that "China is opposed, as always, [...] to the use of unilateral sanctions, or the threat of the use of sanctions freely in international relations";[8] Argentina—"we reject initiatives that seek to isolate one of the parties or impose unilateral economic sanctions that undermine the conditions that could lead to a dialogue that has become very urgent";[9] Nicaragua—"Because we want peace and believe in the prevention and resolution of conflicts by peaceful means, we reject all unilateral methods, such as political or economic sanctions against the Russian Federation, as they violate international law and do not contribute to easing the tense atmosphere."[10]

Consequently, there is a wide consensus that URM do not amount to transnational public policy and that they are illegal under international law.

---

4. Report of the UN Secretary-General "Unilateral economic measures as a means of political and economic coercion against developing countries" No. A/70/152 dated July 16, 2015, para. 5.
5. Report of the UN Special Rapporteur on the negative impact of unilateral coercive measures on the enjoyment of human rights No. A/HRC/42/46 dated July 5, 2019, para. 46.
6. UN General Assembly Resolution No. 2625 (XXV) dated October 24, 1970, Declaration on Principles of International Law concerning Friendly Relations and Cooperation among States in accordance with the Charter of the United Nations, p. 123 "no State may use or encourage the use of economic, political or any other type of measures to coerce another State in order to obtain from it the subordination of the exercise of its sovereign rights"; UN General Assembly Resolution No. 3281 (XXIX) dated December 12, 1974, containing the Charter of Economic Rights and Duties of States, which in its Article 32 calls upon all states to refrain from any unilateral coercive measure not in accordance with international law and the Charter of the United Nations.
7. Report of the UN Special Rapporteur on the negative impact of unilateral coercive measures on the enjoyment of human rights No. A/HRC/42/46 dated July 5, 2019, para. 46; Human Rights Council Resolution No. A/HRC/RES/30/2 dated October 12, 2015, preamble, para 3.
8. UN Security Council Meeting. S/PV.7576, p. 19.
9. General Assembly 80th plenary meeting (A/68/PV.80), p. 20.
10. General Assembly 80th plenary meeting (A/68/PV.80), p. 13.

URM shall not be confused with international sanctions. As opposed to URM, international sanctions are political and economic measures based on a wider international consensus and are imposed by international organizations against states or organizations to protect international law and maintain or restore international peace and security. For example, international sanctions may be imposed by the UN Security Council under Article 41 of the UN Charter. They are defined as measures not involving the use of armed force, which may include complete or partial interruption of economic relations and of rail, sea, air, postal, telegraphic, radio, and other means of communication, and the severance of diplomatic relations.[11] Since 1966, Article 41 of the UN Charter was applied only in exceptional circumstances, and it was always a prevailing majority decision by the UN Member States. In the past six decades, the Security Council has established thirty sanctions regimes, in Southern Rhodesia, South Africa, the former Yugoslavia (2), Haiti, Iraq (2), Angola, Rwanda, Sierra Leone, Somalia and Eritrea, Eritrea and Ethiopia, Liberia (3), DRC, Côte d'Ivoire, Sudan, Lebanon, DPRK, Iran, Libya (2), Guinea-Bissau, CAR, Yemen, South Sudan and Mali, as well as against ISIL (Da'esh) and Al-Qaida and the Taliban.[12]

A distinction between international sanctions and URM bears practical importance, especially when arbitral tribunals are asked to interpret the notion of "public policy." While violation of international sanctions may result in violation of national public policy of a sovereign state, violation of URM imposed by one state does not necessarily lead to violation of national public policy of another sovereign state. That is because each state has a distinct national public policy and may use a different toolbox to achieve its sovereign objectives. As a result, URM programs of different states, even against the same SDNs, differ significantly.

For example, on July 4, 2019, the authorities of Gibraltar detained the Iranian supertanker Grace 1 on suspicion of supplying oil to Syria. The detention ended on August 15, 2019. On August 16, 2019, U.S. court issued a warrant for the seizure of the tanker on the grounds that it had links to Iran's Islamic Revolutionary Guard Corps, which the U.S. have designated as a "terrorist" organization. The U.S. sent a Supplemental Mutual Legal Assistance request to Gibraltar providing information in support of its application to prevent the departure from Gibraltar of Grace 1 and its cargo of oil, in anticipation of forfeiture proceedings to be commenced in the U.S. On August 18, 2019, the Gibraltar Central Authority informed that it was unable to seek an Order of the Supreme Court of Gibraltar to provide the restraining assistance required by the U.S. because:

> "The Central Authority's inability to seek the Orders requested is a result of the operation of European Union law and the differences in the sanctions regimes applicable to Iran in the EU and the US" and also because "The EU sanctions regime against Iran—which is applicable in Gibraltar—is much narrower than that

11. Article 41, Chapter VII of the Charter of the United Nations.
12. https://www.un.org/securitycouncil/sanctions/information.

> applicable in the US" and that "This is a reflection of the very different positions and legal regimes in the US and the EU."[13]

This is one of many examples which demonstrates that: (a) there is no universal acceptance of URM; and (b) URM of one state shall not become mechanically binding in the territories of other nations or on foreign nationals. Considering the unjustified and hostile nature of URM, some targeted states have introduced counter-URM mechanisms to protect their nationals from negative impact of URM.

§8.03 EU'S COUNTER-SANCTIONS MECHANISM

To counter the negative effects of URM, some states introduce counter-sanctions' mechanisms to protect their economic interests. One of such examples is the European Union (EU) Blocking Statute, which makes it illegal for EU companies to comply with certain extraterritorial URM imposed by the U.S.[14] The EU Blocking Statute was originally passed in 1996 in response to illegal extraterritorial United States (U.S.) sanctions on Cuba, specifically the Helms-Burton Act, which codified and expanded the U.S. embargo on Cuba, and the Iran and Libya Sanctions Act which imposed URM on these states. The recitals of the Blocking Statute are self-explanatory:

> Whereas a third country has enacted certain laws, regulations, and other legislative instruments which purport to regulate activities of natural and legal persons under the jurisdiction of the Member State;
>
> Whereas by their *extra-territorial application such laws*, regulations and other legislative instruments *violate international law* and impede the attainment of the aforementioned objectives [emphasis added].

The EU Blocking Statute has been of some use. For example, in 2007, the Austrian government charged an Austrian bank with violating the Blocking Statute when it canceled bank accounts for Cuban citizens as part of its acquisition by a U.S. hedge fund.

On June 6, 2018, the European Commission revived the EU Blocking Statute, to give it a new life by extending the Blocking Statute to the sanctions the Trump administration brought back when it exited the Joint Comprehensive Plan of Action, also known as the Iran deal. Section 1 of the Explanatory Note reads that the EU Blocking Statute:

> constitutes an important achievement of unified EU action against the *unlawful effects of extra-territorial legislation* of third countries;

13. Official Statement of Government of Gibraltar to Further Mutual Legal Assistance Requests from the United States of America. https://www.gibraltar.gov.gi/press-releases/further-mutual-legal-assistance-requests-from-the-united-states-of-america-6042019-5198.
14. European Council Regulation (EC) No. 2271/96 Protecting against effects of the extraterritorial application of legislation adopted by a third country, and actions based thereon or resulting therefrom, dated November 22, 1996.

> The Blocking Statute applies with regard to the extra-territorial legislation mentioned in its Annex ('listed extra-territorial legislation'), which currently consists of U.S. measures concerning Cuba and Iran (emphasis added).[15]

It is yet to be seen how the EU Blocking Statute will develop in the future and which URM programs it may counter in addition to those already listed.

§8.04 RUSSIAN COUNTER-SANCTIONS MECHANISM

Another example of countering URM through national protective regulations is the new Russian law (Law), which extends exclusive jurisdiction of Russian state courts over certain types of disputes and parties affected by URM. The Law was adopted on June 8, 2020, as the "The law amending the Arbitrazh Procedure Code for the purposes of protecting private and legal persons from restrictive measures enacted by a state, union of several states, or a public body of a state or a union of several states." The law was enacted as the new Articles 248.1 and 248.2 of the Arbitrazh Procedure Code (APC).

The Law appears to be a reaction to the anti-Russia URM, which have been introduced against Russian legal and private persons by several states. As of today, around 690 Russian companies and individuals have been designated by the U.S. and 120 by the EU. The number of persons has been continuously growing and URM programs have affected some of the important fields of Russian economy.

[A] Definition of Restrictive Measures

Although the Law is believed to be a reaction to the anti Russia URM, its scope is broader than it may seem. The Law employs a broad definition of "restrictive measures" (*"меры ограничительного характера"*), which may be interpreted much wider than just unilateral trade sanctions. For example, visa restrictions, administrative or criminal restrictions, economic and trade quotas, tariffs, and other unilateral restrictions may theoretically fall within the meaning of the "restrictive measures." Such restrictive measures may originate from a state, union of several states, or a public body of a state or a union of several states. Apparently, the Law does not apply to cases in which the restrictive measures were enacted by international organizations.

[B] Types of Disputes

The Law applies to disputes which may be referred by parties as a result of an international treaty or parties' agreement to arbitral tribunals and courts located outside Russia. Such cases may concern two groups of disputes.

15. European Commission Guidance Note. Questions and Answers: adoption of update Blocking Statute (2018/C 277 1/03).

The first group of disputes involves parties which have become subject to restrictive measures ("a party-based test"). The Law explains that such party ("Designated Party") may be:

(a) a Russian legal or private person, who was designated under the primary restrictive measures; or
(b) a foreign legal person, who was designated under the secondary restrictive measures arising out of the primary restrictive measures against a Russian legal or private person.

The second group of disputes involves Russian or foreign persons. Such disputes shall arise out of restrictive measures against Russian persons ("a subject matter-based test").

Potentially, the Law can make Russia a suitable forum for URM-related disputes between foreign parties. However, such disputes shall arise out of contracts impacted by anti-Russia URM. For example, a dispute between Asian and European parties arising out of a subcontract for construction of a factory in Africa owned by a Russian company could fall within the exclusive jurisdiction of Russian courts if the subject matter of the dispute arises out of URM against the Russian company.

[C] Exclusive Jurisdiction of Russian Courts

The Law provides that parties may refer their disputes to the Russian state commercial court (Arbitrazh court) where private or legal persons are domiciled. For example, if a party is located in Moscow, then the Arbitrazh (Commercial) Court of Moscow will have exclusive jurisdiction.

The Law, however, limits the scenarios when a case may fall within the exclusive jurisdiction of Russian courts. Parties may refer a dispute to the Russian court only if:

(a) there is no case with the same subject matter and between the same parties already pending before a foreign commercial arbitral tribunal or a foreign state court;
(b) the dispute resolution agreement between parties to refer their disputes to a foreign commercial arbitral tribunal or a foreign state court is unenforceable because one of the parties' access to justice is denied due to restrictive measures.

[D] Recognition and Enforcement of Arbitral Awards

If a Designated Party acted as claimant, or, if acted as respondent it did not object to a foreign arbitration or litigation while it was pending, or if the Designated Party did not seek an anti-suit injunction from the Russian court against the initiation or continuation of a foreign arbitration or litigation, such foreign arbitral award or foreign court judgment shall be generally enforceable.

[E] Anti-suit Injunctions

The Law also provides for a new procedural instrument, which was not previously available under Russian law, i.e., anti-suit injunctions. A Designated Person who has become or may become a party to a foreign arbitration or litigation may seek for a Russian court to issue a prohibition to the other party to initiate or continue a foreign arbitration or litigation procedure. The applications are considered by a sole judge, whose ruling may be appealed to a cassation instance within one month. The judge may also award compensation to a Designated Party for a breach of the anti-suit injunction in an amount not exceeding the amount of the relief sought from a foreign arbitration or litigation tribunal and legal costs.

[F] Russian Case Law

The application of the Law was recently considered by Russian courts in a declaratory action brought by JSC NPK Uralvagonzavod (Uralvagonzavod). In 2014, Uralvagonzavod was designated by the U.S. as SDN under the U.S. Executive Order 13661. OJSC Uraltransmash (Uraltransmash) is a leading machinery manufacturer in Russia, owned by Uralvagonzavod (99.23%).

Uraltransmash came into contact with PESA Bydgoszcz SA from Poland (PESA) for the supply of tram carriages for the Moscow transport network. The contract contained an arbitration clause pursuant to which "all disputes arising out of the performance of the present contract shall be resolved in the Arbitration Institute of the Stockholm Chamber of Commerce" (SCC).

In 2018, Uralvagonzavod filed a derivative claim on behalf of its subsidiary Uraltransmash, requesting the court to declare the arbitration agreement between Uraltransmash and PESA invalid and unenforceable.

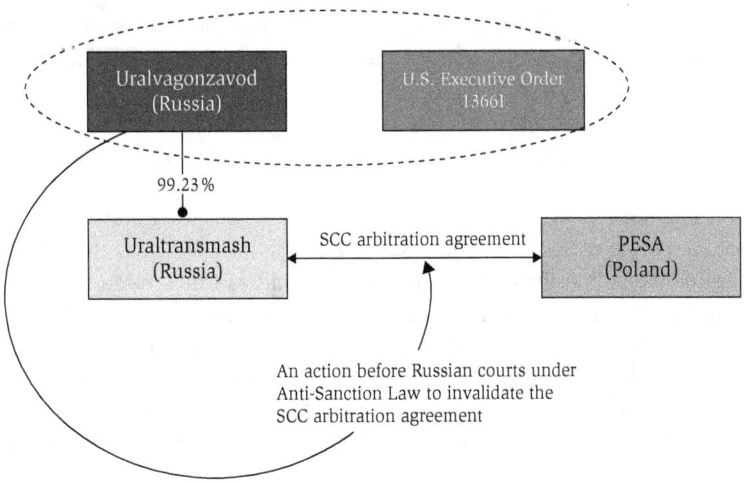

PESA initiated arbitration proceedings under the Arbitration Rules of the SCC pursuant to the arbitration agreement between the parties. Allegedly, due to the U.S. sanctions against its majority shareholder (Uralvagonzavod), Uraltransmash was unable to lodge its share of the arbitration fees to the SCC. It was argued that EU Council Decision No. 2014/512/CFSP dated 31 July 2014 and EU Regulation No. 833/2014 dated 31 July 2014 prohibited EU banks from accepting payments from certain Russian banks.

Furthermore, it was argued that it was impossible to instruct a legal counsel because most of the law firms refused to take instructions due to the SDN status of Uralvagonzavod.

Both the Court of First Instance and the Court of Appeal rejected Uralvagonzavod's claim. However, the Court of Cassation issued a ruling in favor of Uralvagonzavod and held that the lower courts failed to fully analyze the arguments of enforceability of the arbitration agreement. As a result, the Court of Cassation quashed the judgments of the lower courts and transferred the case back to the Court of First Instance for a new trial.

Most importantly, the Court of Cassation held that the Court of First Instance shall take into consideration Articles 248.1 and 248.2 of APC, according to which Russian state courts have exclusive jurisdiction to resolve disputes which involve Designated Parties. The court also noted that Russian courts may also issue anti-suit injunctions prohibiting to initiate or continue arbitration proceedings. In the process of reconsideration of the case by the Court of First Instance, Uralvagonzavod insisted that the arbitration clause is unenforceable because Uralvagonzavod was prevented from paying its share of the arbitration fees to the SCC and was unable to instruct a local legal counsel. The claimant also pleaded that a prospective arbitral award may be unjust due to the possible partiality of the arbitrators based on the designation of Uralvagonzavod.

PESA disagreed and indicated that the provisions of Articles 248.1 and 248.2 of the APC did not prevent the parties from arbitrating under the SCC Arbitration Rules.

PESA also pleaded that the arbitration clause is enforceable since Uralvagonzavod is successfully exercising its rights in the pending process before the SCC. Furthermore, the imposition of sanctions on Uralvagonzavod does not prejudice its rights to a fair trial in the SCC.

The Court of First Instance stated that for the application of Article 248.1 of the APC RF, a party must prove the circumstances preventing consideration of the dispute in arbitration.

In relation to Uralvagonzavod's references to EU Council Decision No. 2014/512/CFSP and EU Regulation 31 July 2014 No. 833/2014, the Court of First Instance indicated that the contract between the parties concerns supply of trams and does not belong to the categories of transactions prohibited by these documents.

The court also rejected Uralvagonzavod's argument on the impossibility of obtaining qualified legal assistance because Uralvagonzavod had a Russian legal representative and Polish legal experts. As for the obstacles in arranging payments to the Polish legal representatives, Uraltransmash unsuccessfully tried to make a transfer through Raiffeisen Bank in Vienna. Uraltransmash could use other banks to make the transfer, but it did not try.

Regarding Uralvagonzavod's arguments on the impossibility of paying the SCC arbitration fee due to the sanctions, the court concluded that Uralvagonzavod made numerous payments to a PESA's bank account in a Polish bank within the past five years while being under the sanctions.

The court found that the U.S. and EU sanctions laws did not prohibit the SCC from accepting payments from Uraltransmash. According to the clarifications received from the Secretary-General of the SCC in August 2020, the SCC was of the opinion that the laws did not contain any instructions which oblige Uraltransmash to apply to Swedish state authorities for obtaining permission to make payments in connection with the arbitration proceedings. The SCC also indicated that in the current circumstances there were no obstacles for Uralvagonzavod to take part in the arbitration.

The court also rejected Uralvagonzavod's argument that the U.S. restrictive measures were effective throughout the EU due to their "extraterritoriality" because Uralvagonzavod did not provide any evidence that the laws and orders of the U.S. President were binding on Sweden or the EU.

Uralvagonzavod's allegations of possible impartiality of the arbitrators have not been accepted by the court either.

Consequently, the Court of First Instance ruled in favor of PESA and specifically said that Uralvagonzavod did not present evidence confirming the existence of circumstances impeding the consideration of the dispute of the SCC.

Although the Court of First Instance refused to accept jurisdiction under the Law, the court has formulated the test for admitting cases for trial—there should be compelling evidence that a Designated Party was unable to pursue its case in arbitration.

§8.05 CHINESE COUNTER-SANCTIONS MECHANISM

On January 9, 2021, the Ministry of Commerce of the People's Republic of China (MOFCOM) published the "Rules on Blocking Unjustified Extraterritorial Application of Foreign Legislation and Other Measures" (Rules).[16]

Article 2 of the Rules provides that they apply to situations where the extraterritorial application of foreign legislation and other measures, in violation of internal law and the basic principles of international relations, unjustifiably prohibits or restricts a citizen, legal person or other organization of China (PRC person) from engaging in normal economic, trade and related activities with another state, or person of that state. In such situations, the PRC person must report it to MOFCOM within thirty days of the situation arising (Article 5).

16. Order of the Ministry of Commerce of the People's Republic of China No. 1, on Rules on Counteracting Unjustified Extraterritorial Application of Foreign Legislation and Other Measures. January 9, 2021.

Under Article 6 of the Rules, MOFCOM should establish a task force to assess the extraterritorial application of URM, and in doing so will take into account:

- whether international law or the basic principles of international relations are violated;
- potential impact on China's national sovereignty, security and development interests;
- potential impact on the legitimate rights and interests of the PRC persons; and
- other relevant factors.

If upon assessment MOFCOM finds unjustified extraterritorial application of foreign legislation and other measures, it will issue a prohibition order against recognition, enforcement and compliance with relevant foreign URM.

Pursuant to Article 9 of the Rules, if a person complies with foreign legislation and other measures within the scope of a prohibition order, and thus infringes upon the legitimate rights and interests of a relevant PRC person, the latter may institute legal proceedings in a people's court, and claim compensation.

Furthermore, if a judgment or ruling made in accordance with a foreign URM within the scope of the prohibition order causes losses to a PRC person, the latter may institute legal proceedings in a people's court, and claim for compensation by a person who benefits from said judgment or ruling.

Where a person (counterparty) refuses to execute an effective judgment or ruling made by the people's court, the PRC person may apply to people's court for enforcement in accordance with law.

§8.06 THE IMPACT OF URM ON INTERNATIONAL ARBITRATION

An avalanche of national URM programs introduced by some states against the nationals of other states as well as counter-URM laws negatively affect global trade, and consequently, international commercial arbitration. Accordingly, to pursue its case in an international arbitration, an SDN must master an ultimate obstacle course of legal restrictions and commercial limitations, which quite often become an insurmountable impediment to "having one's day in court."

Difficulties may arise at each stage when an SDN:

(a) instructs the service providers (legal counsel, expert witness, support services);
(b) initiates arbitration proceedings and pays arbitration fees;
(c) constitutes an arbitral tribunal;
(d) deals with the effect of URM on an underlying commercial contract;
(e) deals with the setting aside of an arbitral award;
(f) pursues the recognition and enforcement of the arbitral award;

Although this list is not exhaustive, the above are probably quite common for the most SDNs, irrespective of which national URM program they are designated by.

[A] Instructing a Legal Representative

The journey kicks off with instructing a legal representative. For example, if an SDN is targeted by the EU, instructing a counsel in the EU may become difficult, if not impossible. Even if an SDN is not targeted by the EU but has been included in the U.S. URM, those law firms which have presence in the U.S., have U.S. nationals as employees or even have U.S. clients, would likely refuse from acting for the SDN.

As a first step, an SDN may approach several law firms. At this stage, the SDN informs the prospective legal counsel of its SDN status and may disclose some information about the case and identity of the counterparty. While some law firms may immediately refuse to be involved, others will carry out an internal compliance check and may eventually require obtaining a state license to represent the client. Understandably, an application for a URM license would require disclosure of information about the parties, contract and dispute, which on its own may harm both parties. The process may take from several weeks to several months and, as a result, the list of potential legal counsel reduces from a dozen to just a few. As the options are limited, often the choice of a legal representative is truncated, vis-à-vis the choice available to the counterparty. Eventually, it cannot be excluded that the SDN will eventually fail to instruct a qualified legal counsel.

In addition, SDNs may be subject to stricter payment terms under various URM programs. For example, some of the URM limit repayment terms under loans (credits) to fourteen days. To avoid allegations of violation of URM, law firms may want to ensure that their services are not credited for longer than fourteen days and therefore frequently invoice SDNs. Consequently, it increases administrative work on the part of law firms and clients.

[B] Instructing an Expert Witness

Expert witnesses (or experts) are commonly used in international arbitration to address legal, accounting, technical and other issues. According to the 2012 International Arbitration Survey: Current and Preferred Practices in the Arbitral Process, "On average, expert witnesses are involved in two-thirds of arbitrations."[17] Furthermore, "in the vast majority of arbitrations, expert witnesses are appointed by the parties (90%) rather than by the tribunal (10%)." Thus, it is a predominant practice that expert witnesses are appointed by parties, not by the tribunal.

Naturally, an SDN which intends to instruct an expert mainly faces similar problems to those when instructing a legal counsel. Again, URM may limit the pool of available candidates, increase time and costs.

One of the common issues which may be put before legal experts is the effect of URM on commercial contracts. For example, if U.S. URM is at the heart of a dispute,

17. 2012 International Arbitration Survey: Current and Preferred Practices in the Arbitral Process, p. 29. http://www.arbitration.qmul.ac.uk/media/arbitration/docs/2012_International_Arbitration_Survey.pdf.

that will require a U.S. qualified and experienced lawyer to act as expert. Under Title 31 of the Code of Federal Regulations §589.506(a)(1), U.S. nationals are permitted to advise on compliance with and the requirements of U.S. law.[18] However, §589.506(a) does not extend to expert testimony in foreign courts or arbitral tribunals on behalf of an SDN without obtaining a license from the Office of Foreign Assets Control (OFAC). In practice, OFAC mostly denies applications for such licenses. In these circumstances, SDNs often try to instruct a non-U.S. person (not a national or a resident of the U.S.), however, who holds a U.S. law degree, has URM-related experience, and has no conflict of interest. It is evident that a search for a legal expert with such qualifications may prove to be difficult. Sometimes, the only practical solution is to dispose of party-appointed experts and ask the arbitral tribunal to appoint its own expert.

Therefore, if an SDN envisages difficulties, it may be worth exploring the idea of tribunal-appointed experts with an arbitral tribunal and the opposite party at the outset of the proceedings.

[C] Procurement of Auxiliary Services

In addition to legal and expert services, parties may also require case support services, e.g., interpreters, court reporters, providers of hearing equipment, hearing facilities, hearing bundles and others. Although these contractors may not look like the most critical element of the arbitration process, usually they are procured as a matter of urgency, and very often not so long before the evidentiary hearing. In such circumstance, one needs to factor in additional time which will be required for supporting contractors to perform compliance checks.

To avoid delays in the proceedings, upon request of parties, an arbitral tribunal may engage directly with service providers to exclude any URM-related issues from the picture. This is something parties and an arbitral tribunal may want to discuss when agreeing on the procedural rules set out in Procedural Order No. 1.

[D] Commencing an Arbitration under the Institutional Arbitration Rules

As a general rule, to initiate the arbitral proceedings under the rules of an arbitral institute (AI), a claimant must file a request for arbitration and pay a registration fee. If an AI is located in a state which has imposed URM against the claimant, it is bound to comply with them. If an AI is not located in or connected with a state which imposed URM, it may want to perform a compliance check to ensure that it does not manifestly violate any URM, which may expose it to penalties or secondary sanctions of a third state. For example, U.S. Executive Orders which impose URM are binding upon "U.S. persons" (U.S. nationals and residents). Because some of the leading European AIs have U.S. persons in their governing bodies and case management teams, it may expose them to the effect of U.S. URM. To avoid such exposure, AIs may employ a "ring

18. https://www.ecfr.gov/cgi-bin/text-idx?node=pt31.3.589&rgn=div5#se31.3.589_1506.

fencing" mechanism by excluding U.S. persons from the decision-making and management of SDN-related cases. For the same reason, an AI may use the currency of a nonsanctioning state to avoid exposure to the financial system of a sanctioning state, such as payments in euro used by the International Chamber of Commerce (ICC).

In 2015, the ICC, London Court of International Arbitration (LCIA) and SCC issued a joint statement on the potential impact of EU sanctions against Russia on international arbitration administered by EU-based institutions. All three arbitration institutes concluded that "A person or entity designated by the EU Regulations is not per se prevented from filing a request for arbitration with the ICC, LCIA or SCC," with the caveat that a designated person or entity is advised to inform the institution of a dispute prior to the request for arbitration, to enable the institutions to discuss with the parties any additional administrative requirement that needs to be fulfilled by either the parties or the institution, for example, filing an application with the relevant national authorities for an exemption under the sanction regulation.[19]

The joint statement by the leading AIs surely gave some comfort to the Russian companies. Indeed, the 2016 Russian Arbitration Association's Survey on the Impact of Sanctions on Commercial Arbitration (2016 RAA Sanctions Survey) revealed that although some users have already had problems with some AIs, the majority continued to place trust in institutional arbitration at large.[20] However, there were some skeptics, who questioned AIs' ability to ensure sustainable administration of SDN-related disputes.

Over the years, the number of skeptics grew, mainly because of their personal experience with AIs. The difficulties primarily related to the lengthy process of obtaining licenses to administer cases by AIs and problems with payment of the arbitration costs to AIs.

Another important consideration is confidentiality. When seeking state permission to administer SDN-related cases, AIs disclose information about the parties, underlying contracts and relevant information about transactions to the state authorities which are responsible for enforcement of URM. Having in mind a high degree of subjectivity and politization of the standards of proof on the part of URM enforcing state bodies, the risk of penalties and secondary sanctions increases dramatically. Therefore, some parties may consider it risky to use institutional arbitration and consider alternative means of dispute resolution, such as ad hoc arbitration.

With that in mind, some of the leading Russian companies (also non-SDNs) have been reconsidering their traditional preferences in arbitration, which have been shaping over decades. Presumably, the change in arbitration preferences will be visible in AIs' annual statistics in the foreseeable future.

By far, the main impediment for institutional arbitration is receiving payments of arbitration costs from SDNs. Even if a money wire is executed in a nonsanctioned currency, banks' compliance departments usually do not allow money transfers

19. https://sccinstitute.com/media/80988/legal-insight-icc_lcia_scc-on-sanctions_17-june-2015.pdf.
20. https://arbitration.ru/upload/medialibrary/e1e/2016-raa-survey-on-sanctions-and-arbitration.pdf.

originating from or relating to SDNs. For example, a local German bank will likely refuse a payment in EUR from a Russian SDN designated under U.S. URM (even if not designated under EU URM). The reason is simple; a bank does not want to take the risk of penalties or the risk of secondary sanctions from the U.S. authorities (OFAC). Ultimately, not having received a claimant's payment of the registration fee or arbitration costs, an AI will discontinue the arbitration pursuant to its arbitration rules.

There have been numerous examples when AIs were unable to arrange for a bank which would accept payments from SDNs. It goes without saying that an AI may face similar problems when returning to parties unused funds from the arbitration costs after the case was completed.

To conclude, payment of arbitration costs is an Achilles heel of institutional arbitration. Commonly, AIs are fixed to their local banks and refuse exploring other payment options. Considering the rapid expansion of URM programs across the globe, URM present a potential risk to many notable market players—there is no guarantee that a person will not be designated as SDN in the future.

Usually, this issue is considered at the stage of drafting a contract. There is an array of contractual tools for minimizing negative effects of potential URM, including alternative dispute resolution clauses (waterfall clauses), currency and payment terms, which enable a party to arbitrate its future contractual claims irrespectively of its SDN status.

However, there is a growing number of SDN-related cases which hover as a result of AIs' payment problems. That raises several important questions.

First, if an AI refuses to administer a case brought by an SDN, what is the effect on the arbitration agreement? Would the arbitration agreement become inoperable, unenforceable, invalid or else? Consequently, can an SDN disregard the arbitration clause and pursue its claims in the court of law, and if yes, in which court? For example, Russian and Chinese counter-sanction laws permit SDNs to disregard arbitration agreements and apply to local courts as if there were no arbitration agreements in place.

Second, if a respondent-SDN intends to bring a counterclaim or a set-off claim, but an AI fails to accept the payment of arbitration fees, what is the effect on the counterclaim or set-off claim and the arbitration agreement? To some extent, this may be resolved by shifting payment obligations onto the other party in arbitration, which is however not always an optimal solution.

Third, if an arbitration agreement is deemed to be unenforceable in connection with the agreed AI's procedures, does it make the parties' intention to arbitrate (as opposed to litigate) unenforceable too? In other words, should the parties still apply their best efforts to arbitrate their dispute, for example, in an ad hoc setup?

Fourth, if an AI fails to administer an SDN-related case, does it amount to a breach of contract by the AI? Indeed, when the parties to an arbitration agreement consent to refer their disputes to a particular AI, they accept the AI's unilateral contract expressed in its arbitration rules. Pursuant to its own arbitration rules, the AI guarantees that it will administer the case.

Fifth, if an AI fails to administer an SDN-related case, does it lead to the AI being liable? Most arbitration rules contain limitation of liability provisions; however, such provisions usually concern "any act or omission in connection with the arbitration."[21] Under many arbitration rules, arbitration commences after an AI receives a request for arbitration and the full amount of registration fee. Formally speaking, at any time before commencement of arbitration (including before payment of registration fee), there is no arbitration. Therefore, it is not obvious whether the limitation of liability provisions in the arbitration rules encompasses pre-arbitration liabilities of the AIs.

Each of these questions requires parties' consideration at the time of drafting an arbitration agreement. As noted above, to some extent, the problem is resolved through "waterfall" clauses, pursuant to which parties may agree on several possible options of AIs, and if one option does not work, they move to another. Such multitier arbitration clauses require careful drafting to avoid parallel proceedings. Another solution is to opt for ad hoc arbitration, which is more flexible than institutional arbitration. Also, for these reasons, in recent years, ad hoc has gained popularity.

As to AIs, there is a possibility to seek license or advisory opinion from state bodies that would enable them to administer URM-related cases.

[E] Constitution of the Arbitral Tribunal

The constitution of the arbitral tribunal may also present difficulties in SDN-related cases. Some arbitrators may hesitate to receive nominations from SDNs, especially if an arbitrator's country imposed URM on an SDN. For the same reason, an agreed chairperson may also refuse to act. That may limit the pool of suitable candidates and slow down the process. The situation may aggravate if the applicable substantive law is the law of the sanctioning state, but suitable candidates from that state would not agree to accept a nomination from the SDN. In that situation, it is hard to ensure that the parties will be on an equal footing in the arbitration.

The 2016 RAA Sanctions Survey revealed that arbitrators were generally ready to accept nominations from the SDNs. The results included answers from ninety-nine arbitrators, sixty-two of whom originated from the states which levied URM against Russian companies, and thirty-seven originated from other nations.

The survey revealed that if the seat of arbitration was in the sanctioning state, seventy-seven arbitrators would accept a nomination as arbitrator from an SDN. Only eight arbitrators would refuse and fifteen did not answer. To sum up, 77% of all interviewed arbitrators would accept a nomination from an SDN if the seat of arbitration was in the sanctioning state.

However, if the seat of arbitration *was outside* the sanctioning state, seventy-two arbitrators would accept a nomination as arbitrator from an SDN. Only seven arbitrators would refuse and twenty-one did not reply. To sum up, 72% of all interviewed

21. See, Article 41 of the ICC Rules of Arbitration (2021); Article 31 of the LCIA Arbitration Rules (2020); Article 52 of the SCC Arbitration Rules (2017).

arbitrators would take a nomination from an SDN if the seat of arbitration *was not* in the sanctioning state.

Although the results of the 2016 RAA Sanctions Survey give some hope, the constitution of the arbitral tribunal may present difficulties in practice. As a practical consideration, parties may avoid choosing the law of a state which has imposed URM as the substantive law of a contract. Similarly, parties may want to avoid selecting a seat of arbitration in a sanctioning state or a state which may potentially impose URM in the future.

[F] The Effect of URM on Commercial Contracts

An arbitral tribunal which considers an SDN-related case may expect to be asked to rule on the issues of public policy, force majeure, hardship, changed circumstances, validity, and enforceability of a commercial contract affected by URM.

Although some of these issues may be agreed in the contract, many other issues depend on the applicable substantive law and its imperative norms. Therefore, the contents of the imperative norms shall be borne in mind when drafting a contract and arbitration clause. One of such norms to bear in mind is Article 11 of the Council Regulation (EU) No. 833/2014 of July 31, 2014, concerning restrictive measures in view of Russia's actions destabilizing the situation in Ukraine, which reads as follows:

> 1. No claims in connection with any contract or transaction the performance of which has been affected, directly or indirectly, in whole or in part, by the measures imposed under this Regulation, including claims for indemnity or any other claim of this type, such as a claim for compensation or a claim under a guarantee, notably a claim for extension or payment of a bond, guarantee or indemnity, particularly a financial guarantee or financial indemnity, of whatever form, shall be satisfied, if they are made by:
>
> (a) entities referred to in points (b) or (c) of Article 5, or listed in Annex III;
> (b) any other Russian person, entity or body;
> (c) any person, entity or body acting through or on behalf of one of the persons, entities or bodies referred to in points (a) or (b) of this paragraph.

Despite the passive voice employed by Article 11 ("no claims shall be satisfied"), one may interpret the language as prohibiting all EU-based AIs and arbitrators to satisfy any claims brought by or on behalf of an SDN and even broader—by "any other Russian person, entity or body." Eventually, Article 11 of the EU Regulation harms both—SDN users and European providers of arbitration services.

Given the difficulties that a national applicable law may entail (e.g., preventing an SDN from instructing legal representatives, experts and service providers, nomination of arbitrators), parties may consider choosing the applicable law of a state which has not imposed and will unlikely impose URM in the future. Alternatively, parties may fully exclude the application of national laws and rediscover *lex mercatoria* as an autonomous legal system. It could be the UNIDROIT Principles of International Commercial Contracts, or sets of other delocalized legal norms (FIDIC, INCOTERMS, etc.).

[G] Setting Aside and Recognition and Enforcement of Arbitral Awards

Validity and enforceability of an arbitral award are the final stop before collecting the debt. A state judge has to decide, ex officio, whether the arbitral award complies with the "public policy" of a particular state, and more precisely with its URM-related restrictions. A lot has been said about public policy, but the following quotes describe it in the most concise yet comprehensive manner:

> Public policy does not admit of definition and is not easily explained. It is a variable quantity; it must vary and does vary with the habits, capacities, and opportunities of the public.[22]
>
> It is impossible to say what the opinion of a man or a Judge might be as to what public policy is.[23]
>
> Public policy is a very unruly horse, and when once you get astride it you never know where it will carry you.[24]

Indeed, it is impossible to say what the opinion of a judge might be as to what public policy is, especially when dealing with URM. After all, it may be less important because in the current circumstances, only a few SDNs may successfully reach the stage of recognition and enforcement of arbitral awards.

§8.07 A WAY FORWARD

An average SDN, be it a Russian, Chinese, or other, is often a company which trades internationally. It is well established that arbitration has become a preferred method for the resolution of international business disputes. Although there is no doubt that it will remain the same, the question is whether institutional arbitration will be able to adapt to the changing circumstances, such as rapid expansion of national URM programs. If not, there is a prospect that a fast-growing global club of SDNs will lean more toward ad hoc arbitration.

A possible way forward would be to exclude arbitration from the scope of URM. It is in the best interest of AIs to lead the discussion and promote a URM free arbitration to: (a) guarantee access to justice as a basic principle of the rule of law; and (b) meet AIs' own contractual obligations under the arbitration rules.

22. Kekewich, J., *Davies v. Davies* (1887), L. R. 36 C. D. 364; see also *Egerton v. Earl Brownlow*, 4 H. L. C. 1.
23. Jessel, M.R., *Besant v. Wood* (1879), L. R. 12 C. D. 620.
24. Burrough, J., *Richardson v. Mellish* (1824), 2 Bing. 252; quoted by Lord Bramwell in Mogul Steamship Co.; McGregor, Gow and others, 66 L. T. Rep. 6.

It is time to recall that international arbitration is a delocalized system with a large degree of contractual procedural freedom. AIs' and tribunals' mandates are not based on national laws or on ever-changing political preferences, but they are based on parties' consent to arbitrate. Users of arbitration have made their conscious choice. It is a turning point for AIs to prove that the choice is correct.

CHAPTER 9

What Is the Governing Law of the Arbitration Agreement? A Comparison Between the English and Swedish Approaches

James Hope & Lisa Johansson

Parties rarely make a specific choice of the governing law of the arbitration agreement. Which law is applicable can, however, have a considerable influence over the outcome of the arbitration. This issue was considered in detail by the UK Supreme Court in *Enka v. Chubb* [2020] UKSC 38, and it was also the subject of a fairly recent case in the Svea Court of Appeal (Judgment of the Svea Court of Appeal, 19 December 2019, Case T 7929-17).

This chapter compares and contrasts the English and Swedish approaches, which differ markedly from each other. The authors find fault with both approaches and suggest ways in which both could be improved. Meanwhile, it is suggested that parties would avoid potential issues by making clear that their choice of governing law in the main contract also relates to the arbitration agreement itself.

§9.01 INTRODUCTION

What is the governing law of the arbitration agreement? This seems at first glance to be a rather straightforward question. It may also initially seem to be a question of somewhat limited interest.

But first impressions can be misleading.

In fact, it is both a complex and important question. The question is complex since there are several different ways of approaching it. The question is important since the governing law of the arbitration agreement can have a considerable influence over the outcome of the arbitration.

This issue has been dealt with in particular depth over recent years by the English courts, most recently by the UK Supreme Court[1] in *Enka v. Chubb* [2020] UKSC 38.[2] This article will compare the English approach with the approach that applies in Sweden. Why England? – because the English approach has been widely publicised. Why Sweden? – because this comparison is a fitting subject for the Stockholm Arbitration Yearbook, and also because the English and Swedish approaches are markedly different from each other.

The reader is invited to consider which approach is preferable.

§9.02 SETTING THE SCENE – SOME BACKGROUND OBSERVATIONS

[A] Three Choices of Law in Arbitration

A standard lecture on choice of law in arbitration starts with the basic observation that there are three choices of law that need to be considered in the arbitration context:[3]

(a) the choice of law of the main agreement between the parties, being the law that governs the contractual rights and obligations of the parties, i.e., the *lex contractus*;
(b) the choice of law of the arbitration agreement; and
(c) the procedural law that governs the arbitration (sometimes also referred to as the 'curial law'), which in almost all cases is the arbitration law of the seat of arbitration, i.e., the *lex arbitri*.[4]

1. As many readers will know, but some may not, the UK Supreme Court is the highest court for all three jurisdictions of the United Kingdom (England & Wales, Scotland, and Northern Ireland).
2. Some minor changes were made to the UK Supreme Court's judgment on 15 March and 12 July 2021, as noted on the Court's website (https://www.supremecourt.uk/cases/uksc-2020-0091.html).
3. It is notable that Lords Hamblen and Lord Leggatt, who gave the judgment of the majority in *Enka v. Chubb*, also started their judgment with this observation.
4. Section 2(1) of the English Arbitration Act 1996 (referred to hereinafter as the 'English Arbitration Act') and section 46 of the Swedish Arbitration Act (SFS 1999:116) (referred to hereinafter as the 'Swedish Arbitration Act') provide that the provisions of those Acts apply where the seat of arbitration is in England and Sweden, respectively, although there are some additional details that ought to be mentioned for completeness:

   - In the case of the English Arbitration Act 1996, it is Part I of that Act that applies, and Part I applies where the seat of arbitration is in England and Wales or Northern Ireland.
   - In the case of the Swedish Arbitration Act, the previous wording provided that the Swedish Arbitration Act applied to arbitrations taking place in Sweden; this was interpreted by the Swedish Supreme Court as referring to the seat of arbitration (*see* NJA 2010 p. 508), but the wording was clarified in connection with the revisions to the Swedish Arbitration Act that were made in 2018 (*see* SFS 2018:1954 and Prop. 2017/18:257).

[B] The Doctrine of Separability: Why the Main Agreement and the Arbitration Agreement Are Two Separate Agreements

In most cases, of course, the main agreement and the arbitration agreement form part of the same written contract.[5] In those circumstances, the arbitration agreement is generally found in the dispute resolution clause of the contract. However, as a legal fiction, the arbitration agreement is deemed to be a separate agreement; pursuant to the doctrine of the separability of the arbitration agreement, this fiction allows the arbitration agreement to remain in place even though the main agreement may be found to be invalid.[6]

It follows that the main agreement and the arbitration agreement should be considered separately.[7] It also follows that the governing law of the main agreement may be different from the governing law of the arbitration agreement.

[C] Two Layers of Procedure: The Distinction Between the Arbitration Agreement and the *Lex Arbitri*

Before turning in more detail to the issues surrounding the governing law of the arbitration agreement, it is also relevant to consider the distinction between the arbitration agreement and the *lex arbitri*.

It is helpful to consider the arbitration agreement and the *lex arbitri* as two layers of arbitration procedure; the arbitration agreement provides the first layer of procedure that is chosen by the parties, while the *lex arbitri* provides the second layer of procedure, including both non-mandatory rules that apply in the absence of any such choice and mandatory rules that apply in any event.[8]

5. Sometimes, the parties enter into a separate arbitration agreement, but this is comparatively rare. It happens in particular when the parties agree to arbitrate after the dispute arises, or where there are several different agreements that are subject to a common arbitration agreement.
6. Both the English Arbitration Act and the Swedish Arbitration Act include express provisions confirming the separability of the arbitration agreement:
   - English Arbitration Act, section 6: 'Unless otherwise agreed by the parties, an arbitration agreement which forms or was intended to form part of another agreement (whether or not in writing) shall not be regarded as invalid, non-existent or ineffective because that other agreement is invalid, or did not come into existence or has become ineffective, and it shall for that purpose be treated as a distinct agreement.'
   - Swedish Arbitration Act, section 3: 'When the validity of an arbitration agreement which constitutes part of another agreement must be determined in conjunction with a determination of the jurisdiction of the arbitrators, the arbitration agreement shall be deemed to constitute a separate agreement' (in-house translation).
7. Whether they should be considered separately for all purposes is an issue that will be considered in more detail below.
8. The distinction between mandatory and non-mandatory provisions is particularly evident in the English Arbitration Act – *see* section 4 of that Act and the list of mandatory provisions in Schedule 1 of that Act.

[1] The Arbitration Agreement

The arbitration agreement is the parties' agreement to resolve their disputes by way of arbitration.

Some arbitration agreements are very brief.[9] However, in most cases, the parties go further by regulating in some detail the scope of the arbitration agreement and the procedure. Thus, the arbitration agreement will typically deal with the following issues:

- the scope of the arbitration agreement, i.e., which issues are deemed to fall within the scope of the arbitration agreement;
- whether the arbitration will be administered by an arbitration institution;
- any agreed rules of arbitration;
- the number of arbitrators;
- the language to be used in the arbitration; and
- the seat of arbitration.

In some cases, the arbitration agreement will also include express (or implied) obligations of confidentiality as between the parties.

[2] The Procedural Law of the Arbitration (The Lex Arbitri)

As noted above, the procedural law of the arbitration is in most cases the arbitration law of the seat of arbitration.[10] It follows, by choosing the seat of arbitration, the parties choose the procedural law of the arbitration. In most seats of arbitration, this arbitration law is to be found in a specific Arbitration Act, together with related case law and legal doctrine.

The procedural law of the arbitration fills in the gaps that may have been left open by the parties in their arbitration agreement. Thus, *inter alia*:

- the procedural law of the arbitration provides for the courts of the seat of arbitration to carry out some of the roles that would otherwise be taken by an arbitral institution,
- the procedural law of the arbitration includes default rules that apply in the absence of a choice by the parties of agreed rules of arbitration,

9. For example, in *Tritonia Shipping Inc v. South Nelson Forest Products Corp* [1966] 1 Lloyd's Rep 114, a clause providing merely for 'arbitration to be settled in London' was enforced.
10. The seat of arbitration is the legal or juridical place of arbitration (section 3 of the English Arbitration Act; section 47 of the Swedish Arbitration Act), but the parties can agree that the hearings can take place at a different location, including in a different country.

    It is also possible for the parties to choose one country as the seat of arbitration but to make the arbitration subject to the procedural rules of another country. In such circumstances, the procedural rules of the seat of arbitration will apply insofar as they are mandatory, but otherwise the parties' choice of procedural law will prevail. To have the arbitration governed by two different procedural laws is, however, unsatisfactory and should be avoided.

- the procedural law of the arbitration includes default rules concerning the number of arbitrators,
- the procedural law of the arbitration sometimes also includes default rules concerning the language to be used in the arbitration, and
- in the absence of a choice by the parties of the seat of arbitration, parties can ask a court to determine the seat of arbitration.[11]

As mentioned above, the seat of arbitration also provides mandatory rules of procedure that apply notwithstanding the parties' agreement. Such rules deal mainly with the role of the courts at the seat of arbitration, including rules concerning the challenge and set-aside of arbitral awards. Depending on the seat of arbitration, there can also be other matters that the legislature has considered to be mandatory.[12]

It is also important to note that the seat of arbitration determines the nationality of the arbitral award for the purposes of the New York Convention on the Recognition and Enforcement of Foreign Arbitral Awards 1958. Article I of that Convention provides for 'the recognition and enforcement of arbitral awards made in the territory of a State other than the State where the recognition and enforcement of such awards are sought'. It follows that, for example, where the seat of arbitration is in Sweden, the arbitral award will be deemed to be a Swedish award for the purposes of the New York Convention, and where the seat of arbitration is in England, the arbitral award will be deemed to be an English award for those purposes.[13]

11. Parties are particularly advised to choose a seat of arbitration since in the absence of such a choice it is unclear which court should determine this issue.
12. Such details vary from seat to seat. For example:
    - Section 40 of the Swedish Arbitration Act provides that the tribunal is not permitted to withhold the award pending the payment of its fees. By contrast, section 56 of the English Arbitration Act gives express power to the tribunal to refuse to deliver an award to the parties except upon full payment of the fees and expenses of the arbitrators, subject to certain provisions that enable parties to apply to the court.
    - Section 60 of the English Arbitration Act provides that an agreement which has the effect that a party is to pay the whole or part of the costs of the arbitration in any event is only valid if made after the dispute in question has arisen. There is no such provision in the Swedish Arbitration Act.
13. Such nationality is deemed to conform to the seat of arbitration, even where the arbitral award is actually signed in a different jurisdiction. There was previously some doubt about this issue, but at least in both England and Sweden this point is now settled:
    - Section 53 of the English Arbitration Act provides that, unless otherwise agreed, where the seat of arbitration is in England & Wales or Northern Ireland, any award shall be treated as made there, regardless of where it was signed, despatched or delivered to any of the parties. This section was expressly enacted in order to reverse the decision in *Hiscox v. Outhwaite* [1992] 1 AC 562 – *see* the DAC Report, para. 253.
    - Section 52, para. 2 of the Swedish Arbitration Act provides that for the purposes of that Act an award shall be deemed to have been made in the country where the seat of arbitration is situated. *See also* the judgment by the Swedish Supreme Court in NJA 2010 p. 508, at para. 4 of the Supreme Court's judgment, criticising an earlier decision of the Svea Court of Appeal in RH 2005:1 ('Titan').

§9.03 GOVERNING LAW ISSUES GENERALLY

[A] A Typical Example

It is most common, and generally most appropriate, for the parties to choose the same law to govern both substantive and procedural issues in the arbitration.

For example, the parties might choose Swedish law as the governing law of the main agreement and Stockholm as the seat of arbitration. In this example, Swedish law is the *lex contractus* which governs the substantive rights and obligations of the parties, and Swedish law is also the *lex arbitri*, being the arbitration law of the seat of arbitration.[14] It is generally appropriate to choose the same substantive and procedural law since that means that the lawyers and the arbitrators only need to concern themselves with one system of law (this situation will be referred to as 'Example A' below).

The situation becomes more complicated if the parties choose different laws. To change the example, the parties might choose English law as the *lex contractus* and Stockholm as the seat of arbitration. In this situation, English law is the *lex contractus*, governing the substantive rights and obligations of the parties, and Swedish law is the *lex arbitri*, being the arbitration law of the seat of arbitration. Here, the lawyers and the arbitrators need to be able to deal with two systems of law, which complicates the arbitration in a number of respects.[15] (this situation will be referred to as 'Example B' below.)

[B] Express Choice of the Governing Law of the Arbitration Agreement?

Notably, in both of these examples, the parties have not expressly chosen the governing law of the arbitration agreement. As readers will know, it is in fact most unusual for parties to make an express choice of the governing law of the arbitration agreement.

By way of further explanation, parties often include a choice of law clause in their contract, but the choice of law in that clause is almost always worded in general terms as governing the contract as a whole. It is very rare for the choice of law clause to state that the parties specifically choose a governing law of the arbitration agreement. Another alternative would be for there to be a separate choice of law provision as part of the arbitration clause by which the parties choose the governing law of the arbitration agreement, but again it is very rare for parties to include such a provision in their contract.

---

14. *See supra* n. 4.
15. Although of course some disputes are determined entirely on the facts, both substantive and procedural legal issues can be determinative. In practice, if one party decides to take procedural points (in this situation, by involving Swedish lawyers regarding issues of Swedish arbitration law), then the other party is also required to respond to such points, although some parties make a deliberate choice to ignore the specifics of the *lex arbitri* in this situation.

[C] The Governing Law of the Arbitration Agreement in the Absence of an Express Choice

So, what is the governing law of the arbitration agreement in Example A? The answer in this example, clearly, is Swedish law, for the simple reason that there is no other law to choose from in these circumstances.

Example B is somewhat more complex since two systems of law have been chosen. As noted above, it is very rare for the parties to make an express choice of the governing law of the arbitration agreement, and it is accordingly necessary for the choice of law to be inferred. There are two main schools of thought as to which law is the governing law of the arbitration agreement in these circumstances:[16]

- A simple solution is to apply the agreed choice of law in the contract to both the main agreement and the arbitration agreement. Even if the parties have not expressly stated the governing law of the arbitration agreement, it may often be inferred that the parties intended their choice of law to apply to every clause of the contract, including the dispute resolution clause that contains the arbitration agreement. In Example B, this would mean that English law would be the governing law of the arbitration agreement. This can be referred to as the 'main contract' approach.
- Alternatively, it might be said that the governing law of the arbitration agreement should be deemed to be the same as the procedural law of the arbitration, i.e., the *lex arbitri*. The rationale for this approach is that both the arbitration agreement and the *lex arbitri* deal with procedural issues. In Example B, this would mean that Swedish law would be the governing law of the arbitration agreement. This can be referred to as the 'seat' approach.[17]

Broadly, English law adopts the first approach, while Swedish law adopts the second approach (although, as will be seen, the details in both jurisdictions are rather more complex). Thus, as was mentioned at the start of this article, the English and Swedish approaches are markedly different from each other.

[D] Why Is This Important?

The reader may be wondering at this point whether this somewhat esoteric choice of law issue is of largely academic importance, or whether in some circumstances it may be of real practical importance.

16. *See, e.g.*, Julian Lew, 'The Law Applicable to the Form and Substance of the Arbitration Clause', in Albert Jan Van den Berg (ed.), *Improving the Efficiency of Arbitration Agreements and Awards: 40 Years of Application of the New York Convention*, Volume 9, International Council for Commercial Arbitration (ICCA) Congress Series, 114, 142-143 (Kluwer Law International; ICCA & Kluwer Law International 1999).
17. The approach that the law of the seat of the arbitration shall govern the arbitration agreement has been adopted in the London Court of International Arbitration (LCIA) Rules. *See* LCIA Arbitration Rules, Article 16.4 (1 October 2020).

The answer is that there are various situations in practice where it is necessary to construe the meaning and effect of the arbitration agreement and where the choice of the governing law of the arbitration agreement can be determinative. For example:

(a) It is quite often necessary to determine the scope, interpretation[18] and effect of the arbitration agreement. This issue can arise *inter alia* where the arbitration agreement is invoked as a bar to court proceedings, or where a challenge is made to the arbitral tribunal's jurisdiction, or where a challenge is made to the arbitral award, or where enforcement proceedings are contested.[19]
(b) Sometimes questions arise concerning the identity of the parties to the arbitration agreement, and (depending on the specific circumstances) this is also an issue that can be determined by the governing law of the arbitration agreement.[20]
(c) The choice of governing law is also particularly important if the arbitration agreement would be invalid under one law but not another.[21]
(d) One unusual situation, which nevertheless features rather often in some of the cases in this area, is where the parties have chosen two different forms of dispute resolution - e.g., arbitration in Sweden and litigation in England - and where it is necessary to determine the meaning and effect of the parties' choice in the particular circumstances of the case at hand.[22]
(e) The governing law of the arbitration agreement can also be of importance in circumstances where the governing law includes an implied term - for example, an implied term of confidentiality.[23]

18. This includes, in theory, the interpretation of any arbitration rules that are adopted by the parties and incorporated by reference into their arbitration agreement. It is interesting to note in this context, however, that the LCIA Rules of Arbitration 2020 provide that those rules 'shall be interpreted in accordance with the laws of England', notwithstanding that the arbitration agreement may be governed by a different law (*see* Articles 16.4 and 16.5 of the LCIA Rules of Arbitration 2020).
19. It is notable that this was the principal issue in the *Enka v. Chubb* case, discussed below. As the Supreme Court judgment makes clear, the parties appear to have accepted that English law interpreted the arbitration agreement more widely than Russian law, in particular since English law regarded tort claims as falling within the scope of the arbitration agreement. It was for this reason that the issue of whether the arbitration agreement was governed by English or Russian law was of such importance. *See* the Supreme Court's judgment, para. 194.
20. *See, e.g.*, *Petersen Farms Inc v. C&M Farming Ltd* [2004] EWHC 121, which concerned the question of whether the 'group of companies' doctrine applied under English law.
21. This situation has occurred in some English cases, notably *Hamlyn & Co v. Talisker Distillery* [1894] AC 202 (where the arbitration clause was valid under English law but invalid under Scottish law), and *Sulamérica Cia Nacional de Seguros SA v. Enesa Engenharia* [2012] EWCA Civ 638 (where the arbitration clause was valid under English law but invalid under Brazilian law).
22. This situation arose in the Svea Court of Appeal Case T 7929-17 of 19 December 2019, as discussed further below.
23. Under English law, there is an implied obligation of confidentiality arising out of the nature of arbitration itself not to disclose or use for any other purposes documents prepared for, used or disclosed during the course of an arbitration: *Ali Shipping Corporation v. Shipyard Trogir* [1999] 1 WLR 314 (CA), *Emmott v. Michael Wilson & Partners Ltd* [2008] EWCA Civ 184, *Glidepath BV v. Thompson* [2005] EWHC 818 (Comm), *Chartered Institute of Arbitrators v. B, C, D* [2019]

§9.04 THE ENGLISH APPROACH

[A] The General Approach

The English approach generally gives priority to the *lex contractus*.

There is substantial authority to support this 'main contract' approach. As Professor Julian Lew has explained:

> There is a very strong presumption in favour of the law governing the substantive agreement which contains the arbitration clause also governing the arbitration agreement. This principle has been followed in many cases. This could even be implied as an agreement of the parties as to the law applicable to the arbitration clause.[24]

This view is also accepted by *Redfern & Hunter on Arbitration*, who state:

> Since the arbitration clause is only one of many clauses in a contract, it might seem reasonable to assume that the law chosen by the parties to govern the contract will also govern the arbitration clause. If the parties expressly choose a particular law to govern their agreement, why should some other law – which the parties have not chosen – be applied to only one of the clauses in the agreement, simply because it happens to be the arbitration clause?[25]

The answer to this rhetorical question is that the doctrine of separability treats the arbitration clause as a separate agreement. However, Professor Lew refers to a position stated by Yves Derains in which he explains:

> [t]he autonomy of the arbitration clause and of the principal contract does not mean that they are totally independent one from the other as evidenced by the fact that the acceptance of the contract entails acceptance of the clause, without any other formality.[26]

EWHC 460 (Comm). It is clear from the case law that such confidentiality applies by reason of a term implied by law 'as a necessary incident' of the arbitration agreement (to quote from Potter LJ in the *Ali Shipping* case). It has also been suggested that this implied agreement is 'really a rule of substantive law masquerading as an implied term' (*Emmott v. Michael Wilson* per Lawrence Collins LJ at paras 84 and 106).

Under Swedish law, it is interesting to note NJA 2000 p. 538 (Bulbank) in this context. In that case, the contract was expressly governed by Austrian law, but there was no express agreement regarding the governing law of the arbitration agreement. The Swedish Supreme Court accordingly found that the arbitration agreement was governed by Swedish law, and the court went on to find that there was no implied obligation of confidentiality upon the parties to an arbitration agreement governed by Swedish law.

24. Lew, *supra* n. 16 at 143.
25. Blackaby, Partasides, Redfern and Hunter, *Redfern and Hunter on International Arbitration*, 158 (6th ed., Oxford University Press 2015).
26. Lew, *supra* n. 16 at 143.

The view that an arbitration agreement shall be governed by the law of the substantive contract also seems to have been adopted by the International Chamber of Commerce (ICC) arbitrators in a number of cases.[27]

[B] *Enka v. Chubb* – An Unusual Case

[1] Introduction

As has already been noted, the UK Supreme Court recently had occasion to consider the law in this area, in the widely publicised decision of *Enka v. Chubb* [2020] UKSC 38.[28] The central issue in this case was which law governs the arbitration agreement when the governing law of the contract containing the arbitration clause differs from the law of the seat of the arbitration.[29]

In short, the UK Supreme Court upheld the traditional English approach, finding that, where the law applicable to the arbitration agreement is not specified, a choice of the governing law of the main contract will generally be inferred to apply to an arbitration agreement which forms part of that contract. The UK Supreme Court further held that the choice of a different country as the seat of the arbitration is not, without more, sufficient to negate this general inference. On the other hand, if the parties have not chosen the governing law of the main contract, the UK Supreme Court held that the arbitration agreement should be governed by the law with which it is most closely connected, and that where the parties have chosen a seat of arbitration, this will generally be the law of the seat.[30]

Interestingly, however, the Court of Appeal judgment, from which the appeal was made to the UK Supreme Court, took a very different approach in this case. As Lords Hamblen and Leggatt state in paragraph 4 of their majority judgment in the UK Supreme Court:

> the Court of Appeal considered that 'the time has come to seek to impose some order and clarity on this area of the law' (para 89) and held that, unless there has been an express choice of the law that is to govern the arbitration agreement, the general rule should be that the arbitration agreement is governed by the law of the seat, as a matter of implied choice, subject only to any particular features of the case demonstrating powerful reasons to the contrary (para 91).

The appellant in the case argued that this conclusion was 'heterodox and wrong'.[31] The UK Supreme Court seem to have agreed.

---

27. For an account of relevant ICC Arbitral Awards *see* Lew, *supra* n. 16 at 143-144 in which he describes the following cases: Case No. 2626, Case No. 6379, Case No. 6752, Case No. 6840 and Case No. 5505.
28. *Enka Insaat Ve Sanayi AS v. OOO Insurance Company Chubb* [2020] UKSC 38.
29. The UK Supreme Court judgment is over hundred pages long and it is impractical to give an account of all the complex details mentioned. Nevertheless, we will attempt to summarise the main issues discussed in the judgment.
30. It is notable that this part of the finding moves away from the traditional 'main contract' approach.
31. The judgment of Lords Hamblen and Leggatt, at para. 5.

[2] The Background Facts and Circumstances

The background of the case is as follows. Following a fire in a power plant in Russia, the insurer OOO Insurance Company Chubb ('Chubb Russia') acquired subrogated rights of the owner of the power plant to claim compensation against third parties, including *inter alia* Enka Insaat Ve Sanayi AS ('Enka'), a Turkish engineering company and a subcontractor in the construction project that was allegedly liable for the fire. Chubb Russia brought proceedings against Enka in the Russian courts. However, pursuant to an assignment agreement, the owner had been given rights to claim against Enka pursuant to a main contract between Enka and the main contractor, which included an ICC arbitration clause providing for arbitration in London. The governing law of the contract was not specified in the agreement, nor was the governing law of the arbitration agreement specified.

Thus, the English courts had jurisdiction by virtue of the parties' choice of London as the seat of arbitration,[32] and English law was the *lex arbitri*,[33] but there was no choice of the governing law of the main agreement (the *lex contractus*) nor of the governing law of the arbitration agreement.

Enka filed a motion with the Russian court seeking dismissal of Chubb Russia's claim on the basis that the claim fell within the scope of the arbitration agreement. However, the Russian court refused to grant Enka's motion for dismissal. At the same time, the Russian court appears to have refused Chubb Russia's claims on the merits.[34]

Both parties filed appeals in the Russian proceedings, but meanwhile Enka brought an arbitration claim[35] in the Commercial Court in London on 16 September 2019 seeking an anti-suit injunction to restrain Chubb Russia from further pursuing the Russian proceedings on the ground that these proceedings were in breach of the arbitration agreement. At first instance, the Commercial Court declined to grant an interim anti-suit injunction and instead ordered an expedited trial. In a judgment dated 20 December 2019, the judge, Andrew Baker J, dismissed Enka's claims on the basis that, in his opinion, the appropriate forum to decide whether Chubb Russia's claim fell within the arbitration agreement was the Moscow Arbitrazh Court.

On 29 April 2020, the Court of Appeal allowed Enka's appeal and issued an anti-suit injunction restraining Chubb Russia from continuing the Russian proceedings. On the governing law issue, the Court of Appeal held that, unless there has been an express choice of the law that is to govern the arbitration agreement, the general rule should be that the arbitration agreement is governed by the law of the seat, as a matter of implied choice. The Court of Appeal further held that there was no express choice of

32. Pursuant to CPR Rule 62.5(1)(c) of the Civil Procedure Rules, the court may give permission to serve an arbitration claim form out of the jurisdiction of England & Wales where the claimant seeks a remedy or requires a question to be decided by the court affecting an arbitration or an arbitration agreement and where the seat of arbitration is in England. *See also* paras 19-20 of the Court of Appeal judgment ([2020] EWCA Civ 574).
33. *See supra* n. 4.
34. These details are taken from the judgment of Lords Hamblen and Leggatt, at paras 13-15.
35. That is, a claim pursuant to Part 62 of the Civil Procedure Rules of the English courts, which provides a specific procedure for bringing claims before the court relating to arbitration matters.

law in this case and that the arbitration agreement was therefore governed by English law.

Meanwhile, Enka had commenced arbitration pursuant to the arbitration clause, seeking a declaration from the arbitral tribunal that Chubb Russia's claims fell within the scope of the arbitration agreement.

Chubb Russia appealed to the UK Supreme Court on 26 May 2020, and the appeal was expedited and heard on 27 and 28 July 2020, with judgment subsequently given on 9 October 2020. As Lord Hamblen and Leggatt stated in their joint judgment at paragraph 24, this timing was impressively quick:

> It is a striking feature of the English proceedings that the trial, the appeal to the Court of Appeal and the appeal to the Supreme Court have all been heard in just over seven months. This is a vivid demonstration of the speed with which the English courts can act when the urgency of a matter requires it.

By a majority (three out of five judges, i.e., Lord Hamblen and Leggatt, with whom Lord Kerr agreed), the UK Supreme Court dismissed the appeal, but as will be seen below the UK Supreme Court came to a different view to the Court of Appeal on the central issues concerning the governing law of the arbitration agreement.

[3] The UK Supreme Court's General Rule That the Arbitration Agreement Is Governed by the Lex Contractus

The UK Supreme Court held that in such situations where the law applicable to the arbitration agreement has not been specified, but where the parties have chosen the law to govern the contract containing the arbitration agreement, this choice will generally apply to the arbitration agreement as an implied choice of law.[36]

Under the heading 'Splitting the contract', the majority of the Supreme Court held that it is 'generally reasonable to assume that parties would intend or expect their contract to be governed by a single system of law', and that this assumption 'applies to an arbitration clause, as it does to any other clause of a contract'.[37] Furthermore, and crucially, the majority of the Supreme Court held that the separability principle 'does not require that an arbitration agreement should be treated as a separate agreement for the purpose of determining its governing law'.[38] The court added that the separability principle 'is a legal doctrine and one which is likely to be much better known to arbitration lawyers than to commercial parties'.[39] For commercial parties, 'a contract is a contract; not a contract with an ancillary or collateral or interior arbitration agreement', and they would therefore 'reasonably expect a choice of law to apply to the whole of that contract'.[40]

36. The majority judgment, paras 43-54.
37. The majority judgment, paras 39-40.
38. The majority judgment, para. 41.
39. The majority judgment, para. 53.
40. The majority judgment, para. 53.

The Supreme Court also referred to leading commentaries and case law, as well as considerations of principle and some international authorities, all supporting the proposition that it is natural to interpret an express governing law clause in the contract as applying to the arbitration clause.[41]

[4] Criticism of the Court of Appeal's Approach

Against this background, the majority of the Supreme Court went on to criticise the approach of the Court of Appeal. As mentioned above, the Court of Appeal came to a contrary conclusion in the present case and held that there is a 'strong presumption' that the parties have, by implication, chosen the law of the seat of the arbitration to govern the arbitration agreement.[42] This was said to be the general rule, 'subject only to any particular features of the case demonstrating powerful reasons to the contrary'.[43] The Court of Appeal justified its approach on the ground that a choice of law to govern the contract 'has little if anything to say about the [arbitration agreement] law choice because it is directed to a different and separate agreement'.[44] This was said to follow from the doctrine of separability.[45]

The majority of the Supreme Court, however, did not agree with this finding, nor with the Court of Appeal's reliance on the principle of separability, which (in the opinion of the majority of the Supreme Court) ' ... puts the principle of separability of the arbitration agreement too high'.[46] The majority of the Supreme Court held that 'the assumption that, unless there is good reason to conclude otherwise, all the terms of a contract are governed by the same law applies to an arbitration clause, as it does to any other clause of a contract'.[47]

Another argument presented by the Court of Appeal in support of the finding that the parties have impliedly chosen the law of the seat to govern the arbitration agreement is what the majority of the Supreme Court refers to as 'the overlap argument'.[48] However, the majority of the Supreme Court rejected this argument and held that any overlap between the scope of the curial law and that of the arbitration agreement does not justify a presumption that the parties have, by implication, chosen the law of the seat of the arbitration to govern the arbitration agreement.[49] The majority

41. The majority judgment, paras 43-58.
42. The majority judgment, para. 59.
43. The majority judgment, para. 59.
44. The majority judgment, para. 61.
45. The majority judgment, para. 61.
46. The majority judgment, para. 61.
47. The majority judgment, para. 40.
48. This argument was first mentioned in *XL Insurance Ltd v. Owens Corning* [2001] 1 All ER (Comm) 530, in which the Court of Appeal held that the parties had impliedly chosen English law to govern the validity of the arbitration agreement despite the choice of New York law as the governing law of the contract. The reasoning in that case was essentially that the substance and process of arbitration 'are closely intertwined' and that the 1996 English Arbitration Act 'contains various provisions which could not readily be separated into boxes labelled "substantive arbitration law" or "procedural law", because that would be an artificial division'.
49. The majority judgment, paras 64-94.

of the Supreme Court held that ' ... the curial law which applies to the arbitration process is conceptually distinct from the law which governs the validity and scope of the arbitration agreement'. [50] Additionally, the Supreme Court held that the content of the English Arbitration Act 1996 does not support such a general inference as suggested by the Court of Appeal.[51]

The Supreme Court, however, identified two exceptions where such an inference as suggested by the Court of Appeal could be made:

(1) One of these exceptions is where the law of the seat of arbitration indicates that the arbitration agreement will also be treated as being governed by that country's law. The Supreme Court gave, as examples, section 48 of the Swedish Arbitration Act[52] and section 6 of the Arbitration (Scotland) Act 2010.[53] However, no provision similar to section 48 of the Swedish Arbitration Act or section 6 of the Arbitration (Scotland) Act 2010 is included in the English Arbitration Act.
(2) The other exception mentioned by the Supreme Court applies to contracts where applying the principle that the law chosen to govern the contract should be applied to the arbitration agreement would mean that there is a significant risk that the arbitration agreement would be ineffective. It is a

50. The majority judgment, para. 69.
51. The majority judgment, paras 73-82. The majority of the Supreme Court noted the fact 'that almost all the provisions of the English Arbitration Act relied on to support the overlap argument are non-mandatory and, where the arbitration agreement is governed a foreign law, by reason of section 4(5) the non-mandatory provisions of the Act which concern arbitration agreements do not apply to it'.
52. The majority judgment, paras 70-71. The Supreme Court referred in this regard to the case of *Carpatsky Petroleum Corpn v. PJSC Ukrnafta* [2020] EWHC 769 (Comm), in which the claimant was seeking to enforce in England and Wales an arbitration award made in Sweden. Enforcement was resisted by the respondent, *inter alia*, on the ground that there was no valid arbitration agreement in the contract between the parties, an argument which was based on the assumption that the validity of the arbitration agreement was governed by the law of Ukraine. The contract provided for the 'law of substance of Ukraine' to apply 'on examination of disputes'. The Court of Appeal found that the parties had not chosen Ukrainian law to govern the arbitration agreement. Instead, under the circumstances, the choice of Stockholm as the seat for any arbitration showed an implied choice that the validity and interpretation of the arbitration agreement should be governed by Swedish law. The following reasons were given for this conclusion: (i) that it was reasonable to conclude that the parties had deliberately chosen a neutral forum to resolve their disputes and hence 'intended the law of that jurisdiction to determine issues as to the validity and ambit of that choice'; (ii) by choosing Sweden as the seat for the arbitration, the parties agreed to the application of the Swedish Arbitration Act, including section 48. Therefore, by providing for a Swedish seat, it followed that the parties were impliedly agreeing that Swedish law should govern the arbitration agreement.
53. Section 6 of the Arbitration (Scotland) Act 2010 provides:

    Where –

    (a) the parties to an arbitration agreement agree that an arbitration under that agreement is to be seated in Scotland, but
    (b) the arbitration agreement does not specify the law which is to govern it,
    then, unless the parties otherwise agree, the arbitration agreement is to be governed by Scots law.

well-established principle of contractual interpretation in English law that an interpretation which upholds the validity of a transaction is to be preferred to one which would render it invalid or ineffective.[54] This is commonly referred to as the 'validation principle'. The majority of the Supreme Court held that this principle 'may apply if, in determining whether the parties have agreed on a choice of governing law, a putative governing law would render all or a part of the contract ineffective'.[55]

[5] The UK Supreme Court's Position in Circumstances Where There Is No Express Choice of Law

In light of these various observations, the majority of the Supreme Court held that, where there is no express choice of law to govern the contract, a choice of the seat of the arbitration does not by itself justify an inference that the contract (or the arbitration agreement) is intended to be governed by the law of the seat.[56]

Thus, in the absence of an express or implied choice of law to govern the arbitration agreement, the court must objectively determine with which system of the law the arbitration agreement is 'most closely connected'. The majority of Supreme Court held that, in general, the default rule will be that the arbitration agreement will be most closely connected with the law of the seat of arbitration if the parties have chosen the seat of arbitration.[57]

The majority of the Supreme Court referred to four principal 'reasons of principle and policy' to justify this general rule that: (i) the seat of arbitration is the place of performance of the arbitration agreement; (ii) this general rule is consistent with international law and legislative policy; (iii) it gives effect to commercial purpose, by being 'likely to uphold the reasonable expectations of contracting parties who have chosen to settle their disputes by arbitration in a specified place but made no choice of law for their contract'; and (iv) such a clear default rule is in the interests of legal certainty.[58]

Under the second heading ('Consistency with international law and legislative policy'), the majority of the Supreme Court referred particularly in this regard to the conflict of laws rule contained in Article V(1)(a) of the New York Convention, which states:

> Recognition and enforcement of the award may be refused, at the request of the party against whom it is invoked, only if that party furnishes to the competent authority where the recognition and enforcement is sought, proof that:
>
> (a) The parties to the agreement referred to in article II [the arbitration agreement] were, under the law applicable to them, under some incapacity, or *the said agreement is not valid under the law to which the parties have subjected it or,*

54. The majority judgment, para. 95.
55. The majority judgment, para. 96.
56. The majority judgment, paras 110-117.
57. The majority judgment, paras 118-124.
58. The majority judgment, paras 120-146.

> *failing any indication thereon, under the law of the country where the award was made* (emphasis added).

The Supreme Court held that, while this provision in the New York Convention only applies in enforcement proceedings, 'it would be illogical to apply different conflict rules to determine which law governs the validity of the arbitration agreement where the arbitration is seated (and the award therefore treated as made) in England'.[59] Referring to Professor van den Berg, one of the leading authorities on the New York Convention, the majority of the Supreme Court also held that 'it would be equally illogical if the law governing the validity of the arbitration agreement were to differ depending on whether the question of validity is raised before or after an award has been made'.[60] For these reasons, in order to ensure consistency and coherence, the same law should be applied in either case.[61]

Under the third heading ('Giving effect to commercial purpose'), the majority of the Supreme Court noted that:

> [i]n such circumstances [where the parties choose a popular neutral seat of arbitration without specifying the governing law of the contract], if the parties had been required to make a common choice of law to govern their arbitration agreement at the time of contracting, it is inherently unlikely that they would have agreed on either of their national systems of law and much more likely that they would have settled on the law of the place which they had chosen as the seat of arbitration.[62]

Moreover:

> [n]ot only does this provide a neutral choice of law but it is already the law of that place which – in countries which have implemented the Model Law or are parties to the New York Convention – will determine the validity of an award if an application is made to set it aside or if its enforcement in the other party's home state is resisted.[63]

[6] Summary of the Principles for Choosing the Governing Law of the Arbitration Agreement, as Stated by the Majority of the Supreme Court

The majority of the Supreme Court summarised its reasoning as follows:[64]

(i) Where a contract contains an agreement to resolve disputes arising from it by arbitration, the law applicable to the arbitration agreement may not be the same as the law applicable to the other parts of the contract and is to be

59. The majority judgment, para. 135.
60. The majority judgment, para. 136.
61. The majority judgment, paras 126-127.
62. The majority judgment, para. 142.
63. The majority judgment, para. 142.
64. The majority judgment, para. 170.

determined by applying English common law rules for resolving conflicts of laws rather than the provisions of the Rome I Regulation.

(ii) According to these rules, the law applicable to the arbitration agreement will be: (a) the law chosen by the parties to govern it or (b) in the absence of such a choice, the system of law with which the arbitration agreement is most closely connected.

(iii) Whether the parties have agreed on a choice of law to govern the arbitration agreement is ascertained by construing the arbitration agreement and the contract containing it, as a whole, applying the rules of contractual interpretation of English law as the law of the forum.

(iv) Where the law applicable to the arbitration agreement is not specified, a choice of governing law for the contract will generally apply to an arbitration agreement which forms part of the contract.

(v) The choice of a different country as the seat of the arbitration is not, without more, sufficient to negate an inference that a choice of law to govern the contract was intended to apply to the arbitration agreement.

(vi) Additional factors which may, however, negate such an inference and may in some cases imply that the arbitration agreement was intended to be governed by the law of the seat are: (a) any provision of the law of the seat which indicates that, where an arbitration is subject to that law, the arbitration will also be treated as governed by that country's law; or (b) the existence of a serious risk that, if governed by the same law as the main contract, the arbitration agreement would be ineffective. Either factor may be reinforced by circumstances indicating that the seat was deliberately chosen as a neutral forum for the arbitration.

(vii) Where there is no express choice of law to govern the contract, a clause providing for arbitration in a particular place will not by itself justify an inference that the contract (or the arbitration agreement) is intended to be governed by the law of that place.

(viii) In the absence of any choice of law to govern the arbitration agreement, the arbitration agreement is governed by the law with which it is most closely connected. Where the parties have chosen a seat of arbitration, this will generally be the law of the seat, even if this differs from the law applicable to the parties' substantive contractual obligations.

(ix) The fact that the contract requires the parties to attempt to resolve a dispute through good faith negotiation, mediation or any other procedure before referring it to arbitration will not generally provide a reason to displace the law of the seat of arbitration as the law applicable to the arbitration agreement by default in the absence of a choice of law to govern it.

Applying these principles, the majority of the Supreme Court found that the arbitration agreement in the case at hand was governed by English law, on the basis that the law of the chosen seat of arbitration was the law with which the arbitration agreement was most closely connected. It was common ground between the parties that, if English law was found to be the governing law of the arbitration agreement, then the arbitration agreement was valid, the dispute between the parties fell within the arbitration agreement, and the injunction granted by the Court of Appeal to restrain Chubb Russia from proceedings against Enka in Russia was properly granted.[65]

[7] The Findings of the Minority of the Supreme Court[66]

Lord Burrows and Lord Sales were in the minority in the Supreme Court, and they each wrote dissenting judgments.[67]

In the judgment of the minority, the governing or proper law of the main contract was 'clearly demonstrated by the terms of the contract or the circumstances of the case' as being Russian law.[68] In these circumstances, the minority considered that the governing or proper law of the arbitration agreement was also Russian law by reason of an implied choice.[69]

The minority of the Supreme Court also considered that there was 'a presumption (or general rule)' 'that the proper law of the main contract is also the proper law of the arbitration agreement; and there is no such presumption (or general rule) that the law of the seat is the proper law of the arbitration agreement'. Thus, in short, the minority favoured 'the "main contract" rather than the "seat" approach'.[70]

Lord Burrows set out eight reasons for favouring this approach:

(i) Dépeçage (i.e., having different laws for different parts of a contract) is the exception, not the rule;
(ii) The rationale of the separability doctrine is that it was devised for a particular purpose, namely to prevent arguments about the validity of the arbitration agreement in circumstances where there are arguments about the validity of the main agreement;
(iii) Dividing the arbitration agreement from the rest of the contract may be problematic;
(iv) In past cases, excessive weight has been given to the seat of arbitration;
(v) In past cases, insufficient weight has traditionally been given to the implied choice of the parties;

65. The majority judgment, para. 186. On the other hand, it is notable that the majority of the UK Supreme Court nevertheless found that the main contract should be deemed to be governed by Russian law on the basis that, pursuant to Article 4(3) of the Rome I Regulation, it was 'clear from all the circumstances of the case that the main body of the construction contract is manifestly more closely connected with Russia than with any other country' (the majority judgment, para. 161).
66. It states at the top of the joint judgment of Lords Hamblen and Leggatt: 'LORD HAMBLEN AND LORD LEGGATT: (with whom Lord Kerr agrees)'. Thus, the opinion expressed in the joint judgment of Lords Hamblen and Leggatt prevailed over the opinion expressed in the judgments of Lord Burrows and Lord Sales, but this was only because Lord Kerr apparently agreed with Lords Hamblen and Leggatt. It is somewhat unfortunate in these circumstances that Lord Kerr did not write a judgment of his own.
67. Lord Sales agreed with Lord Burrows' judgment as well as writing a judgment of his own.
68. Lord Burrows' judgment, para. 205.
69. Lord Burrows' judgment, paras 227-228.
70. Lord Burrows' judgment, paras 229-255.

(vi) The curial law and curial jurisdiction can be separated out from the proper law of the arbitration agreement;

(vii) Section 103(2)(b) of the Arbitration Act 1996 (codifying Article V(1)(a) of the 1958 New York Convention) is neutral – in other words, it is irrelevant where there has been an implied choice of law, and it also only concerns questions of invalidity, not questions of interpretation;

(viii) By analogy, an exclusive jurisdiction clause is normally governed by the law applicable to the contract of which it forms a part.[71]

Furthermore, the minority considered that they would arrive at the same conclusion, i.e., that the proper law of the arbitration agreement was Russian law, even if there had been no implied choice of Russian law as the proper law of the main contract. This was because the minority considered that both the main contract and the arbitration agreement had the closest and most real connection with Russia:[72]

> 256. I would arrive at the same conclusion – that the proper law of the arbitration agreement is Russian law – for the reasons that have been set out in paras 231-255 above, even if the proper law of the main contract was Russian under article 4, rather than under article 3(1), of Rome I Regulation at least if the reason for that was that Russia is the country with which the contract is most closely connected. That would then carry across to the third stage of the common law approach and would mean that, despite the seat for the arbitration being England, the arbitration agreement also has the closest and most real connection with Russia. That one arrives at the same result at common law whether applying the implied choice or the default rule is unsurprising. It has long been recognised that there is a thin distinction between those two stages: they represent the distinction between implied and imputed intention. In *Amin Rasheed Shipping Corpn v Kuwait Insurance Co* [1984] AC 50 the majority, led by Lord Diplock, decided that English law was the proper law by necessary implication whereas Lord Wilberforce came to the same conclusion applying the closest and most real connection test while recognising, at p 69, that the two 'merge into each other'. But although, in general terms, it is important to recognise that one would arrive at the same conclusion if one applied the third stage of the common law approach, this case can be decided without going beyond the choice of the parties. The proper law of the arbitration agreement is Russian because that is the law which they have impliedly chosen.

On the basis of this reasoning, Lord Burrows then summarised his view on how the proper law of the arbitration agreement should be determined, as follows:

> 257. The reasoning above enables me to state the common law on the proper law of an arbitration agreement (contained in a main contract) in the following straightforward and principled way which (had this view found favour) would have been easy to apply and would have been one way of providing the clarity that Popplewell LJ was rightly seeking:
>
> (i) The proper law of the arbitration agreement is to be determined by applying the three stage common law test. Is there an express choice of law? If not, is

71. Lord Burrows' judgment, paras 231-255.
72. Lord Burrows' judgment, para. 256.

there an implied choice of law? If not, with what system of law does the arbitration agreement have its closest and most real connection?

(ii) Where there is an express proper law clause in the arbitration agreement (which is rare) that will be determinative.

(iii) Where there is no such clause, there is a presumption or general rule that the proper law of the main contract is also the proper law of the arbitration agreement. That presumption or general rule can assist the enquiry at any of the three stages of the common law approach. (It is most appropriate to use the language of a presumption where one is considering the parties' choice at the first two stages of the enquiry – ie it is a presumption of the parties' intentions – and to use the language of a general rule where one is considering the third stage of the closest and most real connection.)

(iv) That presumption may most obviously be rebutted, or there is an exception to that general rule, where the standard 'validation principle' (of the English conflict of laws) applies ie where the law of the seat (or another relevant jurisdiction) would treat the arbitration agreement as valid whereas the proper law of the main contract would treat the arbitration agreement as invalid (or, as in the *Sulamérica* case, not binding on one of the parties). In very rare cases that presumption would also be rebutted where it is clear that the parties have chosen the law of the seat as the proper law of the arbitration agreement even though there is no express proper law clause in the arbitration agreement.

[C] Some Conclusions Regarding the English Approach Following *Enka v. Chubb*

It was clearly the intention of the UK Supreme Court that *Enka v. Chubb* would provide an opportunity to clarify English law in this area. Some clarification has indeed been reached, but it must be said that the position would have been considerably clearer if the position of the minority of the UK Supreme Court in *Enka v. Chubb* had prevailed (since the minority was firmly in favour of the traditional 'main contract' approach).

As it is, we are left with a hybrid position following the decision of the majority of the UK Supreme Court in *Enka v. Chubb*, where the traditional English 'main contract' approach has been affirmed where the parties have expressly or impliedly chosen the governing law of the main contract, but where, in the absence of such a choice, the 'seat' approach is applied by default.

§9.05 THE SWEDISH APPROACH

[A] Summary of the Swedish Approach under Section 48 of the Swedish Arbitration Act

Under Swedish law, as has already been referred to, section 48 of the Swedish Arbitration Act (1999:116) governs which law is applicable to the arbitration agreement in international disputes. This section provides:

> If an arbitration agreement has an international connection, the agreement shall be governed by the law agreed upon by the parties. If the parties have not reached

> such an agreement, the arbitration agreement shall be governed by the law of the country where, in accordance with the parties' agreement, the arbitration had or shall have its seat.
>
> The first paragraph shall not apply to the issue of whether a party was authorised to enter into an arbitration agreement or was duly represented.[73]

Thus, section 48 of the Swedish Arbitration Act provides that parties to an arbitration agreement with an international connection may agree on the law governing the arbitration agreement, and the text of the Swedish Arbitration Act does not state anything more about what might be required to constitute such an agreement between the parties on the choice of law. However, according to the Government Bill, a general choice of law clause in the main contract is not considered to be sufficient to constitute an agreement by the parties as to the law governing the arbitration agreement.[74] Instead, the Government Bill suggests that the choice of law clause must explicitly refer to the arbitration agreement in order to govern the law of the arbitration agreement.

In the absence of such an agreement between the parties, section 48 of the Swedish Arbitration Act provides that the arbitration agreement shall be governed by the law of the country where, in accordance with the parties' agreement, the arbitration had or shall have its seat.

As mentioned above, it is very rare for contracts to contain a specific choice of law clause with respect to the arbitration agreement. In practice, therefore, section 48 of the Swedish Arbitration Act provides that in almost all cases the governing law of the arbitration agreement shall be deemed to be the same as the *lex arbitri*.[75]

In situations where the parties have made no choice of law and no agreement has been reached with respect to the place of arbitration, section 48 of the Swedish Arbitration Act provides no guidance on how to establish the law governing the arbitration agreement. In these circumstances, the Government Bill provides that the governing law should be established in accordance with the general conflicts of law rules.[76] Since both the Rome Convention and the Rome I Regulation exclude arbitration agreements from their scope of application, the centre of gravity test must be applied to establish the governing law.[77]

[B] Further Explanation as Set Out in the Government Bill (Prop. 1998/99:35)

Guidance on how to interpret Swedish legislation is generally found by having regard to the detailed government bill that formed the basis for the legislation. In the case of

73. Unofficial translation by the SCC Institute (https://sccinstitute.se/media/1773096/the-swedish-arbitration-act_1march2019_eng-2.pdf).
74. Swedish Government Official Reports 1994:81 pp. 228-229 and Govt. Bill. 1998/99:35 p. 191.
75. Govt. Bill. 1998/99:35 p. 245.
76. Swedish Government Official Reports 1994:81 p. 306 and Govt. Bill. 1998/99:35 p. 245.
77. *See* Rome Convention on the Law applicable to Contractual Obligations, Title 1., Article 1.2d), and Rome I Regulation (Regulation (EC) No. 593/2008), Chapter 1., Article 1.2 e); *see* Stefan Lindskog, *Skiljeförfarande: En kommentar*, 1185 fn 4651 (3d ed., Norstedts Juridik 2020); Kaj Hobér, *International Commercial Arbitration in Sweden*, 79 (2d., Oxford University Press 2021).

the Swedish Arbitration Act, the relevant government bill is Prop. 1998/99:35 (the 'Government Bill'). On pages 190-195 of that Government Bill, there is a detailed explanation of the considerations that formed the basis of section 48 of the Swedish Arbitration Act.

In summary, the Government started from the approach taken in the New York Convention. Pursuant to Article V(1)(a) of the New York Convention, which relates to enforcement of arbitral awards, the agreement under which the award is made must be valid 'under the law to which the parties have subjected it or, failing any indication thereon, ... the law of the country where the award was made'. Thus, Article V(1)(a) of the New York Convention includes a choice of law rule that points to, first, the law chosen by the parties to govern the arbitration agreement, and second, in the absence of such a law, the law of the seat of arbitration.

It was noted that, although this rule in Article V(1)(a) of the New York Convention is only applicable in the context of the enforcement of a foreign arbitral award, it was desirable to have the same basic rule in all situations. In a purely national situation between Swedish parties, it was thought undesirable that such parties should be able to contract out of Swedish contract law as the governing law of the arbitration agreement. However, in any international situation, it should be possible for the parties to choose a law to govern their arbitration agreement.

The Government Bill posits a situation where a German arbitral award is being enforced in Sweden and where the parties have agreed that the contract shall be governed by Swiss law with arbitration taking place in Germany. In that situation, it is stated in the Government Bill:

> The predominant view of the review committee appears to be that the choice of law in applying the Convention must explicitly concern the arbitration agreement. This means that, in the above example, German law should be applied in determining the validity of the arbitration agreement, while Swiss law should be applied to the rest of the contract. It could also be understood in this example that the parties have made an implicit choice of law by referring to arbitration in Germany.
>
> The government considers that, in applying this general rule as sketched out above, concerning the governing law of the arbitration agreement, it should be a requirement that the parties' choice of law concerns the arbitration agreement itself.[78]

On the other hand, if there is no such specific choice of law concerning the arbitration agreement itself, the Government Bill goes on to state that the validity of the arbitration agreement should be determined according to the law of the place where the arbitration takes place. The Government Bill expressly states that this should be the position both where the parties have chosen the seat and also where the seat has been chosen by the arbitrators or by an arbitration institute, since in this situation as well the seat can be said to have been chosen pursuant to the parties' agreement.

78. This is an in-house English translation of the Swedish text.

[C] Criticism of the Swedish Approach

The decision by the Government Bill to apply the law of the seat as the predominant decisive factor in determining the governing law of the arbitration agreement has been criticised by legal commentators. In particular, this is considered to be problematic where the seat is chosen not by the parties but by an arbitral institution, by the arbitral tribunal, or by a court. In these cases, it has been considered that the chosen seat is not a strong connecting factor and, thus, that this may come as a surprise for foreign parties.[79]

Zettermarck argues that '[t]o say the least it is not evident that the language used in Section 48 of the Act (... by virtue of the agreement ...) covers the decision made by an arbitration institute with regard to the place of arbitration'.[80]

Petrochilos argues that '[a]lthough any such choice is made on the strength of an explicit or implicit authority conferred by the parties, it would be entirely artificial to consider this a true choice by the parties'.[81]

Lindskog argues that the arbitrators may have a vested interest in the matter of the applicable law. He therefore suggests that the arbitrators should only be able to choose the law governing the proceedings if this is explicitly supported by the arbitration agreement. Applying this view, a general provision which suggests that the place of arbitration shall be decided by the tribunal should not be sufficient in this respect. Instead, such a provision should only be understood as allowing the tribunal to decide where the proceedings – strictly geographically – shall take place. Pursuant to Lindskog's argument, the law applicable to the proceedings should in such case be decided objectively based on other connecting factors.[82] According to Lindskog, the same objections can, with some modifications, be raised with respect to an arbitration institute.[83] Further, and of particular interest here, Lindskog argues that the same objections can be raised in relation to the arbitration agreement.[84]

It can also be questioned if the view expressed in the Government Bill applies in situations where a court already has determined the law applicable to the arbitration agreement prior to the arbitration proceedings. Questions concerning the applicable law can arise at an early stage before the place of arbitration has been decided, *inter alia*, when an arbitration agreement has been invoked as a bar to court proceedings or when a court or an arbitration institute is to appoint an arbitrator for the respondent and the respondent objects that the arbitration agreement is invalid. The law governing the arbitration agreement must in such cases be established in accordance with general

79. *See, e.g.*, Lars Heuman, *Arbitration Law of Sweden: Practice and Procedure*, 689-690 (Juris Publishing 2003); Claes Zettermarck, 'Determining the Applicable Law to an Arbitration Agreement', in Sigvard Jarvin and Lars Heuman (eds.), *Swedish Arbitration Act of 1999: Five Years on: A Critical Review of Strengths and Weaknesses*, 105, 107 (Juris Publishing 1999).
80. Zettermarck, *supra* n. 79 at 107.
81. Georgios Petrochilos, *Procedural Law in International Arbitration*, 29 (Oxford University Press 2004).
82. Lindskog, *supra* n, 77 at 1170-1171 fn 4594.
83. Lindskog, *supra* n. 77 at 1170-1171.
84. Lindskog, *supra* n. 77 at 1180-1187.

conflicts of laws rules. If such decision has been made by a court, it is questionable if an arbitral tribunal or an arbitral institute would be able to subsequently decide that another law shall apply to the arbitration agreement by choosing the seat of the arbitration.[85]

If the parties have agreed on institutional arbitration, the institution will often determine the place of arbitration in accordance with the rules of the institution if the parties have failed to determine a place of arbitration.[86] Some commentators suggest that if the institution in question does not have provisions of this kind, the law of the country where the chosen arbitration institute has its seat shall be applied.[87] The Arbitration Institute of the Stockholm Chamber of Commerce (SCC) has in a number of cases determined the law applicable on the arbitration agreement on the basis of the seat of the arbitration institution.[88]

Another solution is to extend a general choice of law clause in the contract to the arbitration agreement.[89] Hobér suggests that '[i]t could perhaps be argued that it would be natural to extend the choice of law clause in the main contract to the arbitration agreement' and that '[a]fter all, it would not be unreasonable to assume that this would be in conformity with the expectations of the parties and that the choice of law clause in the main contract should be viewed as an implied term of the arbitration agreement'.[90]

Hjerner argues that '[i]f, however, both parties to the contract are foreigners and, particularly, if a place in Sweden was only later fixed as the venue, it is arguable that the arbitration clause is governed by the proper law of the main contract'.[91]

[D] The Svea Court of Appeal Case T 7929-17 – A Missed Opportunity

As was mentioned briefly above, issues concerning the governing law of the arbitration agreement arose in the Svea Court of Appeal Case T 7929-17.[92]

In this case, the parties had included two conflicting dispute resolution clauses in their contract: one clause providing for disputes to be settled in the courts of Cyprus (the 'jurisdiction clause') and another clause providing for arbitration before 'the International arbitration court in Stockholm' (the 'arbitration clause'). The contract included a general choice of law clause by which the parties chose Cyprus law as the

85. *See also* Lindskog, *supra* n. 77 at 1171 fn 4600.
86. *See, e.g.*, Articles 11 and 25 of the SCC rules according to which the SCC Board will determine the place of arbitration if the parties have failed to do so.
87. Hobér, *supra* n. 77, at 79-80.
88. *See* Stockholm International Arbitration Review 2007, vol. 2, p. 235 which describes SCC Case 10/2005, and Stockholm Arbitration Report 2004, vol. 1, p. 93 which describes SCC Case 12/2002.
89. Lars Hjerner, 'Choice of Law Problems in International Arbitration with Particular Reference to Arbitration in Sweden', in Ulf Franke (ed.), *Swedish and International Arbitration 1982*, 18, 24 (The Arbitration Institute of the Stockholm Chamber of Commerce 1982); Heuman, *supra* n. 79 at 690.
90. Hobér, *supra* n. 77 at 79.
91. Hjerner, *supra* n. 89 at 24.
92. Judgment of the Svea Court of Appeal, 19 December 2019, Case T 7929-17.

governing law of the contract. One of the principal issues for the arbitral tribunal, and also subsequently for the Svea Court of Appeal, was how to reconcile these two conflicting clauses.

It was common ground between the parties that the jurisdiction clause was governed by Cyprus law. It was also common ground that the interrelationship between the two clauses was a matter for Cyprus law. However, the claimant in the arbitration argued, pursuant to section 48 of the Swedish Arbitration Act, that the arbitration clause was governed by Swedish law. The respondent in the arbitration, on the other hand, argued that under Cypriot law the choice of law applied also to the arbitration clause, and thus the parties had chosen Cypriot law as the governing law of the arbitration agreement; alternatively, the parties had not made any choice of Stockholm as the seat of arbitration, Stockholm had been chosen by the SCC Institute, and thus the governing law of the arbitration agreement should be determined on the basis of the law with the closest connection, which in these circumstances would be Cypriot law.

This case was, accordingly, a good opportunity for the Svea Court of Appeal to consider these issues in detail. Sadly, however, the Svea Court of Appeal failed to take advantage of this opportunity. Instead, the court dealt with this part of the case in only a few paragraphs, noting first that under the doctrine of separability the arbitration agreement should be deemed to be a separate agreement.[93] Since the parties' choice of law clause did not specifically relate to the arbitration agreement, the Svea Court of Appeal found that the governing law of the arbitration agreement was the same as the law of the seat pursuant to section 48 of the Swedish Arbitration Act.

Despite the importance of this issue, the Svea Court of Appeal refused leave to appeal to the Supreme Court.[94]

§9.06 DISCUSSION

What conclusions are to be drawn from a comparison of these two approaches? It seems to us that both approaches can be criticised.

[A] The English Approach

As will have become clear, the English approach, as stated by the majority of the UK Supreme Court in *Enka v. Chubb*, can hardly be said to be straightforward. Moreover,

93. The Svea Court of Appeal did not discuss the meaning and effect of the doctrine of separability in any detail, but simply noted that under that doctrine the arbitration agreement was deemed to be a separate agreement for the purpose of determining its validity. However, the court completely failed to address the argument raised by the respondent in the arbitration that the separability principle does not require that an arbitration agreement should be treated as a separate agreement for the purpose of determining its governing law (a point that was accepted by the majority of the UK Supreme Court in *Enka v. Chubb* – *see* the majority judgment in that case, para. 41).

94. It should be noted, in the interests of full disclosure, that James Hope acted for the respondent in the arbitration and also in the Svea Court of Appeal.

the fact that there were such differences of opinion even within the members of the UK Supreme Court suggests that debates will continue to run within English law in relation to these issues.

It is notable that Lord Burrows, who was one of the judges in the minority in that case, is the first member of the UK Supreme Court to have been appointed directly from academia, and before his elevation to the Bench he was a distinguished Professor of Law at the University of Oxford. Lord Burrows' judgment is well reasoned and, in our humble opinion, the approach taken by the minority is preferable. It may be useful to quote paragraph 260 of Lord Burrows' judgment, in which he summarises his criticism of the majority:

> 260. It will be clear from all that I have said above that, while there are large measures of agreement between us (for example, that (at least in general) an express or implied choice of the proper law for the main contract carries across to be the proper law of the arbitration agreement, irrespective of the specified seat of arbitration) I cannot agree, with great respect, with the overall approach or conclusion in this case of my colleagues, Lords Hamblen and Leggatt (with whom Lord Kerr agrees). In their view, the proper law of the arbitration agreement is here English law because there has been no choice of law for the arbitration agreement, express or implied, and the arbitration agreement has the closest and most real connection to England as the seat of the arbitration. Their decision would have been different had the proper law of the main contract been Russian law by reason of an express or implied choice. But because the proper law of the main contract is, in their view, Russian law, only because it has the closest and most real connection to Russia, that means that the proper law of the arbitration agreement is English law. That is to rest crucially different consequences on a divide between the choice and default stages of the Rome I Regulation and between the second and third stages of the common law approach in a way that, with respect, I do not believe to be justified in principle. I also consider that that approach produces undesirable practical and unprincipled consequences (especially by forcing a division of the proper laws) such as those set out in paras 235-239 above. I also have misgivings about the idea that the English common law should depart from a principled solution on the basis of a supposed – but in my view unproven – consensus as to international arbitration policy favouring the seat approach (in the absence of choice). My view is that the proper law of the arbitration agreement is Russian. That is because the proper law of the main contract is Russian by implied choice and that implied choice encompasses, or carries across to constitute, an implied choice of Russian law for the arbitration agreement. Even if my reasoning on the proper law of the main contract is wrong and the proper law of the main contract is Russian by reason of Russia having the closest and most real connection rather than by implied choice – I would still regard the proper law of the arbitration agreement as being Russian law by reason of the arbitration agreement having the closest and most real connection with Russian law. This is to apply the general rule, to which there is here no exception, that the proper law of the main contract is also the proper law of the arbitration agreement.

Lord Burrows' approach, as set out here, has the considerable advantage of simplicity. It starts with the 'main contract' approach and continues with it.

[B] The Swedish Approach

Turning to the Swedish approach, here there is simplicity, in that the Swedish approach adopts almost entirely the 'seat' approach.

However, in deciding that a specific choice of law governing the arbitration agreement must specifically relate to the arbitration agreement itself, it seems to us that the Swedish approach goes too far. In practice, the first sentence of section 48[95] has been rendered inapplicable and superfluous. In practice, parties almost never make a specific choice of law in relation to the arbitration agreement itself.

On the other hand, commercial parties generally assume that their general choice of law will govern all parts of their agreement, including the arbitration clause. Thus, considerations of party autonomy strongly favour giving effect to such a general choice of law. Moreover, the doctrine of separability has a particular purpose – to prevent the arbitration agreement being considered invalid when issues of validity arise in relation to the main agreement – and it should not be used more generally to take precedence over the parties' choice of governing law.

The fact that the Government Bill, more than twenty years ago, included a single sentence stating that the choice of law needed to relate specifically to the arbitration agreement should not prevent this issue from being reconsidered. Sadly, however, the Svea Court of Appeal in Case T 7929-17 failed to consider this issue in any detail, even though the point had been fully argued. It is unfortunate that the Svea Court of Appeal refused to allow the Swedish Supreme Court to consider these issues by denying leave to appeal.

Furthermore, as several commentators have stated, it is particularly questionable to apply the law of the seat of arbitration as determining the governing law of the arbitration agreement in circumstances where the seat has been chosen, not by the parties but by an arbitral institution, or by the arbitral tribunal or by a court.

[C] Concluding Remarks

It will be interesting to see how the law develops in this area, both in England and in Sweden. As can be seen from our comments above, it seems to us that the approach as set out in both jurisdictions could be improved.

In any event, it has to be said that, from the parties' point of view, attempts should be made to avoid the more difficult issues that can arise in these situations. Parties should always include a governing law clause in their contract, and although it is unusual to do so, potential difficulties could easily be avoided if the governing law clause makes clear that it also relates to the arbitration agreement itself. In such circumstances, under both the English approach and the Swedish approach, the parties' choice of law would generally be upheld.

95. 'If an arbitration agreement has an international connection, the law agreed upon by the parties shall apply to the agreement' (in-house translation).

CHAPTER 10

Two Parties – Several Contracts: A Four-Step Method for Assessing Arbitral Tribunals' Jurisdiction Post *Belgor*

Daniel Waerme & Louise Wendleby

A contractual relationship between two commercial parties often consists of multiple contracts that are more or less connected to each other. In such a multi-contract context, it may happen that only one contract (typically the main contract) contains an arbitration clause while the other contracts (successive or ancillary) either lack arbitration clauses or contain other or somewhat different dispute resolution mechanisms. If a dispute arises regarding any of the other contracts, the arbitral tribunal will often have to determine whether such dispute is covered by the arbitration clause in the main contract.

In this chapter, a proposed four-step method for determining arbitral tribunals' jurisdiction in multi-contract contexts under Swedish law is presented. By presenting this method, the ambition is to answer the question of under what circumstances an arbitration clause in one contract may cover disputes regarding another contract between the same parties.

The proposed method addresses the implications from the most recent Swedish precedent on assessing arbitral tribunals' jurisdiction under Swedish law – *Belgorkhimprom v. Koca* (NJA 2019 p. 171, *Belgor*).

§10.01 INTRODUCTION

A contractual relationship between two commercial parties often consists of multiple contracts that are more or less connected to each other. In such a multi-contract context, it may happen that only one contract (typically the main contract) contains an arbitration clause, while the other contracts (successive or ancillary) either lack arbitration clauses or contain other or somewhat different dispute resolution mechanisms.[1] If a dispute arises regarding any of the other contracts, the arbitral tribunal will often have to determine whether such dispute is covered by the arbitration clause in the main contract. In many cases, this will boil down to an interpretation of the scope of the arbitration clause.

Internationally, the trend is to interpret the scope of an arbitration agreement extensively.[2] This seems to be true both when interpreting arbitration agreements in general and when interpreting arbitration clauses specifically in multi-contract contexts, although in the latter case, an assessment shall be made of the particular circumstances in the case at hand.[3]

Overall, Swedish law corresponds to the international trend. However, there are some national aspects that both arbitral tribunals and counsel in arbitral proceedings seated in Sweden would do well to keep in mind.

In this chapter, a method is presented for determining arbitral tribunals' jurisdiction in multi-contract contexts under Swedish law.[4] By presenting this method, the ambition is to answer the question under what circumstances an arbitration clause in one contract may cover disputes regarding another contract between the same parties. The proposed method consists of four steps and may be summarized by asking the following four questions:

(1) Does the claimant, in support of its claim under the other contract, assert grounds that are covered by a legal relationship (Sw. *rättsförhållande*) within the scope of the arbitration clause in the main contract and, if so, is this sufficient in order for the arbitral tribunal to have jurisdiction?
(2) Have the parties agreed (explicitly or implicitly) that the arbitration clause in the main contract shall also cover claims under the other contract?
(3) Do the main contract and the other contract constitute the same legal relationship, with the result that the arbitration clause in the main contract also covers claims under the other contract?
(4) Is the connection (Sw. *anknytning*) between the two contracts so strong – and the circumstances so special – that it motivates the extension of the arbitration clause in the main contract to claims under the other contract?

If the answer to any of these questions is yes, the arbitral tribunal will – with the reservations presented in this chapter – have jurisdiction. There are thus essentially

1. This chapter deals only with multi-contract situations involving *two* parties. Multi-contract arbitrations involving more than two parties give rise to somewhat different as well as additional jurisdictional problems, which will not be addressed here. Cf. Philippe Leboulanger, *Multi-Contract Arbitration*, 13(4), J. Int'l Arb. 43 (1996), at 44 et seq.
2. Gary B. Born, *International Commercial Arbitration*, 2nd ed. (The Hague: Kluwer Law International, 2014), 1326-1338 and Nigel Blackaby, Constantine Partasides, et al., *Redfern and Hunter on International Arbitration*, 6th ed. (Oxford: Oxford University Press, 2015), para. 2.66.
3. *See, e.g.*, Born, *supra* n. 2, at 1345 and 1370-1379.
4. The method is an adaptation of the method presented in Louise Wendleby, *Är skiljenämnden behörig? En probleminriktad studie av skiljenämndens tolkning av skiljeklausuler i sammanhängande avtal* in *Affärsjuridiska uppsatser* (Uppsala: Iustus Förlag, 2020).

four different ways for an arbitral tribunal to determine, on the basis of an arbitration clause in one contract, that it has jurisdiction over a claim under another related contract.

The chapter has the following structure. Section 10.2 introduces some general starting points for the interpretation of the scope of an arbitration agreement under Swedish law. The brief introduction is followed by the presentation of the proposed method in section 10.3. Thereafter, section 10.4 addresses the Swedish Supreme Court's judgment in the case *Belgor* (NJA 2019 p. 171) and its implications for the proposed method. The case is important since it represents the latest of relatively few cases where the Supreme Court has determined whether an arbitration clause in one contract also covers claims under a related contract.[5] Finally, section 10.5 offers some concluding remarks.

§10.02 STARTING POINTS

[A] Points of Departure for the Interpretation of the Scope of an Arbitration Agreement

Under Swedish law, the scope of an arbitration agreement shall be determined according to general principles for contract interpretation.[6] The objective is thus, at least in principle, to ascertain the parties' true intentions in concluding the arbitration agreement. However, arbitration clauses are often the last clauses to be considered – if at all – in the final hour of contract negotiations,[7] and in most cases, the language of the clause is in a standardized form.[8] For these reasons, it is often impossible in practice to determine the parties' true intentions. The wording and other surrounding circumstances may in such situations also allow for different interpretations of the arbitration clause.[9]

5. Apart from in *Belgor*, the Supreme Court has addressed the scope of an arbitration clause in a multi-contract (or multi-agreement) context in the following cases: *G. & L Beijer i Stockholm v. J. Ringborg* (NJA 1910 p. 227), *J. Larsson v. AB nya järnhandeln i Sandviken* (NJA 1919 p. 497), *C.A. Lundborg v. K.I. Gustafsson* (NJA 1922 p. 37), *Hans Schröder AB v. Svenska AB Lebam* (NJA 1964 p. 2), *Byggnadsaktiebolaget Lennart Hultenberger v. Bostadsrättsföreningen Hytten* (NJA 1972 p. 458), *B. Arvold v. Kjellbergs Successors AB* (NJA 1973 p. 620) and *DHL Express (Sweden) AB v. The Bankruptcy Estate of Nordic Logistic Service Oy* (NJA 2005 Note N 8).
6. In *Belgor*, this was explicitly stated by the Supreme Court for the first time (para. 13). However, even before *Belgor* there was a general consensus among legal scholars and practitioners that general principles for contract interpretation should be used when interpreting arbitration agreements, *see, e.g.*, Åke Hassler and Thorsten Cars, *Skiljeförfarande*, 2nd ed. (Stockholm: Norstedt, 1989), 140, Lars Heuman, *Arbitration Law of Sweden: Practice and Procedure* (New York: Juris Publishing, 2003), 54, Kaj Hobér, *International Commercial Arbitration in Sweden* (Oxford: Oxford University Press, 2011), para. 3.31, and Stefan Lindskog, *Skiljeförfarande* (JUNO version 2C, last updated 7 September 2018), section I:0-3.2.1.
7. For this reason, they are often referred to as 'midnight clauses', *see* Blackaby and Partasides, *supra* n. 2, at para. 2.04.
8. *Belgor* para. 13.
9. *Belgor* para. 13.

To handle this common situation, the Supreme Court has established certain 'starting points'[10] when determining the scope of an arbitration clause. It should be stressed that the starting points are to be used only where the intentions of the parties are unclear and where it is not possible to arrive at one single interpretation of the arbitration clause based on its wording and/or other surrounding circumstances.

First, it is assumed that an arbitration clause covers the *entire* legal relationship that has been constituted by the main contract.[11] If parties wish to limit the application of the arbitration clause to certain issues or to a part of the legal relationship, this must be clearly indicated – for example, in the arbitration clause. A standardized arbitration clause will be deemed to cover the entire legal relationship. Importantly, the term 'legal relationship' shall in itself also be interpreted broadly (*see* further section 10.03[D]).

Second, it is assumed that an arbitration agreement fulfils a rational function and regulates the interests of the parties in a reasonable manner. As a result, when interpreting the scope of an arbitration clause, it is assumed that parties in a commercial contractual relationship intended to have all disputes within that relationship resolved swiftly and in one coherent proceeding before an arbitral tribunal appointed by them.[12]

[B] The Identified Legal Relationship Requirement

A common denominator for the two starting points described above is that they allow for and speak in favour of an extensive interpretation of the scope of an arbitration clause. In essence, the point of departure is that arbitration clauses cover the entire legal relationship established through the main contract and shall provide for a coherent arbitral proceeding for all disputes within that relationship. So far, Swedish law is fully in line with the international trend outlined in section 1.

However, the parties' contractual freedom is ultimately limited by the requirements under section 1 of the Swedish Arbitration Act (the SAA or the Act). The requirements are mandatory and applicable in all cases where the seat of the arbitration is in Sweden, even if the dispute has an international connection, unless the parties have specifically agreed that the law of another country shall apply to the arbitration agreement.[13]

When interpreting arbitration clauses in multi-contract contexts, it is primarily one requirement under section 1 of the Act that becomes relevant. This stipulates that

10. *Tupperware* (NJA 2010 p. 734) at para. 7, and *Belgor* in the headline and paras 13 and 19-20.
11. *Tupperware* (NJA 2010 p. 734) para. 7.
12. *Belgor* para. 13.
13. *See* section 48 of the SAA which deals with the applicable law of the arbitration agreement. Unless the parties have agreed on the law to be applied to the arbitration agreement, the arbitration agreement shall be governed by the law of the country where the arbitration had or shall have its seat. As it is fairly uncommon that the parties have made a specific choice of law with respect to the arbitration agreement, usually Swedish law will be applied to the arbitration agreement if the place of arbitration is in Sweden. *See* further Hobér, *supra* n. 6, at paras 2.201-2.207.

an arbitration agreement may only relate to future disputes pertaining to a *legal relationship specified in the agreement.*

This requirement, often referred to as the *identification requirement* in the legal literature,[14] has the effect that two parties cannot simply agree to refer all their future disputes or a specific type of future disputes to arbitration. In order for the arbitration agreement to be valid, the legal relationship(s) that the future disputes pertain to must be specified or *identified* in the arbitration agreement.[15] It is usually not possible to describe a future legal relationship with sufficient clarity and concretization for the identification requirement to be met. Therefore, the legal relationship identified in the arbitration agreement normally already has to exist or be constituted at the time when the arbitration agreement is concluded.[16]

A similar requirement is found in Article II.1 of the 1958 New York Convention, which stipulates that parties can only agree to submit to arbitration future disputes in respect of 'a defined legal relationship'. Many nations have also adopted similar requirements in their national arbitration laws.[17]

However, while the identification requirement seems to be of little practical importance in most countries,[18] in Sweden, the Supreme Court has put weight on the requirement, emphasizing that in order for a dispute to be covered by an arbitration agreement, it must in fact be based on the legal relationship identified in the arbitration agreement. A dispute based on another, separate legal relationship that has arisen out of or in connection with the legal relationship identified in the arbitration clause is thus, as a main rule, *not* covered by the arbitration agreement.[19] This is the case even if an interpretation of the arbitration agreement according to general principles for contract interpretation would allow for a wider scope. In order for a dispute to fall within the scope of an arbitration agreement, it must thus, with a few exceptions,[20] *be based on the actual legal relationship(s) identified therein.*

---

14. Stefan Lindskog, *Skiljeförfarande*, 3rd ed. (Stockholm: Norstedts Juridik, 2020), section I:0-6.2.2.
15. Government Bill, 1998/99:35, 210. *See also* Heuman, *supra* n. 6, at 28 et seq., and Lindskog, *supra* n. 14, at sections I:1-5.1.2 and 5.1.3. It is worth noting that the preparatory works of the SAA do not include any explicit discussion regarding the purpose of the identification requirement. However, in the legal literature, the purpose of the identification requirement has often been described as to enable the parties to comprehend the effects of an arbitration agreement they have entered into and to know which types of contractual dispute it refers to. Further, it has been argued that the identification requirement ensures that a party's right to initiate court proceedings is not more restricted than the party actually anticipated at the time of the conclusion of the arbitration agreement. *See, e.g.*, Lars Heuman, *Översyn av lagen om skiljeförfarande*, JT 2014/15, at 455 et seq. and Lindskog, *supra* n. 14 at section I:1-5.1.2. Cf. also *The Set-Off Agreement* (NJA 2017 p. 226), at para. 13.
16. *See, e.g.*, Heuman, *supra* n. 6, at 29, Fredrik Andersson et al., *Arbitration in Sweden* (Stockholm: Swedish Arbitration Association, 2011), 50. *See also* Lindskog, *supra* n. 14, at sections I:1-5.1.3 who argues that there can be no exceptions to the rule that the legal relationship must already exist when the arbitration agreement is concluded.
17. *See* Born, *supra* n. 2, at 240 and 294.
18. *See* Born, *supra* n. 2, at 294 et seq. with references. Cf. Blackaby and Partasides, *supra* n. 2, at paras 2.25-2.28.
19. *Tupperware* (NJA 2010 p. 734) and *The Set-Off Agreement* (NJA 2017 p. 226).
20. *See* further section 10.03[E] *infra*.

It should be mentioned already at this stage that it has been suggested in the legal literature that the Supreme Court in *Belgor* relaxed or limited the importance of the identification requirement.[21] However, in the authors' opinion, the Supreme Court actually reiterated the importance of the identification requirement in *Belgor*, although the requirement was never really put to the test in the case. The authors will return to this in section 10.04[B] *infra*.

[C] Problematic and Unproblematic Cases Involving the Identification Requirement

In most cases, the identification requirement will not pose any obstacles for the arbitral tribunal when determining its jurisdiction. The model clause for the Arbitration Institute of the Stockholm Chamber of Commerce (the SCC) may be used as an example. It states that:

> Any dispute, controversy or claim arising out of or in connection with *this contract*, or the breach, termination or invalidity thereof, shall be finally settled by arbitration in accordance with the Arbitration Rules of the [SCC] (emphasis added).

In this model arbitration clause, 'this contract' is identified as a legal relationship. Assuming that a dispute arises in the future that is based on the said contract, the identification requirement will be met and, consequently, the arbitral tribunal will have jurisdiction over that dispute.

In other cases, such as in situations involving multiple contracts between two parties, it may however be more problematic to determine whether a dispute is based on a legal relationship that has been identified in an arbitration clause or if the dispute is based on a separate legal relationship. For example, the parties could – following the conclusion of the main contract with the arbitration clause – enter into a subsequent, related contract that lacks an arbitration clause. If a dispute arises based on the subsequent contract, an assessment has to be made as to whether the main contract and the subsequent contract constitute the same legal relationship or if they constitute two separate legal relationships. Only in the first case will the identification requirement be met. This type of problematic situation will be discussed further in section 10.03[D] *infra*.

Lastly, it should be stressed that in practice the identification requirement only becomes an issue if the parties, once a dispute between them has arisen, *disagree* on whether the dispute is covered by the arbitration agreement. If the parties agree that a

21. Anders Reldén and Jacob Frank, *The Belgor Case: Towards an Extensive Interpretation and Application of Arbitration Agreements* in *Stockholm Arbitration Yearbook 2020* (The Netherlands: Kluwer Law International, 2020), 82, and Finn Madsen, *The Swedish 'Belgor' Case and the Scope and Applicability of Arbitral Agreements* in *Tvistlösning inom affärsrätten* (Stockholm: Norstedts Juridik, 2020), 94. Cf. also Lars Heuman, *Har det skett en omsvängning eller omläggning av praxis från restriktiv till extensiv tolkning av skiljeavtalet?*, SvJT 2019, who suggests that the Supreme Court in *Belgor* may have limited the importance of the identification requirement (at 545-547 and 549), while at the same time maintaining that it is not possible to draw any certain conclusions from the case (at 549 et seq.).

dispute that has already arisen shall be resolved in arbitration, or if one party initiates arbitration and the other party does not object to arbitration, then it does not matter whether the dispute is based on another legal relationship than the legal relationship(s) that may have been identified in a previous arbitration agreement. The parties' new agreement will then replace or modify any previous arbitration agreement concluded by the parties.[22]

§10.03 THE PROPOSED METHOD

[A] Introduction

With the general starting points outlined above in mind, this section goes through the different steps which may be included in an arbitral tribunal's assessment of its jurisdiction in a scenario where: (1) the claimant has initiated arbitration on the basis of an arbitration clause in one contract between the claimant and the respondent, (2) the claimant's claim in whole or in part is based on another contract between the parties, and (3) the respondent has, in its statement of defence, made a jurisdictional objection of some sort (i.e., requested that the dispute in whole or in part shall be dismissed due to the arbitral tribunal's lack of jurisdiction).

The proposed method for the arbitral tribunal's assessment of its jurisdiction in this scenario consists of four steps. Depending on the circumstances and the grounds invoked by the parties, it may be relevant for the arbitral tribunal to assess only some of the steps, while in other cases, it may be necessary for the arbitral tribunal to assess all four steps.

For the sake of clarity, the terms 'Contract 1' and 'Contract 2' are used throughout the section to denote the two contracts concluded between the parties. *Contract 1* constitutes the parties' main or original contract containing the arbitration clause which the claimant considers applicable to the dispute, whereas *Contract 2* constitutes the other contract between the parties on which the claimant (partially or wholly) bases his claim. In the scenario discussed in this section, Contract 2 will typically be an ancillary or subsequent contract to Contract 1.

[B] Step 1 – The Doctrine of Assertion

> Does the claimant, in support of its claim under the other contract (Contract 2), assert grounds that are covered by a legal relationship within the scope of the arbitration clause in the main contract (Contract 1) and, if so, is this sufficient in order for the arbitral tribunal to have jurisdiction?

22. Such new agreement may be concluded in writing, orally or through subsequent conduct, *see* Heuman, *supra* n. 6, at 41 et seq., Hobér, *supra* n. 6, at para. 5.11, Anders Reldén and Ola Nilsson, *The Arbitration Agreement* in *International Arbitration in Sweden: A Practitioner's Guide* (The Netherlands: Kluwer Law International, 2013), paras 16-18, and Lindskog, *supra* n. 14, at sections I:0-2.1.2 and IV:0-3.1.2.

When deciding on its jurisdiction, an arbitral tribunal shall always, as the first step, assess if the so-called *doctrine of assertion* (Sw. *påståendedoktrinen*) is applicable. The Supreme Court has stated that it is an 'established principle' under Swedish law that an arbitral tribunal, when deciding on its own jurisdiction, *shall* apply the doctrine of assertion.[23]

The essence of the doctrine has been described by the Supreme Court in the following manner:

> the arbitral tribunal shall not, when deciding on its jurisdiction, assess the existence of the legal facts[24] that a claimant asserts are covered by a legal relationship within the scope of an arbitration agreement. When deciding on its jurisdiction, the arbitral tribunal shall assume the existence of these legal facts.[25]

This statement implies that, as long as the claimant bases its claim on legal facts covered by a legal relationship within the scope of the arbitration agreement, the doctrine of assertion will be applicable.[26] The claimant will then not have to prove the existence of the legal facts invoked in order for the arbitral tribunal to have jurisdiction. The arbitral tribunal shall grant itself jurisdiction solely on what the claimant has asserted.[27] Only later when the arbitral tribunal tries the case on the merits will it determine the existence of the alleged legal facts. Should the arbitral tribunal then find that the claimant has not been able to prove the existence of the legal facts invoked, it shall *reject* the claimant's claim on the merits in the final award (not dismiss it for lack of jurisdiction).

Even though the doctrine of assertion shall be applied as a main rule, there are three important exceptions[28] to the doctrine.[29] Hence, the arbitral tribunal shall not apply the doctrine if:

23. *Petrobart* (NJA 2008 p. 406) at 416 and *The Set-Off Agreement* (NJA 2017 p. 226) at para. 10.
24. Legal facts, in Swedish *'rättsfakta'*, have a special meaning under Swedish law. They are the factual circumstances which, according to a rule of law, have *direct* bearing on the relief sought. This can be compared to so-called evidentiary facts, in Swedish *'bevisfakta'*, which are facts of *indirect* relevance for the relief sought in the sense that they can either prove or disprove the existence of the legal facts.
25. *Petrobart* (NJA 2008 p. 406 at 416). Cf. *The Set-Off Agreement* (NJA 2017 p. 226) at para. 10.
26. *The Set-Off Agreement* (NJA 2017 p. 226) at para. 10.
27. *See, e.g.*, Hobér, *supra* n. 6, at paras 3.33-3.35 and Lindskog, *supra* n. 14, at section I:0-6.1.2.
28. *See, e.g.*, Heuman, *Undantag från påståendedoktrinen och regeln att en skiljeklausul endast avser avtalet*, JT 2017/18, who uses the term 'exceptions'. However, the 'exceptions' could just as well be formulated as 'prerequisites' for the application of the doctrine. Thus, instead of listing the cases where the doctrine is *not* applicable, one could list the conditions for it to *be* applicable, i.e., that: (1) the claimant's claim is *not* manifestly unfounded, (2) it is *undisputed* whether a valid arbitration agreement exists between the parties, and (3) it is *undisputed* whether the arbitration agreement covers the legal relationship on which the claim is based. Cf. Lindskog, *supra* n. 14, at section I:0-6.1.2 note 783. In the authors' opinion, it is however of little practical relevance which terminology is used – the assessment will give the same conclusion no matter if the circumstances are treated as exceptions to, or prerequisites for, the application of the doctrine.
29. These exceptions are generally recognized in court practice and legal literature. It can be noted, however, that there have been discussions in the legal literature regarding further potential exceptions to the doctrine, *see* Heuman, *supra* n. 28, at 900-901.

(1) the claimant's claim is *manifestly unfounded*;[30]
(2) it is disputed whether there is a *valid* arbitration agreement between the parties;[31] or
(3) it is disputed whether the arbitration agreement *covers* the legal relationship on which the claim is based.[32]

In the type of multi-contract situations discussed here, it is usually the third exception to the doctrine of assertion that will become relevant. It follows from this exception that, if the parties disagree on the scope of the arbitration agreement (i.e., whether the arbitration clause in Contract 1 covers a claim based on Contract 2), the disagreement cannot be resolved by application of the doctrine of assertion. Instead, the arbitral tribunal has to move on to the next step in the jurisdictional assessment. The reasoning for this is that a party who has not entered into an arbitration agreement that covers the disputed legal relationship should not be forced into arbitral proceedings as a result of applying the doctrine.[33]

However, if the respondent does not object to the dispute being covered by the arbitration clause but only makes an objection regarding the merits of the claim (e.g., that Contact 2 does not have any bearing at all on the matter of the dispute and therefore the arbitral tribunal shall not have jurisdiction), then the doctrine of assertion becomes applicable.[34] When deciding on its jurisdiction, the arbitral tribunal shall then assume that the legal facts invoked by the claimant exist (e.g., that Contract 2 *does* have a bearing on the dispute) and should, consequently, decide that it has jurisdiction. Whether the claimant actually was right in its assertions will not be settled until the arbitral tribunal determines the case on the merits.

---

30. Cf., e.g., *Nykvarn* (NJA 1982 p. 738) at 741, *PLS Rambøll Management A/S v. A.S.* (NJA 2005 p. 586) at 593 and Svea Court of Appeal, judgment on 5 October 2012 in Case No. T 8399-11. *See* further Lars Welamson, *Recension av Per Olof Bolding. Skiljedom. Studier i rättspraxis beträffande svensk skiljedoms giltighet och verkställbarhet*, SvJT 1964, 278 et seq., Heuman, *supra* n. 6, at 57, and Patrik Schöldström, *Påståendedoktrinen och skiljeförfarande*, JT 2008/09, 140. For another view, *see* Lindskog, *supra* n. 14, at section I:0-6.1.2 note 782 as well as Lindskog's addendum to NJA 2008 p. 406 at 422 et seq.
31. *Petrobart* (NJA 2008 p. 406) at 416 et seq. and *The Set-Off Agreement* (NJA 2017 p. 226) at para. 10.
32. *Petrobart* (NJA 2008 p. 406) at 417 and *The Set-Off Agreement* (NJA 2017 p. 226) at para. 10. Cf. also the Svea Court of Appeal's judgment in *Belgor* at 178.
33. Cf. *Petrobart* (NJA 2008 p. 406) at 416 et seq.
34. It may be added that an arbitral tribunal is normally not obligated to try its jurisdiction *sua ponte* (independent of any motion by the parties), *see Elf Neftegaz v. Interneft OOO et al.* (NJA 2016 p. 264) at para. 11, Heuman, *supra* n. 6, at 340 and Lindskog, *supra* n. 14, at sections I:2-4.3.1 and 4.3.2, as well as sections IV:0-3.1.1 and 3.1.2. This means that if the respondent does not make any jurisdictional objection *at all*, the arbitral tribunal will usually have jurisdiction to try the dispute without having to make any closer jurisdictional assessment. In such a scenario, there is of course no need for the arbitral tribunal to apply the doctrine of assertion (or go through any of the other steps in the method).

[C] Step 2 – Agreement to Extend the Scope of the Arbitration Clause

> Have the parties agreed (explicitly or implicitly) that the arbitration clause in the main contract (Contract 1) shall also cover claims under the other contract (Contract 2)?

As pointed out in the previous section, the arbitral tribunal shall as a main rule apply the doctrine of assertion when determining whether it has jurisdiction over a particular claim. However, if the parties disagree on the scope of the arbitration clause, the doctrine of assertion cannot be applied by the arbitral tribunal to resolve the jurisdictional matter. Instead, the arbitral tribunal will then have to do a proper determination of whether the arbitration clause in Contract 1 covers claims based on Contract 2.

A claimant may invoke several grounds for its assertion that the claim under Contract 2 is covered by the arbitration clause in Contract 1. Step 2 becomes applicable if the claimant as one ground alleges that the parties have *agreed* to extend the scope of the arbitration clause to cover both Contract 1 and Contract 2. If the claimant can prove the existence of such an agreement, then the arbitral tribunal will have jurisdiction.[35] No closer examination is then required of whether Contract 1 and Contract 2 constitute the same legal relationship or two separate legal relationships; the parties' agreement will be sufficient for the arbitral tribunal to have jurisdiction.

The identification requirement will however still affect *the time* at which an agreement can be made to extend the scope of an arbitration clause in one contract to another contract. As mentioned in section 10.02[B], in order for a legal relationship to be identified with the sufficient level of precision in an arbitration agreement, the legal relationship *must have arisen at the time when the arbitration agreement is concluded*. This means that an agreement to extend the scope of an arbitration clause to a new contract may not, as a main rule, be entered into until that new contract has been formed.

There are no restrictions under Swedish law regarding the form of an arbitration agreement. Thus, an arbitration agreement – as well as an extension of an already-concluded arbitration agreement – may be concluded in writing, orally, by conduct or even through inaction/passivity under certain circumstances.[36] It is however usually difficult for the party that has the burden of proof to show that an arbitration agreement has been concluded without a written agreement of some sort.[37] Swedish courts have also often required a fairly high degree of certainty to establish the existence of an

35. In Sweden, the burden of proof for the existence of an agreement (including an arbitration agreement) is normally on the party relying upon the agreement, *see, e.g.*, Lars Heuman, *Bevisbörda och beviskrav i tvistemål* (Stockholm: Norstedts Juridik, 2005), 225 et seq. Cf. also the Svea Court of Appeal's judgment in *Belgor* and Svea Court of Appeal, judgment on 21 February 2007 in Case No. T 6762-05.
36. Government Bill 1998/99:35, 66 et seq. and Hobér, *supra* n. 6 at paras 3.05-3.30.
37. Cf. Hobér, *supra* n. 6, at paras 3.05 and 3.12.

arbitration agreement.[38] The safest way for parties to ensure that an arbitration clause in one contract will also cover disputes under another related contract would therefore be either to add a written addendum to the arbitration clause or to add a specific reference to the arbitration clause in the other contract.[39] The mere fact that one contract contains general references to the other contract would probably not be enough *in itself* to conclude that the parties have intended to incorporate the arbitration clause into both contracts. However, the question has not been clearly addressed in case law.[40]

It has been suggested by some commentators that, in certain multi-contract situations, the arbitration clause in one contract may be implied into future subcontracts once these are concluded. The authors of this chapter agree with this view. A typical situation could be that the parties are in a long-term business relationship regulated by a framework agreement containing an arbitration clause. Should the parties enter into ancillary contracts in the manner set out in the framework agreement, the parties may – by their conduct – be deemed to have agreed to extend the arbitration clause in the framework agreement to these ancillary contracts.[41]

As a final note, it should be stressed that an arbitral tribunal may only determine whether the parties have entered into an agreement to extend the scope of an arbitration clause if this has been *invoked as a legal fact* by either party.[42] If not, the arbitral tribunal must skip this step of the method. The reason for this is that under Swedish law an arbitral tribunal (or court for that matter) may only base an award on legal facts invoked by the parties. If the arbitral tribunal has determined its jurisdiction based on a legal fact that has not been invoked by the right party, the arbitral tribunal will have exceeded its mandate and the award may be set aside.[43]

[D] Step 3 – The Same Legal Relationship

> Do the main contract (Contract 1) and the other contract (Contract 2) constitute the same legal relationship with the result that the arbitration clause in the main contract also covers claims under the other contract?

---

38. *See, e.g.*, RH 1980:48, RH 1982:102, RH 1995:123, and Svea Court of Appeal, judgment on 25 May 2004 in Case No. 1361-02 (p. 18). Cf. also *R. Urhelyi v. Arbetsmarknadens försäkringsaktiebolag* (NJA 1974 p. 573) at 583 where the Supreme Court concluded that a dispute resolution mechanism in a contract between an employee and an insurance company did not 'unequivocally express' that the parties' intention was to resolve disputes in arbitration. *See further* Lindskog, *supra* n. 14, at section I:0-2.1.3. However, as has been pointed out by, e.g., Hobér, *supra* n. 6, at para. 3.04, there is no *express* support in case law that stricter requirements shall apply with respect to entering into arbitration agreements compared to other agreements.
39. Cf. Lars Heuman, *Bevisbördan för skiljeavtal och tolkningsresonemang som grund för skiljebundenhet*, JT 2011/12, 672.
40. However, cf. the Svea Court of Appeal's judgment in *Belgor*, at 179. Cf. also *DHL Express (Sweden) AB v. The Bankruptcy Estate of Nordic Logistic Service Oy* (NJA 2005 Note N 8).
41. *See* Lindskog, *supra* n. 14, at section I:1-5.1.3, notes 1055, 1060 and 1062, and section I:1-5.2.3 *in fine* with note 1097, and Andersson et al., *supra* n. 16, at 44 and 52 et seq.
42. For the meaning of legal fact under Swedish law, *see supra* n. 24.
43. Government Bill 1998/99:35, 143 et seq. and Hobér, *supra* n. 6, at para. 8.79.

In addition to arguing that the parties have reached an agreement to extend the scope of the arbitration clause to cover both Contract 1 and Contract 2, the claimant may also argue that the claim under Contract 2 is covered by the arbitration clause in Contract 1 since the two contracts constitute the *same legal relationship*. The arbitral tribunal will have jurisdiction under this step if it finds that the legal facts invoked by the claimant in support of its claim under Contract 2 are based on the legal relationship identified in the arbitration clause in Contract 1.[44]

As long as Contract 1 and Contract 2 constitute the same legal relationship, the identification requirement will not pose any obstacle for the arbitral tribunal. This is because, in such a case, the claimant's claim under Contract 2 will be based on the legal relationship identified in the arbitration clause in Contract 1, and thus the identification requirement will be met. As discussed in section 10.02[A], it shall as a starting point be assumed that an arbitration clause covers the entire legal relationship identified therein. For the application of this starting point, it does not matter whether the legal relationship is regulated in only one or several contractual documents.

The term 'legal relationship' shall be given a wide interpretation. The Supreme Court has clarified that it covers not only those rights and obligations that have been set forth in the original contract but also subsequent legal facts that alter the content of the contract.[45] Conversely, if the subsequent legal facts (e.g., a new contract) do not only alter or modify the content of the original contract but also establish a completely new and independent relationship between the parties, a separate legal relationship will be formed.

In order to demonstrate the above, commentators have often used as an example the situation where two parties first enter into a main agreement which includes an arbitration clause and then, after some time, enter into a side agreement or an additional agreement. The arbitration clause will cover the side or additional agreement if the agreements have such a strong connection that the subsequent agreement can be said to form a part of the main agreement.[46] However, the subsequent agreement will be deemed a separate legal relationship if it constitutes a complete alteration of, or a significant addition to, the main agreement.[47]

In practice, the assessment will have to consider all the factual circumstances in the case at hand. However, the following circumstances might be of particular interest for the arbitral tribunal.

First, the arbitral tribunal may assess the content of the two contracts to see if there is a substantive connection between them and if they overlap in any way. The

44. This is of course assuming that the scope of the arbitration clause has not been limited to only certain disputes and/or only part of the legal relationship, *see* section 10.02[A] *supra*.
45. *The Set-Off Agreement* (NJA 2017 p. 226) para. 14, and *Belgor* para. 15. In *Belgor*, the Supreme Court has confirmed this further by stating that an arbitration agreement, as well as the term 'legal relationship', shall be interpreted generously. *See* further section 10.04[A] *infra*.
46. *See* Lindskog, *supra* n. 14, section I:1-5.2.3 with notes, and Thorsten Cars, *Lag (1999:116) om skiljeförfarande, 1 §* (Lexino, last updated 2 November 2020), section 2.2.5. Cf. also similar statements in RH 2012:13 and Svea Court of Appeal, judgment on 10 May 2012 in Case No. T 10329-10.
47. *See* Heuman, *supra* n. 39, at 672.

closer the substantive connection and the greater the overlap, the more likely it is that the two contracts shall be deemed to constitute the same legal relationship.[48]

Second, the arbitral tribunal may look to particular phrases in the contracts that may give a clue as to how the parties themselves view the second contract in relation to the first contract. For example, if it is stated in the second contract that it forms an integral part of the first contract, this indicates that the contracts should be viewed as parts of the same legal relationship.[49] This might also be the case if the first contract contains references to the second contract and vice versa.[50] Conversely, if the first contract explicitly states that a certain question will be regulated in a separate contract, and the parties thereafter go on to regulate this question separately, then it is likely that the separate contract will be regarded as a new legal relationship in relation to the first contract.[51]

Third, the arbitral tribunal may pay attention to whether both contracts contain arbitration clauses or if the contracts contain different dispute resolution mechanisms. If both contracts contain an identical arbitration clause, this may – together with other surrounding circumstances – be seen as an indication that the contracts are part of the same legal relationship.[52] However, if the contracts contain different arbitration clauses, or different dispute resolution mechanisms altogether, this might be a reason for treating the contracts as two separate legal relationships.[53]

However, one circumstance that seems to be of little or no relevance when determining whether two contracts constitute the same legal relationship is the standard wording of the arbitration clause. For example, an arbitration clause stating that 'Any disputes arising out of or in connection with *this contract* shall be finally settled by arbitration' will not be limited to disputes under that particular contract but will also cover disputes under other related contracts as long as these contracts constitute the same legal relationship (emphasis added).[54] If the parties wish to limit

48. *See, e.g.*, AD 2012 No. 20 (an employment contract and an oral agreement concluded prior to the employment contract constituted the same legal relationship), *DHL Express (Sweden) AB v. The Bankruptcy Estate of Nordic Logistic Service Oy* (NJA 2005 Note N 8) (a cooperation agreement and some standard agreements did not constitute the same legal relationship), and Svea Court of Appeal, decision on 21 November 1995 in Case No. Ö 3156-95 (a cooperation agreement and some purchase agreements did not constitute the same legal relationship). *See also* Heuman, *supra* n. 39, at 674 et seq. and Andersson et al., *supra* n. 16, at 51.
49. Lars Heuman, *Specialprocess*, 8th ed. (Stockholm: Norstedts Juridik, 2020), 30.
50. Cf. *C.A. Lundborg v. K.I. Gustafsson* (NJA 1922 p. 37), Svea Court of Appeal, judgment on 10 May 2012 in Case No. T 10329-10 and Göta Court of Appeal, judgment on 8 December 2015 in Case No. T 573-15.
51. Svea Court of Appeal, judgment on 21 February 2007 in Case No. T 6762-05 and Court of Appeal for Western Sweden, decision on 29 October 1996 in Case No. Ö 1789-95. Cf. also Heuman, *supra* n. 39, at 673-674.
52. Cf. Svea Court of Appeal, judgment on 21 February 2007 in Case No. T 6762-05.
53. Cf. Heuman, *supra* n. 6, at 71, and Lindskog, *supra* n. 14, at section I:1-5.2.3, note 1091. However, cf. also *Belgor* and Court of Appeal for Western Sweden, decision on 10 February 2005 in Case No. Ö 4204-04.
54. This follows indirectly from, e.g., *J. Larsson v. AB nya järnhandeln i Sandviken* (NJA 1919 p. 497) where the Supreme Court found that an arbitration clause concerning 'disputes regarding the correct interpretation of *the contract*' also covered a dispute under a side agreement to that contract (emphasis added).

the scope of an arbitration clause to only a part of the legal relationship, this has to be clearly indicated in the language of the arbitration clause and/or by other surrounding circumstances.[55]

The above list of circumstances is in no way conclusive but may provide some assistance to an arbitral tribunal when making an assessment under this step.

[E] Step 4 – The Doctrine of Connection

> Is the connection between the two contracts so strong – and the circumstances so special – that it motivates the extension of the arbitration clause in the main contract (Contract 1) to claims under the other contract (Contract 2)?

If the arbitral tribunal concludes under step 3 that Contract 1 and Contract 2 constitute two separate legal relationships, the arbitral tribunal will, as a main rule, *not* have jurisdiction over a claim under Contract 2.[56]

However, in a number of judgments, the Supreme Court has developed a doctrine that is often referred to in the legal literature as the *doctrine of connection* (Sw. *anknytningsdoktrinen*). According to this doctrine, an arbitral tribunal may have jurisdiction over a dispute as long as there is a sufficiently strong connection between the legal relationship identified in the arbitration clause and the legal facts invoked by the claimant, even if these legal facts are based on another legal relationship.

There are several cases where the Supreme Court seems to have applied some variation of the doctrine of connection.[57] The case that perhaps first and foremost has come to represent the doctrine is *The Road Material* (NJA 2007 p. 745). In this case, the Supreme Court found that a ground outside a contractual relationship fell within the scope of the applicable arbitration clause since there was a 'direct connection' between the non-contractual ground and the other two grounds relied upon. Due to this direct connection, and the fact that the two other grounds were based on the legal relationship identified in the arbitration clause, the arbitration agreement was extended to the third ground – despite the fact that it was based on another legal relationship.[58] In a later judgment, *Ystad Harbour* (NJA 2008 p. 120), the Supreme Court also found that a non-contractual ground was covered by an arbitration clause by emphasizing that the claimant's request, which was based on the non-contractual ground, had such a 'strong

55. Cf. section 10.02[A] *supra*.
56. *See* section 10.02[A] *supra*.
57. *Hans Schröder AB v. Svenska AB Lebam* (NJA 1964 p. 2), *Byggnadsaktiebolaget Lennart Hultenberger v. Bostadsrättsföreningen Hytten* (NJA 1972 p. 458), AD 1976 No. 54, *The Road Material* (NJA 2007 p. 745) and *Ystad Harbour* (NJA 2008 p. 120). Cf. also *B. Arvold v. Kjellbergs Successors AB* (NJA 1973 p. 620). In addition, it shall be mentioned that there are a number of older court cases where the courts could have chosen to apply the doctrine of connection but chose not to do so, *see, e.g.*, *Nykvarn* (NJA 1982 p. 738), RH 1985:90, RH 1991:16 and RH 1994:45.
58. *The Road Material* (NJA 2007 p. 475) at 478.

connection' to the contractual relationship that it was covered by the arbitration clause.[59]

In two later judgments, *Tupperware* (NJA 2010 p. 734) and *The Set-Off Agreement* (NJA 2017 p. 226), the Supreme Court has however (partly in obiter dicta) narrowed the scope of the doctrine of connection. Both cases dealt with the question of whether an arbitration clause could be interpreted as covering a ground based on another legal relationship than the legal relationship identified in the arbitration clause, and in both cases the question was answered in the negative.[60] According to the Supreme Court in these cases, the fact that there is a connection between the legal relationship which is covered by an arbitration clause and another disputed legal relationship may only 'in some exceptional cases and under very special circumstances' extend the arbitration clause to cover also the disputed legal relationship.[61]

The Supreme Court has given no further guidance as to when the circumstances would be special enough to motivate an application of the doctrine of connection. What seems clear though is that the doctrine may be applied in situations similar to that in *The Road Material*,[62] i.e., where one party invokes several contractual grounds that are covered by the arbitration clause as well as one additional ground (which either may be non-contractual or based on a separate contractual legal relationship) and where there is a direct or strong connection between the contractual grounds and the additional ground.

In light of this development, the authors' view is that the doctrine of connection may today only be applied if:

(1) there is a sufficiently strong connection between the legal facts invoked by the claimant and the legal relationship identified in the arbitration clause; *and*
(2) it is an exceptional situation where the circumstances are very special, which, for example, may be the case where one party invokes several contractual grounds that are covered by the arbitration clause as well as one additional ground which is based on factual circumstances with a strong or direct connection to the agreement containing the arbitration clause.[63]

As a result of the second point mentioned immediately above, an arbitral tribunal will only rather seldom find that it has jurisdiction under this step 4. The fact that there is a strong or direct connection between Contract 1 and Contract 2 is thus not in itself enough for the arbitration clause to extend to both contracts if it has been concluded under step 3 that Contract 1 and Contract 2 constitute two separate legal relationships.

59. *Ystad Harbour* (NJA 2008 p. 120) at 216.
60. *Tupperware* (NJA 2010 p. 734) actually concerned the scope of a prorogation clause, but the Supreme Court in obiter dicta broadened the scope of all its conclusions to apply also to arbitration clauses.
61. *Tupperware* (NJA 2010 p. 734) at para. 14 and *The Set-Off Agreement* (NJA 2017 p. 226) at para. 12.
62. Cf. *Tupperware* (NJA 2010 p. 734) at para. 14.
63. *See* further Wendleby, *supra* n. 4, at 154-156.

Some commentators have suggested that the Supreme Court in *Belgor* has yet again widened the scope of the doctrine of connection by limiting the importance of the identification requirement. In their opinion, *Belgor* has likely overruled *Tupperware* and *The Set-Off Agreement*.[64] As will be developed in the next section, the authors of this chapter do not believe that it is possible to draw such far-reaching conclusions from *Belgor*. Until the Supreme Court clearly addresses the issue, one should assume that earlier precedents are still valid.

§10.04 THE BELGOR CASE AND ITS IMPLICATIONS FOR THE PROPOSED METHOD

[A] The *Belgor* Case

[1] Background

Belgor has already caused quite a stir among legal scholars and practitioners in the field of Swedish arbitration.[65] In the part of the judgment that has received the most attention, the Supreme Court made some new statements regarding the proper determination of the scope of an arbitration clause. Following a brief introduction to the case and the Supreme Court's judgment, this section addresses *Belgor*'s possible implications on the method presented above.

The *Belgor* case has its origin in a dispute between the Turkish company Koca and the Belarussian company Belgor. In 2010, Belgor, as general contractor, initiated a tender for a project relating to the construction of a mining and processing plant in Turkmenistan. Koca won the tender. In January 2011, the parties entered into a construction contract relating *inter alia* to the construction and sinking of two mining shafts on the construction site (the Construction Contract).[66] The Construction Contract contained an arbitration clause referring all disputes 'emerged because of or in connection with' the Construction Contract to arbitration under the SCC Rules.

In November 2012, the Construction Contract was terminated by Belgor on the ground that Koca had produced defective works. Koca contested the termination, and in February 2013, Koca filed a request for arbitration with the SCC, requesting payment for, e.g., works performed under the Construction Contract as well as for some

64. *See* Madsen, *supra* n. 21, at 87 et seq. and 94, and Reldén and Frank, *supra* n. 21, at 74-77 and 82.

65. *See* Christer Danielsson, *Swedish Arbitration-Related Case Law 2017–2019* in *Stockholm Arbitration Yearbook 2019* (The Netherlands: Wolters Kluwer International, 2019), Patrik Schöldström, *Har Belgor förändrat prövningen av en skiljenämnds behörighet och handläggningsfel?*, JT 2019/20, 222, Heuman, *supra* n. 21 and 49, Reldén and Frank, *supra* n. 21, Madsen, *supra* n. 21, and Lindskog, *supra* n. 14, at sections 0:2.2.8 with note 76, I:1-5.1.2 note 1049, I:1-5.2.4 note 1100, I:2-5.2.3, V:34-4.1.1 note 3677, and IX:54-5.2.3 with note 4915.

66. There was also a third party to the Construction Contract responsible for technical support and supervision of the construction project.

additional works that Koca had performed on the basis of five separate contracts (the Additional Works).[67]

In its final award in April 2015, the arbitral tribunal ruled in favour of Koca (albeit not in full) and ordered Belgor to compensate Koca for *inter alia* the Additional Works. Belgor challenged the award and requested that it be set aside in its entirety or at least in part. As one of the grounds for setting aside the award, Belgor maintained that the arbitral tribunal lacked jurisdiction to resolve claims in respect of the Additional Works as they fell outside the scope of the arbitration clause in the Construction Contract.

[2] The Arbitral Tribunal's Assessment of Its Jurisdiction

The arbitral tribunal found that it had jurisdiction to try the claims concerning the Additional Works based on the following reasoning.[68]

According to the arbitral tribunal, the Construction Contract did not *directly* refer to the Additional Works, and thus disputes concerning the Additional Works could not be said to 'arise out of the [Construction] Contract'. The arbitral tribunal noted however that it was undisputed between the parties that: (1) the Additional Works were ordered after the termination of the Construction Contract and while the parties were trying to agree on the terms and conditions for the termination of the Construction Contract,[69] and (2) the Additional Works related to the construction and sinking of the shafts (i.e., to the subject matter of the Construction Contract). For these reasons, and particularly in light of the fact that the Additional Works were ordered and performed while the parties were negotiating the consequences of the termination of the Construction Contract, the arbitral tribunal found that the Additional Works had been performed 'in connection with' the Construction Contract, 'indeed within the contractual framework between the Parties established by the [Construction] Contract'. Claims concerning the Additional Works therefore fell within the scope of the arbitration clause in the Construction Contract.

The arbitral tribunal then went on to note that the Additional Works had been performed under five separate contracts, which did not have arbitration clauses, but which stipulated that the parties had a right (but not an obligation) to refer disputes to the Economic Court in Minsk. However, according to the arbitral tribunal, the prorogation clauses in the separate contracts did not displace the arbitration clause in the Construction Contract. Thus, even though the Construction Contract and the Additional Works contained different dispute resolution mechanisms, the arbitration

67. In the award (para. 84), the arbitral tribunal stated that it was 'undisputed' between the parties that the Additional Works had been performed under five separate contracts. This was however later on denied by Koca in the challenge proceeding where Koca claimed that the parties had never entered into any written, separate agreements in respect of the Additional Works, *see* Koca's submission to the Supreme Court on 21 September 2018, file appendix 37, para. 2.1.5.
68. *See* paras 79-86 of the award.
69. This was also later on denied by Koca in the challenge proceeding where Koca argued that the Additional Works had been ordered and carried out *before* the termination of the Construction Contract. *See* Koca's submission to the Supreme Court on 21 September 2018, file appendix 37, para. 2.1.6.

clause in the Construction Contract could still be applied to disputes concerning the Additional Works.

[3] The Case Before the Supreme Court

Belgor's challenge action was examined by the Svea Court of Appeal as the first instance. Contrary to the arbitral tribunal, the court made the assessment that the arbitration clause in the Construction Contract did not cover the dispute concerning the Additional Works.[70] For this reason, the award was partially set aside.[71]

Koca appealed to the Supreme Court and argued, in summary, that the Additional Works were covered by the arbitration clause in the Construction Contract since: (1) it followed explicitly from the Construction Contract that the arbitration clause also encompassed the Additional Works (cf. step 2 of our proposed method), and (2) the Construction Contract and the Additional Works constituted the same legal relationship (cf. step 3 of the proposed method).[72] Koca did not claim that the doctrine of connection was to be applied (cf. step 4 of the proposed method).[73]

Belgor contested Koca's claims and maintained that the arbitration clause in the Construction Contract did not cover the Additional Works since: (1) the parties had not agreed to extend the scope of the arbitration clause in the Construction Contract to cover disputes concerning the Additional Works, and (2) the Additional Works had been performed under five separate contracts which constituted other legal relationships than the legal relationship identified in the arbitration clause in the Construction Contract.[74]

The Supreme Court ruled in Koca's favour and concluded that there was no reason to reject the arbitral tribunal's determination of its jurisdiction. The Supreme Court reached this conclusion by first laying out some legal starting points (Sw. *rättsliga utgångspunkter*) and then applying these to the current case.[75] As regards the legal starting points, the following should be mentioned in particular:

- The Supreme Court started off by referring to the identification requirement under section 1 of the SAA, reiterating that an arbitration agreement has to pertain to a specific legal relationship.
- The Supreme Court thereafter went on to establish the second 'starting point' described under section 2.1 *in fine*, regarding the interpretation of the scope of an arbitration clause, stressing that in a case where it is not possible to

70. For a brief summary of the Svea Court of Appeal's judgment in English, *see* Reldén and Frank, *supra* n. 21, at 69 et seq.
71. The Svea Court of Appeal also found that there was one additional ground for partially setting aside the award, which, however, will not be discussed here.
72. Koca's submission to the Supreme Court on 15 June 2018, file appendix 30, section 3, and Koca's submission to the Supreme Court on 21 September 2018, file appendix 37, section 2. *See also* legal opinion by legal scholar Marcus Radetzki submitted by Koca, file appendix 39.
73. Cf. Koca's submission to the Supreme Court on 21 September 2018, file appendix 37, section 2.
74. Belgor's submission to the Supreme Court on 21 September 2018, file appendix 40, section C.1.
75. *Belgor* paras 12-24.

determine a common intention of the parties – and where neither the wording nor other surrounding circumstances give any guidance – it shall be assumed that the parties have intended to resolve all their disputes swiftly and in one cohesive proceeding before an arbitral tribunal appointed by them.

- With reference to the underlying principles of the 1958 New York Convention, the Supreme Court then emphasized that arbitration agreements and the term 'legal relationship' shall be given a generous interpretation. The Supreme Court also reiterated that a legal relationship may cover more than those rights and obligations that have been set forth in an original agreement.
- Lastly, the Supreme Court stated that when a court in a challenge proceeding is tasked with reviewing the arbitral tribunal's decision on its jurisdiction, the court shall pay regard to the fact that the arbitral tribunal typically is best positioned to determine the issue of its own jurisdiction. A starting point should therefore be that the arbitral tribunal's interpretation and evaluation of evidence is correct.

Based on these starting points, the Supreme Court stated that, in a challenge proceeding, it shall be reviewed whether the party contesting jurisdiction has shown that the arbitral tribunal has made an incorrect assessment of the scope of the arbitration agreement. The Supreme Court then went on to summarize the arbitral tribunal's assessment of whether the Additional Works were covered by the arbitration clause in the Construction Contract. The Supreme Court concluded that what Belgor had asserted in the challenge proceeding did not constitute grounds for rejecting the arbitral tribunal's assessment.

[B] Discussion

In *Belgor*, the Supreme Court upheld the arbitral tribunal's determination of its own jurisdiction. Some commentators have argued that the Supreme Court by doing so widened the scope of the doctrine of connection and relaxed the identification requirement. They seem to arrive at this conclusion by putting emphasis on the fact that the arbitral tribunal in its decision stated that the Additional Works could not be said to 'arise out of' the Construction Contract but had been performed 'in connection with' the Construction Contract. According to these commentators, this shows that the arbitral tribunal determined that the Construction Contract and the Additional Works constituted separate legal relationships (cf. step 3 of our proposed method) but nevertheless gave itself jurisdiction by applying the doctrine of connection (cf. step 4 of the proposed method).[76]

In the authors' opinion, it is difficult to draw such far-reaching conclusions from the arbitral tribunal's decision. The arbitral tribunal did not refer to any Swedish case

76. Cf., e.g., Reldén and Frank, *supra* n. 21, at 68 et seq. It is worth mentioning that this was also one of Belgor's arguments in the proceeding before the Supreme Court, *see, e.g.*, Belgor's submission on 16 March 2018, file appendix 24, section A.1, and Belgor's submission on 28 September 2018, file appendix 47, para. 6.

law and it is unclear which meaning the arbitral tribunal gave to the words 'in connection with'. Having concluded that the Additional Works had been performed in connection with the Construction Contract, the arbitral tribunal added however that this indeed meant that the Additional Works had been performed 'within the contractual framework' established by the Construction Contract. This additional finding by the arbitral tribunal does not suggest that the arbitral tribunal concluded that the Additional Works constituted separate legal relationships. Rather, it implies that the arbitral tribunal considered the Additional Works to constitute part of the legal relationship that had been established by the Construction Contract.

Interestingly, it is only the addition ('within the contractual framework ... ') which is quoted by the Supreme Court in *Belgor*. In fact, this is the *only* direct quote from the arbitral tribunal's decision included in this part of the Supreme Court's judgment.[77] This indicates that the Supreme Court attached great significance to this particular finding by the arbitral tribunal. Thus, it is possible that the Supreme Court interpreted the arbitral tribunal's assessment on the basis that the arbitral tribunal *did not* apply the doctrine of connection, but rather confirmed its jurisdiction by concluding that the arbitration clause in the Construction Contract covered the Additional Works as they constituted part of the same legal relationship.[78]

This conclusion does not seem unreasonable.[79] A construction contract and additional contracts to such a contract may very well be regarded as the same legal relationship depending on the circumstances in the given case.[80] The arbitration clause in the Construction Contract would then be assumed to cover the entire legal relationship, i.e., also the additional contracts.[81]

If the Supreme Court intended to limit the importance of the identification requirement in *Belgor*, one may also ask why the Supreme Court did not make its intention clear. After all, it had plenty of opportunities to do so. For example, the Supreme Court began the legal starting points by referring to the identification requirement, reiterating that an arbitration agreement has to pertain to a specific legal relationship, but made no statement indicating a limitation of the requirement. Also, in the legal starting points, the Supreme Court discussed the scope of the term 'legal relationship', emphasizing *inter alia* that it should be given a generous interpretation

77. *Belgor* para. 22.
78. On this note it should be stressed that not even Koca argued before the Supreme Court that the arbitral tribunal had applied the doctrine of connection or that the doctrine should be applied in the case, *see* section 10.04[A][3].
79. It should be mentioned that the Svea Court of Appeal found that the Construction Contract and the Additional Works did not constitute the same legal relationship, *see Belgor* at 179 et seq. However, the Court of Appeal arrived at this conclusion partly due to the fact that it could not make a more comprehensive assessment of the connection between the Construction Contract and the Additional Works since Koca had not presented any further investigation into this question. In the proceeding before the Supreme Court, Koca did however make a thorough presentation of the connection between said contracts, *see, e.g.*, Belgor's submission on 15 June 2018, file appendix 30, sections 3.2-3.4. It is possible that if this investigation had been presented already to the Svea Court of Appeal, the court would have deemed that the Construction Contract and the Additional Works constituted the same legal relationship.
80. Cf., e.g., Lindskog, *supra* n. 14, at I:1-5.2.3 note 1095, and Heuman, *supra* n. 39 at 675.
81. *See* section 10.02[A] *supra*.

and not only cover those rights and obligations that have been set forth in an original agreement. These statements would seem irrelevant if the court actually sought to limit the importance of the identification requirement, but on the other hand they make perfect sense if the court intended to confirm that the term 'legal relationship' shall be given a wide application.

Further, it has been suggested that the Supreme Court, by making references to *Tupperware* and *The Set-Off Agreement* in *Belgor* without stating explicitly that it follows from these cases that the doctrine of connection may only be applied under exceptional circumstances, has made it clear that these statements should no longer be guiding and authoritative when determining the scope of an arbitration agreement.[82] However, in the authors' view, one should be careful about interpreting the Supreme Court's silence on a particular matter as if previous precedents regarding that matter have been overruled. One shall have in mind that there might have been reasons why the Supreme Court did not consider it relevant to delve into previous precedents regarding the application of the doctrine of connection in *Belgor*. For instance, if the Supreme Court interpreted the arbitral tribunal's assessment on the basis that it did not apply the doctrine of connection (and if the Supreme Court had no intention to apply the doctrine itself), there would be no need for the Supreme Court to discuss it further under its discussion of the legal starting points.

However, there are several important new points that may be deduced from *Belgor*.

First, in *Belgor*, the Supreme Court has made it even clearer that arbitration agreements (to the extent allowed for by the identification requirement) shall be interpreted extensively. *Belgor* shows that the assumptions that: (1) an arbitration clause covers the entire legal relationship identified therein and (2) parties intend to have all their disputes settled in one single forum are very strong.[83] Thus, even in a situation where the underlying contracts contain completely different (albeit voluntary) dispute resolution mechanisms than the main contract containing an arbitration clause, this is not enough in itself to determine a clear intention of the parties to limit the scope of the arbitration clause to only cover the main contract. [84] Thus, the parties need to be even more explicit if they wish to limit the scope of an arbitration clause to only some disputes or to only a part of the legal relationship.

Second, and perhaps most importantly, *Belgor* has introduced the idea that the 'starting point' for a court's determination of an arbitral tribunal's jurisdiction shall be that the arbitral tribunal's interpretation and evaluation of evidence is correct since it is typically the arbitral tribunal that is best positioned to determine the issue of its own jurisdiction. Therefore, the party contesting jurisdiction will have to show that the arbitral tribunal's assessment of the scope of the arbitration agreement was incorrect.

82. Cf. Reldén and Frank, *supra* n. 21, at 76, and Heuman, *supra* n. 21, at 546-547.
83. Cf. section 10.02[A].
84. This has been criticized by, e.g., Schöldström, *supra* n. 65, at 245 and 247.

The Supreme Court's statements in this respect are in line with previous statements made in cases regarding the enforcement of foreign arbitral awards.[85] Through *Belgor*, these statements now seem to have been extended from enforcement proceedings to challenge proceedings as well. Moreover, the Supreme Court's statements correspond well to the more general notion that the emphasis of the administration of justice should be on the first instance (which, if the notion were to be applied to arbitral proceedings, would be the arbitral tribunal) and that the task of the appellate courts above all shall be to review decisions and correct any errors.[86]

It is difficult to predict the practical implications of the Supreme Court's statements. In the authors' view, *Belgor* is likely to result in a higher threshold for setting aside arbitral awards in the future on the ground that the arbitral tribunal has exceeded its jurisdiction.[87] It should however be stressed that, at least in the authors' opinion, *Belgor* does not mean that a court in a challenge proceeding should completely refrain from making its own interpretation and evaluation of evidence. The court still has to ascertain that the arbitral tribunal's conclusions are based on an acceptable analysis.[88]

However, the core of the principle established through *Belgor* seems to be that when the question of the arbitral tribunal's jurisdiction boils down to an *interpretation and evaluation of evidence*, the starting point for the court's assessment is that the tribunal's interpretation and evaluation of evidence is correct. In practice, questions regarding an arbitral tribunal's jurisdiction often come down to interpretation and evaluation of evidence. This is, for example, the case when the question for the arbitral tribunal is whether the parties have agreed that claims under a second contract shall be covered by the arbitration clause in the first contract (cf. step 2 *supra*) or whether several contracts constitute the same legal relationship or, in the terms used by the arbitral tribunal in *Belgor*, fall within the same contractual framework (cf. step 3 *supra*).

§10.05 CONCLUDING REMARKS

This chapter has explored the different steps that may be included in an arbitral tribunal's assessment of its own jurisdiction in multi-contract situations where the parties have entered into one contract containing an arbitration clause, but where the dispute relates – in whole or in part – to another contract between the parties. It is important to stress that a mere assertion from the claimant that a claim under one contract is covered by the arbitration clause in another contract is not enough for the arbitral tribunal to have jurisdiction if this fact is disputed by the respondent (cf. step

85. *Fruits et Légumes* (NJA 2003 p. 379) and *Carbaque International Aktiebolag v. Fabryka Wyrobó* (NJA 2009 Note N 9).
86. Cf. Government Bill 2004/05:131, 82, Government Bill 1998/99:35, 170 et seq., and Government Bill 2017/18:257, 17.
87. However, it is worth mentioning that even before *Belgor* it was very rare that courts set aside arbitral awards, *see, e.g.*, Swedish Governmental Official Report SOU 2015:37, 79-81.
88. This also seems to be the way that the appellate courts at least so far have interpreted *Belgor*, *see, e.g.*, Svea Court of Appeal, judgment on 19 December 2019 in Case No. 7929-17 and Svea Court of Appeal, judgment on 10 June 2019 in Case No. T 4155-19.

1 of the proposed method). Likewise, a strong connection between the contracts is not enough in itself for the arbitral tribunal to have jurisdiction over disputes based on both of them (cf. step 4 of the proposed method). Usually, in order for the arbitral tribunal to have jurisdiction, the parties must have agreed to extend the scope of the arbitration clause to both contracts (cf. step 2 of the proposed method) or the two contracts must constitute the same legal relationship (cf. step 3 of the proposed method).

In the authors' opinion, through *Belgor*, the Supreme Court has provided arbitral tribunals with two important starting points when assessing its jurisdiction, namely that: (1) an arbitration clause generally covers the entire legal relationship identified therein and (2) parties generally intend to have all their disputes settled in one single forum. The Supreme Court has also provided Swedish courts with an important starting point when examining arbitral tribunal's assessment of its jurisdiction, namely that the starting point for the court is that the arbitral tribunal's interpretation and evaluation of evidence is correct since it is typically the arbitral tribunal that is best positioned to determine the issue of its own jurisdiction.

In the authors' opinion, it is too early to conclude that the Supreme Court in *Belgor* has also limited the importance of the identification requirement and rejected previous precedents regarding the scope of the application of the doctrine of connection. Although the authors personally would have favoured such a development, it is not clear that it was actually achieved through *Belgor*.

CHAPTER 11

Protecting Confidentiality Within Arbitral Proceedings

Anna-Maria Tamminen & Viktor Saavola

Disputes being resolved in international commercial arbitration often involve confidential information such as trade secrets, know-how, price calculations, sources of supply or intellectual property rights. Situations where a party would need to present material containing confidential information that requires increased protection may arise in various situations during an arbitration. The desire to protect confidentiality is on the other hand in conflict with general principles of due process, including the equal treatment of the parties and the right to be heard. The chapter presents established measures with the function of protecting confidential information within arbitral proceedings, and which have been employed by practitioners in practice and reported in preceding legal literature. Further, the chapter provides an analysis of how these measures conform to the general due process requirements of international arbitration, especially under the Swedish Arbitration Act. In addition to presenting measures which the parties may agree to and the arbitral tribunal may assist in implementing, e.g., by issuing confidentiality orders, the chapter argues that arbitrators have the authority to restrict access to sensitive material presented in the arbitration upon the application of one the parties. While no precedent confirming such authority under Swedish law yet exists, it is the view of the authors that a tribunal may restrict access within the limits set by Article 24 of the Swedish Arbitration Act when a legitimate need to protect confidential information exists and the procedural rights of the other party are upheld as far as possible.

§11.01 INTRODUCTION

One of the decisive reasons for parties to choose arbitration over domestic court proceedings is the confidentiality provided by arbitral proceedings.[1] Disputes being resolved in international commercial arbitration often revolve around or, at least, involve confidential information such as trade secrets, know-how, price calculations, sources of supply or intellectual property rights. The significance of confidential information and the measures available to protect it are both increasingly prevalent in arbitration, due to not only the growing amount of regulation to which companies are subject but also the number of possible participants involved in an arbitration. Arbitrators, parties, and their counsel are expected to be aware of the ever-increasing mandatory rules and regulation regarding, e.g., competition law, intellectual property law, data protection, market abuse and business secrets in general, while simultaneously being conscious of the amount of participants an arbitration may include, especially in a cross-border arbitration: the parties themselves (especially in a multi-party arbitration), their counsel (with possible additional local counsel), the members of the tribunal as well as possible third parties, such as third-party funders, insurers, translators, and so on.

Situations where one party would need to present material containing confidential information that requires increased protection may arise on various occasions during an arbitration. For example, such confidentiality concerns may arise when a party presents evidence in support of its case, as either claimant or respondent, or when a party is requested to produce such documentation during document production. Parties to arbitration have legitimate expectations to be able to effectively present their cases without compromising sensitive information.

The desire to protect confidentiality is on the other hand in conflict with general principles of due process, including the equal treatment of the parties and the right to be heard. These principles require that the opposing party has an opportunity to review and comment on all material submitted to the arbitral tribunal. In Sweden, these principles are expressly enshrined in section 24 of the Swedish Arbitration Act (SAA), which is based on the Model Law on International Commercial Arbitration drafted by the United Nations Commission On International Trade Law (UNCITRAL Model Law).

The present chapter intends to present measures which arbitrators can use to protect confidential information within arbitration proceedings, and provide an analysis of how these measures conform to the general due process requirements of international arbitration, especially in proceedings governed by the SAA.

However, the above-mentioned rules and guidelines do not provide practical guidance on how to protect the confidentiality of sensitive material in a way that would

1. *See, e.g.*, *Queen Mary, University of London, 2018 International Arbitration Survey: The Evolution of International Arbitration*, 7: '87 % of respondents believe that confidentiality in international commercial arbitration is of importance. Most respondents think that confidentiality should be an opt-out, rather than an opt-in, feature.' Further, according to the survey, 'confidentiality and privacy' was selected among one of the most valuable characteristics of arbitration, and more so emphasized by in-house counsel respondents (pp. 7 and 27).

not infringe the right to access the case file. This chapter seeks to present alternatives for protective measures to which parties can agree or which an arbitral tribunal could order to ensure due protection of confidential information while respecting the other party's right to access the case file. In doing so, the chapter also examines the interplay between the parties' right to confidentiality and due process during arbitral proceedings. The focus is on a Swedish perspective on these issues, coupled with some comparative research.

§11.02 DUE PROCESS IN INTERNATIONAL ARBITRATION UNDER THE SAA

Due process is an essential principle and a fundamental requirement in both court litigation and arbitration. In brief, and in somewhat simplified terms, due process requires that judges and arbitrators act fairly and impartially and treat the parties equally during the proceedings. Due process entails *inter alia* that a judge or an arbitrator must ensure that each party has a reasonable opportunity to present its case, i.e., a right to be heard. Equal treatment is a prerequisite for the parties to properly exercise their right to be heard.[2]

The right to be heard and to present one's case include the right to access to file. A party must have the right to access and review the material, which has been submitted to the arbitral tribunal and which relates to the dispute at hand, as well as the right to present its arguments and comments on the submitted material.

Section 24 of the SAA sets out the requirements of due process for an arbitration conducted under Swedish law:

> The arbitrators shall afford the parties, to the extent necessary, an opportunity to present their respective cases in writing or orally. Where a party so requests, and provided that the parties have not otherwise agreed, an oral hearing shall be held prior to the determination of an issue referred to the arbitrators for resolution.
>
> A party shall be given an opportunity to review all documents and all other materials pertaining to the dispute which are supplied to the arbitrators by the opposing party or another person.[3]

According to section 24(1) SAA, no party should be judged without a fair hearing in which each party is given the opportunity to respond to the evidence presented against them (*the contradictory principle*). Section 24(2) sets out the requirement for access to file (*the principle of communication, kommunikationsprincipen*), whereby a party must be granted access to any material pertaining to the dispute that is presented to the arbitral tribunal, including all documentation submitted by the opposing party, reports submitted by experts and any other material. The principle of communication is built upon the premise of two opposing parties presenting evidence to an impartial

2. *See, e.g.*, Fouchard Gaillard Goldman on International Commercial Arbitration 1999, 609.
3. Unofficial translation of the Swedish Code of Statutes (SFS) 1999:116 as updated per SFS 2018:1954, provided by the Arbitration Institute of the Stockholm Chamber of Commerce (SCC), available at https://sccinstitute.com/about-the-scc/digital-library/legislation/.

arbitral tribunal. Together, sections 24(1) and (2) of the SAA set out the framework for ensuring a due process for the parties.[4] If a party is not provided with the opportunity to access and comment upon, e.g., a submission or written evidence, both rules are breached. In such a situation, the injured party can have the arbitral award set aside according to section 34(1) of the SAA if the error most likely affected the outcome of the case.

Per the *travaux préparatoires* of the SAA, the right to access to file is limited to the material that is submitted to the arbitral tribunal from an 'external source' and does not apply to material that is directly related to the arbitral tribunal's own deliberations, e.g., internal legal memoranda and enquiries as well as drafts of the award.[5] Further, issues caused by an absent respondent in this regard were also considered during the drafting of the SAA. All submissions and other written procedural material submitted to the arbitral tribunal should be provided to the respondent to ensure that a passive respondent would not be given the opportunity of challenging the award.[6] However, the Arbitration Commission tasked with preparing a proposal for a new arbitration act proposed a rule whereby materials presented at the hearing would not need to be transmitted to the absent party.[7] The Swedish government opted for a less absolute approach and rejected the proposed provision. Instead, the legislator found that the arbitrators should decide to what extent the communication principle should be applied and whether material presented at the hearing would need to be transmitted to an absent party. According to the SAA, this should be decided on a case-by-case basis.[8]

While the general rule is that any documents submitted to the arbitral tribunal in relation to the dispute should be sent to the opposing party as well, it is worth noting that the *travaux préparatoires* for the SAA also mention that section 24(2) of the SAA does not require that 'bulky material' is sent to the opposing party. Instead, it is sufficient that such bulky material is only made available for review at, e.g., the

4. *See, e.g.*, Lars Heuman, *Arbitration Law of Sweden: Practice and Procedure* (Juris Publishing, 2003), 385-386; Bengt Lindell, *Alternativ tvistlösning: särskilt medling och skiljeförfarande* (Iustus Förlag, 2000), 188.
5. Statens offentliga utredningar (SOU) 1994:81, 279; Government Proposition ('Gov. Prop') 1998/99:35, 225. *See also* Lindell, *supra* n. 4, 188. Lindell notes that limiting the right to access to file to material submitted by external parties to the arbitral tribunals is closely related to the principle that arbitral tribunals are allowed to take generally known facts into consideration. In borderline cases, where there is doubt whether a fact is generally known or not, the arbitral tribunal should give the parties an opportunity to be heard before rendering an award based on the application of said generally known fact. Lindell also opines that the same applies when the arbitral tribunal is considering whether to apply a different legal rule than what the parties themselves have invoked in the proceedings. The underlying rationale is that both parties would otherwise be subject to an unexpected judgment in the matter. *See also* Heuman, *supra* n. 4, 386-387, who notes that if the arbitrators are contemplating an extensive interpretation of a certain claim after the end of the final hearing, and nothing in the opposing party's pleadings or in the evidence produced by the parties supports that interpretation, the opposing party's right to defend his case speaks strongly in favour of rejecting the extensive interpretation.
6. Heuman, *supra* n. 4, 388.
7. SOU 1994:81 p. 28.
8. Gov. Prop. 1998/99:35, 111-112.

presiding arbitrator's office. Per the wording of the *travaux préparatoires*, the requirement set by section 24(2) of the SAA is that the submitted documents must be shared with the opposing party.[9]

The aforementioned exceptions to a party's right to review all of the material submitted to the arbitral tribunal are the only exceptions addressed in the *travaux préparatoires*. The *travaux préparatoires* of the SAA do not address whether the right to review material could be limited in order to safeguard confidential material. Thus, the clear starting point is the principal rule that the parties must have the same access to all the material as the arbitral tribunal whether it includes confidential information or not.

§11.03 CONFIDENTIALITY IN INTERNATIONAL COMMERCIAL ARBITRATION

[A] Does Arbitration Entail an Implied Obligation of Confidentiality?

Although the focus of this chapter is on the treatment and protection of confidential information when it cannot be disclosed to the opposing party in an arbitration (i.e., absolute confidentiality),[10] a brief overview of the opinions expressed regarding the confidentiality of arbitration in general is due in order to give context to the role confidentiality plays in arbitration.

In legal literature and case law, discussion regarding 'confidentiality' in the context of arbitration typically refers to whether the parties are obligated not to disclose information concerning the arbitration to third parties or the public, i.e., relative confidentiality.[11] Obligations of confidentiality extend to prohibiting third parties from attending arbitral hearings as well as to prohibiting the parties to an arbitration from disclosing any of the material related to the arbitration proceedings to third parties.[12] The confidentiality of the proceedings serves to centralize the parties' dispute in a

9. Gov. Prop. 1998/99:35, 225; SOU 1994:81, 279: 'Det förutsätts att alla handlingar skall komma motparten till del, om de kan sägas röra själva tvisten. Som regel bör handlingen sändas till motparten. Något krav på delgivning finns inte. Bestämmelsen utesluter inte att skrymmande material hålls tillgängligt t.ex. hos skiljenämndens ordförande och att parten i fråga underrättas om detta.'
10. This article adopts the terminology used by, e.g., Yves Derains, *Evidence and Confidentiality*, Special Supplement 2009 Confidentiality in Arbitration, ICC International Court of Arbitration Bulletin, paras 14-16, where *relative confidentiality* refers to any information regarding the arbitration being confidential in relation to any third parties not involved in the arbitration, and *absolute confidentiality* refers to such confidential information that the party holding the information does not wish to disclose to the opposing party in the arbitration.
11. *See, e.g.*, Gary Born, *International Commercial Arbitration* (3rd ed., Wolters Kluwer, 2021), Chapter 20.
12. Material related to the arbitral proceedings includes, e.g., hearing transcripts, written pleadings and submissions, submitted evidence, materials produced during disclosure and the arbitral awards and orders.

single forum and to provide an objective, efficient and commercially sensible resolution of the dispute, while limiting disclosure of the parties' confidences to the press, public, competitors and others.[13]

Despite the general characterization of arbitration as an alternative form of dispute resolution perfectly suitable for discreet resolution of commercial disputes, it would be misleading to state that the confidential character of arbitration is a given. Rather, the confidentiality of arbitration remains debated, and this also applies to confidentiality within arbitration vis-à-vis the parties.[14] Until the mid-1990s, there was little discussion about confidentiality in arbitration as the widespread assumption was that arbitration was a private process excluding any third parties, and that any documents related to the arbitration were protected from disclosure to third parties not involved in the arbitration. Judgments rendered by Australian and Swedish courts changed the situation as the courts rejected the idea of a general duty or obligation of confidentiality in relation to the parties to an arbitration. In the cases *Esso Australia Resources Ltd v. Plowman* ('*Esso v. Plowman*') and *Bulgarian Foreign Trade Bank Ltd v. A.I. Trade Finance Inc.* ('*Bulbank*'), the courts found that there is no authority providing for an implied obligation of confidentiality in arbitration, which would prevent the parties from disclosing information regarding the arbitration to third parties. The courts held that an express intent of the parties is required to keep the arbitration confidential. The cases drew attention to confidentiality in arbitration and prompted discussion regarding the issue. This discussion drove some states to legislative action by leading them to incorporate confidentiality obligations into their laws or to enact laws providing for a default rule of non-confidentiality. Some states left the matter to be developed by case law. Certain arbitral institutions also addressed the issue by including provisions regarding confidentiality in their rules. As a result, the laws of international arbitration vary significantly when it comes to the existence and extent of an obligation of confidentiality. The most common feature is arguably that legislation leaves a lot of room for party autonomy.[15]

In contrast to the *Esso v. Plowman* and *Bulbank* cases, there are English and Singaporean cases, which are often cited in support of the existence of an implied obligation of confidentiality in arbitration. In the latter cases, the courts expressed the general sentiment that an implied obligation of confidentiality that binds the parties arises from the very nature of arbitration, while certain acceptable circumstances allow for disclosure of material or information relevant to an arbitral proceeding. Such acceptable circumstances include, most notably, the consent of the parties, which can be either express or implied, and the reasonable necessity of disclosure for the

13. Born, *supra* n. 11, Chapter 20.01. In contrast, the 'privacy' of the proceedings refers only to the arbitral hearings being closed off for any third parties and to the public.
14. Domitille Baizeau & Juliette Richard, *Addressing the Issue of Confidentiality in Arbitration Proceedings: How Is This Done in Practice?*, 43 ASA Special Series, 53, 53 (2016).
15. The Committee on International Commercial Arbitration of the International Law Association, *Report on The Hague Conference: Confidentiality in International Commercial Arbitration* (2010), pp. 4-5 and 8-9.

protection of legitimate interests of a party.[16] The Singaporean High Court considered in *Myanma Yaung Chi Oo Co. Ltd v. Win Nu and Another [2003] SGHC* the argument for an implied obligation of confidentiality to be more convincing with emphasis on the parties' expectations. According to the court, parties who opt for arbitration rather than litigation are likely to be aware of, and be influenced by, the fact that the former are private hearings while the latter are open hearings. Therefore, the court concluded that rather than to say that there is nothing inherently confidential in the arbitration process, it is more in keeping with the parties' expectations to take the position that the proceedings are confidential, and that disclosures can only be made under acceptable circumstances, e.g., with the consent of both parties or when disclosure is necessary to protect legitimate interests of a party.

Given the above, there are clearly differing opinions on whether arbitration entails an implied obligation of confidentiality. Therefore, the exact scope of confidentiality in arbitration and the enforceability of any confidentiality orders[17] is uncertain. Considering the diverse international backgrounds that come into play in international arbitration, the proceedings are often subject to several different legal regimes, which at times include conflicting legal principles. As a consequence, the participants do not always share the same expectations as to whether a confidentiality obligation exists, what is covered by such a confidentiality obligation and how it may be enforced.[18]

There is no uniform definition or concept of confidentiality in international arbitration. There is no international convention that defines the concept of confidential information, or generally provides for a right, or an obligation to confidentiality. There is also no uniform definition of the term 'confidentiality' or 'business secrets'.[19] In the absence of an internationally binding definition, the content and scope of a right to confidentiality could be found in the parties' agreement, including the arbitration clause,[20] arbitration rules, statutory national law, or case law.[21] However, no uniform

16. *Dolling-Baker v. Merrett & Another* [1990] 1 WLR 1205, *Hassneh Insurance Co of Israel v. Mew* [1993] 2 LI LR 243, *Ali Shipping Corporation v. Shipyard Trogir* [1999] 1 WLR 314, and *Myanma Yaung Chi Oo Co. Ltd v. Win Win Nu and Another* [2003] SGHC 124.
17. That is, orders issued by the arbitral tribunal regarding the treatment of confidential information outside of and/or within the arbitral proceedings.
18. *See, e.g.*, Baizeau & Richard, *supra* n. 14; Born, *supra* n. 11, Chapter 20.02.
19. Lukas F. Wyss, *How to Protect Business Secrets in International Commercial Arbitration*, 6/2009 Int. A.L.R. 158, 158-159 (2009); Karl Pörnbacher & Inken Knief, *Protection of Confidentiality in International Arbitration* in *Arbitraż i Mediacja: Księga Jubileuszowa Dedykowana Doktorowi Andrzejowi Tynelowi* (ed. Maciej Łaszczuk et al., Sąd Arbitrażowy przy Krajowej Izbie Gospodarczej w Warszawie, 2012), p. 466.
20. Many contractual agreements contain extensive and detailed confidentiality clauses specifying the term 'confidentiality' or 'confidential information' that should, in the opinion of the parties, be confidential information and business secrets. With a carefully drafted confidentiality clause, the parties lay the grounds for the restricted use of whatever information is defined as 'confidential' in a potential arbitration (*see* Wyss, *supra* n. 19, 160). However, even where confidentiality is addressed by the agreement or a similar instrument, the need may arise to identify the law which governs that instrument's validity, effects or interpretation (ILA Report, *supra* n. 15, 11).
21. Wyss, *supra* n. 19, 160. Relatively few national arbitration statutes contain provisions prescribing general standards of confidentiality in international arbitration, though (Born, *supra* n. 11, Chapter 20.03).

standard for confidentiality obligations in arbitration can be derived from national arbitration laws, either.[22]

Following the *Bulbank* judgment, the starting point in Swedish arbitration law is that there is no implied duty or obligation of confidentiality in arbitration. In an arbitration conducted under Swedish law, any obligation of confidentiality must thus be derived from the parties' agreement. The Arbitration Rules of the Arbitration Institute of the Stockholm Chamber of Commerce (the 'SCC') do not provide for the confidentiality of the proceedings either.[23] As such, the parties would expressly have to agree on the confidentiality of the proceedings in order for there to be a relative confidentiality obligation binding the parties themselves. In the absence of such a provision, it would be advisable for the arbitrators to draw the attention of the parties to the confidentiality of the proceedings at the outset.[24]

[B] The Right to Confidentiality Within Arbitral Proceedings

The principles of due process do not apply unrestrictedly. It is generally accepted that the rights to be heard, to equal treatment, and to be able to present one's case are subject to limitations. Especially, requirements of conducting the proceedings expeditiously and cost-effectively set certain limitations that require due process considerations to be balanced. The tribunal may, for example, limit the number of submissions, restrict the examination of witnesses to a certain extent or set deadlines for introducing new factual allegations or evidence (provided that the parties do not agree otherwise) in order to conduct the proceedings efficiently.[25] This limitation of due process is also reflected in the wording of Article 24(1) of the SAA, which provides that 'the arbitrators shall afford the parties, *to the extent necessary*, an opportunity to present their respective cases in writing or orally' (emphasis added). In contrast to the UNCITRAL Model Law, which the SAA was inspired by on several points, the SAA does not require that the parties be given a *full opportunity* to present their case. Article 24(1) of the SAA thus recognizes that there are certain limits to the procedural rights of the parties, such as the aforementioned limitations.[26]

---

22. Pörnbacher & Knief, *supra* n. 19, 457-458. One of the reasons given as to why certain legislators (and even arbitral institutions) have abstained from adopting rules on the confidentiality of arbitration is the difficulty in defining the exceptions to confidentiality (ILA Report, *supra* n. 15, 16).
23. The SCC Rules do, however, rule that the arbitral tribunal, any administrative secretary of the tribunal and the SCC shall maintain the confidentiality of the arbitration and the award (Article 3 and Article 9).
24. ILA Report, *supra* n. 15, 20. For further discussion regarding the drafting of a procedural order regarding confidentiality at the outset of the proceedings, *see* Michael Hwang & Nicholas Thio, *A Proposed Model Procedural Order on International Arbitration: A Comprehensive and Self-Governing Code*, 29/2 J. Int. Arbitr, 137 (2012).
25. *See, e.g.*, Karl Pörnbacher & Sebastian Baur, *Confidentiality and Fundamental Rights of Due Process and Access to the File: A Comparative Overview*, 43 ASA Special Series 21, 28 (2016).
26. Heuman, *supra* n. 4, 385. As examples of this limitation, Heuman mentions for the example cutting off the exchange of submissions in the name of procedural efficiency and reduction of costs as well as an apportion of time available to the parties to present their cases at the hearing.

It has also been generally considered that the right to confidentiality may conflict with the rights of equal treatment and of access to the file to a certain extent. A party is entitled to keep their business secrets and internal documents confidential and may be obliged to do so in cases where the file involves, e.g., information regulated by competition law, other important public policy considerations or contractual obligations.[27]

While Sweden is not a Model Law country, the SAA is inspired by the UNCITRAL Model Law. In matters concerning the recognition and enforcement of arbitral awards under the SAA, the Swedish Supreme Court has looked to international case law and the underlying principles of the UNCITRAL Model Law.[28] The same should apply when assessing the application of section 24(2) SAA as the statute is based on Article 24(3) of the UNCITRAL Model Law. When drafting Article 24(3) of the UNCITRAL Model Law, the Working Group tasked with drafting the Model Law discussed its underlying principles. The Working Group concluded that parties generally must be given an opportunity to study all documents upon which the arbitral tribunal might rely in making its decision. However, it also raised the point of protecting professional secrecy. As stated by the Working Group's United States representative, the concerned party should together with the arbitral tribunal find some means of permitting professional secrecy to be respected.[29]

However, the scope and extent of the right to protection of confidentiality can be quite unclear. Even in situations where the parties have agreed on a relative confidentiality obligation, the parties have seldom agreed on anything regarding the protection

27. *See, e.g.*, the judgment C-450/06 Varec SA / Belgium of the Court of Justice of the European Union (which predates the Trade Secrets Directive) and the case law referred therein (paras 47-49 and 52): 'The adversarial principle means, as a rule, that the parties have a right to a process of inspecting and commenting on the evidence and observations submitted to the court. However, in some cases it may be necessary for certain information to be withheld from the parties in order to preserve the fundamental rights of a third party or to safeguard an important public interest ... One of the fundamental rights capable of being protected in this way is the right to respect for private life, enshrined in Article 8 of the ECHR ... The Court of Justice has, moreover, acknowledged that the protection of business secrets is a general principle. ... The principle of the protection of confidential information and of business secrets must be observed in such a way as to reconcile it with the requirements of effective legal protection and the rights of defence of the parties to the dispute.' *See also* Pörnbacher & Baur, *supra* n. 25, 28-30.
28. *See, e.g.*, Swedish Supreme Court cases NJA 2018 p. 504 (para. 16) and NJA 2018 p. 291 (para 16).
29. Summary record of the 324th meeting, held at Vienna International Centre, Vienna, on Thursday, 14 June 1985: United Nations Commission on International Trade Law, 18th session, A/CN.9/SR.324, paras 12-13 and 15 regarding discussions of the formulation of Article 24(4):

> 12. Mr. VOLKEN (Observer for Switzerland) inquired whether, if the words "or other document" were deleted, a party would be able to provide the arbitral tribunal with documents which contained professional secrets which it did not wish the other party to see.
>
> 13. Mr. HOLTZMANN (United States of America) said that under the first sentence, all documents supplied to the arbitral tribunal by one party must be communicated to the other party. It was up to the party concerned and the arbitral tribunal to find some means of permitting professional secrecy to be respected. The deletion of the second sentence would not affect the preservation of professional secrecy, however.

of confidential information, such as business secrets, between themselves in any potential arbitral proceedings.[30] In the absence of explicit provisions, guidance may be found from other parts of the parties' agreement, e.g., the arbitration clause and confidentiality clauses. Guidance on confidentiality, disclosure and protection of business secrets may be derived from the applicable substantive law as well. Within the EU, the Trade Secrets Directive[31] provides for a harmonized definition of 'trade secrets'[32] and sets out rules for Member States regarding the protection against unlawful acquisition, use and disclosure of trade secrets.[33]

Any protective measures taken must, however, be proportional and take into account the fair and equal treatment of the parties.[34] In choosing and formulating the appropriate measure for the sake of protecting confidentiality, proportionality is key. The legitimate interest of a party to protect its business secrets must be respected to the extent possible, while at the same time the principle of the right to be heard requires that parties must be given the possibility to comment on all items on the record.

[C] The Arbitral Tribunal's Discretion to Issue Confidentiality Orders

As a starting point, parties may empower the arbitral tribunal, either in the terms of reference or ad hoc, to order measures to protect the parties' business secrets. Documents such as the terms of reference or first procedural orders are binding upon the tribunal and therefore define the boundaries for the taking of evidence and the treatment of business secrets within the arbitration. In some cases, the parties have included in their arbitration agreement a reference to specific arbitration rules that expressly empower the arbitral tribunal to take or order protective measures with regard to business secrets.[35] This is the case for, e.g., the Arbitration Rules of the International Chamber of Commerce (ICC Rules) (Article 22(3)) and the Arbitration Rules of the World Intellectual Property Organization (WIPO Arbitration Rules) (Article 54).

30. Pörnbacher & Knief, *supra* n. 19, 466.
31. Directive (EU) 2016/943 on the protection of undisclosed know-how and business information (trade secrets) against their unlawful acquisition, use and disclosure.
32. According to Article 2 of the Directive, 'trade secret' means information which meets all of the following requirements: (a) it is secret in the sense that it is not, as a body or in the precise configuration and assembly of its components, generally known among or readily accessible to persons within the circles that normally deal with the kind of information in question; (b) it has commercial value because it is secret; (c) it has been subject to reasonable steps under the circumstances, by the person lawfully in control of the information, to keep it secret.
33. Article 1 of the Trade Secrets Directive.
34. Pörnbacher & Baur, *supra* n. 25, 43; Roman Khodykin & Carol Mulcahy, *A Guide to the IBA Rules on the Taking of Evidence in International Arbitration* (Oxford University Press, 2019), para. 12.328.
35. Wyss, *supra* n. 19, 162. However, Wyss notes that rules which explicitly empower the arbitral tribunal to order protective measures to protect confidentiality are rarely included in the terms of reference or in procedural orders.

The parties seldom include express provisions in their confidentiality clause dealing with the disclosure of confidential information in a dispute between themselves.[36] Thus, it is unlikely that the parties will have included any provisions for the handling of confidential information within the proceedings. However, if the subject matter of an arisen dispute or the industry sector in which the parties operate is one where sensitive or highly valuable commercial information is likely to be generated, there may be good reason to anticipate issues of confidentiality. In such a situation, the arbitral tribunal may, for example, issue a confidentiality order included in its first procedural order. However, it is impossible to foresee all possible issues related to confidentiality that may arise during arbitral proceedings. In such situations, it may be necessary for the arbitral tribunal to react by ordering protective measures to ensure the protection of confidential information even when the parties cannot agree on an arrangement for the taking of evidence that includes confidential material.

As mentioned above, issues related to confidentiality tend to arise in two distinct situations within arbitration: first, when a party is requested to produce documents by the opposing party, and second, when a party wishes to submit evidence in support of their case. While the differences in said scenarios should not be exaggerated,[37] certain considerations should still be given to whether the confidential information is being submitted as evidence at the initiative of the party in possession of the material or at the request of the other party.[38] The bottom line is, however, that the arbitral tribunal must decide whether to depart from ordinary procedure by adopting special measures to protect the confidential information and, if so, what measures should be adopted.[39]

The IBA Rules on the Taking of Evidence in International Commercial Arbitration (IBA Rules) are frequently relied on as a guideline by arbitrators in matters of taking of evidence. This is the case even in disputes where the parties have not agreed to the application of the rules.

Under Article 3.5 and Article 9.2(e) of the IBA Rules, a party may object to a request for production on the grounds of commercial or technical confidentiality. Where it finds that there are compelling grounds to do so, the tribunal is permitted to exclude that evidence or production altogether. In cases where the tribunal deems that the threshold has not been met, the tribunal may still find, either on its own motion or upon the application by the relevant party, that measures should be implemented to protect the confidentiality of the relevant evidence.

Article 9.5 of the IBA Rules allows a tribunal to arrange matters so that evidence of a confidential nature may be introduced into the arbitration subject to protections designed to prevent unnecessary disclosure or dissemination. The discretion granted to the tribunal is a wide one. The tribunal may make such arrangements where it considers it 'appropriate' to do so. The provision does not specify the nature of the arrangements either with the only requirements being that they be 'necessary' to

36. *Ibid.*, *supra* n. 19, 160.
37. Yves Derains, *Evidence and Confidentiality,* Special Supplement 2009 Confidentiality in Arbitration, ICC International Court of Arbitration Bulletin, paras 7-8 (2009).
38. These considerations will be discussed further for each specific measure below.
39. Derains, *supra* n. 37, para. 8.

permit the evidence to be used. It is also noteworthy that the power given to the tribunal under Article 9.5 is not limited to situations where confidentiality concerns have been raised as part of document production under Article 9.2.[40] The tribunal may propose or agree to confidentiality safeguards whenever it considers it appropriate to do so. Such safeguards may be issued in relation to documents produced by a party, taking of witness evidence (written and/or oral), proprietary materials used or relied on by experts in preparing their evidence, or premises and technology inspected during the course of the proceedings. The application of any protective measures such as the ones that may be arranged under Article 9.5 of the IBA Rules must be considered in tandem with any eventual arrangements regarding confidentiality that the parties have already agreed to or orders the arbitral tribunal has already ordered.[41]

As examples of measures that the arbitral tribunal may take, the IBA Task Force for the revision of the IBA Rules mentions prohibiting further disclosure of the evidence (a confidentiality order) or directing the parties to enter into a non-disclosure agreement. Further, when a party's legitimate interests call for non-disclosure of confidential information, an arbitral tribunal may order production of documents in redacted form. It may also, where permitted by applicable laws and rules, order that the documents should be exchanged between counsel only, without granting the parties access to them. Finally, the arbitral tribunal can appoint an independent and impartial expert to review the document concerned in order to report to the arbitral tribunal and the parties about the non-confidential content (*see also* Article 3.8 of the IBA Rules about the appointment of the expert).[42] These measures, in addition to certain others, and their application under the SAA will be analysed in the following.

§11.04 POSSIBLE CONFIDENTIALITY MEASURES UNDER THE SWEDISH ARBITRATION ACT

[A] Redaction

Redaction of documents is a straightforward means of protecting confidential material and its use is commonplace in arbitration. The confidential parts of a document are simply excised from the copy of the document produced. An obvious example is minutes of board meetings containing confidential material on different topics, only one of which is relevant to the arbitration.

40. This distinction has been made more explicit in the most recently revised version of the rules, which state that the 'Arbitral Tribunal may, where appropriate, make necessary arrangements to permit *Documents to be produced, and* evidence to be presented or considered, subject to suitable confidentiality protection' (the emphasized part has been added in the most recent revision of the rules).
41. Roman Khodykin & Carol Mulcahy, *A Guide to the IBA Rules on the Taking of Evidence in International Arbitration* 2019, p. 488.
42. IBA Task Force for the Revision of the IBA Rules on the Taking of Evidence in International Arbitration, *Commentary on the revised text of the 2020 IBA Rules on the Taking of Evidence in International Arbitration* (January 2021), 30.

When the parties agree that the redacted information is irrelevant or immaterial to the outcome of the dispute, such redaction should not raise any concerns regarding the principle of due process. However, in situations where a disagreement exists, redaction may not be appropriate, as that could give rise to issues regarding a party's possibility to present its case. Such a disagreement could be settled by having the proposed redactions reviewed against the originals in order to assess whether the redaction was appropriate. Such review could be performed by, e.g., the opposing party's counsel only or by a confidentiality expert.[43] In such case, the comparative analysis must take into account the same due process considerations that had applied if the relevant material would be submitted for 'counsel only' review or for review by a confidentiality expert.[44]

Another solution would be to allow the tribunal to verify the redacted documents against the original ones. Such solutions are not suitable if the redacted information requires protection from disclosure to any third parties, including the tribunal.[45] Some authors have raised the point that there might be doubts about the true independence of a party-appointed arbitrator, which in turn leads to the risk of the arbitrator divulging the confidential information to the other party.[46] As a solution, it has been suggested that the presiding arbitrator alone may examine the documents or assign the task to the administrative secretary of the tribunal. This solution was applied by an arbitral tribunal in an ICC arbitration in which the respondent was concerned that the claimant might disclose certain information outside of the arbitration.[47] This approach would, however, per a strict interpretation of Article 24(2) of SAA, be in breach of the SAA without the approval of the party not in possession of the unredacted documentation. This is because of the risk that tribunal or presiding arbitrator may be influenced by the redacted parts of the material which would not be available to both parties.[48]

[B] Synopsis or Summary

An option quite similar to redaction would be to provide a synopsis of the key elements of the content of a document. In one ICC arbitration, the claimant requested production of contracts that the respondent had concluded directly or indirectly with designated customers. The contracts formed the basis of the claimant's claim for commission from the respondent. The respondent objected to production on grounds that 'disclosure as requested ... would violate confidentiality of Respondent's contracts with third parties

43. *See, e.g.*, Khodykin & Mulcahy, *supra* n. 41, 492; Baizeau & Richard, *supra* n. 14, 55.
44. *See* Chapters 4.3.1.2 and 4.3.1.3 *infra*.
45. Baizeau & Richard, *supra* n. 14, 55-56.
46. Derains, *supra* n. 37, paras 20-22; Baizeau & Richard, *supra* n. 14, 56.
47. *See* Baizeau & Richard, *supra* n. 14, 56.
48. Cf. Derains, *supra* n. 37, para. 19. Derains notes that any knowledge the arbitral tribunal has of the redacted information remains outside of the proceedings as the tribunal cannot make any use of such details in their final award. Still, Derains states that the arbitrators should be asked to return the non-redacted documents after checking them to ensure that the knowledge of the information therein remains 'fleeting'.

and legitimate interest of Respondent for "non-disclosure and secrecy" of its commercial and contractual practices'. In order to protect the respondent's concerns regarding confidentiality, the tribunal decided not to compel the respondent to produce copies of the contracts, but only a list containing the date of each contract, the subject matter of the contract, the original contract price (and any variation), payments received, and payments pending or anticipated.[49]

It should be without question that an arbitral tribunal should be able to give a similar order in an arbitration conducted under Swedish law and the SAA. As long as the synopsis is provided to both the arbitral tribunal and the opposing party, and no other documentation is submitted to the arbitral tribunal as material related to the dispute, there should be no risk of the proceedings being in breach of Article 24(2) of the SAA.

[C] Restricted Access to Some Individuals

The redaction of certain confidential information may not be appropriate if the information proposed to be redacted is material to the outcome of the dispute. If the arbitral tribunal finds, either prima facie or after having compared the proposed redactions to the original documentation, that the confidential information is more likely than not material to the dispute, but still in need of protection for the sake of confidentiality, the arbitral tribunal could, instead of redacting, resort to restricting the access to certain information to a designated group of individuals. As noted by Baizeau and Richard, this is one of the most common tools used in practice.[50]

[1] 'Confidentiality Clubs'

The simplest form of restricted access to the confidential information consists of limiting access to it to selected individuals, often referred to as a 'confidentiality club'. Restricted access limited to selected individuals has been described as a straightforward measure for protecting confidentiality. Of course, plenty of consideration needs to be given to the number of people included in the 'club'. The narrower the circle of people, the higher the risk of breach of due process. On the other hand, the wider the circle, the weaker the protection of confidentiality.[51] To avoid this risk, the clubs are in most cases set up by agreement of the parties.[52]

---

49. Final award in ICC Case 15583 (Extract), 1 ICC Dispute Resolution Bulletin 139, paras 273-274 (2016).
50. Baizeau & Richard, *supra* n. 14, 57.
51. Khodykin & Mulcahy, *supra* n. 41, para. 12.340. *See* also Waincymer, *Procedure and Evidence in International Arbitration* (Kluwer Law International, 2012), 799 and 877; Trevor Cook & Alejandro I. Garcia, *International Intellectual Property Arbitration* (Kluwer Law International, 2010), Chapters 3.3.1 and 3.3.4-3.3.6; Derains, *supra* n. 37, para. 28; Baizeau & Richard, *supra* n. 14, 57.
52. Baizeau & Richard, *supra* n. 14, 57.

[a] In Camera, or Tribunal-Only Review

The most extreme form of restricted access would be review of the confidential information only by the arbitral tribunal (so-called in camera or ex parte proceedings). This approach is uncommon, but not unheard of in practice.[53] The method raises obvious due process concerns as both the tribunal and the party producing or submitting the confidential information would have the opportunity to review the material while the other party would be denied access to the material. The other party would not be able to challenge or test the evidence and present any challenges or arguments regarding the material to the tribunal.

There is a general opposition against the admissibility of in camera proceedings in international arbitration expressed by legal authors as such proceedings would violate the right to be heard.[54] However, some authors have noted that in camera proceedings could be viable where the party bearing the burden of proof has requested a confidential document from the other side and the document would otherwise not be submitted due to, e.g., a successful objection during the document production phase, citing the confidentiality of the material. In such a situation, the party requesting the documentation may prefer to waive the right to be heard (i.e., review and comment on the documentation) in order to have the arbitral tribunal review the document in camera if the only other alternative is that the documentation is not submitted to the proceedings at all.[55]

However, tribunal-only review without the agreement of both parties would be in violation of SAA 24(2) and the principle of due process expressed therein. Tribunal-only review could thus not be ordered by an arbitral tribunal in an arbitration conducted under Swedish law in a situation where the parties cannot agree on the measures for the protection of the confidential material. An award rendered after such proceedings could be subjected to a challenge by the aggrieved party.

[b] Counsel-Only Review

The arbitral tribunal could also order the confidential material to be made available only for review by counsel to the party not in possession of the confidential documentation. The potential advantage of this approach over simple redaction is that the relevant material can be included in complete form in the development of a case strategy. The disadvantage is, however, that in many cases the material in question

53. As reported in Khodykin & Mulcahy, *supra* n. 41, para 12.347, who refer to a BCLP Survey on the use of the IBA Rules where respondents from Spain and Argentina reported orders by an arbitral tribunal permitting tribunal-only review of documents.
54. *See, e.g.*, Baizeau & Richard, *supra* n. 14, 57; Khodykin & Mulcahy, *supra* n. 41, para. 12.341; Cook & Garcia, *supra* n. 51, 263. Cook & Garcia cite the use of ex parte disclosure in certain arbitral proceedings where the tribunal accepted that detailed blueprints were submitted to the tribunal, while more general blueprints were submitted to the opposing party. Similar approaches have reportedly also been taken with, for example, contracts entered into with third parties used to substantiate damage claims for breach of contract.
55. Pörnbacher & Knief, *supra* n. 19, 472.

could be of technical character. As a result, counsel may be unable to assess the material without input from the client or a client-appointed expert, thereby hindering an effective presentation of that party's case.[56]

In addition, this solution would require counsel to issue an undertaking not to disclose to the client the confidential information made available. However, such an undertaking without the client's express consent could be problematic, or even impossible, in certain jurisdictions.[57] In any event, the proper execution of this protective measure would require that the client gives counsel express consent to take part of the documentation without disclosing it to the client. The arbitral tribunal could not compel the client to do so. Therefore, to be able to rely on counsel-only review, the consent of the party not in possession of the confidential information is ultimately necessary in order to be put into practice. Such a measure could thus not be relied on in a situation where the parties are unable to reach an agreement on the protective measures.

[c] Expert-Only Review

As an alternative to counsel-only review, the confidential information could be shared solely with the experts for each of the parties. Similar complications as those that arise when only sharing the material with opposing counsel may, however, become apparent with this approach as well. The experts may have the necessary knowledge to assess the technical evidence but, on the other hand, the effective use of that assessment is weakened if the expert is unable to consult with counsel in order to facilitate arguments against or on the basis of the evidence presented containing confidential information. This in turn may infringe a party's right to be heard.[58] The practical solution to this problem, which affects both counsel- and expert-only review, is to grant both counsel and expert the opportunity to review the evidence, thereby giving them the opportunity to consult with each other regarding the confidential information, and to build an effective case.[59]

However, the same issue as with counsel-only review remains. If the party not in possession of the confidential agreement does not agree to such an approach, they have not, in fact, been given an opportunity to review the material that would be submitted into evidence if the arbitral tribunal were to order such a measure without consent. Neither counsel nor an independent expert can by any stretch of imagination be identified with the party itself within the meaning of section 24(2) of the SAA. Such a measure could thus not be ordered without the consent of both parties.

---

56. *See, e.g.*, Khodykin & Mulcahy, *supra* n. 41, 492, Waincymer, *supra* n. 51, 877-879, Baizeau & Richard, *supra* n. 14, 57-58.
57. *See* Pörnbacher & Knief, *supra* n. 19, 477. Pörnbacher & Knief note, e.g., that the German Constitutional Court has emphasized the client's right vis-à-vis its counsel to obtain full access and to comment in detail on the content of legal submissions; *see also* Baizeau & Richard, *supra* n. 14, 56-57.
58. Khodykin & Mulcahy, *supra* n. 41, paras 12.342-12.344.
59. *See, e.g.*, Baizeau & Richard, *supra* n. 14, 58 and the ICC arbitration reported therein.

[d] Designated Party Representatives

One further possibility is to extend the 'confidentiality club' to designated party representatives. Such representatives could include, e.g., in-house counsel, employees with the relevant technical knowledge, or employees with first-hand knowledge of the facts of the dispute (i.e., usually the same people that would be heard as fact witnesses in the matter).[60]

In certain disputes, it may not be sufficient to allow only counsel and experts to have access to and work with the confidential information. They may need instructions from party representatives or to be able to seek clarifications on specific facts known by the parties alone. Therefore, it may be necessary to include key party representatives in the 'confidentiality club'. This measure was implemented in an investor-state dispute, where a party's counsel had to sign a confidentiality undertaking providing that confidential information would only be disclosed to its signatories and to certain named party employees and other counsel if required, upon their signing a similar undertaking:

> [Counsel for Party X] also undertakes that it will share such information or documentation only with members of [Party X]'s counsel team (constituted by all the undersigned) and with directors, managers or employees of [Party X] [named], or additional members of the counsel team, who have a need to know such information (each the 'authorized Recipient') [named] who will [...] cause each such Authorized Recipient, whose names will be disclosed to [counsel for the other party] 5 days in advance, to provide undertakings identical in substance to those above as a condition to provision of access to such information or documentation.[61]

This approach would undoubtedly be in line with section 24(2) of the SAA as both parties would de facto be able to review any material submitted in evidence to the arbitral tribunal.

[2] Other Practical Arrangements to Restrict Access to the Material

The arbitral tribunal could also order the parties to undertake certain practical measures or arrange restricted access to the confidential information. Such measures could be, for example, imposing a requirement that the documents containing the confidential information (as well as any copies) are to be returned or destroyed,[62] or restricting the visual inspection of the confidential information, e.g., to a single location, with no (or limited) right to take notes, make copies or take photographs or

60. *See, e.g.*, Khodykin & Mulcahy, *supra* n. 41, para. 12.345.
61. Baizeau & Richard, *supra* n. 14, 60.
62. *See, e.g.*, Derains, *supra* n. 37, para. 19; *see also* Bazieau & Richard, *supra* n. 14, 60-61, who see the issue with this method is the balancing act needed between, on one hand, the need to destroy or return documents as soon as possible to preserve confidentiality, and, on the other, the need to retain documents that may be required for potential enforcement or challenge proceedings.

videos.[63] Such arrangements are often used in combination with 'confidentiality clubs'.[64]

Regarding the requirement to destroy or return documents with confidential information, the solutions adopted in practice appear to vary greatly. The procedural orders given, and the undertakings made by the parties, differ significantly both in clarity and extent. A frequent issue is the timing of the return or destruction of the confidential documents. Thus, it appears to be common practice either to agree, or for the tribunal to order, a specific time limit by which documents and any possible copies must be returned or destroyed, by referring to the issuance of the award (or settlement of the dispute), i.e., that the documents should be destroyed or returned, e.g., 'immediately after issuance of the award' or a few weeks or a few years later. The time limits may also vary for different recipients, in particular allowing counsel longer possession.[65]

In a further effort to prevent the release and dissemination of confidential information, the visual inspection of confidential material may be restricted, either physically or virtually, to a single location. When the inspection of the confidential material is restricted to a single location, usually the right to take notes, make copies or take photographs or videos is also prohibited, or at least restricted. The inspection could be conducted at a 'neutral' place, such as at the office of the presiding arbitrator, or, alternatively, at the office of counsel. If the material is comprehensive, this approach could entail the setting up of an entire data room. However, in the context of international arbitration, where the parties are located in different countries, the most practical and effective approach would in most cases be to set up a virtual data room.[66] This, of course, requires that the data room is adequately secured.[67]

---

63. Derains, *supra* n. 37, para. 21.
64. Baizeau & Richard, *supra* n. 14, 60 and 64.
65. *See* Baizeau & Richard, *supra* n. 14, 61-63 for examples of procedural orders and undertakings. Baizeau and Richard refer to an UNCITRAL investor-state arbitration where the parties sought to agree a specific date by which the investor should destroy its two copies of the raw footage of a film about the alleged wrongful actions of the investor, which the state had submitted in the arbitration. At the request of the film maker, who was a third party to the proceedings, the state requested that the copies be destroyed 'at the end of the arbitration or at the latest at the end of any setting aside or enforcement proceedings relating to an award issued upon the completion of the Arbitration'. The investor contended that this undertaking was overly broad since it was impossible to determine when enforcement proceedings would take place. The tribunal agreed and did not order any destruction. Notably, however, only two copies were held by counsel at their premises subject to an undertaking that no further copies could be made, and that the footage could only be viewed by certain named persons at the premises.
66. *See* Baizeau & Richard, *supra* n. 14, 63-64 for an example of a protective order limiting access to confidential material to an electronic data room.
67. The party gaining access through a virtual data room would, in any event, be able to take notes, and even if the software used in conjunction with the data room would prevent the copying of the material and the taking of 'print-screens' or 'snapshots' of the material, the party would also have the possibility to take pictures of the computer screen with a camera. Therefore, adopting this approach necessitates at least some level of trust between the parties.

[3] Restricted References in Written Submissions and the Award

In cases where the arbitral tribunal orders measures to protect sensitive information, such as redaction or restricted access, the measures taken would prove pointless if the information is referred to and cited in the parties' submissions, witness statements, experts reports, etc. Therefore, such measures are often combined with an order for restricted reference in future submissions.

This approach can be implemented through various means. One approach is to only allow for references to the confidential documents to be made in general terms only, while sections that necessitate quotes or more substantive references to the sensitive information would have to be submitted separately, marked as 'confidential', and these documents would be treated as other documentation with sensitive information. Another approach is to file a redacted and a non-redacted version of the same submission, the non-redacted version only available to the 'confidentiality club'.[68]

[D] A Confidentiality Advisor or a Third-Party Expert

In certain cases, the disclosure of the confidential information to any individuals connected to the dispute, i.e., the members of the tribunal, the parties and counsel, may need to be avoided due to its particularly sensitive nature. The parties' dispute may also concern the confidential nature of the material itself, e.g., in connection with document production. In such situations, the tribunal and parties may have to resort to more drastic measures involving third parties to review the confidential information and determine any dispute regarding the confidentiality of the material. As such measures may raise serious due process concerns, any such arrangements must be formulated with care in order to avoid any challenges based on the arbitral having improperly delegated its powers. Any such measures would preferably only be taken after reaching an agreement between the parties on the arrangements to be put in place.[69]

Article 54 of the WIPO Arbitration Rules, which regulates the conduct of the proceedings, refers to a confidentiality advisor:

> (d) In exceptional circumstances, in lieu of itself determining whether the information is to be classified as confidential and of such nature that the absence of special measures of protection in the proceedings would be likely to cause serious harm to the party invoking its confidentiality, the Tribunal may, at the request of a party or on its own motion and after consultation with the parties, designate a confidentiality advisor who will determine whether the information is to be classified, and, if so, decide under which conditions and to whom it may in part or in whole be disclosed. Any such confidentiality advisor shall be required to sign an appropriate confidentiality undertaking.

68. Baizeau & Richard, *supra* n. 14, 64-65.
69. Khodykin & Mulcahy, *supra* n. 41, para. 12.348, Baizeau & Richard, *supra* n. 14, 65.

Article 3(8) of the IBA Rules also provides for a similar measure:

> In exceptional circumstances, if the propriety of an objection can be determined only by review of the Document, the Arbitral Tribunal may determine that it should not review the Document. In that event, the Arbitral Tribunal may, after consultation with the Parties, appoint an independent and impartial expert, bound to confidentiality, to review any such Document and to report on the objection. To the extent that the objection is upheld by the Arbitral Tribunal, the expert shall not disclose to the Arbitral Tribunal and to the other Parties the contents of the Document reviewed.

The rationale of such provisions and the role of the confidentiality advisor's role are in practice limited to determining whether a confidentiality objection presented by a party during the document production phase of the arbitral proceedings holds true. When a confidentiality objection against the production of specified documentation becomes contested, the tribunal may rather than review the documents itself (and therefore also possibly becoming influenced by the contents of the documents) have a third party review the disputed documentation.[70] The confidentiality advisor can then report on the alleged confidentiality and even propose measures to protect the confidentiality during the proceedings.[71] Notably, both the WIPO Arbitration Rules and the IBA Rules provide that the appointment of a confidentiality advisor should only be resorted to under 'exceptional circumstances'. While the confidentiality advisor should generally and formally speaking have no decision-making power,[72] the line is not always easy to draw, as the process of identifying the nature of the alleged confidential information inevitably entails a decision-making process. Thus, it is important to set out the detailed terms of reference of the advisor's mission and power to avoid uncertainty. It is also advisable for both parties to expressly agree to the advisor's nomination, although the consensus in legal writing appears to be that such an appointment of a confidentiality advisor would be admissible even without the parties' consent, depending on the applicable law and rules.[73] A lack of agreement, however, further emphasizes the importance of a well-formulated and detailed appointment by the tribunal.[74]

The role of the third-party expert may also need to be broader, in the sense that the expert may, in lieu of the arbitral tribunal and the party not in possession of the

70. *See, e.g.*, Pörnbacher & Knief, *supra* n. 19, 479; Hans van Houtte, *The Document Production Master and the Experts' Facilitator: Two Possible Aides for an Efficient Arbitration* in *Liber Amicorum Bernardo Cremades* (eds Miguel Angel Fernandez-Ballester and David Arias Lozano, Wolters Kluwer España, 2010), p. 1149.
71. *See, e.g.*, Waincymer, *supra* n. 51 para. 11.8.1, Derains, *supra* n. 37 paras 25-26 and 30-31, Khodykin & Mulcahy, *supra* n. 41 para. 12.348.
72. Waincymer, *supra* n. 51, Chapter 11.8.1. *See also* IBA Working Party's Commentary, *supra* n. 42, 12: 'The expert, who need not necessarily be appointed pursuant to the terms of Article 6 of the IBA Rules of Evidence, would provide a report on the objection, but the arbitral tribunal is to make the final ruling as to its validity.'
73. Pörnbacher & Knief, *supra* n. 19, 479-480; Baizeau & Richard, *supra* n. 14, 67-68; van Houtte, *supra* n. 70, 1152-1153; Derains *supra* n. 37, 25.
74. Baizeau & Richard, *supra* n. 14, 68.

documentation, review the documentation containing sensitive information and prepare a report answering specific questions put by the parties and the tribunal. Such an exceptional measure is specifically referred to in Article 54(e) of the WIPO Arbitration Rules and has reportedly also been adopted in practice in an ICC arbitration. The dispute in that case related to a technology licence agreement in the defence and security industry and involved reliance on extremely sensitive evidence by both parties, which each party refused to disclose to the opposing party. The solution proposed by the arbitrator, and accepted by the parties, consisted in appointing a third party to collect the evidence, review the sensitive information and answer the factual and technical questions deemed relevant by each party, and which could be supplemented by the arbitrator, pursuant to detailed 'Third-Party Neutral Procedural Rules'. Just like a tribunal-appointed expert, the parties (and the arbitrator) had the opportunity to comment on the third-party neutral's report. However, any requests for access to sensitive information had to be presented to the tribunal for a decision.[75]

§11.05 CONCLUSIONS

International business disputes involve an increasing amount of confidential information that requires protection as between the parties within an arbitration. When the parties to a dispute can agree on the handling of such confidential information, the arbitral tribunal can assist the parties by issuing, e.g., confidentiality orders confirming the parties' agreement.

If the parties are unable to agree on the treatment of confidential information within the arbitral proceedings, the arbitral tribunal will have to decide whether to order measures to protect the sensitive information upon application by one party. An arbitral tribunal can order the protection of confidential information, e.g., by allowing for redaction of parts of the sensitive material or by restricting access to the sensitive material. While an arbitral tribunal should be cautious when limiting one party's access to documentation presented by the other party, in the view of the authors, an arbitral tribunal has the required authority to restrict access to sensitive material if so requested. While there is not yet any precedent under Swedish law that would confirm the arbitral tribunal's authority to order the restriction of access to confidential information, an arbitral tribunal can do so within the limits set by Article 24 SAA. While any arbitral tribunal is likely to strive to have the parties reach an agreement on the subject of confidentiality, an arbitral tribunal should not deny a requesting party a confidentiality order if the request for confidentiality is based on a legitimate need and if the procedural rights of the other party are upheld as far as possible.

An arbitral tribunal's efforts in this regard are much aided by advance party agreement on, e.g., the application of the IBA Rules on the Taking of Evidence to the

75. Baizeau & Richard, *supra* n. 14, 69-70.

given dispute. The authors thus recommend that parties anticipating the need for increased confidentiality measures within the arbitration proceedings also seek to agree upon the application of the IBA Rules on the Taking of Evidence at the outset of a dispute.

CHAPTER 12

Expert Determination – Interaction with the Arbitral Tribunal and the Conflict of Competences Between Both: An International Perspective

Anna Tujakowska

The majority of disputes arising out of the post-closing phase relate to determination or adjustment of the purchase price, which is done through an expert determination (ED) procedure. ED is recognized by various jurisdictions and is a well-known and frequently exploited legal feature in the commercial reality. The gist of the ED procedure consists of allowing a third party, usually an independent accountancy firm, to determine the level of the price adjustment or the final price itself. If any dispute between the parties pertaining to the outcome of the ED should arise, the same expert is involved in resolving such dispute by providing their own determination. Such determination is designed to be fact specific, based on financial documents only, fast and efficient. The parties agree that once the expert's procedure is completed, the ED's decision shall be final and binding. At the same time, it is not uncommon for the same M&A contract to include an arbitration agreement which stipulates that 'any dispute' arising out of said contract shall be solved by an arbitral tribunal. This duality often leads to these two proceedings overlapping which creates conflicts of competences between the arbitral tribunal and ED.

This chapter aims to focus on analysing what the interrelation between ED and arbitration is, what the possible conflicts of competences between both institutions are, and how such conflicts are and should be tackled from the international arbitration practice perspective.

§12.01 INTRODUCTION

According to the inventory of merger and acquisition (M&A) cases, '[t]he most common disputes arising out of the post-closing phase are those relating to the determination or adjustment of the purchase price'.[1] Usually, the determination or adjustment of the purchase price in M&A contracts is done through an expert determination (ED) procedure. ED is recognized by various jurisdictions and is a well-known and frequently exploited legal feature in commercial reality. The gist of the ED procedure consists of allowing a third party, usually an independent accountancy firm, to determine the level of the price adjustment or the final price itself. If any dispute between the parties pertaining to the outcome of the ED should arise, the same expert is involved in resolving such dispute with its determination. Such determination is designed to be fact specific, based on financial documents only, fast and efficient. The parties agree that once the expert's procedure is completed, the ED's decision shall be final and binding. At the same time, it is not uncommon for the same M&A contract to include an arbitration agreement which stipulates that 'any dispute' arising out of the said contract shall be solved by an arbitral tribunal.

While the parties' 'view, or hope [is] that the two [the ED clause and arbitration agreement,] would not encroach on each other and lead their own lives',[2] the reality is that they do overlap more than one would have expected, creating conflicts of competences. It is said that '[e]very practitioner probably has at least an intuitive understanding of expert determination, but its precise limits are difficult to discern'.[3]

Unlike arbitrators, experts typically do not have the authority to interpret an M&A contract's language or address legal issues, such as liability for improper performance of the contract. Instead, experts are limited to deciding specific factual questions. Nevertheless, sometimes these legal issues may have an impact on the data which constitutes the basis for the answer to a specific factual question. Consequently, the scope of the expert's mandate overlaps with the jurisdiction of the arbitral tribunal (i.e., assessing whether a breach of the contractual obligations of one of the parties has reduced or increased the final price or value of the assets or had an impact on the level of an earn-out).

Indeed, drawing the demarcation line between the ED clause and arbitration agreement is not an easy task. This might be because, as some French scholars argue, ED is 'very fuzzy [and] ... very difficult to handle'[4] or because 'many practitioners assume that the Purchase Process Adjustments Clause [i.e. ED] must be an arbitration agreement because, if it's not an arbitration agreement, then it is not clear what else it could be'.[5]

This chapter aims to focus on analysing what the interrelation between ED and arbitration is, what the possible conflicts of competences between both institutions are,

1. Andrea Carlevaris, *The Arbitration of Disputes Relating to Mergers and Acquisitions: A Study of ICC Cases*, 24 ICC Int. Court Arbitr. Bull. (2013).
2. *X v. S, case study presented by White & Case during the conference – M&A disputes in Warsaw (2019).*
3. Martin Valasek & Frederic Wilson, *Distinguishing Expert Determination from Arbitration: The Canadian Approach in a Comparative Perspective*, 29 Arbitr. Int., 64 (2013).
4. Klaus Sachs, *The Interaction Between Expert Determination and Arbitration*, 24 ASA Spec. Ser., 240 (2005).
5. NYC Bar, *Report by the Committee on International Commercial Disputes 'Purchase Price Adjustment Clauses and Expert Determinations: Legal Issues, Practical Problems and Suggested Improvements'* 2 (2013).

and how such conflicts are and should be tackled from the international arbitration practice perspective.

§12.02 DEFINITION AND LEGAL IMPLICATIONS OF ED

[A] Definition of ED

The parties to commercial contracts frequently decide to include an expert determination clause (ED clause).[6] By virtue of this clause, the parties elect that an expert will deal with various factual controversies or determine some factual issues that may arise during the lifetime of the contract. Experts are called upon by the parties also to establish a fact or a limited set of facts. They may also be called upon to supplement, amend or replace the intentions of the parties.[7] The experts are rarely or even never lawyers, most often being accountants, engineers or other technical specialists.[8] Their qualifications depend on the type of contract and the potential issues to be solved or determined. The process will typically end with a final and binding decision. However, unlike in cases of arbitration or domestic litigation, the outcome of the ED does not result in an enforceable outcome in the form of an award.[9]

[B] Recognition of ED by Various Legal Systems

ED is recognized by various legal systems, both common and civil. As far as it is possible to agree on what ED is, procedural aspects, requirements and powers of an expert will vary in various jurisdictions.[10]

ED roots date back to Roman law.[11] For instance, ED has a long standing tradition under English law going back for almost 250 years.[12] In other common law countries, like Canada, Australia, New Zealand or Singapore, ED is also commonly used and is accompanied by a wealth of case law.[13] In the United States (US), ED is also often called 'appraisal' and has been commonly used in a commercial context since at least

6. Gary B. Born, International Commercial Arbitration 259 (2nd ed. 2014).
7. Eliane Fischer & Michael Walbert, *Efficient and Expeditious Dispute Resolution in M&A Transactions*, Austrian Yearb. Int. Arbitr., 41 (2017), https://www.walbert.law/wp-content/uploads/2018/04/Efficient-And-Expeditious-Dispute-Resolution-In-MA-Transactions.pdf.
8. *Id.*, at 41. The ED mechanism has been used in various types of the contracts, such as: (i) the review of the amount of rent payable by the tenant under a long-term lease; (ii) the valuation of shares in a company whose shares are not listed on a stock exchange; (iii) disputes over certain representations and warranties, such as environmental issues; (iv) the value, quality or quantity of goods or commodities being sold; (v) disputes of a technical nature, in particular under the FIDIC Rules. *See also* NYC Bar, *supra* note 5 at 13.
9. Sachs, *supra* note 4 at 235.
10. Wolfgang Peter & Daniel Greineder, Conflicts between Expert Determination Clauses and Arbitration Clauses [in:] GAR: The Guide to M&A Arbitration (3rd. ed. 2021).
11. Born, *supra* note 6 at 259. Ali Yesilimak, *Expert Determination in Turkey*, 33 ASA Bull., 308 & fn. 8 (2015).
12. John Kendall, *Expert Determination: Its Use in Resolving Art and Antiquity Disputes*, 2 Art Antiq. Law, 325 (1997).
13. Valasek and Wilson, *supra* note 3 at 76.

the beginning of the twentieth century.[14] However, in some states, such as California or Nevada, the institution has been abolished 'altogether by introducing a concept of arbitration broad enough to include expert determination as a form of arbitration'.[15]

ED is also recognized in civil law countries. For instance, the wide use of ED in Germany - where it goes by the name of 'Schiedsgutachten' - has enabled the development of a substantial body of case law. There is however no separate legal provision that would govern it. The practice is to apply by analogy Article 317 of the German Civil Law which deals with the specification of performance by a third party.[16] Similarly, in Austria as well there is no legal provision which would be solely devoted to ED. The Austrian Supreme Court considers provisions of Austrian civil law - which deal with section 1056 of Austrian Civil Code (ACC) - as providing a legal basis for the ED.[17] Both Austrian case law and legal literature consider ED a permissible and acceptable tool routinely exploited by parties.[18]

Also, in Switzerland, there is no explicit provision in the Swiss Code of Obligations pertaining to ED; however, this institution is recognized as a contractual concept and references can be found in cantonal codes of civil procedure.[19] In Italy, ED is called 'arbitraggio' which might create some confusion. It does not however have any relation with arbitration.[20] It is also known in Denmark, where it is called 'bindend advices' (binding advice).[21] In Sweden, ED is recognized to constitute contractually binding procedure and not arbitration; however, as pointed by Elofsson, there is a lack of clear rules and practice.[22] Nevertheless, according to Elofsson, ED is a quite popular feature in the M&A contracts with surveys conducted in 2006/2010/2013 showing that more than one-third of the Swedish transfer agreements surveyed contained the ED clauses.[23]

On the other hand, there are two views as to the status of ED under French law. According to Sachs, ED in France is not only not recognized as a legal concept but is also criticized.[24] French scholars describe ED as 'very fuzzy' ('très floue') and 'very difficult to handle' ('fort peu maniable').[25] There is a similar institution under Article 1592 of the French Civil Code which deals with price determination by a third person

14. NYC Bar, *supra* note 5 at 10-11. One of the first US cases which deals with ED is City *of Omaha v. Omaha Water* from 1910.
15. Sachs, *supra* note 4 at 240.
16. Anke Sessler & Corina Leimert, *The Role of Expert Determination in Mergers and Acquisitions under German Law*, 2004 20 Arbitr. Int., 152.
17. However, neither the Austrian Code of Civil Procedures (ACCP) nor the Austrian Civil Code (ACC) contains express provisions on expert determination. Christian Klausegger, *The Arbitrator and the Arbitration Procedure, Ad Hoc Expert Determination – Useful Tool or 'Too Much of a Headache'*, 2013 Austrian Yearb. Int. Arbitr., 169.
18. *Id.*, at 169.
19. For instance, a reference can be found in Article 258 of the Zurich ZPO. Sachs, *supra* note 4 at 240.
20. Sachs, *supra* note 4.
21. *Id.*, at 235.
22. Niklas Elofsson, *Tvistlösningsklausuler i kommersiella avtal*, Juridisk Tidskrift 2014-15, p. 644-645.
23. *Id.*, at 644.
24. *Id.*, at 240.
25. *Id.*, at 240.

acting as price determiner. This is, however, different from ED as understood by German or Swiss law. This is because under French law, the third person acting as price determiner under Article 1592 is deemed to be their joint representative, whose task is to finalize the contract by determining the price. As explained by K. Sachs, '[w]ithout such price determination, the contract is null and void'.[26] A different position is presented by Besson, who equates German 'Schiedsgutachten' to French 'expertise amiable' and argues that ED is a concept recognized under French law.[27]

[C] ED in Price Adjustment Clauses

Despite many possibilities of application, nowadays the ED clause is most commonly used in cross-border commercial transactions in the adjustment of the final price payable under a share sale-purchase agreement. Under such a clause, the expert is authorized to calculate certain adjustments, either upward or downward depending on certain factors or to establish the final price based on the valuation of the net equity of the target company as a basis for calculating the purchase price or the company's future earnings in the context of EBIT (earnings before deducting interest and taxes) or EBITDA (earnings before interest, taxes, depreciation and amortization) guarantees or earn-out clauses.[28]

Given its inherent purpose, i.e., dealing with an issue of fact and not a legal dispute, the ED clause is typically inserted in the substantive part of a contract. Usually, the clause describes various procedural steps in a very detailed and systematic manner. It usually consists of two parts, which correspond to two phases.

The *first part* covers a process which allows for arriving at the necessary adjustment of the purchase price or determining the final price. This includes either submission of the parties' respective positions or exchange of accounting and/or financial documents between the parties and the expert, usually an independent accounting firm.[29] In this phase, the final purchase price is determined under the contract either by the parties themselves or via the expert. This allows for a final price to be adjusted upward or downwards so as to reflect the true value of the company.[30]

There are various reasons for the parties to include such a provision, in particular, the time between the execution of the contract and the closing, competition law issues or tax considerations that require more time to be resolved, the necessity of obtaining consent from third parties or from the board of directors, or the need for confirmatory due diligence.[31]

26. *Id.*, at 240.
27. Sebastien Besson & Jean-Francois Poudret, Comparative Law of International Arbitration 14 (2nd ed. 2007).
28. Sachs, *supra* note 4 at 235.
29. There is no requirement for an expert to be a person, the ED clause can also provide for an institution.
30. NYC Bar, *supra* note 5 at 1.
31. Wolfgang Peter, *Arbitration of Mergers and Acquisitions: Purchase Price Adjustment Arbitrations*, 24 ASA Spec. Ser., 59 (2005). NYC Bar, *supra* note 5 at 1.

As explained by Peter:

> price adjustment provisions mitigate the buyer's risk of suffering from the target company's financial deterioration in the event that the seller should fail to manage the company efficiently until the closing of the transaction. Furthermore, the balance sheet, on the basis of which the provisional purchase price is determined, is obviously drawn up well before closing and unless the target company is a static enterprise, there will invariably be changes by the time of closing.[32]

In the case of price adjustment provisions based on future earnings of the company (earn-outs), the philosophy is different, as the buyer wants to ensure that the company's future income is in line with the projections.[33]

The *second part* is optional and is triggered when one of the parties disagrees with the determination (valuation) either proposed by the other party or prepared by the expert. Such a party usually submits a notice of disagreement, which describes the disputed issues. Typically, the parties agree to settle the dispute amicably. If a settlement is not reached, the disputed issues are directed to an expert for resolution. The ED clauses may differ here regarding the procedural steps on how the parties choose the expert. The expert usually has a limited period of time to solve the dispute. It is common practice not to hold a hearing or exchange the parties' positions as to their differences.

Finally, the expert issues a decision. Commonly, such decision is final and binding on the parties as the parties explicitly agreed that the expert decision would have such an effect. The contract usually stipulates that the expert does not act in the capacity of an arbitrator.[34] The parties either share the expert's costs or decide that the entire cost will be borne by the party whose position on adjustment was the furthest from the expert's decision.

The inclusion of ED clauses in M&A contracts seems to be a suitable solution. As explained by K. Sachs:

> [i]t particularly makes sense [to include an ED clause] in cases where the issue is a limited factual one and of such nature that an arbitral tribunal would also call in an expert, or hear party-appointed expert witness, to clarify the issue. This is true, for example, when the result of the valuation depends on the proper application of accounting rules, such as specified national Generally Accepted Accounting Principles (GAAP) or the International Financial Reporting Standards (IFRS). By choosing expert determination, the parties can thus rely on the specific know-how of the expert and avoid time-consuming and costly arbitration proceedings.[35]

32. Peter, *supra* note 31 at 59.
33. Peter and Greineder, *supra* note 10 at 34.
34. Gerald Hansen, Managing Expert Determinations [in:] The Guide to M&A Arbitration (1st ed. 2018).
35. Sachs, *supra* note 4 at 235. Sessler and Leimert, *supra* note 16 at 151.

§12.03 THE DISTINCTION BETWEEN ED AND ARBITRATION

A leading treatise on arbitration states that '[j]ust as arbitration is not litigation, so too arbitration is not expert determination or valuation'.[36] While the distinction between arbitration and ED is clear in theory, it is not so easy to distinguish both in practice. Nevertheless, the distinction even if 'uneasy [is] necessary':[37] depending on the qualification given to ED, different legal regimes will apply, producing different legal consequences.

Usually, under ED clauses, the parties authorize the expert to resolve all the disputes that may arise out of the price adjustment process. At the same time, the contract often includes a choice of forum clause under which the parties agree that all disputes arising out of the contract will be resolved either by an arbitral tribunal or by a court. In practice, the scope of disputes under the price adjustment process and general disputes arising out of the contract often overlap. While for one party determining the level of Working Capital might be a pure accounting issue that falls squarely under the expert's authority, for the other party it might be a case of contract interpretation that belongs to the jurisdiction of the arbitral tribunal.

The parties may further add to this confusion if they are not rigorous in drafting their ED clause. Sometimes, an ED clause may stipulate that disputes pertaining to the price adjustments shall be submitted to an 'expert arbitrator' or foresee that an expert who will not act as an arbitrator shall resolve 'any dispute aris[ing] out of [the] Agreement'.[38] Therefore, it might not be clear whether the parties intended these disputes to be solved by an expert in a final and binding ED procedure or by an arbitral tribunal. According to Fischer and Walbert, in the case of doubt 'it is the content of the agreement, i.e., the tasks entrusted upon and powers vested in the expert or arbitrator and not the terminology employed by the parties that determines whether the parties agreed on expert determination or on arbitration'.[39] The scope of the mandate entrusted to the expert also has a bearing. The narrower the scope of such mandate 'the more it is an indication that the parties intended the dispute to be decided by an expert rather than an arbitrator'.[40]

As pointed out by Peter and Greineder, the parties may also:

> provide for a tiered provision, where a matter must be referred to expert determination and then subject to review by an arbitral tribunal. It is also possible for a dispute resolution provision to leave the parties with a choice of referring a matter to either an expert or arbitral tribunal. In that case, an arbitral tribunal would have the authority to decide any matter that might equally be referred to expert determination, in addition to any other dispute arising under the M&A agreement and covered by the arbitration agreement.[41]

36. Born, *supra* note 6.
37. Frank Spoorenberg, *Expert Determination and Arbitration: An Uneasy but Necessary Distinction (blog post)* (2009).
38. Sachs, *supra* note 4 at 237-238.
39. Fischer and Walbert, *supra* note 7 at 41.
40. *Id.*, at 41.
41. Peter and Greineder, *supra* note 10.

Nevertheless, courts and arbitral tribunals also struggle with distinguishing ED and arbitration. In the United Kingdom, the jurisdiction where ED has been exploited for 'at least 250 years',[42] there are a plethora of cases that discuss the distinguishing features. In *Holt v. Cox*, judge Santow J explained that 'the distinction is that an arbitrator exercises a quasi-judicial function to whom is submitted for decision a formulated dispute to be decided between the competing contentions of the parties, while an expert determines matters from the expert's own experience and expert knowledge, making his or her own investigations'.[43] In the seminal case of *Barclays Bank v. Nylon Capital*, Thomas LJ found that in contrast to arbitration, ED 'is a very different form of dispute resolution to which neither the Arbitration Act 1996 nor any other statutory codes apply'.[44] In a subsequent case, *Wilky Property Holdings v. London & Surrey Investments*, Deputy Judge of the High Court, Richard Snowden QC added that '[a]s such, at least prima facie, parties who have, in a carefully drafted written agreement, expressly chosen to refer their disputes to an expert should not be taken to have intended a reference to arbitration'.[45] The English courts have also found the question of immunity to be a clear distinguishing factor between ED and arbitration.[46]

In the US, the close interrelation between both institutions has caused a lot of tension. Despite the enactment of the Federal Arbitration Act (FAA) in 1925 to provide clear guidelines on how to properly distinguish ED and arbitration, the courts have often confused them.[47] This chaotic landscape prompted the New York Bar association to prepare in 2013 a report on 'Purchase Price Adjustment Clauses and Expert Determinations: Legal Issues, Practical Problems and Suggested Improvements'.[48] The report provides an inventory of the case law and recommends clearly distinguishing ED from arbitration. It is however limited to one state only.

In more general terms, currently approx. twenty-four states in the US clearly recognize ED and arbitration as distinct legal institutions.[49] The same position is taken by the Restatement Third of the US Law of International Arbitration and Investor-State Arbitration.[50] Twenty-two states do not recognize any distinction between the two, and in four states the matter has been resolved ambiguously or not at all. At the federal level, the US Courts of Appeals are split on whether ED constitutes arbitration under the FAA.[51]

42. John Kendall, Expert Determination (4th ed. 2008).
43. Andrew Lacey, *How 'Final and Binding' Is An Expert Determination? (blog post)* (2017).(citing *Holt v. Cox* (1994) 15 ACSR 313).
44. Adham Kotb, *Alternative Dispute Resolution: Arbitration Remains a Better Final and Binding Alternative Than Expert Determination*, 8 Queen Mary Law J., 127 (2017).
45. *Id.*, at 127.
46. Besson and Poudret, *supra* note 27 at 17.
47. NYC Bar, *supra* note 5 at 11.
48. NYC Bar, *supra* note 5.
49. *Penton Business Media Holdings, LLC v. Informa PLC and Informa USA, INC (2018).*
50. Restatement of the Law, The US Law of International Commercial and Investor-State Arbitration (Proposed Final Draft), 55 (2019).
51. *Penton Business Media Holdings, LLC v. Informa PLC and Informa USA*, INC, *supra* note 47.

In Switzerland, it was not until 2006 that the Swiss Federal Tribunal finally crystallized its distinction analysis, setting forth a long list of factors distinguishing arbitration from ED. In the judgment of 17 November 2006, the court found that:

> [t]he distinction between an arbitral award and an expert determination is that the former enjoys the formal and material authority of res judicata and may be modified if the requirements of a request for revision are met whilst the latter, even when it decides factual or legal issues in a way binding the parties, may be invalidated only in an ordinary proceeding, in which it must be established that the findings of the expert are manifestly inaccurate, arbitrary, faulty, gravely contrary to equity or relying on an erroneous factual statement, or affected by a failure to consent ... Case law set forth various criteria allowing such a distinction; it suggests to take into consideration, among other things, the terms of the agreement of the parties, the scope of the powers given to the third party to be appointed according to that agreement, as well as the capacity of that third party's decision to be enforceable. ... Moreover, arbitration and expert determination do not necessarily exclude each other, so that it is possible to encounter a combination of these two institutions.[52]

To summarize, 'two factors can usefully serve to distinguish arbitration from expert adjudication: the duty of an arbitrator to adjudicate between the competing arguments of the parties (without being able to rely on his or her own subjective opinion, as can an expert adjudicator) and the relate duty to comply with rules of procedural fairness'.[53]

§12.04 THE INTERACTION BETWEEN ED AND THE ARBITRAL TRIBUNAL

Most often, when the parties decide to include both an ED clause and an arbitration agreement in their M&A contract, their 'view, or hope [is] that the two would not encroach on each other and lead their own lives'.[54] In practice, however, both proceedings very often overlap, which in turn creates a conflict of competence. Depending on the forum selection clause in a particular M&A contract, these conflicts might be solved by either a state court or an arbitral tribunal. The discussion below focuses on conflict resolution by arbitral tribunals. However, since a plethora of case law on ED, in particular from England, pertains to the interaction between ED and the courts, for illustrative purposes, some reference to court cases is provided as well.

An arbitral tribunal may approach the conflict of competence in a number of ways. In particular, it can:

(i) dismiss a claim pertaining to price adjustment as inadmissible or premature;

52. Judgment in case no. 4A_428/2015 (2016), https://www.swissarbitrationdecisions.com/; Phillip Landolt, *SWITZERLAND: Expert Determination, or Arbitration?*, Global Arbitr. Rev. (2009).
53. Valasek and Wilson, *supra* note 3 at 69.
54. *X v. S*, case study presented by White & Case during the conference – M&A disputes in Warsaw, *supra* note 2.

(ii) stay the arbitration proceedings;
(iii) absorb the ED procedure into the arbitration proceedings;
(iv) issue an award which validates the ED's decision; or
(v) review the ED's decision.

[A] Possibility to Dismiss a Claim Pertaining to Price Adjustment as Inadmissible or Premature

The first scenario to consider is when one of the parties wishes to initiate arbitral proceedings but fails to undergo the ED process. Here the principal claim may be submitted as either:

(i) a claim for damages which overlaps with the price determination; or
(ii) a claim for determination by the arbitral tribunal of the purchase price.

If the arbitration agreement in the underlying contract grants the authority to the arbitral tribunal to hear 'any disputes', then such tribunal will have jurisdiction to hear all the claims, including the ones under (i) and (ii) above. However, one may argue that these claims should be dismissed as inadmissible. This is because in both cases, the claimant is requesting the arbitral tribunal to effectively disregard the parties' contractual agreement. The parties explicitly agreed in the contract to a particular sequence of events or that certain elements of their contractual relationship, such as the final purchase price, which were left open, should first be determined by an expert. Thus, submission of a claim that overlaps with the scope of the ED's mandate, without exhaustion of the ED process first, would not yet be due.

There are divergent positions on whether the obligation to undergo the ED affects the jurisdiction of the arbitral tribunal or the admissibility of a claim.

The first position considers that 'it is generally held in both civil and common law jurisdictions that to the extent a matter has been contractually referred to expert determination, the arbitral tribunal or state court lacks jurisdiction. Under German and Swiss law, this effect is referred to as "Ausschlusswirkung," and this effect of exclusion of competence is reciprocal between the two mechanisms'.[55] As explained by Frey and Müller, in Switzerland 'the arbitral tribunal must decide whether it may determine the subject-matter of the expert determination itself (e.g., by performing a new valuation or by appointing an expert for this task) or if the expert retains the exclusive jurisdiction for the determination of this subject-matter. The answer to this question depends on the specific distinction between the jurisdiction of the arbitral tribunal and the expert as agreed by the parties in the M&A contract'.[56]

A second view is that failure to refer to the ED is a matter of an admissibility issue since the objection goes to a claim which is premature. This is the position under Austrian and German law where the failure to obtain a binding ED affects the merits of the case rather than the tribunal's jurisdiction. The Austrian and German courts will

55. Sachs, *supra* note 4 at 236.
56. Harold Frey & Dominique Muller, Arbitration in Switzerland: The Practitioner's Guide 1137 (2nd ed. 2018).

find requests initiating court proceedings premature if the parties failed to go through ED.[57] Klausegger underscores that '[s]uch decision creates only a limited res judicata effect. The claimant can therefore refile the same claim once the expert determination has been obtained'.[58] Furthermore, as explained by K. Sachs who discusses the concept of ED in broader terms, not anchored in any particular jurisdiction:

> [I]f a party were to start an arbitration, in which it brought a claim based on facts that were the subject of contractually agreed expert determination (e.g. a claim for a reduction in the purchase price on grounds of an alleged shortfall in the target company's net equity), the request for arbitration would have to be dismissed as not admissible, or at least premature. It is only once the expert determination has been made that arbitration can be commenced, and only then with a request for the expert determination to be declared non-binding because of manifest errors.[59]

[B] Possibility to Stay the Arbitration Proceedings

Another possibility for the arbitral tribunal is to order a stay of proceedings and allow the ED to take its course.[60]

The practice of courts in common law countries in this respect is instructive. Freedman argues that if the parties agreed to include an ED clause in a contract and one of the parties disregards such clause and initiates proceedings, a court or arbitral tribunal will have the authority to stay the proceedings. The prerequisites for such a stay vary depending on whether the proceedings take place before a court or before an arbitral tribunal. In the case of a court, according to Freedman, a stay of proceedings might be granted only if the ED clause meets the following conditions:

(i) the process must be sufficiently certain, in that there should not be the need for an agreement at any stage before matters can proceed;
(ii) the administrative processes for selecting a party to resolve the dispute and to pay that person should also be defined;
(iii) the process or at least a model of the process should be set out so that the detail of the process is sufficiently certain.[61]

Nevertheless, even if the above conditions are met, the court, under its discretion, may still refuse to stay the proceedings. As explained by Freedman, '[t]he court may decide that having regard to the circumstances of the particular case, it would be better to allow court proceedings to continue, rather than expert determination'.[62] An example here might be *Thames Valley Power Ltd. v. Total Gas & Power Ltd*, where Justice Christopher Clarke declined to stay the proceedings on the grounds that the matter related to the interpretation of a contract between the parties, and that the issue

57. Klausegger, *supra* note 17 at 173.
58. *Id.*, at 172.
59. Klaus Sachs, *Solving Tensions Between Expert Determination and Arbitration Under M&A Contracts*, International Arbitration Under Review: Essays Honour John Beechy (2015), 3.3.
60. Kendall, *supra* note 12.
61. Filip J.M. De Ly & Paul A. Gelinas, *Dispute Prevention and Settlement Through Expert Determination and Dispute Boards*, 29 Kluwer L. Int. (2017).
62. *Id.*, at 29.

in dispute had been fully argued in the due course of the court proceedings.[63] Justice Christopher Clarke concluded that the position of one of the parties was unsustainable and that a reference to an expert would involve the duplication of effort and expense. Furthermore, the matter was urgent and reference to an expert would cause delay. Thus, the court proceeded to adjudicate the matter itself. Such position seems to be accepted only if the dispute between the parties in the ED procedure pertains to a legal issue. If the dispute is of a financial/accountancy character, it would be unacceptable for the court (the arbitral tribunal) to replace the expert, as such a decision would clearly be in violation of the parties' intentions.

The discretion of the court in cases of ED consists also in the possibility to decide that the dispute is unsuitable for ED. According to Freedman, 'the burden is on the party seeking to litigate in breach of the expert determination clause to show grounds for refusing a stay'.[64]

It seems that the grounds proposed by Freedman can be easily extrapolated to arbitration and used by arbitral tribunals for application when confronted with requests for the stay of proceedings.

[C] Possibility to Absorb ED Proceedings into Arbitration

Yet another solution is for the arbitral tribunal to 'absorb' the ED into the arbitration proceedings in such a way that the arbitral tribunal could use the ED as its own and treat the expert as a tribunal-appointed expert. According to Gross, '[i]f a request for arbitration is submitted before the terms of engagement of the expert are finally agreed, then the arbitral tribunal should be constituted before the expert determination proceedings continue. The expert then provides his determination within the arbitration proceeding, and holds a position that is similar to the position of a tribunal-appointed expert'.[65] Under this scenario, the arbitral tribunal may:

- (i) appoint the expert if the person nominated in the agreement is unavailable and the parties disagree on who should be appointed in their place;
- (ii) replace an expert who has become unavailable or unfit;
- (iii) decide preliminary legal questions in connection with the establishment of the drawing up of the closing accounts;
- (iv) assist in the preparation of the expert's report, in particular by:
  - (a) giving guidance on procedural issues or conducting the proceedings;
  - (b) requiring the parties to assist the expert, produce evidence or provide information;
  - (c) deciding on the consequences of a party's refusal to comply with a request, in particular by making negative inferences.

63. *Thames Valley Power Ltd v. Total Gas & Power Ltd*, [2006] 1 Lloyd's Rep. 441,.
64. De Ly and Gelinas, *supra* note 61 at 30.
65. Blaz Gross, *M&A Disputes and Expert Determination: Getting to Grips with the Issues (blog post)* (2010).

(v) make the expert's mandate more precise, or even amend it if the parties' original agreement on ED no longer fulfils the needs of the parties; and/or
(vi) mitigate defects in an expert's determination by giving a party their right to be heard, have the parties provide additional facts, and so on.[66]

This proposition, however, puts into question whether the ED still enjoys the finality and binding force stipulated by the parties under the ED clause and whether the standard of conduct differs. It seems that once the arbitral tribunal treats the ED as a quasi tribunal-appointed expert, the ED loses its original character. Prado underscores that if the arbitral tribunal has the authority to change the ED's mission, the ED's decision issued during the arbitration proceedings losses its original independent character as it 'aims only to contribute to inform the Arbitral Tribunal about issues it considers ... necessary or useful to support its decision'.[67]

[D] Possibility to Review the ED's Decision

If one of the parties does not agree with the ED's decision, they may challenge it before the arbitral tribunal under certain grounds such as excess of mandate fraud and material mistake.[68] From a formal point of view, a party seeking to challenge an expert decision should submit twofold relief. First, they should request a declaratory award finding that the ED's decision is not binding and final due to particular grounds (be it fraud or manifest error, etc.).[69] Second, they should request an award that would substitute ED's decision with a proper determination of the price adjustment or a final price. Such a twofold relief sought is practised in Germany.[70]

[E] Possibility to Validate the ED Decision in an Arbitral Award

Despite being final and binding, the ED's decision does not constitute an enforceable title. If one of the parties does not accept the ED's decision, the other party may ask the arbitral tribunal to confirm (validate) such decision in an arbitral award, which could then be enforced under the New York Convention.

An illustration of what such a validation process should look like is afforded by an London Court of International Arbitration (LCIA) case where the sole arbitrator issued an interim award found that an ED against Pakistan was final and binding and ordered Pakistan to pay USD 167 million to a group of nine local power companies pursuant to the ED's decision.[71] Similarly, in ICC Case 14691, the arbitral tribunal issued an award validating the ED's decision. In this case, the share purchase agreement provided for an additional price to be paid by the buyer to the seller in the

66. *Id.*
67. De Ly and Gelinas, *supra* note 61 at 44.
68. For detailed analysis of the ground for challenge *see Id.*, at 31.
69. Sachs, *supra* note 59.
70. Sessler and Leimert, *supra* note 16 at 164.
71. Lacey Yong, *LCIA Arbitrator Rules Against Pakistani State Entity*, Global Arbitr. Rev. (2017).

event that the target company met certain earn-out targets. The seller had received an advance on the earn-out portion of the price. In the arbitration initiated by the buyer, the seller raised several counterclaims with respect to the earn-out, in particular regarding: (i) the inclusion of certain recurring credits in the company's accounts; (ii) the time of payment of the earn-out sum; and (iii) the currency in which payment was to be made and the relevant exchange rate. The arbitral tribunal found that the ED, which had excluded the recurring credits for purposes of determining the earn-out, was final and binding. It further held that the buyer should have paid the earn-out amount immediately after sending the seller the notice containing their calculation of the amount due. Therefore, the seller was entitled to interest from such date until the date of actual payment. Finally, the advance on the earn-out had been paid in US dollars, while the earn-out was to be paid in Brazilian reais. The arbitral tribunal considered that the advance payment could only be credited at the time the main payment became due and payable, and based its decision on the exchange rate as of that date.[72]

[F] Practical Examples of Ways to Resolve Conflicts of Competence Between ED and Arbitral Tribunals

Three recent cases provide an interesting insight into how conflicts of competences between arbitral tribunals and ED are resolved in practice.

In the *first case*, a Dutch Holding ('X') concluded a share purchase agreement ('SPA') with a seller ('S'), owner of the target company ('Company'). The Company cooperated with X's subsidiary. The SPA contemplated a price consisting of three components, a Base Price (a percent of 7 x the Company's operating income (OI)); an Earn-Out (7 annual deferred payments of 7 x the Company's OI); and an Additional Payment. The SPA included an ED clause dealing with an Annual Determination, under which the expert was to determine, among other things, the Company's OI. The parties agreed that the expert 'shall act as an expert and not as an arbitrator' and that its decision 'shall be binding, final and conclusive upon all the parties'.[73] The SPA also included a broad arbitration agreement with arbitration under Vienna International Arbitral Center (VIAC) Rules, seated in Vienna, Austria.

The problems arose when the last deferred payment was to be calculated. X claimed that S allegedly manipulated the revenue in order to artificially increase the Company's OI and, at the same time, had increased the payments due under the earn-out. Consequently, X blocked the process of calculating the Annual Determination by refusing to disclose the Company's financial documents to S. X also refused to pay the Additional Payment. S initiated arbitration for payment of the Additional Payment only and sought X to engage in ED procedure. X continued to refuse to participate in the ED procedure. It brought, however, a counterclaim for determination by the arbitral

72. Carlevaris, *supra* note 1 at 29-30.
73. *X v. S*, case study presented by White & Case during the conference – M&A disputes in Warsaw, *supra* note 2.

tribunal of the final sale price, which included determination of the last year OI and determination of the impact of the alleged 'schemes' on previous earn-out payments.

S raised jurisdiction and admissibility objections, stating that the claim for determination is premature as X disregarded the ED procedure; and that determination of the Annual Determination was beyond the scope of the arbitral tribunal's jurisdiction. Furthermore, S claimed that ED was a precondition to arbitrate any disputes associated with the Annual Determination.

X's counterarguments regarding the jurisdiction and admissibility were that ED was not a precondition for arbitration, that ED did not limit the arbitral tribunal's jurisdiction, and that ED pertained to other issues than the counterclaim for determination of the price.

The arbitral tribunal issued an award on jurisdiction where it found that the contract 'itself contains an unrestricted arbitration clause' and that 'the Independent Expert's task is very specific and narrower than the tasks attributed to ... the Arbitral Tribunal'.[74] The arbitral tribunal further noted that the:

> arbitration clause does not refer to the Independent Expert [ED] clause, nor does the latter mention the former. It appears to have been the Parties' view, or hope, that the two would not encroach on each other and lead their own lives. ... The absence of any reference to the Independent Expert procedure as another prerequisite for arbitration supports the argument that [the ED clause] is not a prerequisite to arbitration and does not affect jurisdiction or admissibility of a claim. ... Therefore, on whatever construction, [the ED clause] cannot affect jurisdiction or admissibility of the Respondent's counterclaims to the extent that they are broader than the Annual Determination.[75]

The arbitral tribunal, however, emphasized that the situation pertaining to the claims which rely on the Annual Determination, i.e., the scope of the Independent Expert's mandate, is different. With respect to those claims:

> the parties must obtain [an ED's decision] through the process set out in [the ED clause] in a first stage, i.e. before the Arbitral Tribunal decides the broader counterclaim. ... The Arbitral Tribunal finds that [the ED clause] vests the Independent Expert with a priority right only, not with an unfettered one ... The Parties cannot have meant in good faith that the result of a cursory review, in a process where no legal issues are decided, would have such far reaching effects without any safety net for either of them. ... Irrespective of the applicable law and the degree and conditions of finality of the Independent Expert's decision, the Arbitral Tribunal considers that the Parties can be presumed to have wanted some restraints.[76]

In conclusion, the arbitral tribunal dismissed both jurisdictional and admissibility objections. At the same time, it stated that 'the Parties are required to conduct the Independent Expert procedure foreseen in [the ED clause] in order to establish the

74. *Id.*
75. *Id.*
76. *Id.*

Annual Determination to the extent that it has an impact on the claims or counterclaims in this arbitration'.[77]

Interestingly, although the arbitral tribunal did not dismiss the counterclaims as inadmissible (as it should have, it did honour the parties' intention to keep separate the mandates of the expert and the arbitrators), it de facto compelled X to honour its contractual obligation to direct all the issues arising out of the Annual Determination to the ED. Only once the ED decision had been issued, the tribunal would be able to assume the authority to hear X's claims.

The *second case, General Electric v. Alstom,* also confirms that in the end, the parties' intention to resolve factual disputes through the ED first, before the arbitral tribunal assumes its jurisdiction, will usually be respected.

In 2014, Alstrom agreed to purchase a rail-signalling business from General Electric (GE) for USD 800 million, subject to a post-closing purchase price adjustment process, including Final Positive (or Negative) Working Capital Adjustments.[78] The contract included the ED clause under which the parties foresaw a detailed procedure to 'determine whether they have any disputes as to the specific working capital adjustment items, and for working capital disputes to be decided by an Independent Accounting Firm' (IAF).[79] The parties agreed that 'any matters identified in [the] Dispute Notice that remain in dispute ... shall be finally and conclusively determined by' an IAF and that the IAF was to function as 'an expert and not as an arbitrator'.[80]

The contract also provided for arbitration in New York under the ICC Arbitration Rules. The parties carved out from the jurisdiction of the arbitral tribunal all the issues to be dealt with by the expert under the ED clause.[81]

At the stage of the post-closing purchase price adjustment process, GE delivered its position as to possible adjustments of the purchase prices. Alstrom disagreed and submitted its own position, taking issue with thirty-eight items in GE's position. With the exact amounts not being public, it appears there was a substantial difference between the parties as to the scope of adjustment. Alstrom sought the IAF to determine the final purchase price. GE replied stating that while half of the items disputed by Alstrom should be decided by the IAF, the other half 'have little or no connection to accounting matters at all'[82] and 'challenged its business and engineering judgements rather than its application of accounting principles [that] were for'[83] the arbitral tribunal to resolve.

GE, instead of participating in the ED procedure, submitted a request for an emergency arbitrator followed by a request for arbitration to the ICC in May 2016.[84] In its request for arbitration, GE explained that it aimed to prevent Alstrom 'from abusing a "working capital adjustment" proceeding before an accounting firm to seek a ... price

77. *Id.*
78. *General Electric v. Alstom et.al.*, Request for Arbitration (2016).
79. *Id.*, at 26.
80. *Alstom, et. al., v. General Electric*, Opinion and Order (2017).
81. *General Electric v. Alstom et.al.*, Request for Arbitration, *supra* note 78.
82. *Id.*, at 44.
83. *Alstom, et. al., v. General Electric*, Opinion and Order, *supra* note 80 at 44.
84. Ali Khan, *Amber Signal for GE-Alstom Rail Dispute*, Global Arbitr. Rev. (2016).

reduction on an $ 800 million sale of GE business ... to Alstrom'.[85] The gist of the dispute was a distinction between 'working capital issues' which ought to be decided by an IAF and the legal claims which ought to be decided by the arbitral tribunal. The GE explained that Alstrom sought to 'disguise baseless legal claims as working capital adjustments and assert those claims in a forum that it considers advantageous to it'.[86] According to GE, Alstom tried to introduce claims relating to representations and warranties that it failed to obtain from GE during the contract negotiations.[87] Consequently, GE requested, among other things, that the arbitral tribunal 'declare[s] that an Independent Accounting Firm appointed under the [contract] would not have authority to render a binding determination concerning'[88] the final purchase price.

A few days later, Alstrom asked the New York City court to issue a summary judgment and compel ED procedure. GE requested the court to either stay the procedure pending arbitration before the ICC or compel such arbitration. [89] Initially, Alstom obtained a temporary restraining order that prevented GE from pursuing an ICC claim against Alstrom. The order was vacated a month later.[90] The judge however ordered the parties to promptly act for the limited purpose of constituting an arbitral tribunal before the ICC within the prescribed deadlines, and also to promptly and jointly appoint an IAF.[91] The parties were also ordered to refrain from presenting any substantive arguments to the ICC tribunal or the IAF pending their decision on which forum had jurisdiction.

In his order of 10 January 2017, the judge discussed first the arbitrability issue, and explained that the important question in the case was 'who should decide the very question of who decides', i.e., the tribunal or the court. In the course of the proceedings, GE argued that this question falls under the kompetenz-kompetenz principle squarely into the arbitral tribunal's jurisdiction. Alstrom was of the opinion that the arbitrability issue (under the US meaning of the institution) is for the court to decide.[92]

At the outset of his analysis, the judge first found that the ED clause is in 'itself an arbitration clause'. Second, he underscored that the existence of both the ED clause and an arbitration agreement 'creates an ambiguity'.[93] Consequently, the judge found that the question put by Alstrom should be decided by the court, and not the arbitral tribunal.

As to the central dispute between the parties, i.e., whether all or only some of the issues raised by Alstrom should be submitted to the IAF (ED), the judge found that the ED clause was a narrow one, as it was limited to certain disputes over the proposed

85. *General Electric v. Alstom et.al.*, Request for Arbitration, *supra* note 78 at 1.
86. *Id.*, at 1.
87. Ali Khan, *GE Gets Red Light for Claim Against Alstom*, Global Arbitr. Rev. (2016). *Id.*
88. *General Electric v. Alstom et.al.*, Request for Arbitration, *supra* note 78 at 70.
89. *Alstom, et. al., v. General Electric*, Opinion and Order, *supra* note 80 at 5.
90. Khan, *supra* note 84.
91. *Alstom, et. al., v. General Electric*, Stipulation and Order (2016).
92. It should be born in mind that the issues of arbitrability are differently understood in Europe and in US.
93. *Alstom, et. al., v. General Electric*, Opinion and Order, *supra* note 80 at 6.

Working Capital Statement and Net Debt Statements. Therefore, he agreed with Alstrom that the thirty-eight issues raised by it should be submitted to the IAF (ED), in the first instance.[94] The court paid attention to the language of the ED clause which stated that 'any matters identified in [the] Dispute Notice that remain in dispute ... shall be finally and conclusively determined by the IAF'.[95]

Furthermore, the court found that the ED clause 'do[es] not substantively limit the kinds of disputes to be delegated to the IAF; [it] require[s] only that a dispute be included in the Dispute Notice and remain unresolved'. However, the court cautioned that this does not mean that:

> any claim would be subject to resolution by the IAF simply because Alstom chose to include it in the Dispute Notice ... Although GE contends that the disputed items impermissibly challenge its engineering and business judgments ..., the issues raised by Alstom are not merely collateral to the determination of the Final Working Capital; to the contrary, Alstom has laid out – in a more than plausible manner – the specifics of its objections and the accounting principles upon which each objection is based. ... The mere fact that the issues raised by Alstom call for more than 'bean-counting' does not take them outside the scope of the purchase price adjustment dispute-resolution provisions.[96]

The court also made reference to the carve-out in the arbitration agreement which excluded from the scope of the arbitral tribunal's jurisdiction disputes arising out of the price adjustment process. It found that the decision whether a dispute falls within the scope of such a carve-out or not should be interpreted by the IAF (ED). The parties to the dispute were clear that they wish such issues to be decided by the IAF (ED) and not the arbitral tribunal. Therefore, the question which of thirty-eight disputed items can be entertained by the IAF (ED) should be submitted in the first instance to the IAF (ED), even if the IAF (ED) might subsequently agree with GE that these issues do not have an accountancy character. The court emphasized the sequence of events, and quoted *XL Capital* case, where the court 'caution[ed] that [its] conclusion . . . [was] not a back door permitting' non-accounting issues 'to be brought before' the IAF, and 'note[d] that disputes may well remain for the ICC to decide even after the IAF "resolves the issues before it." But these are arguments that GE must make in the first instance to the IAF, not to this Court or to the ICC'.

This judgment is interesting for a number of reasons. First, the court found that the ED clause was in fact an arbitration agreement, and consequently applied to the FAA. The judge relied on older case law where the court had noted that '[c]ourts have consistently found that purchase price adjustment dispute resolution provisions ... constitute enforceable arbitration agreement'.[97] He did so, despite the fact that the parties included in the ED clause the statement that the IAF 'shall function as an expert and not as an arbitrator'. At a glimpse, this order seems to disregard not only the parties' explicit intention to maintain a clear distinction between ED and arbitration but

94. *Id.*, at 10.
95. *Id.*, at 11.
96. *Id.*, at 11-12.
97. *Id.*, at 6.

also a rather consistent New York case law which takes the opposite view, clearly distinguishing ED from arbitration. However, once one takes into account the final result, the judge in fact respected the parties' intention; i.e., he compelled GE to honour its contractual obligation to direct a certain type of dispute to the expert first for final and binding determination. Only after that, under a broad arbitration agreement, could GE request the arbitral tribunal to hear GE's challenge to the ED decisions. While this case is very US specific, it nevertheless illustrates how important it is to be very careful while drafting ED clauses and also very vigilant in designating different dispute resolution methods for different types of dispute.

Finally, the *third case*, ICC Case 11587 is illustrative of how an arbitral tribunal may 'absorb' the ED procedure into the arbitration proceedings. In that case, the claimant agreed to sell to respondents all the shares of several companies incorporated in various jurisdictions. The purchase contract provided for two different closing dates, at each of which 50% of the shares of the target companies were to be transferred against payment of 50% of the purchase price which was subject to adjustment depending, among other things, on the determination of the consolidated net equity of the target business. A dispute arose between the parties over the method of determining the price adjustment. The buyers claimed that any dispute relating to the calculation of the price was to be settled by ED pursuant to the dispute settlement clause contained in the contract and requested the appointment of a contractual expert. The seller objected, arguing that the dispute extended beyond mere price determination and covered the buyers' compliance with their contractual obligations with respect to the exchange of documents and information relating to price adjustment. The arbitral tribunal rendered three partial awards dealing with the preliminary issues. In its first partial award, the arbitral tribunal 'postponed' the decision on whether to appoint a contractual expert to determine the matters in dispute relating to price adjustment, as requested by the respondents. It decided to appoint a procedural expert under Article 20(4) of the 1998 ICC Rules of Arbitration to assist it in assessing the parties' conduct with respect to the price adjustment mechanism provided in the contract. In the second partial award, the tribunal endorsed the conclusions of the expert it had appointed and decided that none of the parties had forfeited their rights with respect to price adjustment. Accordingly, the arbitral tribunal granted the respondents' claim for the appointment of a contractual expert to assess the accounting issues required for determining the final sale price. In the third partial award, the arbitral tribunal determined the cut-off dates on the basis of which the price adjustment should be assessed.[98]

§12.05 CONCLUSIONS

The analysis of the case law which has emerged in international arbitration thus far suggests that it is possible to draw a demarcation line between ED and arbitration. It

98. Carlevaris, *supra* note 1 at 23.

seems that there is no dispute on how to distinguish an ED clause from an arbitration agreement.

The best test to distinguish ED from arbitration 'can be found in the type and scope of authority that is being delegated by the parties to the decision maker'.[99] This is because the authority granted to an expert is limited to deciding a specific factual issue or dispute concerning a matter which is within the special expertise of the expert, usually concerning an issue of valuation. The expert's authority is limited to their mandate to use their specialized knowledge to resolve a specified issue of fact. The parties do not, however, normally grant the expert the authority to make binding decisions on issues of law or legal claims, such as legal liability.[100] In the absence of clear language in a contract suggesting that the expert is not an arbitrator, this author agrees that the scope of the ED's mandate should be decisive in assessing whether the clause under analysis is an ED clause or an arbitration agreement.

The real problem with ED, however, seems to be the conflict of competences between the ED and arbitral tribunal's jurisdiction. There does not seem to be a good or final answer to how that conflict of competence should be resolved. The overlap between the two seems unavoidable and, most importantly, impossible to prevent. Thus, it seems that the best and most logical solution when the parties decided to include both an ED clause and an arbitration agreement and the ED process has not been complied with is for the arbitral tribunal to stay the proceedings and compel the parties to go through the ED first. This is in line with the general concept of admissibility which pertains to the claim and not the jurisdiction of the arbitral tribunal. Only once the ED is finalized can the claims pertaining to the scope of the ED be entertained by the arbitral tribunal. Otherwise, the ED clause would have been devoid of its purpose and would be made redundant. Indeed, the practical examples provided herein confirm that the intention of the parties to keep a certain order of events (first the ED procedure, and only after that arbitration) should be the decisive factor.

99. NYC Bar, *supra* note 5 at 4.
100. *Id.*, at 4.

CHAPTER 13

Witness Examination in International Arbitration – Best Practices Regarding Cross-Examination and Related Issues

Rikard Wikström-Hermansen & Christopher Spreigl

A main feature of international arbitration is the arbitral tribunal's discretion to decide on most procedural issues that may arise during the proceedings. When deciding on such procedural issues, the arbitral tribunal usually turns to what constitutes best practice. However, what constitutes best practice is not always entirely clear, and it is therefore of interest to examine it so as to provide some degree of clarity. In this chapter, best practice is examined and evaluated in relation to what is often the main event of an oral hearing – witness examination.

The following issues are discussed: (i) whether an arbitral tribunal should allow and/or mandate written witness statements, (ii) the evidentiary weight of written witness statements when the witness does not attend the oral hearing, (iii) how direct examination ought to be conducted when written witness statements have been used, (iv) admissibility of questions during cross-examination, (v) whether to allow new evidence during cross-examination to prove a witness is lying, (vi) how digital hearings affect cross-examination, and (vii) issues of witness sequestration, including how digital hearings affect the possibility for sequestration.

§13.01 INTRODUCTION

In international arbitration, parties normally only agree on a broad procedural framework. In the absence of a detailed and uniform procedural framework, many aspects of the arbitral process will be subject to the discretion of the arbitral tribunal. In an international setting, deciding on procedural issues can be a challenging task. The arbitral tribunal is often faced with having to reconcile differing cultural backgrounds and approaches to procedural issues in a manner that is considered reasonable by both parties, and concurrently conforms to best international practice.

This becomes particularly clear in relation to witness examination. Different legal systems take (sometimes considerably) different approaches when dealing with witnesses as evidence. Consequently, parties from different legal backgrounds will have differing attitudes towards witness examination. For example, lawyers from common law backgrounds will generally underline the importance of cross-examination, whereas lawyers from civil law backgrounds often take a more sceptical attitude towards it.[1] As witness hearings often constitute the main events in a hearing, it is of interest to examine best practice in this area. Best practice ought to reconcile the different attitudes towards witness examination. As witness examinations generally are costly and time-consuming events, best practice ought to balance the interest in conducting an efficient arbitration against the parties' right to present their cases.

In this chapter, we examine best practice in international arbitration for some common procedural issues related to witness examination. Initially, the concept 'best practice' is discussed in brief (§13.02), before going into specific issues. The rest of the chapter deals with issues related to witness statements (§13.03), direct examination (§13.04), cross-examination (§13.05), and witness sequestration (§13.06). The chapter ends with some concluding remarks (§13.07).

§13.02 SOME REMARKS ABOUT THE CONCEPT 'BEST PRACTICE'

Before we look at what solutions to common procedural issues are, or ought to be considered, best practice, a few words should be said about the concept 'best practice'. In our opinion, best practice can be described as: an existing practice that arbitrators and arbitration litigators as a collective consider most prudent. However, it is much more difficult to say exactly what practices the collective agrees upon. As practitioners come from different legal backgrounds around the world, many different opinions are expressed. However, the trend in international arbitration has been towards developing an international set of standards that try to bridge the gap between different legal cultures.[2] Therefore, in the authors' opinion, it is possible to 'nail down' what constitutes best practice in specific situations, with at least a certain degree of precision.

For the purposes of this chapter, we have used the following definition of what constitutes best practice as a working method. We suggest that 'best practice' is comprised of two components:

(i) Common practice, i.e., prevailing solutions that most arbitral tribunals will apply to certain problems.
(ii) Rationality, i.e., the solution that is purported to be best practice must have a rational justification.

1. Gary B. Born, *International Commercial Arbitration* (3d ed., Kluwer Law International 2021), 2453-2454.
2. *See* Klaus Peter Berger, *Common Law vs. Civil Law in International Arbitration: The Beginning or the End?*, Journal of International Arbitration, Volume 36, Issue 3, 295, 295-298 (2019).

It can be argued that common practice tends to be rational as the practice became common due to the rationality generally convincing arbitrators to apply the solution. However, it is important to not simply accept *common* practice as *best* practice, as alternative solutions may be more rational.

It is of course not always simple to ascertain what is the prevailing practice. Rationality may also prove a problem as it is seldom the case that one alternative solution to a procedural issue is obviously the most rational one. Therefore, what constitutes best practice must be evaluated on an ongoing basis, both in terms of what is common practice, and in terms of the rationality of the common practice. In a sense, best practice will evolve over time.

That being said, for issues on evidence, the International Bar Association (IBA) Rules on the Taking of Evidence in International Arbitration have a widespread acceptance and can thus be taken to be an expression of what constitutes best practice.[3] We frequently cite these rules in this chapter. However, so as to meet the requirements of our definition, we will also assess the rules to determine their rationality.

§13.03 WRITTEN WITNESS STATEMENTS

[A] Allowing Written Witness Statements

When relying on evidence from a fact witness, it is common practice in international arbitration to present witness testimony in the form of a written witness statement.[4] The witness statement often replaces the direct oral examination. According to the IBA Rules on the Taking of Evidence, the statement should contain:

> [A] full and detailed description of the facts, and the source of the witness's information as to those facts, sufficient to serve as that witness's evidence in the matter in dispute.[5]

The witness statement is provided in advance of the oral hearing to both the arbitral tribunal and the other party.[6] Notwithstanding the common use of written witness statements, a party may oppose the use of witness statements, and request to hear the witnesses orally. There may be several reasons for such a request. The party may be principally opposed to witness statements, as they deprive witnesses of their

3. Berger, *supra* n. 2, at 302-303. It is stated in the Foreword to the IBA Rules on the Taking of Evidence in International Arbitration 2020: 'Since their issuance in 1999, the IBA Rules on the Taking of Evidence in International Commercial Arbitration have gained wide acceptance within the international arbitral community.'
4. Born, *supra* n. 1, at 2423-2424; Blackaby Nigel, Constantine Partasides, Alan Redfern & Martin Hunter, *Redfern and Hunter on International Arbitration* (6th ed., Oxford University Press 2015), 390; Roman Mikhailovich Khodykin, Carol Mulcahy, Nicholas Hugo & Martin Fletcher, *A Guide to the IBA Rules on the Taking of Evidence in International Arbitration* (Oxford University Press 2019), 7.60.
5. Article 4.5(b).
6. Born, *supra* n. 1, at 2423.

'day in court'.[7] Alternatively, the party may consider that an oral testimony may be advantageous for strategic reasons. Perhaps the party's witnesses are skilled orators, whereas the other party's witnesses are assumed to be less well spoken.

If the parties are not in agreement as to the use of witness statements, the arbitral tribunal must decide whether they should be allowed. It is the authors' opinion that best practice in international cases is that the tribunal should allow witness statements.[8] As mentioned above, the use of witness statements is widespread in international arbitration.[9] In the authors' view, the predominant use of witness statements is prompted by the fact that witness statements provide *greater efficiency* and contribute to a *fair process*.

With regard to efficiency, witness statements drastically shorten the direct examination, as the witness generally only needs to confirm that the facts provided in the written statement are correct.[10]

Witness statements also contribute to a fair process as they often provide parties with detailed information about the other side's evidence.[11] Due to the use of witness statements, the parties can better prepare their counterarguments and decide how the witness should best be examined.[12] This is of course much more difficult without witness statements.[13] Another benefit of each party being provided with information about the other party's evidence in advance is that the parties' presentations of their respective cases generally become more succinct, which also furthers efficiency.[14]

Witness statements have been criticized for being an inferior alternative to hearing the witness' factual observations orally. As the party's counsel often assists in drafting the statement, questions might be raised about how genuine the witness statement is.[15] While this is a legitimate concern, it should be noted that the criticism is just as applicable to an oral examination of a witness who has been prepared by counsel.[16] We consider that the above-mentioned benefits of witness statements

---

7. Cf. Born, *supra* n. 1, at 2425.
8. This view is supported by Born, *see* Born *supra* n. 1, at 2425, and Lindskog, *see* Stefan Lindskog, *Skiljeförfarande: en kommentar* (3rd ed., Norstedts Juridik 2020), 732-733. Lindskog notes that, in international arbitral proceedings, the arbitral tribunal as a rule should allow witness statements, even if one of the parties protests.
9. Born, *supra* n. 1, at 2423-2424. Blackaby, et al., *supra* n. 4 at 390. Both the IBA Rules on the Taking of Evidence and the Prague Rules have provisions on witness statements, *see* Articles 4.4-5 and 5.3-8, respectively.
10. Born, *supra* n. 1, at 2425. Article 8.5 of the IBA Rules on the Taking of Evidence provides that the witness statement can serve as the witness' direct testimony. *See also* the Commentary on the 2020 IBA Rules on the Taking of Evidence, at 18.
11. Cf. the Preamble to the IBA Rules on the Taking of Evidence, paras 1 and 3.
12. *See* the Commentary on the 2020 IBA Rules on the Taking of Evidence, at 18.
13. Khodykin et al., *supra* n. 4, at 7.64.
14. In the Commentary on the 2020 IBA Rules on the Taking of Evidence, at 18 it is noted that the written statements also benefit the tribunal, as it is 'in a better position to appreciate the testimony and put its own questions to the witness'.
15. Born, *supra* n. 1, at 2425. As Khodykin et al. notes, some critics make the point that witness statements are simply a vehicle for the counsel to make further submissions, *see* Khodykin et al., *supra* n. 4, at 7.67.
16. Born, *supra* n. 1, at 2425. However, Blackaby, et al. note that experienced arbitrators may see through overly prepared witnesses, *see* Blackaby, et al., *supra* n. 4 at 392. Therefore, oral examination might be a better alternative if one only considers the issue of genuineness.

outweigh the drawbacks. We also note that the fact that the other party has access to the witness statement prior to the hearing means that the party can better prepare a cross-examination by which potential issues of genuineness can be brought to light.

[B] Mandating Written Witness Statements

If one party opposes written witness statements, an arbitral tribunal should, in general, nevertheless allow witness statements. It has been suggested that, even though it is best practice for the arbitral tribunal to *allow* witness statements, the arbitral tribunal should not, in general, *mandate* that a party who opposes witness statements must hand in a witness statement for a witness to be heard during the oral hearing.[17] We submit that this cannot be considered best practice. Instead, the arbitral tribunal should in general mandate that a witness statement must be submitted for a witness to be heard. Otherwise, the above-mentioned benefits of witness statements would be undercut. A party will likely not hand in a witness statement if it knows that the counterparty will refrain from doing likewise, as this would provide the counterparty the opportunity to better prepare its cross-examination.[18] Thus, by only allowing, and not mandating, witness statements, the proceedings would in most cases be conducted without witness statements.

It is therefore not surprising that Article 4.4 of the IBA Rules on the Taking of Evidence expressly grants the tribunal the right to order the submission of witness statements:

> The Arbitral Tribunal may order each Party to submit [...] to the Arbitral Tribunal and to the other Parties Witness Statements by each witness on whose testimony it intends to rely.[19]

That being said, there is always room for nuance when an issue is decided in the tribunal's discretion. The wishes of the parties and the specific circumstances of the case can make mandating witness statements unsuitable.[20]

[C] Evidentiary Weight of a Written Witness Statement Without a Testimony

A question which arises when using written witness statements in an arbitration is what evidentiary weight should be placed on the witness statement if the witness does

17. Lindskog, *supra* n. 8, at 733, footnote 2891 ('[d]äremot bör i regel inte skiljenämnden mot en parts bestridande bifalla den andres begäran om att förhören skall föregås av vittnesattester. Det måste således stå en part fritt att avstå från att ge in vittnesattester').
18. It could be argued that the submitting party's rights to know in advance what evidence the other party relies on is sufficiently ensured by the arbitral tribunal requiring the parties to identify their witnesses and the subject matter of their testimony, cf. Article 4.1 in the IBA Rules on the Taking of Evidence. There is, however, a considerable difference between knowing the subject matter of a testimony and knowing exactly what the testimony consists of.
19. *See also* Article 5.5 of the Prague Rules.
20. *See* the Commentary on the 2020 IBA Rules on the Taking of Evidence, at 18.

not appear at the hearing. The problem touches on an important aspect of arbitration, namely the other party's right to cross-examine the witness. The value of cross-examination can be debated.[21] Without going further into this discussion, we merely note that cross-examination is common practice in arbitration. There is also a case to be made that, if a party is allowed to submit a witness statement, the other party ought to be allowed to question this evidence.[22] Cross-examination is generally a useful tool for this.

When a witness refuses to appear at the hearing, the other party is denied the opportunity to cross-examine that witness.[23] Thus, to ensure the party's right to present its case, the witness statement's evidentiary weight ought to be affected. Article 4.7 of the IBA Rules on the Taking of Evidence provides as follows:

> If a witness whose appearance has been requested pursuant to Article 8.1 fails without a *valid reason* to appear for testimony at an Evidentiary Hearing, the Arbitral Tribunal shall disregard any Witness Statement related to that Evidentiary Hearing by that witness unless, in *exceptional circumstances*, the Arbitral Tribunal decides otherwise (emphasis added).

For the arbitral tribunal to attach evidentiary weight to the witness statement, either the witness must have provided a valid excuse or exceptional circumstances must exist. This rule reflects common practice.[24] The inclusion of exceptions to the rule that a witness statement without a witness to back it up at the hearing is prudent. The party who has submitted the witness statement has a right to present its case and the reasons for the witness not showing up may be outside of the party's control.[25] However, the exceptions should be interpreted restrictively.

A *valid reason* for not attending the hearing could be some kind of considerable hindrance to attend the hearing. Examples include serious illness and having to undergo a medical procedure with a certain degree of urgency. The excuse ought to be substantiated by some kind of documentation, such as a doctor's note.[26] The death of the witness is of course also a valid excuse.[27] When considering whether the witness' excuse constitutes a valid reason, the arbitral tribunal ought to consider the possibilities of conducting the examination via videoconference.[28] This will exclude many excuses that would previously have been valid, such as being hindered from attending physically by travel restrictions.[29]

21. *See* Khodykin et al., *supra* n. 4, at 7.140-7.145 for an overview of the debate.
22. Khodykin et al., *supra* n. 4, at 7.144.
23. Note that the other party may not have called the witness for cross-examination. In such cases, the party's rights are not infringed by the witness not showing up, cf. Article 4.8 of the IBA Rules on the Taking of Evidence.
24. Born, *supra* n. 1, at 2456.
25. Cf. Khodykin et al., *supra* n. 4, at 7.158.
26. Khodykin et al., *supra* n. 4, at 7.148.
27. Anne-Véronique Schlaepfer, 'Chapter 4. Witness Statements', in Laurent Lévy and V.V. Veeder (eds), *Arbitration and Oral Evidence, Dossiers of the ICC Institute of World Business Law, Volume 2* (Kluwer Law International 2004), 70.
28. Born, *supra* n. 1, at 2456.
29. Note that if the parties are opposed to videoconferencing, or the arbitral tribunal has mandated against it, not being able to attend physically will generally be a valid excuse.

As some authors have observed, it is difficult to imagine what could constitute *exceptional circumstances*, but not a valid reason.[30] There may be some situations where a reason provided is not sufficient to be considered valid, but the specific circumstances of the case justify attaching at least some evidentiary weight to the witness statement.

Even if the witness statement is accepted in accordance with Article 4.7, questions might be raised as to its evidentiary weight. The fact remains that the witness has not been cross-examined and the witness statement's evidentiary weight should be diminished accordingly.[31]

§13.04 DIRECT EXAMINATION

During an oral hearing, fact witnesses are usually initially examined by the party who presented the witness. This examination is referred to as the direct examination. As mentioned in §13.03[A] above, the direct examination is often rendered redundant in international cases by the use of witness statements. Instead, the examining party simply asks the witness some initial questions such as his or her name, followed by the witness confirming the witness statement.[32] Though this procedure is efficient, it is conceivable that a party may still want to conduct a full-length direct examination.

By way of example, take the above-mentioned party who was opposed to the use of written witness statements. Dissatisfied with the arbitral tribunal's decision to order written witness statements, the party nevertheless submits them. At the hearing, the party insists on conducting a complete direct examination. An alternative scenario is that the party provides a witness statement which only includes the broad strokes of the witness' testimony. The party intends for the witness to elaborate on the witness statement in further detail during the direct examination, thus in practice accomplishing the party's goal of conducting a complete direct examination. Should the arbitral tribunal allow such procedural manoeuvres?

Article 8.5 of the IBA Rules on the Taking of Evidence provides that:

> [T]he Arbitral Tribunal may order that the Witness Statement or Expert Report shall serve as that witness's direct testimony, in which event the Arbitral Tribunal may nevertheless permit further oral direct testimony.

In our opinion, best practice is that the arbitral tribunal should, in general, order that the witness statement is to replace a full-length direct testimony. One of the main reasons for using witness statements is that they eliminate the need for direct examinations, which generally shortens the duration of the hearing. It is also common

30. Khodykin et al., *supra* n. 4, at 7.151.
31. Cf. Schlaepfer, *supra* n. 27, at 72-73 where the author presents a sceptical view to witness statements' evidentiary weight in general.
32. Cf. Article 8.5 in the IBA Rules on the Taking of Evidence.

practice in international arbitrations for witness statements to replace direct examinations.[33]

That being said, the parties ought to be provided with an opportunity to conduct a brief direct examination, as long as the questions are limited to the contents of the witness statement. The benefit of such an examination is that it provides the arbitral tribunal with a better idea of the witness' character. As the cross-examining party will often attempt to tarnish the witness' credibility, it would be unfair if the other party could not present the witness in a better light during direct examination.[34] A brief direct examination provides the arbitral tribunal with a 'baseline' from which to evaluate the evidentiary weight of the witness' testimony.[35] For this purpose, we suggest that as a rule of thumb, it is enough for such an examination to be limited to ten to twenty minutes. In our opinion, this balances the interest of efficiency against the parties' right to present their case.

Apart from the above-mentioned brief direct examination, there are situations where further oral direct testimony might be necessary. In certain cases, the unfolding of events between the submission of the witness statement and the oral hearing may justify further testimony from the witness.[36] It is mainly for these situations that the stipulation that 'the Arbitral Tribunal may nevertheless permit further oral direct testimony' is provided in Article 8.5 the IBA Rules.[37] Such testimony will likely be outside of the scope of the witness statement. It is therefore important that the arbitral tribunal is restrictive in allowing such further testimony and provides the other party with an opportunity to respond to the new facts. Otherwise, the further testimony will have the effect of an 'ambush' testimony, potentially limiting the other party's right to present their case. We suggest that the contents of the witness statement ought to be the basis for deciding what further testimony is to be allowed.

It may also be necessary for the examining party to ask questions to clarify certain issues in the witness statement and correct any inaccuracies. Such questions should be allowed, but once again the arbitral tribunal ought to be careful to make sure that the questions confine themselves to the contents of the witness statement.[38] It should also be noted that such questions can often be conducted in the ten to twenty minutes that we suggest for the brief direct examination.

If we return to the party who has submitted a written witness statement that is lacking in detail, it is clear that this strategy entails considerable risk. The witness statement is the basis for which questions should, in general, be allowed. If the witness statement is lacking in detail, this will generally limit the examining party's range of available questions. Furthermore, there is a difference between simply clarifying certain issues in the witness statement (which is generally allowed) and filling gaps

33. *See* Born, *supra* n. 1, at 2458 and the Commentary on the 2020 IBA Rules on the Taking of Evidence, at 27.
34. Cf. Khodykin et al., *supra* n. 4, at 7.67.
35. Cf. Schlaepfer, *supra* n. 27, at 72-73 where the author notes a scepticism among arbitral tribunals towards witness statements that have not been tested orally.
36. Born, *supra* n. 1, at 2458.
37. *See* the Commentary on the 2020 IBA Rules on the Taking of Evidence, at 27.
38. *See* Schlaepfer, *supra* n. 27, at 72. *See also* Khodykin et al., *supra* n. 4, at 11.58.

(which the arbitral tribunal will be restrictive in permitting). We therefore recommend that parties refrain from attempting to circumvent the arbitral tribunal's order to submit witness statements in this manner.

Born has argued that, in principle, a party who wishes to conduct a full-length direct examination on facts already presented in the witness statement should be allowed to do so.[39] The examining party may consider that the witness' testimony is best presented orally.[40] Born notes that such examination must be limited to the facts in the witness statement *and be conducted in the party's allotted hearing time.*[41] Nevertheless, we submit that the arbitral tribunal ought to be restrictive in allowing lengthy direct examinations. There is generally little point in allowing a witness to repeat the contents of the witness statement.[42] The party who wishes to conduct a detailed direct examination should be required to present compelling arguments for why the particular evidence is best presented orally, regardless of the witness statement and the already provided brief direct examination. If lengthy direct examination is allowed, it should be conducted within the allotted hearing time.[43]

§13.05 CROSS-EXAMINATION

[A] Admissible Questions During Cross-Examination

Due to the predominance of written witness statements replacing direct examination, the cross-examination is often the main event in a witness examination. As discussed above, best practice is that the witness statement limits or replaces the direct examination. A further question is whether the witness statement also limits the cross-examination.

Practice regarding this question is varied. One view is that the cross-examination should be strictly limited to the contents of the witness statement (*the restrictive view*). The other is that the examining party should be allowed to ask questions outside the scope of the statement (*the generous view*).[44] Born considers that the generous view is more common.[45] The issue is, of course, not binary, and arbitral tribunals will in varying degrees be restrictive or generous. We examine the merits of the respective views below.

Before doing so, we wish to underline the fact that the primary purpose of cross-examination is to weaken the other side's case. This is often achieved by calling

39. Born, *supra* n. 1, at 2458.
40. Cf. Khodykin et al., *supra* n. 4, at 11.60-11.61.
41. Born, *supra* n. 1, at 2458. *See also* Khodykin et al., *supra* n. 4, at 11.64.
42. Cf. Article 8.3 of the 2020 IBA Rules on the Taking of Evidence which empowers the arbitral tribunal to exclude questions that are duplicative. *See also* Schlaepfer, *supra* n. 27, at 72.
43. Considering the 'chess clock' principle, a party who wants to conduct a lengthy direct examination must carefully weigh the benefit of orally presenting the evidence against the loss of valuable hearing time.
44. Khodykin et al., *supra* n. 4, at 11.65-11.66.
45. Born, *supra* n. 1, at 2458.

the witness' credibility into question.[46] When discussing what questions an arbitral tribunal ought to accept from the cross-examiner, it is important to keep this fact in mind.

The main benefit of the restrictive view is efficiency. First, it can be argued that, by reducing the range of questions the cross-examiner can ask, the cross-examination will, in general, be shorter. This is true to a certain extent, but if the witness statement is a formidable document, the cross-examiner will likely have little problem asking a large array of questions. Second, the restrictive view makes it easier for parties to plan their case. Knowing that the cross-examiner will be limited to the contents of the witness statement provides foreseeability, which enables the other party to more efficiently plan its rebuttal. Another benefit of the restrictive rule is that it ensures that the parties are not ambushed with new evidence from the examining party.[47]

The main drawback of the restrictive view is that it leaves the cross-examining party's opportunity to undermine the other party's case at the mercy of the other party. For example, the other party can present a witness statement which only contains matters of secondary relevance to the case.[48] The cross-examining party would then be hindered from asking questions about the main issues of the case, limiting its 'access to truth'. However, this issue should not be exaggerated. Generally, a party will not refrain from including matters of primary relevance to the case if its case relies, in whole or in part, on the evidence provided by the witness. Also, if the cross-examining party believes that the witness in question has information of primary relevance to the party's case, it can also call the witness for examination on the relevant issues.

The benefits and drawbacks of the generous view are inverse to the benefits and drawbacks described above. In short, it provides the cross-examining party with a greater opportunity to undermine the other party's case, but at the cost of efficiency. It also entails a larger risk of the cross-examining party ambushing the other party.

We submit that best practice ought to be slightly more generous than the restrictive view. In general, the questions asked should be limited to the contents of the witness statement. However, in addition to this, we suggest that questions can also be asked on submitted documents and oral evidence from other witnesses. Such a rule lessens the above-mentioned risk of the other party limiting the cross-examining party by providing a limited witness statement. We believe that such a rule provides the cross-examining party with a sufficient degree of flexibility to enable it to successfully weaken the other side's case. At the same time, limiting the questions to the evidence that is already a part of the proceeding promotes efficiency and lessens the risk of ambushing the other party.

A related issue is how the arbitral tribunal should deal with an objection that a question is irrelevant. There are different methods for the arbitral tribunal to determine whether a question is irrelevant. In some cases, the question might be so obviously

46. Kaj Hobér, *International Commercial Arbitration in Sweden* (Oxford University Press 2011), 232. *See also* Kaj Hobér & Howard S. Sussman, *Cross-Examination in International Arbitration: Nine Basic Principles* (Oxford University Press 2014), 32.
47. Cf. the Preamble to the IBA Rules on the Taking of Evidence, para. 3.
48. Schlaepfer, *supra* n. 27, at 72.

irrelevant that the arbitral tribunal could accept the party's objection immediately. Otherwise, the arbitral tribunal could hear the parties' views on why they consider the answer to the question to be relevant/irrelevant.

An alternative is for the arbitral tribunal to accept the examining party's argument that the relevance of the answer will become clear by subsequent evidence. If the answer proves to be irrelevant, the arbitral tribunal can simply disregard the witness' answer.[49] This method is advantageous when the relevance of the answer is complicated. However, a legitimate objection is that the arbitral tribunal may be psychologically prejudiced by the irrelevant answer, regardless of it formally disregarding the evidence.[50] We therefore recommend that arbitral tribunals generally refrain from using this method.

[B] Providing New Evidence to Prove a Lie

It is common for the arbitral tribunal to provide a cut-off date, i.e., a deadline for presenting documents and other evidence to the tribunal. In general, this prevents parties from presenting evidence at a late stage in the proceedings, such as during the oral hearing. The purpose of a cut-off date is to ensure that each party can effectively argue its respective case, having been presented with all of the evidence the other party relies on. Cut-off dates also ensure efficient proceedings, as new evidence during the hearing can lead to delays since the other party must generally be allowed the time to consider the new evidence.

Cut-off dates raise a certain question for cross-examination, namely whether a party can present documents that have not been previously submitted during cross-examination to prove a point. The most common example is where the examining party presents the document to catch the witness in a lie. By way of illustration, take the following example.

During document production, a party has come across an e-mail sent by Witness X in which the witness admits that Company X's product was faulty. Witness X is supposed to be heard by the other party on the quality of Company X's products. The party can use the documents in two possible ways: either submit the document to the arbitral tribunal before the hearing or wait until asking Witness X during the cross-examination whether he or she considers Company X's products to be without fault. In the example, the arbitral tribunal has provided a cut-off date before the hearing.

Of course, the value of presenting the document at the hearing varies from case to case, but there are two main benefits. First, by catching the witness in a lie, the witness' credibility is likely to be tarnished in the eyes of the arbitral tribunal. Second,

49. Cf. Judge Coleridge's opinion in *Haigh v. Belcher* (1836) 7 Carrington and Payne 389, 173 ER 173.
50. Cf. Lindskog, *supra* n. 8, at 729.

the examining party catches the other party off guard, instead of providing them with an opportunity to address the evidence in their written submissions.[51]

Whether to allow the new evidence is within the discretion of the arbitral tribunal.[52] There is disagreement as to what constitutes best practice in this regard.[53] We suggest that whether or not witness statements have been submitted in the proceedings is a deciding factor. If witness statements are used, the parties have little excuse not to submit documents that prove that something in the witness statement is a lie before the cut-off date. Allowing such documents to be produced during the hearing without having been first submitted would undermine the above-mentioned purpose of a cut-off date. Although there is a dramatic effect to producing the document during the cross-examination, the witness' credibility can just as easily be tarnished by submitting the document before the cut-off and pointing out that the witness statement is not to be relied upon.

However, the party may present a document to prove a lie after the cut-off date if it has a valid excuse for not submitting it earlier. For example, a valid excuse could be that the witness has testified to something during the hearing that was not included in the witness statement (assuming such evidence is admissible). In these cases, the cross-examining party ought to be allowed to present a document proving that the witness is lying.

It can be argued that such an excuse is invalid, as a party who catches a witness in a lie by producing a document on the spot obviously anticipated that the witness might lie. This may be true. However, it is important to distinguish between the knowledge that people sometimes lie (even when in court) and the legal assumption that people tell the truth during legal proceedings.[54] Parties to an arbitration must be allowed to conduct their case on the basis of this legal assumption. Otherwise, it may be rightfully questioned whether the practice of witnesses affirming that they will tell the truth is simply procedural window dressing.

If witness statements are not used in the proceedings, arbitral tribunals ought to be more generous in allowing documents to be produced during cross-examination. This is because the parties in this situation have considerably less knowledge about the contents of the witness' testimony.

Regardless of whether witness statements are used or not, there are limitations as to what evidence can be submitted to prove that the witness is lying. By providing a new document after the cut-off date, the party is in effect ambushing the other party with evidence that it has not had time to prepare for. Born suggests that evidence must

51. Although not uncommon, the possibility of catching a witness in a lie should not be exaggerated. Due to document production and witness prep, the witness is often aware of inconsistencies in their testimony before the oral hearing and has been prepared for possible ambushes. Cf. Hobér & Sussman, *supra* n. 46, at 31.
52. *See, e.g.*, Article 9.1 of the 2020 IBA Rules on the Taking of Evidence and the Commentary on the 2020 IBA Rules on the Taking of Evidence, at 28.
53. *See* Born, *supra* n. 1, at 2428 and Hobér, *supra* n. 46, at 233-234.
54. Cf. Article 8.5 of the 2020 IBA Rules on the Taking of Evidence, which provide that the witness should affirm that he or she commits to tell the truth.

comprise 'documents which are genuinely relevant for purposes of impeachment'.[55] The arbitral tribunal ought to be restrictive in allowing a document which contains other information not directly relevant to this purpose. Furthermore, even when allowing the evidence, the arbitral tribunal ought to provide the other party with a reasonable opportunity to examine the evidence and provide a response.

[C] Issues of Digitalization in Relation to Cross-Examination

A problem that arises from digital hearings is the possibility of a party coaching the witness during cross-examination. The party can be present in the same room as the witness and covertly provide notes to them in response to questions from the cross-examiner. If the party has no scruples when it comes to underhand tactics, the witness can also feign 'technical difficulties' to buy time in which to prepare an answer to a particularly difficult question. This issue is virtually non-existent in a live hearing as it would be blatantly obvious if opposing counsel attempted to assist the witness.[56]

A simple technical solution is to require opposing counsel to be visible during cross-examination in their own 'window' of the videoconferencing tool used. We cannot see any valid objections to the arbitral tribunal mandating this. It is natural that a digital hearing should use the technological solutions available to make sure that the hearing maintains the same integrity as a live one. We submit that this ought to be considered best practice.

The main drawback of the solution is that it does not fully ensure that the witness is not influenced by the other party. Counsel could potentially arrange for a colleague to sit with the witness *incognito* and provide coaching. It is impossible for the arbitral tribunal to control exactly who is working on the case in the counsel's organization. An alternative is to mandate that an independent observer should be present with the witness during their testimony. This solution ensures that the witness is not influenced. It is, however, an impractical solution, encumbering the hearing with extra logistics.[57]

We therefore submit that, although an independent observer solves the issue entirely, it cannot be considered best practice. However, the parties are of course free to agree on the use of independent observers.

---

55. Born, *supra* n. 1, at 2428.
56. However, there is the possibility of discussing the case with the witness during breaks. *See* §13.06 below regarding witness sequestration.
57. For the purpose of increasing cost-efficiency while still ensuring procedural integrity, another solution is to set up two cameras: one showing the witness, and the other showing the hearing room from the side. This enables the arbitral tribunal to monitor whether someone is covertly trying to coach the witness.

§13.06 WITNESS SEQUESTRATION

[A] Before the Witness Testifies

[1] General

When a witness is to testify at a hearing, the question arises whether the witness ought to be sequestered before giving their testimony. It is common for the arbitral tribunal to mandate that a fact witness not be allowed to attend the proceedings before the witness has testified.[58] It can be discussed whether this is best practice, as the IBA Rules on the Taking of Evidence are intentionally silent on this issue.[59] The rationale for sequestration is that the witness could otherwise tailor his or her testimony in accordance with what occurs during the proceedings.[60] Some authors suggest that the witness can attend the hearings if it is unlikely that the witness will be able to tailor the testimony so that a party will receive an unfair advantage.[61] We submit that, since it can generally be assumed that the witness will be able to tailor the testimony, arbitral tribunals ought to be restrictive in allowing witnesses to attend. Another benefit of witness sequestration is that the proceedings will also appear fairer. The parties can rely on there being no testimony tailoring, regardless of whether the particular witnesses would have actually altered their testimonies or whether a party would actually gain an advantage. Considering this, we therefore submit that this should be best practice.

Another aspect of sequestration is that the witnesses should not be allowed to discuss the case with the party representatives, counsel, or other witnesses. The rationale for this rule is the same, namely that the witness could otherwise tailor their testimony.[62] The arbitral tribunal can enforce this with varying degrees of strictness, mandating that the witness should refrain from any communication with the other members of the 'team' during the hearing or simply admonishing the witness not to discuss the case, but otherwise allowing conversation between the different individuals involved in the case. We suggest that the stricter rule is to be preferred, but the logistics of the proceedings may make this position untenable.

58. Born, *supra* n. 1, at 2462. However, cf. Nigel Rawding, Gregory Roy Fullelove & Penny Martin, 'Chapter 18: International Arbitration in England: A Procedural Overview' in, Julian David Mathew Lew, Harris Bor, Gregory Roy Fullelove & Joanne Greenaway (eds), *Arbitration in England, with chapters on Scotland and Ireland* (Kluwer Law International 2013), 389. The authors submit that the arbitral tribunal will generally permit the witness to attend the hearing 'unless there are particularly contentious factual questions in issue'.
59. The Commentary on the 2020 IBA Rules on the Taking of Evidence, at 26.
60. Born, *supra* n. 1, at 2462.
61. Blackaby, et al., *supra* n. 4, at 407.
62. Blackaby, et al., *supra* n. 4, at 407.

[2] *Party Representatives Acting as Witnesses*

The same considerations that justify sequestering fact witnesses are of course applicable to a party witness. However, if the witness is the party representative, there is often a legitimate interest in the party attending the entire hearing, such as the need to instruct counsel. A balance can be struck between these opposing interests by scheduling the witness examinations of the party representatives first and limiting the number of party witnesses who are allowed to be present.[63] We consider that this practice generally is sound. However, the issue of testimony tailoring remains, as some of the party witnesses will be allowed to hear the other party's witness testimonies before giving their own. The arbitral tribunal ought to consider this when attaching evidentiary weight to the witness in question's testimony.

[3] *Expert Witnesses*

With regard to expert witnesses, arbitral tribunals generally allow them to attend the hearing. Their attendance is justified as the expert witness is not being heard on matters of fact. Furthermore, it has been held that exposing the expert to the evidence is 'beneficial, rather than harmful'.[64] There is merit to this view, but it must be kept in mind that the expert is party appointed. One can assume that experts generally provide evidence based on their professional opinion and not simply based on what the party wants them to say. However, as the expert is generally paid by the party to testify, they may have an incentive to tailor their testimony. We therefore question the prudence of allowing party-appointed experts to attend the entire hearing.[65]

[B] After the Witness Has Testified

After witnesses have testified, there is generally no objection to them attending the rest of the hearing. However, we wish to raise an issue, namely that the witness may need to provide new testimony. Arbitral tribunals will generally frown upon a witness being heard a second time. However, an example of when this might be allowed is where evidence provided after the testimony affects the testimony's evidentiary weight. If the party who relies on the witness ought not to have foreseen this, a new testimony may be allowed.[66] Considering this possibility, however small, we suggest that witnesses should not be allowed to attend hearing even after testifying.

63. Born, *supra* n. 1, at 2463.
64. Born, *supra* n. 1, at 2462. Khodykin et al. concur with this opinion, *see* Khodykin et al., *supra* n. 4, at 11.100.
65. For tribunal-appointed experts there is no such issue.
66. Lindskog, *supra* n. 8, at 730.

[C] Issues of Digitalization in Relation to Witness Sequestration

As a result of digital hearings, witness sequestration becomes harder to uphold. In principle, the sequestered witness is not allowed to view the proceedings via video-feed. However, it is difficult for the arbitral tribunal to control this. If the hearing is conducted via videoconference, the witness can in theory be present in the same room as the party, keeping outside of the view of the camera. A possible solution is to mandate that an independent observer should be present together with the witness during the hearing. This solution is impractical. The independent observer must be present with the witness (whether physically or digitally) for a sizeable portion of the hearing, at least until the witness has testified. This will entail additional costs for the parties, not to mention inconvenience to the witness who may have other matters to attend to. If the proceedings last for several days and there are several witnesses who need to be observed, this solution may border on the absurd.

We also wish to point out that the issues of keeping the witness effectively sequestrated also exist in live hearings. It is difficult for the arbitral tribunal to ensure that the parties do not inform their witnesses of what has occurred during a break, or provide the witness with a transcript. The arbitral tribunal must generally rely on admonishing the witness that they are not to discuss the case during breaks and rely on the ethical conduct of the parties, counsel, and witnesses. We submit that these methods are sufficient and that independent observers should only be mandated if both parties request them.

§13.07 CONCLUDING REMARKS

In this chapter, we have discussed best practice in relation to some common issues on witness examination. When dealing with evidentiary matters, the IBA Rules on the Taking of Evidence are a good starting point as they generally reflect best practice. However, as the IBA Rules often provide broad rules, they do not always provide clear answers. An example of this is the rule in Article 8.5 that allows further direct testimony even if witness statements are submitted. The article does not provide how restrictively or generously the rule should be applied. As we have suggested in §13.04, best practice is that, apart from a brief direct testimony to 'warm up' the witness, further direct testimony should generally not be permitted. Some other issues are left outside of the IBA Rules entirely, such as whether a witness ought to be sequestered.

Based on our experience and review of international literature on the subject, our conclusions as to what constitutes best practice in relation to the issues discussed in this chapter can be summarized as follows:

(i) The use of written witness statements is best practice in international cases. A party can be mandated to submit witness statements if it wishes to rely on a witness. *See* §13.03[A]-[B].

(ii) If a witness does not appear at the hearing, it is best practice to disregard the witness' written witness statement, unless the party can present a valid excuse, or exceptional circumstances exist. If the arbitral tribunal decides not to disregard the witness statement, it ought to carefully consider the fact that the witness has not been cross-examined when determining the evidentiary weight of the statement. *See* §13.03[C].

(iii) Written witness statements ought to replace direct examination. However, we suggest that the parties should be allowed to conduct a brief direct examination, as long as the questions are kept within the scope of the witness statement. Such an examination provides the arbitral tribunal with a 'baseline' from which to better evaluate the witness' credibility and ensures that the witness is not flung directly into cross-examination. As a rule of thumb, we suggest that such an examination should be limited to ten to twenty minutes in length.

During direct examination, the party may also ask questions to clarify and correct inaccuracies in the witness statement. This can generally be achieved within the above-mentioned time frame, but there may be instances where more time is needed. In certain cases, the unfolding of events may justify the witness providing further testimony. The arbitral tribunal ought to be restrictive in allowing this and should in any event provide the other party with an opportunity to respond to the new evidence. If the examining party can present compelling arguments, the arbitral tribunal may in exceptional cases allow a full-length direct testimony. This should come at the cost of the party in question's allotted hearing time. *See* §13.04.

(iv) If written witness statements are mandated in an arbitration proceeding, questions during cross-examination should generally be limited to the contents of the witness statement. However, questions about submitted documents and oral evidence from other witnesses should be allowed. *See* §13.05[A].

(v) In arbitrations where written witness statements are used, the cross-examining party ought to generally be hindered from confronting a witness with new evidence during cross-examination to prove a lie. If the cross-examining party has a valid excuse why the evidence was not submitted before the cut-off date, the arbitral tribunal may allow it. A valid excuse exists if the witness testifies to something that was not included in the witness statement (but for one reason or another is still admitted as evidence). If witness statements are not used, the arbitral tribunal can be less restrictive in allowing the production of documents during cross-examination. Regardless of whether witness statements are used or not, the document must clearly prove that the witness is lying. The arbitral tribunal must also provide the other party with an opportunity to respond to the new evidence. *See* §13.05[B].

(vi) So as to ensure that a witness is not being covertly coached during a digital cross-examination, it is best practice for the other party and its counsel to be visible in their own 'windows'. *See* §13.05[C].

(vii) Fact witnesses ought to be sequestered before giving testimony. Exceptions can be made for party witnesses. In the authors' view, arbitral tribunals should also be restrictive in permitting expert witnesses to attend the hearing. *See* §13.06[A].

(viii) Permitting the witness to attend the hearing after giving testimony is generally not considered an issue. However, we suggest that there is a case to be made for sequestration to continue after testimony has been given, in light of the (albeit small) possibility of the witness testifying a second time. *See* §13.06[B].

(ix) The use of independent observers to ensure that witness sequestration is upheld during digital hearings cannot be considered best practice. It is sufficient that the arbitral tribunal admonishes the witnesses not to take part in the proceedings in any way until they have been heard. *See* §13.06[C].

CHAPTER 14

The Alleged Failure of Arbitration to Address Due Process Concerns: Is Arbitration under Attack?

Giuditta Cordero-Moss

Arbitration is a mechanism for settling disputes that has gained considerable success, first in international commercial disputes and later in investor-state disputes. More recently, both types of arbitration, but especially investment arbitration, have been exposed to harsh criticism.

Both types of arbitration are facing an erosion of their credibility, mainly based on doubts about the lack of efficiency in the proceedings, the impartiality and independence of the arbitrators and suspicions about the ability to accurately apply the law. To a large extent, these doubts are based on perceptions or misperceptions, rather than on factual circumstances. With reference to the main issues for which arbitration is being criticized, this chapter explores whether there is reason to fear that the institution of arbitration is not compatible with the principle of due process.

§14.01 INTRODUCTION

Arbitration is a mechanism for settling disputes that has gained considerable success, first in international commercial disputes, and later in investor-state disputes. More recently, both types of arbitration, but especially investment arbitration, have been exposed to harsh criticism.

With reference to the main issues for which arbitration is being criticized, this chapter explores whether there is reason to fear that the institution of arbitration is not compatible with the principle of due process.

Commercial arbitration is criticized particularly for having lost of sight its original feature as a method for dispute settlement: its flexibility and closeness to the parties. Arbitration proceedings are often described as having become unnecessarily costly and time-consuming, as well as overregulated.[1] In addition, arbitral tribunals are increasingly scared of being criticized for violating procedural rights of the parties, and indulge the parties in sometimes unreasonable requests that new claims or new evidence be admitted, that terms be extended, etc. – falling for what is often called 'due process paranoia' and unnecessarily inflating the duration and cost of the proceedings. As a reaction, arbitration institutions sometimes reform their rules, in the name of expedience, to an extent that may overreach and lead to the opposite extreme.

Furthermore, critical voices are increasingly being raised against one of the pillars of commercial arbitration, the principle of confidentiality. While calls for transparency in commercial arbitration do not achieve the intensity that can be registered in investment arbitration, significant developments in the practice of commercial arbitration are introducing some transparency.

Also, the sometimes possibly excessive enthusiasm professed by part of the arbitration community about the autonomy of arbitration and its independence from national laws and national courts seems to increasingly give rise to a mistrust towards the appropriateness of permitting arbitration for those disputes in which an accurate application of the law is deemed to be crucial. As a consequence of the suspect that arbitration might exceed in its autonomy, the scope of the disputes that may be arbitrated has been in several instances reduced. The scope of arbitrability is threatened also by the risk that court control may be restricted so as to prevent the courts from meaningfully verifying whether the award is compatible with fundamental principles.

As far as *investment* arbitration is concerned, loud criticism has been moved questioning its legitimacy and its ability to properly have regard to the public interests involved. Criticism against investment arbitration led to, among other things, a mandate by the United Nations Commission on International Trade Law (UNCITRAL) to its Working Group III to work on the possible reform of investor-state dispute settlement. As summarized in the note prepared by the UNCITRAL Secretariat for the first session held in the UNCITRAL Working Group III, the criticism regards these main points: (i) inconsistency in arbitral decisions, (ii) limited mechanisms to ensure the correctness of arbitral decisions, (iii) lack of predictability, (iv) appointment of arbitrators by parties ('party-appointment'), (v) the impact of party appointment on the impartiality and independence of arbitrators, (vi) lack of transparency, and (vii) increasing duration and costs of the procedure.[2] While not all the issues mentioned in this list may raise due process concerns, some may potentially be relevant to questions such as access to justice or fairness of the proceedings, which are usually considered to be part of the due process principle.

1. Queen Mary and White&Case 2015 Survey 'Improvements and Innovations in International Arbitration', available at http://www.arbitration.qmul.ac.uk/media/arbitration/docs/2015_International_Arbitration_Survey.pdf.
2. Working Group III (Investor-State Dispute Settlement Reform), thirty-fourth session, Vienna, 27 November-1 December 2017, Possible reform of investor-State dispute settlement (ISDS) – Note by the Secretariat, A/CN.9/WG.III/WP.142, para. 20.

Criticism against investment arbitration has prompted certain developments in the legal framework. Nevertheless, recent investment treaties restrict arbitration considerably.[3] Furthermore, the European Union (EU) took the political decision to discontinue the choice of arbitration contained in the existing investment treaties entered into between Member States and took an active position against arbitration also as far as regards treaties with third states. [4]

The need to ensure an accurate application of EU law, furthermore, has led the Court of Justice of the European Union (CJEU) to exclude the arbitrability of investment disputes between EU Member States.[5] While it is possible to draw some parallels with analogous developments in commercial arbitration, the CJEU seemed to accept that commercial tribunals may solve disputes relating to EU law, as long as appropriate court control is possible. For investment arbitration, the CJEU denied arbitrability of disputes relating to EU law. The different treatment of commercial and investment arbitrability was explained, quite unconvincingly, with a distinction between the respective sources of the arbitral power.

The criticism against investment arbitration has not only a legal but also a political dimension. In this framework, it has been observed that the debate on the legitimacy of investment arbitration is not necessarily only about facts but also about perceptions.[6]

Hence, the ability of arbitration to comply with due process may sometimes be questioned more from a political perspective or from the point of view of perceptions, than on the basis of objective and technical legal arguments.

All the above has created a climate of suspicion against arbitration that can be summarized with an observation made by one of the grey eminences of arbitration, Yves Derain:[7] 'arbitration is under attack'.

This chapter explores to what extent the institution of arbitration as such is capable of safeguarding, as a dispute settlement mechanism, the principle of due process. To this aim, I will briefly address possible sources for determining the specific content of the principle of due process (in section 14.02), attempt to define the content of the principle (in section 14.03), discuss to what extent compliance with the legal framework applicable to arbitration may be deemed to be a necessary condition to meet the requirements of the principle of due process (in section 14.04), examine, in light of the criticism mentioned above, to what extent the legal framework applicable to arbitration may be deemed to be a sufficient condition to comply with the principle of due process (in section 14.05), and consider whether there is a basis to distinguish, in this context, between commercial and investment arbitration (in section 14.06).

---

3. For references, *see* UNCTAD, World Investor Report 2017 (WIR 2017), p. 120.
4. For references and comments, *see* Albert Jan van den Berg, 'Appeal Mechanism for ISDS Awards: Interaction with the New York and ICSID Conventions' (2019) 34 *ICSID Review*, 1-34, 8f.
5. Case C- 284/16 *Slovak Republic v. Achmea BV*.
6. Working Group III Note by the Secretariat, A/CN.9/WG.III/WP.142, cit., paras 42, 63; Report of Working Group III (Investor-State Dispute Settlement Reform) on the work of its thirty-fifth session (New York, 23-27 April 2017), A/CN.9/935, paras 94-96.
7. At the 39th ICC Institute Annual Conference, 'Explaining why you lost – Reasoning in arbitration', 17 December 2019.

§14.02 DUE PROCESS: SOURCES

Due process is a cornerstone for every adjudicative system, including arbitration. Each legal system has fundamental principles safeguarding the integrity and fairness of the process, often rooted in constitutional law. Also, in international law, due process is deemed to be one of the generally recognized principles.[8] In the field of transnational disputes, however, the notion of due process is elusive. An extensive comparative exercise, carried out by the International Institute for the Unification of Private Law (UNIDROIT) and the American Law Institute (ALI) and resulted in a soft law instrument on Transnational Civil Procedure, gives an idea of what procedural principles are generally recognized.[9] Among the principles emphasized in this instrument, are the necessity to respect each of the parties' right to be heard,[10] the principle of equality of arms,[11] and the requirement that the adjudicating body be independent and impartial.[12] It can be readily accepted that these principles are an integral part of the concept of due process.[13] However, these notions are quite vague. While it may be relatively easy, in case of evident violations in a specific case, to determine whether the principle of due process was breached, it is more difficult to define on general terms the exact content of the principle of due process.

For arbitration, the principle of due process is enshrined, among other sources, in Article 18 of the UNCITRAL Model Law of International Commercial Arbitration, [14] according to which 'the parties shall be treated with equality and each party shall be given a full opportunity of presenting its case'. Analogous requirements can be induced from the sources that permit to exercise judicial control on the decision rendered by an arbitral tribunal, and that will be discussed in section 14.03. Arbitral awards may be set aside or may be refused enforcement if certain fundamental principles were not respected during the process. Setting aside of arbitral awards is regulated by the national law of the country under the law of which the award was rendered; an instrument that successfully harmonized the arbitration law of eighty-five countries is the UNCITRAL Model Law.[15] This applies both to commercial arbitration and to investment arbitration that is carried out under the rules designed for commercial

8. *See* Charles T. Kotuby Jr. and Luke A. Sobota, *General Principles of Law and International Due Process*, Oxford University Press 2017, with extensive references.
9. The text of the Principles and the accompanying commentary, adopted by the American Law Institute (ALI) in May 2004 and by the International Institute for the Unification of Private Law (UNIDROIT) in April 2004, is available at https://www.unidroit.org/english/principles/civilprocedure/ali-unidroitprinciples-e.pdf.
10. Article 5 of the ALI/UNIDROIT Principles of Transnational Civil Procedure.
11. Article 3 of the ALI/UNIDROIT Principles of Transnational Civil Procedure.
12. Article 1 of the ALI/UNIDROIT Principles of Transnational Civil Procedure.
13. Kotuby, Sobota, *General Principles of Law and International Due Process*, cit., 157-202, identify the following principles as the main content of the principle of due process: notice and jurisdiction, impartiality and independence, procedural equality and right to be heard, condemnation of fraud and corruption, evidence and burden of proof, res judicata.
14. UNCITRAL, 1985 Model Law on International Commercial Arbitration, revised in 2006, http://www.uncitral.org/pdf/english/texts/arbitration/ml-arb/07-86998_Ebook.pdf.
15. For an updated status, *see* http://www.uncitral.org/uncitral/en/uncitral_texts/arbitration/1985Model_arbitration_status.html.

arbitration, such as the UNCITRAL Arbitration Rules, the Arbitration Rules of the Stockholm Chamber of Commerce (SCC) or of the International Chamber of Commerce (ICC). For investment arbitration that is carried out under the International Centre for Settlement of Investment Disputes (ICSID) Convention,[16] annulment of awards is regulated in Article 52 of the convention itself, without reference to national law.

Enforcement of awards is regulated by the 1958 New York Convention on the Recognition and Enforcement of Foreign Arbitral Awards.[17] The New York Convention applies to commercial awards, as well as to investment awards rendered under the procedural rules for commercial arbitration. For investment arbitration that is carried out under the ICSID Convention, enforcement of awards is regulated in the convention itself, which creates in Article 54 an obligation to enforce the award as if it was a final court decision rendered in that state.

All these sources determine the grounds upon which arbitral awards may be set aside or refused recognition and enforcement. These grounds are meant to prevent that awards are effective if they have been reached as a result of unfair proceedings. Hence, it is possible to consider them as a measure of the due process principle in arbitration.

In a broader context, a possible basis to define due process may be found in the sources of international obligations for states. States may be deemed to have violated their international obligations if they permit and give effect to a process that disregarded certain fundamental principles.[18]

An obligation to grant access to a justice system capable of safeguarding certain fundamental principles can be found in international treaties on human rights. The European Convention on Human Rights[19] states, in Article 6, that 'everyone is entitled to a fair and public hearing within a reasonable time by an independent and impartial tribunal established by law'.

However, these criteria cannot necessarily be identified with the content of the principle of due process. As the European Court of Human Rights (ECtHR) has repeatedly affirmed, some of the guarantees contained in Article 6 can be waived,[20] as long as certain conditions are met – particularly, the waiver must be voluntary and clear.[21] An agreement to arbitrate fulfils the conditions for waiving the Article 6 requirements, at least when the agreement is freely entered into by the parties.[22] Some

16. Convention on the Settlement of Investment Disputes between States and Nationals of Other States (adopted 18 March 1965, entered into force 14 October 1966) UNTS 575 (ICSID Convention or Washington Convention).
17. Convention on the Recognition and Enforcement of Foreign Arbitral Awards (adopted 10 June 1958, entered into force 7 June 1959) UNTS 330 (New York Convention).
18. On this basis, the ECtHR assessed Swiss law on arbitration in *Mutu and Pechstein v. Switzerland*, Decision of 2 October 2018, Application No. 40575/10 and 67474/10, paras 62-67.
19. Convention for the Protection of Human Rights and Fundamental Freedoms (adopted 4 November 1950, entered into force 3 September 1953), UNTS 213 (ECHR).
20. *Osmo Suovaniemi v. Finland*, Decision of 23 February 1999, Application No. 31737, p. 4. *Mutu and Pechstein v. Switzerland* para. 145; *Tabbane v. Switzerland*, Decision of 1 March 2016, Application No. 41069/12, paras 33-36.
21. *Tabbane v. Switzerland*, paras 26f. In *Mutu and Pechstein v. Switzerland*, paras 94ff., the ECtHR confirms the distinction between voluntary and compulsory arbitration. The guarantees set forth in Article 6 may be waived only in case of voluntary arbitration.
22. *Mutu and Pechstein v. Switzerland*, paras 95f.

of the guarantees contained in Article 6, however, cannot be waived, not even when arbitration has been chosen voluntarily by the parties.[23] It is fair to assume that these non-waivable guarantees constitute an important part of the principle of due process. Which guarantees are non-waivable, however, has not been specified by the ECtHR. Hence, the specific content of the principle of due process in arbitration escapes a clear definition on the basis of Article 6.

Requirements similar to those contained in Article 6 of the European Convention on Human Rights (ECHR) are to be found in the Universal Declaration of Human Rights,[24] which in Article 10 reads: 'Everyone is entitled in full equality to a fair and public hearing by an independent and impartial tribunal [...].'

Similarly, in the field of criminal procedure, the International Covenant on Civil and Political Rights[25] requires, in Article 14, equality before the courts and tribunals and a fair and public hearing by a competent, independent and impartial tribunal established by law.

The above overview shows that the international sources set out the principle of due process in rather general terms. The legal sources specifically applicable to arbitration must, in principle, be assumed to comply with this general framework: The New York Convention and the ICSID Convention are treaties in force in, respectively, 168[26] and 154[27] states, and the UNCITRAL Model Law is a soft law instrument adopted by the UNCITRAL and used as a model for arbitration law in eighty-five states.[28] This large support must be taken as a consensus that these instruments' conditions for validity, recognition and enforcement of awards are acceptable from the point of view of the states' more general obligations of safeguarding due process. To what extent this assumption is sound will be discussed in section 14.05 below.

That the legal framework for arbitration is compatible with the principle of due process appears also from a recently issued instrument of soft law, the Hague Rules on Business and Human Rights Arbitration.[29] The Hague Rules emphasize that arbitration can assist in implementing the UN Guiding Principles on Business and Human Rights.[30]

23. *Osmo v. Finland*, p 4.
24. Universal Declaration of Human Rights (adopted by the UN General Assembly Resolution 217 A(III) of 10 December 1948).
25. International Covenant on Civil and Political Rights (adopted 16 December 1966 and entered into force 23 March 1976), UNTS 999.
26. For an updated status, *see* https://uncitral.un.org/en/texts/arbitration/conventions/foreign_arbitral_awards/status2.
27. For an updated status, *see* https://icsid.worldbank.org/en/Pages/icsiddocs/ICSID-Convention.aspx.
28. https://uncitral.un.org/en/texts/arbitration/modellaw/commercial_arbitration/status.
29. Hague Rules on Business and Human Rights Arbitration, launched 12 December 2019, by the Centre for International Legal Cooperation and the Business and Human Rights Arbitration Working Group, chaired by former ICJ Judge Bruno Simma, available at https://www.cilc.nl/cms/wp-content/uploads/2019/12/The-Hague-Rules-on-Business-and-Human-Rights-Arbitration_CILC-digital-version.pdf.
30. Hague Rules on Business and Human Rights Arbitration, Preamble, Comment No. 2. The UN Guiding Principles are available at https://www.ohchr.org/Documents/Publications/GuidingPrinciplesBusinessHR_EN.pdf.

The Hague Rules are based on the UNCITRAL Arbitration Rules,[31] and have identified six features of human rights disputes that may require improvement of the UNCITRAL Arbitration Rules:[32] (a) the particular characteristics of disputes related to the human rights impacts of business activities; (b) the possible need for special measures to address the circumstances of those affected by the human rights impacts of business activities; (c) the potential imbalance of power that may arise in disputes under these Rules; (d) the public interest in the resolution of such disputes, which may require, among other things, a high degree of transparency of the proceedings and an opportunity for participation by interested third persons and states; (e) the importance of having arbitrators with expertise appropriate for such disputes and bound by high standards of conduct; and (f) the possible need for the arbitral tribunal to create special mechanisms for the gathering of evidence and protection of witnesses.

As will be discussed in section 14.05, the Hague Rules make some additions to the UNCITRAL Arbitration Rules for the purpose of adjusting the regulation to the needs of human rights disputes. These additions reveal that, while human rights disputes may require a special attention to the mentioned areas, the structure and principles of the UNCITRAL Arbitration Rules are not deemed to be inadequate. The UNCITRAL Arbitration Rules, in turn, are a soft law instrument providing procedural rules for arbitration proceedings that are carried out under the legal framework applicable to arbitration - including the above-mentioned rules on court control. Hence, according to the Hague Rules, the legal framework of arbitration is capable of solving human rights disputes and does not create due process concerns.

§14.03 DUE PROCESS: CONTENT

If, as discussed above, the rules on court control may be a useful framework to determine the content of the principle of due process, the main elements of the principle can be broadly summarized to be the principle that each party must be heard, the principle of equality of arms, the principle of independence and impartiality of the tribunal, the principle that the tribunal shall not exceed the power that the parties voluntarily conferred on it. This is a distillate of the main safeguards contained in the sources on validity and enforceability of awards, as will be briefly presented below.

The body who controls the validity or the enforceability of an award derives its jurisdiction from the applicable law. In case of challenge to the award's validity, the applicable law is the arbitration law prevailing in the place of arbitration. For investment arbitration that is carried out under the ICSID Convention, annulment of awards is regulated in Article 52 of the convention itself, without reference to national law.

31. The UNCITRAL Arbitration Rules are a model contractual regulation of arbitral procedure. They were first issued in 1976, and revised in 2010. In 2013, a new edition accompanied by the UNCITRAL Transparency Rules was published. *See* https://uncitral.un.org/en/texts/arbitration/contractualtexts/arbitration.
32. Hague Rules on Business and Human Rights Arbitration, Preamble, point 6.

In case of the award's enforcement, the applicable law is, in the 168 countries who ratified it, the New York Convention. For investment arbitration that is carried out under the ICSID Convention, enforcement of awards is regulated in Article 54 of the convention itself.

National arbitration law differs from country to country; therefore, the court's process in case of a challenge to the award's validity need to be analysed on the basis of the national law that is applicable in the specific case. For the sake of simplicity, however, we will assume here that the national arbitration law corresponds to the UNCITRAL Model Law, as it does, more or less literally, in the eighty-five countries that are considered to be 'Model Law countries'.

As the court's powers, to the extent that is relevant here, are equivalent in the New York Convention and in the Model Law,[33] the analysis can be made without distinguishing between court control carried out in connection with challenge to the award's validity and court control carried out in connection with enforcement of the award. It should be emphasized, however, that, if the law applicable in a specific case does not belong to a Model Law country, or if it implements the Model Law with some discrepancies from the original, it will be necessary to verify whether the law applicable to annulment has diverging regulation.

The criteria contained in the New York Convention and the Model Law largely correspond to the criteria contained in Article 52 of the ICSID Convention.

Thus, an award rendered by an arbitral tribunal whose jurisdiction did not rest on a valid and binding arbitration agreement is not valid[34] and not enforceable;[35] an award rendered as a result of a proceeding that did not give each of the parties the possibility to present its case is not valid[36] and not enforceable;[37] an award rendered in excess of the jurisdiction granted on the arbitral tribunal is not valid[38] and not enforceable;[39] an award rendered by an arbitral tribunal that was not constituted in accordance with the parties' agreement or the applicable law, or as a result of proceedings that did not comply with the parties' agreement or the applicable procedural rules, is not valid[40] and not enforceable;[41] an award rendered on a non-arbitrable subject matter is not

33. This correspondence is intentional, *see* Gary Born, *International Commercial Arbitration*, 2nd ed., Kluwer Law International 2014, pp. 3186, 3340; Giuditta Cordero-Moss, *International Commercial Contracts*, Cambridge University Press 2014, p. 224.
34. Article 34(2)(a)(i) of the Model Law; Article 52(1)(a) and (b) of the ICSID Convention.
35. Article 36(1)(a)(i) of the Model Law and Article V(1)(a) of the New York Convention; Articles 25 and 26 of the ICSID Convention.
36. Article 34(2)(a)(ii) of the Model Law; Article 52(1)(d) and (e) of the ICSID Convention.
37. Article 36(1)(a)(ii) of the Model Law and Article V(1)(b) of the New York Convention.
38. Article 34(2)(a)(iii) of the Model Law; Article 52(1)(b) of the ICSID Convention.
39. Article 36(1)(a)(iii) of the Model Law and Article V(1)(c) of the New York Convention.
40. Article 34(2)(a)(iv) of the Model Law; Article 52(1)(a) and (c) of the ICSID Convention.
41. Article 36(1)(a)(iv) of the Model Law and Article V(1)(d) of the New York Convention.

valid[42] and not enforceable;[43] an award infringing fundamental principles (public policy) is not valid[44] and not enforceable.[45]

In addition, in the New York Convention and in the UNCITRAL Model Law there is a rule on public policy, which covers not only the procedural public policy but also the substantive public policy. While the ICSID Convention does not mention public policy as a ground to annul an award, it has a specific rule on the necessity that the award be reasoned. Regarding enforcement, ICSID awards are subject to the same regime as final court decisions in the enforcement country. To the extent the enforcement country has a public policy exception, therefore, it will apply also to ICSID awards.

The applicable provisions make it clear that judicial control is not meant to be an appeal. Judicial control is not the same as a review of the award on the merits, neither in respect of the assessment of facts nor in respect of the application of law. The direct consequence of this limitation of judicial control is that an award is final and binding, even if it contains errors of fact or errors of law. This is the basis upon which the system of arbitration, as we know it today, rests: international conventions, national laws, courts of law, legal doctrine and practitioners support the aim that arbitration is to be an effective and efficient means of dispute resolution. To achieve this aim, they widely recognize that awards must be final and binding. Effectiveness and efficiency of arbitration are important principles of arbitration law, and at the origin of the widespread arbitration-friendly attitude that has characterized legislation and case law in the past decades.

The provisions regulating judicial control on arbitral awards represent the limit of tolerance that legal systems have in respect of arbitral awards. They can, therefore, to a large extent be deemed to concretize the due process principle in arbitration.

The next sections 14.04 and 14.05 will discuss to what extent these requirements contained in the New York Convention, the UNCITRAL Model Law and the ICSID Convention are necessary or sufficient basis to comply with due process.

§14.04 COMPLIANCE WITH LEGAL FRAMEWORK AS A NECESSARY CONDITION OF DUE PROCESS?

An award rendered in a process that did not comply with the requirements deriving from the rules on judicial control is not necessarily invalid or unenforceable, and thus does not necessarily violate the principle of due process.

As will be discussed immediately below, this is due not only to the circumstance that court control may be waived but also to the fact that the guarantees contained in the legal framework are not necessarily absolute.

42. Article 34(2)(b)(i) of the Model Law; Article 52 (1)(b) of the ICSID Convention.
43. Article 36(1)(b)(i) of the Model Law and Article V(2)(a) of the New York Convention; Articles 25 and 26 of the ICSID Convention.
44. Article 34(2)(b)(ii) of the Model Law; Article 52(1)(d) of the ICSID Convention, with respect to procedural public policy.
45. Article 36(1)(b)(ii) of the Model Law and Article V(2)(b) of the New York Convention.

Some national laws, such as Belgian, French, Swedish and Swiss law, permit the parties to exclude in advance their right to challenge the validity of the arbitral award. By permitting to exclude challenge of the award, these legal systems give effect to awards that may or may not be in compliance with the requirements for validity of awards.

That waiver of challenge is compatible with Article 6 of the ECHR has been confirmed by the ECtHR.[46] The ECtHR evaluated Swiss arbitration law that permits to exclude court control on the award, and concluded that it did not violate Article 6 of the ECHR. The court considered that the possibility to exclude court control was justified by the intent to promote an efficient arbitration system in Switzerland. In the eyes of the ECtHR, the interest in promoting an efficient arbitral system outweighed the interests protected by Article 6 of the convention. Hence, it is not necessarily a violation of due process if an award does not meet general criteria for validity, such as those set out in the Swiss Private International Law Act, which broadly correspond to the criteria for invalidity laid down in the UNCITRAL Model Law.

Furthermore, courts retain a discretion in the exercise of their control on the award. This confirms that the court's function as a safeguard of procedural principles does not respond to an absolute duty. Under Article 34 of the UNCITRAL Model Law, courts may set aside an award on the basis of the listed annulment grounds, but are not obliged to do so. Likewise, Article 52(3) of the ICSID Convention gives the ad hoc committee the authority to annul an award on any of the grounds for annulment, but does not create an obligation to do so.

Likewise, under the New York Convention, courts may refuse recognition and enforcement of an award that presents the procedural or substantive flaws listed in Article V, but are not obliged to do so.[47]Thus, an award that does not meet the requirements for recognition and enforcement derived from Article V may nevertheless be recognized and enforced. It must be concluded that the award does not necessarily violate the principle of due process, even though it breaches some of the criteria set out in Article V.

Moreover, the New York Convention permits states to apply their own law instead of the provisions of the convention if domestic law is more favourable to the

46. *Tabbane v. Switzerland*, paras 33-36.

47. In a past debate on this topic, this position was also supported by a linguistic argument, *see* Jan Paulsson, 'Rediscovering the N.Y. Convention: Further Reflections on Chromalloy', 12 *Mealey's International Arbitration Report* 4, 1997, 20-34, 24f. According to this argument, the English text ('recognition and enforcement [...] may only be refused if [...]') could be seen as a basis for the courts' discretion, because of its use of the verb 'may'. In reality, the verb 'may' is coupled with 'only if', and is meant to express that the only allowed grounds for refusing recognition and enforcement are those listed in the provision. The text, in other words, says nothing about the court's discretion to recognize and enforce an award notwithstanding that there is a ground for refusal. This is confirmed by a look at other language versions (I can only express a considered opinion on the French and the Russian versions, and also the Spanish version seems to suggest the same). Although the court's discretion may not necessarily be based on the language of the provision, there are good reasons for asserting it. If a process was flawed by a violation which is not very serious or which did not affect the outcome of the decision, reasons of effectiveness suggest that the award be recognized and enforced.

recognition and enforcement of the award.[48] If a state has a more arbitration-friendly regulation than Article V, the award may be recognized and enforced on the basis of that state's law, and the New York Convention will not be deemed violated, although the criteria set out in Article V may have been breached. Hence, the requirements for recognition and enforcement of awards that are listed in Article V of the New York Convention cannot necessarily be equated with the principle of due process.

It can be concluded that the principle of due process is not automatically violated even though the requirements laid down in the sources applicable to arbitration are not met, as long as these sources permit to give effect to the award on alternative bases. However, in these situations, the presumption that the due process principle was not violated may be weaker.

§14.05 COMPLIANCE WITH THE LEGAL FRAMEWORK AS A SUFFICIENT CONDITION FOR DUE PROCESS?

The next question is whether arbitration may be deemed to give institutional guarantees of due process at least as long as it is carried out within the borders of what the applicable sources require for the validity and enforceability of an award. In other words: is due process automatically deemed to be safeguarded if the requirements for validity and enforceability of the award are met?

Generally, it can be assumed that the structure created by the legal framework applicable to arbitration is sufficient to ensure the respect of due process. As was mentioned above, the large support of the New York Convention, the UNCITRAL Model Law and the ICSID Convention must be assumed to represent a consensus that states do not breach their obligations relating to due process when they give effect to an award that meets the requirements imposed by that legal framework. Where due process is infringed in the specific case, normally the system for review of the award by the courts or, in the case of ICSID awards, by ad hoc committees permits to remedy.

The system of award review is meant precisely to safeguard the integrity and fairness of the process. The idea is that, notwithstanding the principle of finality of the awards, which is fundamental in arbitration law, there must be a possibility to review the award to ensure that fundamental principles have not been infringed in the process that led to the award. The two conflicting principles of awards' finality and need to safeguard basic procedural rights have to be balanced against each other. The result of the balancing is the existing system of court control (or ad hoc control for ICSID awards): the award is final on the merits, but it can be subject to control as far as due process issues are concerned.

In light of the growing criticism against arbitration, however, it is appropriate to enquire whether it is legitimate to assume that the existing legal framework captures all issues related to due process, and whether it does so in an efficient way. Based on recent practice and doctrinal debate, it seems that there are several issues that may have relevance to due process, and where it is often argued that an improvement of the

48. New York Convention, Article VII.

legal framework, or at least a more assertive application of the existing rules, may have beneficial effects. The question is whether potential for improvement is equal to violation of due process.

[A] Length of the Proceedings: Costs

One of the main criticisms moved against arbitration is that arbitral proceedings have become too complicated and time-consuming. [49] The hypertrophy of arbitration has also a financial dimension, as it implies costs that are sometimes extremely high, possibly not proportionate to the value in dispute. [50]

This may have relevance to the principle of due process. On the one hand, the high costs may be an insurmountable obstacle for impecunious parties, thus preventing their access to justice.

On the other hand, too lengthy proceedings may result in a justice system that is so inefficient, that in practice it denies justice. The former aspect will be analysed immediately below, the latter in the subsequent section.

As regards the issue of access to justice by indigent parties, criticism has been raised in the context both of commercial and of investment arbitration.

To a large extent, however, the existing legal framework seems to be capable of providing acceptable solutions.

In the field of commercial arbitration, an example is a French Supreme Court decision[51] setting aside an award that had disregarded the respondent's counterclaim.

The arbitral tribunal had ruled that the counterclaim was inadmissible on the ground that the respondent, who was subject to insolvency proceedings, was not able to pay the advance deposit on costs that, according to the applicable arbitration rules, had to be paid for the counterclaim to be admitted.

By way of general explanation, the advance deposit for arbitration costs is calculated as an aggregate of the dispute's value, and is divided between the parties. If one party does not pay its share, payment of that share may be effected by the other party. In this way, the proceedings may be instituted and continue. If the advance deposit is not paid, arbitration costs are not covered, and the proceedings do not go forward. The arbitration rules of some institutions permit to allocate payment of the

49. The choice of devoting various sessions of the UNCITRAL Working Group II to an instrument for the promotion of mediation, which resulted into the adoption of the United Nations Convention on International Settlement Agreements Resulting from Mediation, is a symptom of the declining hegemony of arbitration. The same Working Group is presently working on an instrument for expedite arbitration, precisely to meet the growing criticism against the excessive features of arbitration, *see* Report of the United Nations Commission on International Trade Law Fifty-first session (25 June-13 July 2018), A/73/17, para. 244. *See also* the Working Group II (Dispute Settlement) sixty-ninth session New York, 4-8 February 2019, Note by the Secretariat, A/CN.9/WG.II/WP.207.
50. Queen Mary and White&Case 2018 International Arbitration Survey: The Evolution of International Arbitration, available at http://www.arbitration.qmul.ac.uk/media/arbitration/docs/2018-International-Arbitration-Survey---The-Evolution-of-International-Arbitration-(2).PDF.
51. Cour de Cassation, 1e civ., 28 March 2013, No. 11-27.770 (*Pirelli*).

advance deposit between the parties in proportion to the respective claims or counterclaims.[52] If one party does not effect payment of its share, that party's claim is not admitted. In the case before the Cour de Cassation, the respondent did not have the possibility to pay its share of the deposit because of its insolvency situation.

The court found that the claim and the counterclaim were necessarily interlinked, and that not admitting the counterclaim, while rendering a decision on the claim, would have deprived the respondent of the possibility to have the counterclaim heard at a later stage. This annulment decision is an example of how the existing legal framework may safeguard the due process principle in the specific case.

While the arbitration rules that led to the annulled award may be applied in a way that leads to unacceptable results, it does not seem that there is a compelling need to modify them: the allocation of the deposit between the parties is in the discretion of the arbitration institute (in the case at hand, of the International Court of Arbitration of the ICC), and so is the decision to consider a claim inadmissible.

In many cases, the decisions on allocation and on admissibility will not create due process issues;[53] in the cases in which due process may be relevant, it can be expected that the discretion of the arbitration institute will be exercised so as not to infringe it; should, in a specific case, due process be infringed, court control will intervene.

As far as investment arbitration is concerned, it has been put forward that its excessive costs may prevent developing states from having access to justice. [54]

Admittedly, investment proceedings may achieve costs that can be prohibitive. However, it has convincingly been argued that it is not correct to evaluate the cost of arbitration in absolute terms: the costs should be evaluated in relation to alternative, comparable mechanisms of dispute resolution.

When compared to the alternatives, the cost of investment arbitration becomes less outstanding. In particular, it has been pointed out that between 80% to 90% of the costs of investment arbitrations are represented by attorney and expert fees.[55]These are costs that would arise irrespective of the type of dispute resolution mechanism that is applied.

It is, on the one hand, correct that arbitration proceedings may become exceedingly lengthy and thus the costs increase accordingly. This may in part be explained in terms of the already mentioned due process paranoia that will be commented on below.[56]

52. *See*, for example, Article 37(3) of the ICC Arbitration Rules and Article 51(3) of the SCC Rules.
53. The same Cour de Cassation, for example, confirmed an award under similar circumstances, because in this case the claims were not necessarily interlinked: Cour de Cassation 1e civ., 17 October 2018, No. 17-21411.
54. Working Group III Note by the Secretariat, A/CN.9/WG.III/WP.142, cit., paras 40, 41, 64.
55. Report of Working Group III (Investor-State Dispute Settlement Reform) on the work of its thirty-fourth session (Vienna, 27 November-1 December 2017), A/CN.9/930, paras 36, 43, 62.
56. Report of Working Group III on the work of its thirty-fourth session, A/CN.9/930, cit., para. 45.

Other reasons for the length of arbitration proceedings, however, are specific to disputes involving states: [57] the circumstance that investment disputes are solved on the basis of treaties, and treaty law may be fragmented and may require more thorough investigation than national law; or the circumstance that states may be constrained by domestic laws and may need more time than private parties to act in legal proceedings.[58]

Another aspect that has been mentioned is that investment arbitration generally follows the public international law approach characteristic of disputes between states, according to which each party bears its own costs, as opposed to allocating costs between the parties according to the outcome of the dispute. This prevents states from absorbing their costs even in case they win and is deemed to be an important disadvantage for states with a small economy.[59]

The matters described above can be addressed by the sound use of the arbitral tribunal's or the arbitral institution's discretion.[60]

[B] Length of the Proceedings: Efficiency

Both in commercial and in investment arbitration, there is an emerging criticism against what is being perceived as an excessive deference to procedural requests by one of the parties (what has become fashionable to call the due process paranoia).

It can first of all be mentioned that, in case the parties agree on procedural measures that increase the duration or the level of complication of the proceedings, the arbitral tribunal is bound to follow the parties' instructions. The parties may agree on extensive discovery, on the use of multiple experts, on extensions of terms, on the admission of late claims, etc. In these cases, the excessive length of the proceedings is due to the parties' own determination, not to the inefficiency of arbitration.[61]

Due process paranoia arises when procedural requests are made by one party, and often opposed to by the other party. The tribunal's indulgence is in this case not dictated by the desire to comply with the parties' agreement; it is rather dictated by the fear that the party whose request was rejected attacks the award claiming that the tribunal violated due process guarantees by not admitting a new claim, by not requesting discovery of documentation, by not allowing multiple experts, by not

57. Report of Working Group III on the work of its thirty-fourth session, A/CN.9/930, cit., paras 45-52.
58. Report of Working Group III on the work of its thirty-fifth session, A/CN.9/935, cit., para. 36.
59. Report of Working Group III on the work of its thirty-fourth session, A/CN.9/930, cit., paras 39-41 and 53. *See also* Report of Working Group III (Investor-State Dispute Settlement Reform) on the work of thirty-sixth session (Vienna, 29 October-2 November 2018), A/CN.9/964, paras 110-123.
60. A consequence of the high costs of arbitration is the development of different schemes for third-party funding of litigation. While the topic is attracting considerable attention, it is not exclusive to arbitration, but regards all kinds of litigation. Therefore, it will not be discussed here.
61. For similar considerations *see* Diego P. Fernández Arroyo, 'Nothing Is for Free: The Prices to Pay for *Arbitrabilizing* Legal Disputes', Loïc Cadiet, Burkard Hess, Marta Requejo Isidro (eds.), *Privatizing Dispute Resolution*, Nomos 2019, 617-646, 624.

granting an extension of terms, etc. Indulging the party's procedural requests burdens the process, but only rarely may itself become a violation of the other party's due process rights. The arbitral tribunal may thus reason that avoiding the risk that the award be set aside or refused enforcement on the basis that a party's requests were rejected outweighs the disadvantages of indulging excessive procedural requests by one party. The consequence of this calculation is that a dissatisfaction may grow among the users of arbitration, who witness that insufficiently assertive case management by the arbitral tribunal renders the proceedings inefficient and unnecessarily expensive. In extreme cases, hypertrophic proceedings may affect the efficiency to an extent that due process is violated.

To the extent these causes for long and costly proceedings do not depend on the parties' agreement or, as was mentioned above, on the participation of a state in a dispute, it seems to be possible to meet the concerns encouraging a more assertive case management.

The fear that courts may, in the name of due process, set aside or refuse enforcement as a consequence of the arbitral tribunal's case management is exaggerated.[62] Rather than a structural due process problem, therefore, the paranoia seems to be curable by enhancing an informed and sound use of the arbitral tribunal's discretion.

Arbitration rules are increasingly emphasizing the tribunal's procedural discretion: in her seminal 2016 Queen Mary School of International Arbitration – Freshfield Lecture,[63] Lucy Reed pointed out, for example, a change in the UNCITRAL Arbitration Rules. While the 1976 version, in Article 15(1), used to provide that parties would be given a 'full' opportunity of presenting their case 'at any stage of the proceedings', the 2010 version provides, in Article 17(1), that the parties are given a 'reasonable' opportunity of presenting their case at 'an appropriate stage'.

Furthermore, the UNCITRAL Commission launched a work on the efficiency of arbitration, with the aim of enhancing efficiency without losing sight of the quality of the proceedings and thus of due process.[64] Currently, in this framework, the Working Group II is drafting rules for expedited arbitration in ad hoc proceedings.[65]

Regarding investment arbitration, already in 2006, the ICSID Rules were amended introducing measures to expedite the proceedings, and in 2016 the ICSID Secretariat initiated a consultation process to introduce further improvement of the rules.[66]

62. A comparative study analysing this subject matter in seventeen different countries is forthcoming: Dietmar Czernich, Franco Ferrari, Friedrich Rosenfeld (eds.), *Due Process in Arbitration*, forthcoming 2020, with general report by Friedrich Rosenfeld.
63. Lucy Reed, 'Ab(use) of Due Process: Sward vs Shield' (2017) 3 *Arbitration International*, 361-377.
64. Report of the Commission's fifty-first session, cit., para. 252.
65. Report of the Working Group II seventieth session (Vienna, 23-27 September 2019), A/CN.9/1003, para. 2.
66. For an overview and references, *see* https://icsid.worldbank.org/sp/amendments/Pages/Resources/A-Brief-History-of-Amendment-to-the-ICSID-Rules-and-Regulations.aspx, *See also* https://icsid.worldbank.org/en/Documents/about/List%20of%20Topics%20for%20Potential

Even in disputes relating to human rights, it seems that the existing mechanism is deemed to be capable of ensuring due process. Article 5 of the Hague Rules has added a provision to the existing UNCITRAL Arbitration Rules. However, this provision does not seem to create new powers for tribunals or to create mechanisms that are not already present in arbitration.

Thus, in case of inequality of arms between the parties, Article 5(2) of the Hague Rules states that the 'arbitral tribunal shall, without compromising its independence and impartiality, ensure that such party is given an effective opportunity to present its case in fair and efficient proceedings'. It is doubtful that this provision creates more than an obligation for the tribunal to exercise its discretion so as to permit a fair process, even when there is an unbalance between the parties in terms of resources, information, etc. The commentary to the Hague Rules concludes its explanation of this provision as follows: 'Thus, the tribunal should make efforts to ensure that an unrepresented party can present its case in a fair and efficient way, including by adopting more proactive and inquisitorial, as opposed to adversarial, procedures.'[67]

While it is commendable that the Hague Rules explicitly mention the inequality of arms and the intention to remedy it, they do not seem to add considerably to the discretion that arbitral tribunals already have under the UNCITRAL Arbitration Rules and under other arbitration rules.

The Hague Rules' suggestion that arbitral tribunals may take an active role already flows from the existing legal framework: as I have discussed elsewhere, arbitration law and courts give arbitral tribunals a considerable leeway in developing their own independent reasoning.[68] As long as the award does not exceed the scope of power that the parties conferred on the tribunal, as long as the parties were given the possibility to comment on the basis for the decision, and as long as the tribunal acts impartially, the tribunal has a considerable autonomy and may have an active role even under the existing legal framework, depending on the peculiarities of each domestic arbitration law. If the Hague Rules are intended to extend the tribunal's role beyond this autonomy, it is doubtful that they will be capable of having effect: the award is exposed to annulment or its enforcement may be refused on the basis of the applicable arbitration law and of the New York Convention, if these borders are overstepped. Likewise, disregard of these criteria would violate the due process principle.

Other additions made by the Hague Rules to the UNCITRAL Arbitration Rules are meant to highlight the need for culturally appropriate and rights-compatible process,[69]

%20ICSID%20Rule%20Amendment-ENG.pdf, and Working Group III Thirty-fourth session, Submissions from International Intergovernmental Organisations, A/CN.9/WG.III/WP:143, paras 1-5.

67. Hague Rules on Business and Human Rights Arbitration Article 5, comment 2.
68. Giuditta Cordero-Moss, 'The Arbitral Tribunal's Power in Respect of the Parties' Pleadings as a Limit to Party Autonomy (On Jura Novit Curia and Related Issues)', Franco Ferrari (ed.), *Limits to Party Autonomy in International Commercial Arbitration*, Juris 2016, 289-330. For a comparative analysis of this issue in fourteen national jurisdictions, as well as in international law, *see* Giuditta Cordero-Moss and Franco Ferrari (eds.), *Jura Novit Curia in International Arbitration*, Juris 2018, with general report by Giuditta Cordero-Moss (463-487).
69. Hague Rules on Business and Human Rights Arbitration Articles 18, 19, 27 and 32.

without, however, introducing structural changes. Yet other additions are meant to implement mechanisms already present in other arbitration rules,[70] thus not adding new elements to the existing arbitration landscape.

In summary, the Hague Rules that were developed for the purpose of adapting the existing arbitration mechanism to human rights disputes have introduced provisions that highlight the advisability of using the tribunal's power in a way that ensures a balanced, culturally appropriate and rights-compatible process. While enhancing the visibility of these guidelines, these provisions do not bring significant structural changes to the legal framework for arbitration as is reflected in today's legal framework.

Based on the foregoing, it seems that concerns about the efficiency of proceedings to a large extent may be addressed by a sound case management within the existing legal framework.

[C] Reasoning

In an eagerness to reinstate and enhance efficiency of arbitral proceedings, some institutional rules are pushing the line between legitimate case management and the principle of due process.

For example, under the SCC Rules for expedited arbitration, the award is to state reasons only if one of the parties requests so.[71] This means that, in SCC expedited processes, as a general rule, an award needs not stating reasons.

In a similar vein, for ordinary (non-expedited) arbitration proceedings, the UNCITRAL Model Law permits the parties to agree that the award shall not state any reasons.[72] As I have discussed elsewhere,[73] however, the reasons of the award may be necessary for the purpose of rendering court control meaningful.

Most rules for expedited arbitration have not gone as far as the SCC Rules, and awards are usually expected to state reasons even in expedited proceedings. The ICC Expedited Procedure Rules,[74] for example, do not permit to derogate from Article 32(2) of the Arbitration Rules, according to which awards must state the reasons upon which they are based. As a matter of fact, the ICC Notes to the Parties and Arbitral Tribunals state that: [75] 'Any award under the Expedited Procedure Provisions shall be reasoned. Arbitral tribunals may limit the factual and/or procedural sections of the award to what they consider to be necessary to the understanding of the award, and state the reasons of the award in as concise a fashion as possible.' In my experience as member of the ICC Court of Arbitration, the scrutiny of the draft awards rendered under the Expedited

70. Hague Rules on Business and Human Rights Arbitration, Articles 26 and 31, respectively, on summary dismissal and emergency arbitrator.
71. Article 42(1) of the 2017 Stockholm Rules for Expedited Arbitrations.
72. UNCITRAL Model Law Article 31(2).
73. Giuditta Cordero-Moss, 'Reasons in Arbitral Awards and Court Control', *Dossier XVIII: Explaining Why You Lost: Reasoning in Arbitration*, ICC Institute of World Business, forthcoming 2020.
74. *See* Article 1 of Appendix VI to the ICC Arbitration Rules.
75. ICC Notes to the parties and arbitral tribunals, cit., para. 117.

Procedures takes into consideration the need for an expedited processing, but is no less thorough in substance than for ordinary arbitration.

Regarding investment arbitration, under the ICSID Convention, lack of reasoning is a ground for annulment.

The UNCITRAL Working Group II on dispute resolution, which is currently working on matters relating to expedited arbitration, discussed at its sixty-ninth session in February 2019 whether it is desirable to eliminate the requirement that the award states the reasons for the decision.[76] The outcome of the discussion was not favourable to eliminating the requirement, but the simple fact that the matter was discussed shows that any measures are contemplated for the purpose of enhancing efficiency.

Given that the award's reasons are necessary or important to permit court control, how can this be reconciled with the systems that permit the parties to agree that the award shall not state any reasons, or even that assume that awards shall not have reasons unless one party requests so? Permitting the parties to exclude reasons may create considerable problems if the applicable arbitration law does not permit to exclude court control and may create difficulties in case of enforcement. As an award that does not state reasons prevents or at least hampers court control, it must be assumed that an award without reasons will not be deemed acceptable by a court. While there is no specific basis to assume that reasoning is a necessary requirement of due process, in the field of criminal decisions, the ECtHR has repeatedly affirmed that, while an unmotivated verdict in criminal cases in itself is not a violation of the principle of fair trial, the principle of fair trial is breached by a process that does not provide sufficient guarantees to rule out any risk of arbitrariness and enable the accused to understand the reasons for his conviction.[77]

Furthermore, the increased interest in transparency, that will be mentioned below, suggests that the general expectations towards arbitration are not going in the direction of releasing arbitral tribunals from any obligation to state the reasons for their decisions.

The intention, when permitting that an award does not state reasons, is to enhance arbitration and increase its effectiveness. The risk is that exactly the opposite result is obtained, i.e., that arbitration loses its credibility and, instead of being promoted, is restricted.

It can be expected that, to the extent the exercise of the power granted by arbitration rules violates due process, court control will put a remedy.

76. *See* the Report of Working Group II (Dispute Settlement) on the work of its sixty-ninth session (New York, 4-8 February 2019), A/CN.9/969, https://undocs.org/en/A/CN.9/969, at item No. 7.

77. *Taxquet v. Belgium*, Decision of 16 November 2010, Application No. 926/05, as well as *Agnelet v. France* and *Legillon v. France*, Decisions of 10 January 2013, Application Nos 61198/08 and 53406/10.

[D] Transparency

Traditionally, arbitration is a confidential process to which only the involved parties are privy. Indeed, confidentiality is often mentioned as one of the advantages of arbitration as opposed to court litigation. The ECtHR considered the lack of public hearing to be a feature of arbitration that is unacceptable from the point of view of due process in a case where arbitration was deemed to be compulsory and not voluntary, and the dispute regarded disciplinary measures that carried a degree of stigma and was likely to affect the respondent's professional honour and reputation.[78] Under these circumstances, the ECtHR found that holding proceedings in public protects the parties against injustice being administered in secret. The ECtHR in the same decision made a distinction between voluntary and compulsory arbitration and affirmed that the guarantees set forth in Article 6 of the European Convention of Human Rights may be waived in voluntary arbitration. In particular, 'proceedings devoted exclusively to legal or highly technical questions may comply with the requirements of Article 6 even if there has been no public hearing'.[79]

However, transparency has increasingly been called for in arbitration, particularly, but not only, investment arbitration.

In investment arbitration, there is a clear public interest in the dispute and its outcome. The arbitral tribunal is called upon to evaluate the conduct of the state, and this may involve scrutinizing, *inter alia*, the state's policies, its balancing of conflicting policies, its management of public interests, etc. The award, furthermore, may have an impact on the state's regulations and future policies, with effects that go far beyond the legal relationship between the disputing parties. The public, therefore, has a clear interest in being informed about investment disputes, and stakeholders have an expectation to be able to present comments. Facing growing criticism for lack of legitimacy and accountability,[80] already in 2006, the ICSID Rules were amended, introducing transparency.[81] In 2013, the UNCITRAL adopted the Rules on Transparency in Treaty-Based Investor-State Arbitration.[82] A new provision was added in Article 1, paragraph 4 of the UNCITRAL Arbitration Rules (that had just been revised in 2010), to incorporate the Rules on Transparency for arbitration initiated pursuant to an investment treaty concluded on or after 1 April 2014. Furthermore, with the 2014 Mauritius Convention on Transparency,[83] parties to investment treaties concluded before 1 April 2014 express their consent to apply the Rules on Transparency also to disputes based on investment treaties concluded prior to 1 April 2014.

78. *Mutu and Pechstein v. Switzerland* para. 182.
79. *Mutu and Pechstein v. Switzerland* para. 177.
80. For references, *see* UNCTAD, Transparency in IIAS: A Sequel, UNCTAD Series on Issues in International Investment Agreements (2012), p. 36, and UNCTAD, World Investment Report 2015, p. 148.
81. https://icsid.worldbank.org/sp/amendments/Pages/Resources/A-Brief-History-of-Amendment-to-the-ICSID-Rules-and-Regulations.aspx.
82. http://www.uncitral.org/pdf/english/texts/arbitration/arb-rules-2013/UNCITRAL-Arbitration-Rules-2013-e.pdf.
83. https://uncitral.un.org/en/texts/arbitration/conventions/transparency.

For human rights disputes, the Hague Rules suggest a regulation that is largely based on the UNCITRAL Transparency Rules.

The calls for transparency that have recently turned around the world of investment arbitration seem to be affecting also commercial arbitration. [84] Commercial awards are being published to a larger extent than earlier, [85] institutions are being more transparent regarding the appointment and removal of arbitral tribunals,[86] and initiatives flourish to increase transparency in commercial arbitration.[87]

As long as confidentiality is the main rule for arbitral proceedings, however, transparency measures will require the parties' consent – either given specifically in each case or given by choosing arbitration rules containing transparency mechanisms. A possible way to enhance transparency is to change the statutory rules governing arbitration. Under Norwegian arbitration law,[88] for example, confidentiality is not the main rule, but assumes that a specific agreement on confidentiality was entered into between the parties in relation to the particular dispute.

[E] Impartiality and Independence

The appointment mechanism of arbitral tribunals is heavily criticized, particularly in investment arbitration. The circumstance that arbitrators are appointed by the parties for the particular dispute is deemed to prejudice the legitimacy and accountability of

84. Calling for transparency in commercial arbitration, *see* Diego P. Fernández Arroyo, 'Nothing Is for Free', cit., 635ff. In 2016, the then Lord Chief Justice of England and Wales, Lord Thomas, held a lecture in which he pointed out that, since many commercial parties choose arbitration to solve their disputes and appeal from arbitral awards is very restricted, courts are not participating to the desirable extent to the development of the law: Lord Thomas of Cwmgiedd, Lord Chief Justice of England and Wales, Bailii Lecture: Developing Commercial Law Through the Courts: Rebalancing the Relationship Between the Courts and Arbitration (9 March 2016). The same criticism had been put forward, decades earlier, by the then Chief Justice of the Norwegian Supreme Court, Carsten Smith. «Voldgift – domstolenes konkurrent og hjelper», in *Tidsskrift for Rettsvitenskap,* 1993, p. 474ff. The Norwegian Arbitration Act of 2004 acted upon this criticism and assumes that confidentiality of the awards must be agreed to by the parties. In contrast, most arbitration laws still assume confidentiality as the main rule in arbitration.
85. Many arbitration institutions publish, in anonymized version, a selection of the awards rendered under their rules. For example, following an amendment to the ICC Notes to the parties and arbitral tribunals on the conduct of the arbitration under the ICC Arbitration Rules dated 1 January 2019, https://cdn.iccwbo.org/content/uploads/sites/3/2017/03/icc-note-to-parties-and-arbitral-tribunals-on-the-conduct-of-arbitration.pdf, section III.D, all awards rendered after 1 January 2019 may be published, unless one party objects. In addition, awards are collected in data bases such as the database Case Law on UNCITRAL Texts (CLOUT, https://www.uncitral.org/clout/) or the database on UNIDROIT Principles and CISG Unilex (http://www.unilex.info/).
86. *See*, for example, the publication by the Stockholm Arbitration Institute in 2017 of its policy for appointing arbitrators: https://sccinstitute.com/media/220131/scc-policy-appointment-of-arbitrators-2017.pdf. As from 2016, the ICC publishes information about arbitrators sitting in tribunals administrated under the ICC Rules: *see* the ICC Notes to the parties and arbitral tribunals, cit., section III.B.
87. *See*, for example, Arbitrator Intelligence, https://www.arbitratorintelligence.org/.
88. 2004 Norwegian Arbitration Act, § 5.

investment arbitration.[89] Arbitrators appointed by the parties are suspected of being biased[90] and of being inclined to decide in favour of the party who appointed them, for the purpose of being appointed again by the same party in new disputes.[91] The system of party appointment is criticized for preventing diversity by confirming pre-existing connections,[92] and for creating conflict of interests when professionals belonging to the same environment appoint each other or alternatively appear as counsel and as arbitrator (so-called double hatting).[93]

Indeed, there are noticeable examples of double hatting, and, in some cases, this is detrimental to the credibility of arbitration. Also, the method for selection, although significantly improved in the course of the past decade, can certainly be made more objective and professional.[94]

However, the system according to which the arbitral tribunal is appointed by the parties is the fundament of this dispute settlement mechanism. It permits to select arbitrators for their expertise and their understanding of the specific area of the dispute. Even the Hague Rules recognize, for human rights disputes, the importance of ensuring that the arbitral tribunal has the relevant expertise.[95] There may be few qualified experts in sophisticated areas, and it may be more important to ensure that the tribunal understands the law and the underlying issues, than to avoid appointing anyone who has involvement in similar disputes.

However, it is undoubtedly important to exercise a sound use of the discretion that characterizes the selection of arbitrators.

It must be pointed out that the existing legal framework governing arbitration reflects the importance of ensuring the independence and impartiality of the arbitral tribunal. It provides mechanisms to challenge arbitrators, and it permits to set aside or refuse enforcement of awards rendered by a tribunal that was not impartial or independent.[96] Also, arbitration rules give the parties the possibility to challenge arbitrators. Therefore, mechanisms are in place to ensure this fundamental element of the due process principle. When called upon to scrutinize the appointment mechanism

89. Jan Paulsson, 'Moral Hazard in International Dispute Resolution' (2010) 25 *ICSID Review* 339; Jan Albert Van den Berg, 'Dissenting Opinions by Party-Appointed Arbitrators in Investment Arbitration', M H Arsanjani, J Cogan, R Sloane, S Wiessner (eds.), *Looking to the Future: Essays on International Law in Honor of W. Michael Reis- man*, Martinus Nijhoff 2011; for further references, *see* Diego P. Fernández Arroyo, 'Nothing Is for Free', cit., 627.
90. Report of Working Group III on the work of its thirty-fifth session, A/CN.9/935, cit., para. 54.
91. Report of Working Group III on the work of its thirty-fifth session, A/CN.9/935, cit., paras 56, 73.
92. Report of Working Group III on the work of its thirty-fifth session, A/CN.9/935, cit., para. 70.
93. Working Group III Note by the Secretariat, A/CN.9/WG.III/WP.142, cit., paras 40, 41, 64; Report of Working Group III on the work of its thirty-fifth session, A/CN.9/935, cit., para. 78. *See* Malcolm Langford, Daniel Behn and Runar Lie, 'The Ethics and Empirics of Double Hatting' (2017) *SSRN Electronic Journal*, 0.2139/ssrn.3008643.
94. For an anecdotal observation based on my experience *see* Giuditta Cordero-Moss, 'Interpretation of contracts in International Commercial Arbitration: Diversity on More Than One Level'(1-2014) *European Review of Private Law*, 13-36, 33f.
95. Hague Rules on Business and Human Rights Arbitration, Preamble, point 6(e).
96. Articles 34(2)(a)(iv) and 36(1)(a)(iv) of the Model Law of the Model Law; Article 52(1)(a) and (c) of the ICSID Convention; Article V(1)(d) of the New York Convention.

of the Court of Arbitration for Sport (CAS), the ECtHR found that it did not violate the principle of independence and impartiality laid down in Article 6 of the ECHR.[97]

What can be improved is the predictability and effectiveness of how this mechanism of challenge is applied. To this end, the International Bar Association (IBA) has developed the Guidelines on Conflicts of Interest in International Arbitration,[98] a soft law instrument that enjoys a widespread success.[99] Furthermore, rules on conflict of interest and codes of conduct are being developed,[100] including improvements to the ICSID Rules.[101]

As far as the method for the selection of arbitrators is concerned, the increased transparency measures will gradually lead to a more systematic information about arbitrators and their activity.

That the mechanism of party appointment as such is capable of meeting the requirements of due process seems to be confirmed by the Hague Rules that, for human rights disputes, suggest a system that largely corresponds to the system provided for by the UNCITRAL Arbitration Rules. The most important addition made by the Hague Rules is the introduction of a code of conduct, with which arbitrators have to comply. Otherwise, the Hague Rules emphasize 'the importance of impartiality, independence and expertise to the legitimacy of business and human rights arbitration under these Rules'.[102] Furthermore, they insert a requirement that arbitrators shall be of high moral character and exercise independent and impartial judgment,[103] and the requirement that the presiding arbitrator has demonstrated expertise in international dispute resolution and in areas relevant to the dispute.[104] While it is commendable to spell out these requirements, it does not seem to make a structural difference from the UNCITRAL Arbitration Rules, and the Hague Rules preserve the autonomy of the parties in the selection of their party-appointed arbitrators.[105]

[F] Accuracy of the Application of the Law

As was mentioned above, one of the pillars of the institution of arbitration is that arbitral awards are final and are not subject to any form of appeal on the merits – be it on the evaluation of evidence and assessment of the facts, or on the application of the

97. *Mutu and Pechstein v. Switzerland*, paras 150ff.
98. https://www.ibanet.org/Document/Default.aspx?DocumentUid=e2fe5e72-eb14-4bba-b10d-d33dafee8918.
99. Although not all of its provisions are always deemed to reflect sound principles, *see* the English High Court case [2016] EWHC 422 (Comm) and the Austrian Supreme Court case 15 May 2019 Docket 18 ONc 1/19w.
100. For references, *see* Report of Working Group III on the work of its thirty-sixth session, A/CN.9/964, cit., paras 72, 76.
101. *See* https://icsid.worldbank.org/sp/amendments/Pages/Resources/A-Brief-History-of-Amendment-to-the-ICSID-Rules-and-Regulations.aspx. *See also* Report of Working Group III on the work of its thirty-sixth session, A/CN.9/964, cit., paras 84-90.
102. Hague Rules on Business and Human Rights Arbitration, Article 11, Comment No. 1.
103. Hague Rules on Business and Human Rights Arbitration, Article 11(1)(b).
104. Hague Rules on Business and Human Rights Arbitration, Article 11(1)(c).
105. Hague Rules on Business and Human Rights Arbitration, Article 11(1)(c).

law. The tribunal's autonomy in determining and applying the substantive law is a fundamental feature of arbitration. However, there is a growing mistrust against this autonomy.

In commercial arbitration, some domestic courts have recently denied the arbitrability of disputes on commercial agency contracts out of a fear that the important policies of agency law may not be accurately applied.[106] In investment arbitration, concerns are voiced about the ability of arbitrators to understand public interest issues,[107] about the consistency of awards, and about the lack of appeal. [108]

Quite apart from the observation that inconsistency in the application of the law is not a characteristic exclusive of arbitration, [109] it should be pointed out that the absence of an appeal mechanism does not mean that the fairness of proceedings cannot be reviewed.

As was mentioned above, the New York Convention and the Model Law are based on the assumption that courts may review awards in respect of due process, public policy and arbitrability. Likewise, the ICSID Convention opens for review of due process issues. Any further review would directly undermine the efficiency of arbitration: arbitration would be nothing but an additional, introductory phase to court proceedings if there was an appeal on the merits. That court control does not entail review of the award in the merits, therefore, is the result of a balancing between the need to safeguard due process and the interest in efficiency.

As I have explained elsewhere, [110] however, a word of caution is due regarding the ambitions to restrict court control for the purpose of enhancing arbitration.

Thirty years ago, the famous *Mitsubishi* decision[111] opened an era of arbitration friendliness, and permitted arbitrability of disputes relating to competition law - which until that time had been considered to involve too important and general interests to be arbitrable. The condition for extending the scope of arbitrability was that courts be permitted to give a 'second look' on the accurate application of the law - notably, in the occasion of court control and, in particular, through the rule on public policy. A similar opening was made by the CJEU with the *Eco Swiss* case.[112] This approach permits the courts to review the determination of whether important policies (such as, in these cases, competition law) are applicable, as well as their application - as long as the interests at issue are such that they qualify to fall into the realm of public policy, and for the only purpose of verifying whether these interests were seriously infringed. The

106. *See*, for references, *infra* n. 114-118.
107. Report of Working Group III on the work of its thirty-fifth session, A/CN.9/935, cit., paras 82-88; Report of Working Group III on the work of thirty-sixth session, A/CN.9/964, cit., paras 64-108.
108. Report of Working Group III on the work of its thirty-fifth session, A/CN.9/935, cit., paras 35, 38; Report of Working Group III on the work of thirty-sixth session, A/CN.9/964, cit., para. 30.
109. Report of Working Group III on the work of its thirty-fifth session, A/CN.9/935, cit., paras 36, 39; Report of Working Group III on the work of thirty-sixth session, A/CN.9/964, cit., para. 58.
110. Giuditta Cordero-Moss, 'Mitsubishi: Balancing Arbitrability and Court Control,' Horatia Muir Watt, Lucia Bíziková, Agatha Brandão de Oliveira and Diego Fernández Arroyo (eds.), *Global Private International Law, Adjudication without Frontiers*, Elgar 2019, 82-91.
111. *Mitsubishi Motors Corp. v. Soler Chrysler-Plymouth, Inc.*, 473 U.S. 614, 628 (1985).
112. Case C-126/97, *Eco Swiss China Time Ltd. v. Benneton Int'l NV*, 1999 E.C.R. I-3079.

large scope of arbitrability, therefore, is directly linked to the existence of judicial control on the awards, albeit restricted.

The legitimacy of arbitration is threatened by the fear that arbitration may become a mechanism by which the parties circumvent the application of important policies reflected in overriding mandatory rules such as competition law. By exercising their party autonomy, the parties may choose a governing law that permits them to avoid these rules. The fear is that arbitral tribunals, feeling bound by the parties' choice of law, lend themselves to the circumvention of important policies. Arbitral tribunals may in fact fear that, if they consider these policies notwithstanding the parties' agreement on a different law, they may exceed their power and thus render an invalid and unenforceable award.

As I have discussed elsewhere,[113] the fear that courts may, in the name of excess of power, set aside or refuse enforcement of an award as a consequence of the tribunal's independent selection or application of the law is ill-founded. While there are nuances particular to each legal system, most arbitration laws give the tribunal the power to make its own, independent legal reasoning. What the principle of due process requires in many systems, however, is that the tribunal informs the parties of its legal considerations, so that the parties are given the possibility to comment or present new evidence that becomes relevant in view of the tribunal's legal reasoning.[114]

There seems to be a growing awareness, in the arbitration community, of the necessity to ensure that the award gives due consideration to the law applicable to the merits.[115] Coupled with the courts' possibility to give a second look at awards to ensure that fundamental principles are not violated, this should be a sufficient basis to ensure the arbitration-friendly attitude opened by *Mitsubishi* – although the second look does not provide a perfect system.[116]On the contrary, ambitions to enhance the autonomy of arbitration and correspondingly restrict court control on awards may turn out to be counterproductive. Fears about the accuracy with which arbitral tribunals apply the law may affect the scope of arbitrability. Likewise, the scope of arbitrability is linked to the intensity of judicial control that will be discussed below.

[G] The Intensity of Judicial Control

As was seen above, judicial control is restricted; for what is relevant here, it consists mainly in ensuring that the award does not infringe public policy (*ordre public*).

113. Cordero-Moss, 'The Arbitral Tribunal's Power in Respect of the Parties' Pleadings as a Limit to Party Autonomy', cit.; Giuditta Cordero-Moss, 'EU Overriding Mandatory Provisions and the Law Applicable to the Merits', Franco Ferrari (ed.), *The Impact of EU Law on International Commercial Arbitration*, Juris 2017, 317-349.

114. For a description of due process requirements in this context *see* Cordero-Moss and Ferrari, *Iura Novit Curia in International Arbitration*, cit.

115. Luca Radicati di Brozolo, 'Mandatory Rules and International Arbitration' (2012) 23 *American Review of International Arbitration* 49, 66ff.

116. Massimo Benedettelli, '"Communitarization" of International Arbitration: A New Spectre Haunting Europe?' (2011) 73(4) *Arbitration International* 583, 597; William Park, 'Private Adjudicators and the Public Interest: The Expanding Scope of International Arbitration,' (1986) 12 *Brook. J. Int'l L.*, 642.

Elsewhere, I have discussed the different theories regarding the intensity that court control may have in respect of the award's conformity with public policy, and have commented the dichotomy between minimalist and maximalist theory.[117] Briefly, the minimalist theory postulates that courts are bound by the evaluation the arbitral tribunal made of the award's compliance with public policy; according to the maximalist theory, courts may independently verify whether the award infringes public policy.

For commercial arbitration, the CJEU has so far tacitly recognized that a uniform interpretation of EU law may be ensured, thanks to the control that courts of Member States exercise on arbitral awards. For investment arbitration, in the *Achmea* case,[118] the CJEU took a different position that will be discussed below. The Bundesgerichtshof ('BGH'), in its referral of the *Achmea* case to the CJEU,[119] as well as the Advocate General (AG) in the opinion for the *Achmea* case,[120] endorsed the maximalist theory. The BGH and the AG assumed that the controlling court of the Member State shall be entitled to independently evaluate whether EU law has been properly applied in the award. This would mean that, since the controlling Member State court may submit requests for preliminary rulings, court control on awards would ensure uniformity of interpretation of EU law also in arbitration. This maximalist approach is in accordance with the above-mentioned *Mitsubishi* and *Eco Swiss* approaches. The minimalist approach, on the contrary, assumes that Member State courts shall owe deference to the arbitral tribunal's evaluation made in the award.[121] In a previous case, the AG had affirmed that the minimalist approach would deprive court control of its meaning and would not be compatible with EU law. This is because having to accept the arbitral tribunal's evaluation effectively means delegating the matter to the arbitral tribunal. As arbitral tribunals may not request preliminary rulings under Article 267 of the TFEU, the uniformity of the interpretation of EU law is not ensured.[122]

Notwithstanding that the AG had several times brought up the relationship between court control and the compatibility of (commercial) arbitration with EU law,[123] the CJEU had, prior to *Achmea*, never expressed an opinion on the matter. It had, however, tacitly accepted that (commercial) disputes relating to EU law may be arbitrable, as pointed out by the AG in the *Achmea* opinion.[124] The CJEU seems in *Achmea*, indirectly and as an obiter dictum, to endorse the AG's opinion that

117. Giuditta Cordero-Moss, 'Inherent Powers and Competition Law' (2017) 6.2 *European International Arbitration Review* 69-94; Cordero-Moss, 'Mitsubishi: Balancing Arbitrability and Court Control', cit.
118. Case C-284/16 (*Achmea*).
119. Bundesgerichtshof, 3 March 2016, I ZB 2/1.
120. Case C-284/16 (*Achmea*), Opinion of AG Wathelet., paras 251-260.
121. Radicati di Brozolo, 'Mandatory Rules and International Arbitration', cit.; *see also*, criticizing this approach, Christophe Seraglini and Jérôme Ortscheidt, *Droit de l'arbitrage interne et international*, Domat Montchrestien, 2013, para. 982.
122. Case C-567/14 *Genentech v. Hoechst and Sanofi-Aventis Deutschland*, Opinion of AG Wathelet.
123. In addition to the already mentioned opinions in the *Genentech* and the *Achmea* case that were both rendered by Whatelet, *see also* Case C-352/13 *CDC Hydrogen Peroxide v. Evonik Degussa and Others*, Opinion of AG Jääskinen.
124. Case C-284/16 (*Achmea*), AG Opinion para. 243.

commercial disputes regarding the interpretation of EU law may be subject to arbitration, as court control permits the court to review the interpretation of EU law made by the tribunal and, by requesting preliminary rulings, to ensure uniformity of the interpretation of EU law.[125]Thus, the CJEU endorses the maximalist theory.

However, as will be discussed in section 14.06 below, the CJEU has denied arbitrability of investment disputes based on intra-EU treaties, based on the lack of an effective method to control the uniform application of EU law.[126] The decision was based on an unconvincing distinction between commercial and investment arbitration, which gives reason to fear that the distinction may be abandoned, expanding the inarbitrability also to commercial disputes. Courts in EU states, such as Austria,[127] Belgium,[128] Germany[129] and England,[130] already denied the arbitrability[131] of disputes regarding contracts of commercial agency. EU agency law is deemed to be necessary for the achievement of the internal market. Hence, some courts have affirmed that disputes concerning commercial agency should be decided by courts of EU Member States: choosing a court outside the EU, or choosing arbitration, may endanger the effective enforcement of EU law.

In such a climate of mistrust against arbitration, it does not seem that arbitration can be promoted by insisting on a minimalist approach to court control – quite to the contrary. In the context of corruption and economic crime, the minimalist theory seems to have been abandoned in its country of origin, France.[132] As long as court control is not deprived of its significance – in other words, as long as the maximalist theory is embraced – it seems that arbitration does not raise issues of due process in this context.

§14.06 CONCLUSION

The overview made in section 14.05 shows that, although much of the criticism has been voiced in relation to investment arbitration, the features that are being criticized are present both in commercial and in investment arbitration. It should also be

125. Case C-284/16 (*Achmea*), para. 54.
126. Case C-284/16 (*Achmea*).
127. OGH 1 March 2017, 5ob 72/16y, Ecolex 520 (2017).
128. Cour de Cassation, 16 November 2006, PAS. 2006, I, No. 11; Cour de Cassation, 14.1.2010, PAS. 2010, I, No. 12; Cour de Cassation, 3 November 2011 PAS. 2011, I, No. 1.
129. Bundesgerichtshof, 5 September 2012, *Neue juristische Wochenschrift* (2012).
130. *Accentuate Limited v. Asigra Inc.* [2009] EWHC (QB) 2655.
131. Or they deny the recognition of a contractual choice of forum in favour of a court not located within the EU. This responds to the same rationale, i.e., that matters relating to commercial agency shall be decided by courts located in the EU in order to ensure a uniform application of EU law. Therefore, it can be expected that the same courts would also deny arbitrability if the contract contained an arbitration clause.
132. *See*, in the areas of corruption and money laundering: Cour d'appel de Paris, 4 November 2014, nr. 13/10256; Cour d'appel de Paris, 25 November 2014, nr. 13/1333; Cour d'appel de Paris, 7 April 2015, nr. 14/00480; Cour d'appel de Paris, 14 April 2015, nr. 14/07043; Cour d'appel de Paris, 21 February 2017, nr. 15/01650; Cour d'appel de Paris, 16 January 2018, nr. 15/21703. *Contra*, *see* Cour d'appel de Paris, 20 January 2015, nr. 13/20318; Cour d'appel de Paris, 24 February 2015, nr. 13/23404. In the area of procedural fairness, *see* Cour d'appel de Paris, 8 November 11.2016, nr. 13/12002.

remembered that a considerable part of investment disputes is carried out under the rules applicable to commercial arbitration. Certainly, the specificities of investment disputes may require considerations that are not generally made in commercial disputes, in particular due to the public interests involved in investment arbitration. However, there does not seem to be a structural reason to distinguish between investment and commercial arbitration in the context of due process.[133]

This chapter examined some of the main issues for which arbitration is currently criticized and that can have relevance to the structural compatibility of arbitration with the principle of due process.

It argues that, with the possible exception of transparency, there does not seem to be a structural need to use different criteria for, respectively, commercial or investment arbitration, when evaluating whether the principle of due process has been respected.

Both types of arbitration are facing an erosion of their credibility, mainly based on doubts about the lack of efficiency in the proceedings, the impartiality and independence of the arbitrators and suspicions about the ability to accurately apply the law. To a large extent, these doubts are based on perceptions or misperceptions, rather than on factual circumstances.

To the extent that inefficient or abusive practices have developed, a proper application of the existing legal framework seems to be adequate to put a remedy. Much can be achieved by a sound exercise of the arbitral tribunal's discretion in the field of case management and in respect of an independent development of the tribunal's reasoning (without, however, exceeding the power conferred by the parties and without depriving the parties of the possibility to comment on the basis for the decision).

Considering the existing legal framework on court control can also contribute to contain the development of inefficiencies or abuses. Accepting that an effective court control, without being a review on the merits, is a necessary condition for arbitrability would be a significant step. It would lead to a higher degree of self-discipline, which, in turn, would meet much of the criticism to which arbitration is being exposed.

In other areas, an improvement of the regulation may be appropriate, such as ensuring transparency and developing codes of conduct.

Hence, there does not seem to be a sound foundation for the fears that the institution of arbitration is not capable of meeting the requirements of the due process principle.

There is, certainly, room for making the legal framework more efficient. But this can be achieved by improving specific areas of the existing legal framework, rather than by excluding arbitration as a method to solve disputes.

Restricting arbitrability in the name of a more effective implementation of due process is equivalent to throwing the baby out with the bathwater.

133. Affirming that legitimacy issues shall be taken into consideration both in investment and in commercial arbitration, *see also* Arroyo, 'Nothing If for Free', cit., 632 ff.

CHAPTER 15

Virtual Arbitration Hearings under Swedish Law

Edward Jansson Stiernblad

Videoconferencing is increasingly used to conduct entire remote hearings, i.e., virtual hearings. This raises the question if it is possible under Swedish law to hold a virtual hearing against the objection of one of the parties. The fundamental principle relevant to the question of virtual hearings is the universally recognized principle of due process and equality in the treatment of the parties, established in section 24 of the Swedish Arbitration Act. Section 24 of the Swedish Arbitration Act is an expression of due process as expressed in Article 6 of the European Convention on Human Rights. The European Court of Human Rights considers videoconferencing in general to be compatible with due process. Virtual hearings are also accepted as meeting the standards of due process according to the Swedish Code of Judicial Procedure. It can also be noted that there is nothing under the Arbitration Institute of the Stockholm Chamber of Commerce Arbitration Rules from 2017 or the IBA Rules on the Taking of Evidence that prohibits a hearing by virtual means. Moreover, many arbitration institutes explicitly accept virtual hearings. It would therefore appear reasonable to assume that section 24 of the Swedish Arbitration Act permits virtual hearings, also against the objection of one of the parties. Whether a virtual hearing can be held against the objection of a party is yet to be tried under Swedish law. Consequently, time will tell if virtual hearings are compatible with the Swedish Arbitration Act.

§15.01 INTRODUCTION

In early 2020, at the onset of the COVID-19 pandemic, it was initially difficult to imagine that the situation would last longer than a few weeks or, at the most, a couple of months. However, the pandemic became the 'new normal' during 2020 and at least for parts of 2021. Strategies were thus adopted worldwide to limit and cope with the spread of the virus. Although the worst is luckily behind us in terms of the pandemic, it did indeed raise a number of interesting, albeit complex, issues within the field of arbitration that may change the way we look at certain aspects in the aftermath of the pandemic.

A highly relevant issue is how arbitration hearings should be conducted during the midst of a pandemic. For many years now, technology has been used in arbitrations for, e.g., remote witness examinations, either by telephone or by videoconference. The pandemic has accelerated the developments of the use of technology. Notwithstanding the pandemic, there is overall an increased demand for hearings by virtual means as this saves both time and cost. Videoconferencing is increasingly used as a means to conduct entire remote hearings, i.e., virtual hearings.

Given the apparent longevity of the pandemic, it has been difficult to argue that arbitration hearings, as a general rule or principle, should be postponed until the pandemic was over. However, during the midst of the pandemic, it was not always possible (or appropriate for that matter) due to travel and other restrictions to gather a room filled to the brim with tribunal members, counsel, party representatives, witnesses, experts, translators, court reporters, etc., for a traditional physical hearing. Instead, an alternative has been to conduct the hearing virtually.

Party autonomy is one of the cornerstones of arbitration allowing the parties much freedom to decide how to conduct the proceedings. Can the parties agree that a virtual hearing is held instead of a traditional hearing where the participants are physically present? That the parties agree on procedural issues is nevertheless not always the case. The claimant is often keen to have the dispute tried as speedily as possible and may thus opt for a virtual hearing, especially if the alternative is an indefinite postponement of the hearing. The respondent usually does not have the same wish for a speedy procedure and may reject the idea of a virtual hearing.

If this is the case, is it possible to hold a virtual hearing against the objection of one of the parties? If so, to what degree can a hearing be held virtually – can a partially virtual hearing be held where, e.g., the arbitral tribunal and counsel are physically present, but where witnesses and experts participate virtually, or can the hearing be fully virtual? Can 'asymmetry' be accepted, e.g., where one of the parties is physically present through counsel whereas the other party's counsel participates virtually?

§15.02 FUNDAMENTAL PRINCIPLES OF RELEVANCE

Swedish arbitration procedure is governed by a few fundamental principles.

First, and as already mentioned, the principle of party autonomy is fundamental, and pursuant to section 21 (second sentence) of the Swedish Arbitration Act (hereinafter the SAA), the arbitrators shall 'act in accordance with the decisions of the parties, unless they are impeded from doing so'.[1] The arbitration procedure is to a significant

1. Translated by the Swedish Ministry of Justice (Ds 1999:22) and revised and updated by Joel Dahlquist on behalf of the Arbitration Institute of the Stockholm Chamber of Commerce, https://sccinstitute.se/media/1773096/the-swedish-arbitration-act_1march2019_eng-2.pdf (accessed 2021-04-22).

degree governed by the agreement of the parties, subject, however, to a small number of statutory requirements.[2]

Second, the arbitrators shall adhere to the principles of impartiality, practicality and speed. This is expressed in section 21 of the SAA, which stipulates that the arbitrators shall 'handle the dispute in an impartial, practical, and speedy manner'.[3]

Third, and of particular interest for the subject matter of this chapter, the universally recognized principle of due process and equality in the treatment of the parties is established in section 24 of the SAA. This principle is considered perhaps the most fundamental procedural principle[4] and means that the parties shall be afforded the opportunity not only to present their case[5] but also to respond to the statements made and evidence invoked by the opposing party.[6]

§15.03 THE RIGHT TO AN ORAL HEARING UNDER THE SWEDISH ARBITRATION ACT

The SAA is from 1999. At that time, the legislator did probably not consider the possibility or the necessity of virtual hearings. Nor did the legislator do so when the SAA was amended in 2018.[7]

The first two paragraphs of section 24[8] of the SAA read as follows:

> The arbitrators shall afford the parties, to the extent necessary, an opportunity to present their respective cases in writing or orally. Where a party so requests, and provided that the parties have not otherwise agreed, an oral hearing shall be held prior to the determination of an issue referred to the arbitrators for resolution.

2. Kaj Hobér, *International Commercial Arbitration in Sweden*, 203-204 (Oxford University Press 2011).
3. Translated by the Swedish Ministry of Justice (Ds 1999:22) and revised and updated by Joel Dahlquist on behalf of the Arbitration Institute of the Stockholm Chamber of Commerce, https://sccinstitute.se/media/1773096/the-swedish-arbitration-act_1march2019_eng-2.pdf (accessed 22 April 2021).
4. Stefan Lindskog, *Skiljeförfarande: En kommentar*, 579 (3d ed., Norstedts Juridik 2020).
5. *See, e.g.*, Lindskog, *supra* n. 4, at 579-580; Marie Öhrström, *En handbok och regelkommentar för skiljeförfaranden*, 198 (Norstedts Juridik 2009); Finn Madsen, *Commercial Arbitration in Sweden*, 269 (5th ed., Jure 2020); Thorsten Cars, *Lagen om skiljeförfarande: En kommentar*, 117 (3d ed., Fakta Info Direkt Sweden AB 2001).
6. *See, e.g.*, Lindskog, *supra* n. 4, at 694; Lars Heuman, *Skiljemannarätt*, 402 (Norstedts Juridik 1999); Öhrström, *supra* n. 5, at 198; Madsen, *supra* n. 5, at 269; Cars, *supra* n. 5, at 117.
7. For the 2018 amendments to the SAA, *see* SFS 2018:1954.
8. The SAA is largely based upon the UNCITRAL Model Law on International Commercial Arbitration (hereinafter the 'Model Law'). Pursuant to Article 24(1) of the Model Law, the arbitrators shall decide whether the proceedings shall be oral or in writing, subject to any contrary agreement of the parties. It is thus a matter for the parties to decide whether an oral hearing shall be held or not. If the parties have agreed that no oral hearing shall be held, the arbitral tribunal is bound by this agreement.

> A party shall be given an opportunity to review all documents and all other materials pertaining to the dispute which are supplied to the arbitrators by the opposing party or another person.[9]

The second sentence of the first paragraph stipulates that a hearing shall be held if requested by a party. Accordingly, a party has an absolute right to a hearing; the necessity of the hearing is irrelevant. However, as expressly stated in the provision, this is only the case unless the parties have agreed otherwise. The principle of party autonomy means that the tribunal may not decide that a hearing shall be held if the parties have agreed on an exclusively written procedure. Correspondingly, an arbitral tribunal may not deny the parties a hearing if the parties have agreed that a hearing shall be held.[10]

According to the first sentence of the first paragraph, the parties have the right, to the extent necessary, to present their respective cases in writing or orally. It is expressed in *travaux préparatoires* and legal doctrine that the provision is mandatory in the sense that a party cannot *in advance* waive its right to present its case to the extent necessary.[11] One commentary to the SAA goes one step further by stating that the parties cannot, with binding effect, agree in advance on an exclusively written procedure since such a procedure does not live up to the standards of due process.[12] However, this does not prevent the parties from jointly agreeing on an entirely written procedure once the arbitration has been initiated.[13] If the parties so agree, a party thereby waives its right to challenge the award on the basis that it was not given a proper opportunity to present its case.[14] This follows from the second paragraph of section 34 which states that a party is not 'entitled to rely upon a circumstance, through participation in the proceedings without objection, or in any other manner, the party may be deemed to have waived'.[15]

9. Translated by the Swedish Ministry of Justice (Ds 1999:22) and revised and updated by Joel Dahlquist on behalf of the Arbitration Institute of the Stockholm Chamber of Commerce, https://sccinstitute.se/media/1773096/the-swedish-arbitration-act_1march2019_eng-2.pdf (accessed 22 April 2021).
10. Lindskog, *supra* n. 4, at 695.
11. Govt. Bill 1998/99:35, p. 227; Lindskog, *supra* n. 4, at 695-696; Cars, *supra* n. 5, at 117; Heuman, *supra* n. 6, at 273; Bengt Lindell, *Civilprocessen*, 722 (4th ed., Iustus 2017); Johan Kvart & Bengt Olsson, *Tvistlösning genom skiljeförfarande*, 103 (3d ed., Norstedts Juridik 2012). It should be noted that the parties' right to present their case pursuant to section 24 is restricted through the words 'to the extent necessary' (*translated by the author*) meaning that a party is prevented from relying on section 24 in order to obstruct the proceedings by submitting superfluous documents and materials, *see* Cars, *supra* n. 5, at 117.
12. Lindskog, *supra* n. 4, at 691-692 and 695-696. Cf. Heuman, *supra* n. 6, at 273-274.
13. Lindskog, *supra* n. 4, at 691-692 and 697.
14. Lindskog, *supra* n. 4, at 692 n. 2691.
15. Translated by the Swedish Ministry of Justice (Ds 1999:22) and revised and updated by Joel Dahlquist on behalf of the Arbitration Institute of the Stockholm Chamber of Commerce, https://sccinstitute.se/media/1773096/the-swedish-arbitration-act_1march2019_eng-2.pdf (accessed 22 April 2021).

§15.04 ACCEPTABLE FORM OF HEARING UNDER THE SWEDISH ARBITRATION ACT

As cited above, section 24 stipulates that an 'oral hearing' shall be held if requested by a party. A hearing in the traditional sense is where the arbitral tribunal and counsel meet physically and where the parties are afforded the opportunity to present their case before the tribunal.[16] There is nothing under Swedish law, the Arbitration Institute of the Stockholm Chamber of Commerce (hereinafter the SCC) Arbitration Rules from 2017 (hereinafter the 'SCC Arbitration Rules'), or the International Bar Association (hereinafter the IBA) Rules on the Taking of Evidence in International Arbitration that expressly prohibits a hearing by virtual means.[17] Nonetheless, whether an 'oral hearing' can be conducted virtually as opposed to a traditional hearing is a topic which has been subject to much debate.

The common view in Swedish arbitration law is that virtual hearings can fully replace traditional hearings where the participants are physically present.[18] It is suggested that with the necessary technology now available, a virtual hearing may be the only way to comply with the fundamental arbitration requirements of efficiency and speed, subject to the principles of party autonomy and equal treatment of the parties.[19]

One contrasting view is found in Swedish arbitration law where it is argued that a virtual hearing is not an adequate substitute for a hearing where the hearing participants meet physically.[20] However, it should be stressed that it seems that this view is held by one author alone and cannot be considered to constitute the general opinion on the matter.

§15.05 THE IMPACT OF TECHNOLOGICAL DEVELOPMENTS IN OTHER LEGAL AREAS

Although the focal point of this chapter is virtual hearings, it is relevant to consider what impact the technological developments have had on other areas.

16. Lindskog, *supra* n. 4, at 699.
17. *See* further sections 15.08 and 15.09 *infra*.
18. Kristoffer Löf, Aron Skogman & Sara Johnsson, 'Chapter 9: The Proceedings', in Annette Magnusson, Jakob Ragnwaldh, et al. (eds), *International Arbitration in Sweden: A Practitioner's Guide*, paras 188-193, (2d ed., Kluwer Law International 2021); Velislava Hristova & Malcom Robach, *Legal and Practical Aspects of Virtual Hearings During (and After?) the Pandemic: Takeaway from the SCC Online Seminar Series*, Kluwer Arbitration Blog, http://arbitrationblog.kluwerarbitration.com/2020/05/16/legal-and-practical-aspects-of-virtual-hearings-during-and-after-the-pandemic-takeaway-from-the-scc-online-seminar-series/ (accessed 19 April 2021); Lars Edlund, *Om virtuell förhandling – en replik*, SvJT 2021 p. 401; Kristoffer Lööf, *Remembrance of Things Past – a reply to Stefan Lindskog's argument that only a traditional hearing is a hearing in arbitration*, SvJT 2021 p. 406.
19. Löf, Skogman & Johnsson, *supra* n. 18, at 217, 264-265.
20. Stefan Lindskog, *Virtuella slutförhandlingar i skiljeförfaranden mot parts bestridande*, SvJT 2021 p. 293.

By way of example, it is now a widely accepted view in the Swedish courts that written documents not only are limited to physical paper documents but also include electronic documents such as emails. In two rather recent cases, the Swedish Supreme Court has found that electronic documents should be deemed equivalent to a paper document. In a case from 2015, the Supreme Court found that the prohibition against confiscation of documents in certain situations should be equally valid for electronic documents. The Supreme Court pointed out that this was in line with the purpose of the regulation in question.[21] Further, in a case from 2017, the Supreme Court stated that an electronic document can be a valid negotiable debt instrument subject to certain requirements.[22]

Considering the technological advancements and the impact it has had on other areas of the law, it does not appear too far-reaching to suggest that a 'hearing' or indeed an 'oral hearing' may mean something else today than what it did when the SAA was drafted and entered into force some twenty years ago. The question remains if an interpretation that would allow virtual hearings under the SAA is in line with the purpose of the provision.

§15.06 THE PURPOSE OF SECTION 24 OF THE SWEDISH ARBITRATION ACT

The *travaux préparatoires* to the SAA state that the purpose of the right to an oral hearing pursuant to section 24 of the SAA is to ensure the right to due process and a fair trial.[23] Therefore, the use of videoconferencing seems to be in line with the purpose of section 24.

As discussed above (*see* section 15.02), section 24 of the SAA affords the parties an equal right to fully present their case orally. Furthermore, it is also clear that a party has an absolute right to an oral hearing, if so requested.

This raises the question what an oral hearing entails. Is it limited to a hearing in the traditional sense, i.e., in a hearing room with the arbitrators, parties, witnesses and experts physically present? Or can it include a hearing conducted merely by telephone, or does it need to be by means of videoconferencing in order to count as a hearing?

The words 'oral' (Sw. *muntlig*) and 'oral hearing' (Sw. *muntlig förhandling*) suggest that a hearing in the form of a telephone conference would be permissible under Swedish arbitration law. There is no explicit requirement for the oral hearing to take place through physical participation, it just needs to be oral.

The *travaux préparatoires* to the SAA are silent as to what an oral hearing is. It is however stated that an oral hearing under the SAA is rather equivalent to a main hearing according to the Swedish Code of Judicial Procedure.[24] Hence, the statement in

21. 'Husrannsakan på tidningsredaktionen' which means 'the Search of the premises at the newspaper office', NJA 2015 p. 631.
22. 'Collectors elektroniska skuldebrev', which means 'Collector's electronic promissory note', NJA 2017 p. 769.
23. Govt. Bill 1998/99:35 p. 110.
24. Govt. Bill 1998/99:35 p. 110.

the *travaux préparatoires* is aimed at a hearing in the Code of Judicial Procedure's traditional sense, i.e., a hearing where the participants are physically present. As already discussed, virtual hearings were most likely not envisioned at the time when the SAA entered into force. What was intended with an 'oral' hearing at the time was thus a physical hearing.

The legislative process leading up to the SAA may shed some light on the Act's concept of 'oral' hearing.[25] In the *travaux préparatoires* to the SAA, it is stated that the purpose of the right to an oral hearing pursuant to section 24 is to ensure the right to due process and a fair trial. Section 24 is thus an expression of the fundamental principles of due process expressed in Article 6 of the European Convention on Human Rights (hereinafter the ECHR).[26] Although the ECHR was designed primarily for court proceedings, it is not lacking in relevance with regard to arbitrations.[27] Article 6(1) of the ECHR is relevant in that it can be said to express a 'common core of essential safeguards for the integrity of the arbitral process'.[28]

There are several cases, primarily criminal cases, from the European Court of Human Rights (hereinafter the ECtHR), which acknowledge videoconferencing as a means of satisfying the right to a fair trial.

In the criminal case *Marcello v. Italy*, a person with connections to the mafia had been accused of a serious crime. The person was not allowed to be physically present in the court and instead participated via videoconference. The ECtHR found that it was acceptable for a person accused of a criminal offence to participate in the hearing through videoconferencing for security reasons.[29] The ECtHR came to the same conclusion in the criminal case *Golubev v. Russia*.[30] Furthermore, in the criminal case *Schatschaschwili v. Germany*, the court stated that even cross-examination of witnesses can be conducted through special means such as videoconferencing.[31] In addition, the ECtHR has stated in the case *Yevdokimov and others v. Russia* that the use of videoconferencing instead of appearing in person is generally acceptable in civil matters.[32]

25. Stig Strömholm, Max Lyles & Filippo Valguarnera, *Rätt, Rättskällor och rättstillämpning: En lärobok i allmän rättslära*, 450 (6th ed., Norstedts Juridik 2020); Lars Heuman, *Metoder för rättstillämpning och lagtolkning: Generaliseringar, logik och argumentation*, 333 (Jure 2018).
26. Govt. Bill 1998/99:35 p. 110.
27. Georios Petrochilos, *Procedural Law in International Arbitration*, 130 para. 4.51 (Oxford University Press 2004).
28. Petrochilos, *supra* n. 27, at 151 para. 4.95.
29. *Marcello Viola v. Italy*, case no. 45106/04, http://hudoc.echr.coe.int/eng?i=001-77246 (accessed 19 April 2021); *See* also Hans Danelius, *Mänskliga rättigheter i europeisk praxis*, section 6.9 298, (Norstedts Juridik, Juno Version 5 2015).
30. *Golubev v. Russia*, case no. 26260/02, http://hudoc.echr.coe.int/eng?i=001-78357 (accessed 19 April 2021).
31. *Schatschaschwili v. Germany*, case no. 9154/10, https://hudoc.echr.coe.int/eng#{%22itemid%22:[%22001-159566%22]} (accessed 19 April 2021); *see* also *Al-Khawaja and Tahery v. The United Kingdom*, https://hudoc.echr.coe.int/eng#{%22tabview%22:[%22document%22],%22itemid%22:[%22001-108072%22]} (accessed 19 April 2021) which also refers to the possibility to use special measures such as videoconferencing.
32. *Yevdokimov v. Russia*, case nos 27236/05, 44223/05, 53304/07, 40232/11, 60052/11, 76438/11, 14919/12, 19929/12, 42389/12, 57043/12 and 67481/12, http://hudoc.echr.coe.int/eng?i=001-160620 (accessed 19 April 2021).

To sum up, the use of videoconferencing is not considered by the ECtHR to be incompatible with the notion of a fair and public trial. The views of the ECtHR and its interpretation of Article 6 of the ECHR are well described by the court in the above-cited case *Golubev v. Russia*, in which the following is stated with regard to participation through means of videoconferencing:

> Thirdly, even assuming, in the applicant's favour, that he did not waive his right and had no other choice but to participate in the hearing through a video communication system, the Court recalls that the physical presence of an accused in the courtroom is highly desirable, but it is not an end in itself: it rather serves the greater goal of securing the fairness of the proceedings, taken as a whole.[33]

The above reasoning of the ECtHR demonstrates that the crucial point of Article 6 is due process, not that the participants are physically present during the hearing. The ECtHR is evidently of the opinion that the principle of due process can be satisfied through the use of videoconferencing systems.

As mentioned, section 24 of the SAA does not regulate the form for the hearing. If the parties have not agreed on the form for the hearing, this decision is left to the tribunal.[34] In the *travaux préparatoires* of the SAA, the possibility for the tribunal to examine witnesses via telephone or 'TV monitor' is mentioned.[35] The *travaux préparatoires* expressly mention that the boundaries for witness examinations are not determined by law, but by technology.[36]

In this respect, it may also be noted that examination of witnesses in an arbitration pursuant to the SAA can, at the request of a party, be held at and administered by a Swedish District Court. The SAA does not require the tribunal to attend such witness examination. It is sufficient that the tribunal has access to a video recording of the witness examination.[37] This is thus an acceptable form for the taking of evidence pursuant to the SAA.

In summary, the *travaux préparatoires* to the SAA state that the purpose of the right to an oral hearing pursuant to section 24 is to ensure the right to due process and a fair trial. Section 24 is thus an expression of due process as expressed in Article 6 of the ECHR. It is evident from the above-mentioned case law from the ECtHR that the ECtHR does not consider videoconferencing in general to be incompatible with the notion of a fair and public trial. The use of videoconferencing for a virtual hearing is thus in line with the purpose of section 24 of the SAA.

33. *Golubev v. Russia*, case no. 26260/02, http://hudoc.echr.coe.int/eng?i=001-78357 (accessed 19 April 2021).
34. Govt. Bill 1998/99:35 pp. 110-111.
35. Govt. Bill 1998/99:35 p. 114.
36. Govt. Bill 1998/99:35 p. 114.
37. *See* section 26 of the SAA.

§15.07 A GLANCE AT THE SWEDISH CODE OF JUDICIAL PROCEDURE

It is stated in the *travaux préparatoires* for the Code of Judicial Procedure that the ECHR should not be considered an obstacle to a virtual hearing.[38] Virtual hearings are thus accepted as meeting the standards of due process according to the Swedish Code of Judicial Procedure.

The Swedish Code of Judicial Procedure regulates a large number of issues that have been left unresolved in the SAA. The principles and rules in the Code of Judicial Procedure should not be applied automatically in arbitrations[39] and should not be considered a complement to the SAA. [40] Even though the Code of Judicial Procedure has had a significant impact on the SAA, the SAA should be applied independently of the Code of Judicial Procedure.[41] However, the procedures before the general courts and the general principles of the Code of Judicial Procedure may serve as inspiration where the arbitrators can seek guidance when faced with procedural issues.[42] This would reasonably be limited to Swedish arbitrations, whereas in international arbitrations seated in Sweden, it is perhaps more appropriate for the arbitrators to apply international best practice than to glance at the Code of Judicial Procedure.[43]

The Code of Judicial Procedure contains a brief requirement in Chapter 43, section 5, namely that 'the hearing shall be oral'. The general rule is that the parties shall be physically present at the hearings.[44] However, according to Chapter 5, section 10 of the Code of Judicial Procedure, the court may decide that a party or other person who is to be present at a meeting, such as a hearing, shall participate by audio only or audio visually, i.e., videoconference. When someone participates through videoconference, that person is deemed to be participating in the hearing. Since the general rule is that the parties shall be physically present at the hearings, participation through videoconference against the will of a party is generally not permitted. However, exceptions are allowed if it appears justified. It is the court that has the ultimate responsibility to determine whether participation through videoconferencing should take place.[45]

When assessing whether participation should take place through videoconferencing, consideration should be taken to the parties' views on the matter although, ultimately, it is the decision of the court. The court must, when evaluating the matter, make an overall assessment of all relevant circumstances and in particular consider the

38. Govt. Bill 2004/2005:131 p. 90.
39. Heuman, *supra* n. 6, at 306; Finn Madsen, *Skiljeförfarande i Sverige*, 60-61 (2d ed., Jure 2009); Hans-Gunnar Solerud, 'Har skiljemannalagen och rättegångsbalken ett förhållande?', in Jan Hellner (ed), *Festskrift till Ulf K. Nordenson*, 411, 428 (Carlsson Law Network 1999); Lindskog, *supra* n. 4, at 645.
40. Bengt Westerling, 'Rättegångsbalken och skiljeförfarandet', in Stockholms handelskammares skiljedomsinstitut (ed), *Svensk och internationell skiljedom 1981: Årsbok*, 17 (Stockholms handelskammare 1981).
41. Govt. Bill 1998/99:35, p. 47; Swedish Government Official Reports 1994:81, p. 74.
42. Lindskog, *supra* n. 4, at 68.
43. Lindskog, *supra* n. 4, at 68 n. 234; Westerling, *supra* n. 40, at 17.
44. Govt. Bill 2004/2005:131 p. 224.
45. Govt. Bill 2004/2005:131 pp. 224-225.

role of the person in question, the nature of the case and the topics to be addressed during the hearing. If the parties agree that a person can participate through videoconference, there is generally no reason for the court to make a different assessment. In the case of a hearing for evidentiary purposes, the wishes of the party invoking the evidence must generally be considered. However, the other party's opinion can also be relevant in many cases and should therefore be taken into account.[46]

In the *travaux préparatoires* to the so-called En modernare rättegång (hereinafter the EMR) Revision of 2008 of the Code of Judicial Procedure, it is expressly stated that participation through videoconference is consistent with the ECHR.[47] Consequently, a virtual hearing conducted through means of videoconferencing even against the will of one party must thus still be considered to meet the requirements of due process under the Code of Judicial Procedure.

The audiovisual alternatives as a means for party participation in hearings as well as a means for the taking of evidence are common in Swedish courts. In fact, the *travaux préparatoires* conclude that the taking of evidence through audiovisual participation is generally considered to work well.[48]

In a decision from the Swedish Office of the Chancellor of Justice, an individual had claimed damages from the Swedish State on the basis that his right to a fair trial according to the ECHR had been violated in criminal proceedings before the Svea Court of Appeal. More specifically, he had demanded that witnesses should attend the hearing physically rather than through videoconference in order for him to be able to duly question them. The Chancellor of Justice found that the use of videoconferencing was not in conflict with Article 6 of the ECHR with reference to the fact that he was, albeit with some difficulties, afforded the opportunity to examine the witnesses through the available videoconferencing system.[49]

In a recent case from the Court of Appeal for Western Sweden, the issue of a virtual hearing in light of the pandemic was addressed.[50] The Court of Appeal found that the District Court had committed a procedural error when cancelling a hearing in a case in which the main hearing had been delayed. The case itself had been going on for a long time. The Court of Appeal found that it was not acceptable to cancel a hearing with reference to the pandemic and the regulations from the Swedish Public Health Authority. The Court of Appeal stated that the District Court had an obligation to conduct the proceedings in an expeditious manner and in order to do so it should have utilized the existing possibilities to allow for participation through telephone or videoconference.

In summary, virtual hearings are accepted as meeting the standards of due process according to the Swedish Code of Judicial Procedure. As also mentioned, it is

46. Govt. Bill 2004/2005:131 pp. 224-225.
47. Govt. Bill 2004/2005:131 p. 90.
48. Govt. Bill 2018/19:81 p. 28.
49. Decision from the Office of the Chancellor of Justice dated 13 October 2016, Reference number 5024-16-40.
50. Court of Appeal for Western Sweden, case no. Ö 4485-20.

stated in the *travaux préparatoires* for the EMR Reform of the Code of Judicial Procedure that the ECHR should not be considered an obstacle to a virtual hearing.

§15.08 HEARINGS UNDER THE SCC ARBITRATION RULES

The SCC has conducted a survey with SCC arbitrators to learn more about the use of, and attitudes towards, using virtual hearings.[51] The survey demonstrates that the pandemic has resulted in an increase in virtual hearings. Moreover, the survey concludes that the arbitrators are generally satisfied with and positive towards using virtual hearings also after the pandemic. In sum, the survey suggests that virtual hearings will be the norm for the duration of the COVID-19 crisis and also remain as a viable option thereafter. It seems that the possibility to conduct a virtual hearing under the SCC Rules against the will of one party is compatible with the SCC Arbitration Rules, especially considering the requirement of speed in arbitration.

As stated above, there are views that the parties cannot, with binding effect, agree *in advance* on an exclusively written procedure since such a procedure does not meet the standards of due process.[52] It can be noted that it is always possible for the parties to agree to an exclusively written procedure once the arbitration has commenced.[53] Nonetheless, would it be possible for the parties to agree in advance on a virtual hearing instead of a traditional hearing? It is unlikely that the parties' agreement contains any specific or detailed agreements or instructions for the proceedings in the event of a dispute. Instead, the arbitration agreement normally refers to a set of arbitration rules such as in Sweden (and elsewhere), the widely used SCC Arbitration Rules. What effect does a reference to the SCC Arbitration Rules in the arbitration agreement have in terms of the possibility to conduct a virtual hearing against the will of one party? Do the SCC Arbitration Rules only accept an oral hearing in the traditional sense or could a virtual hearing be accepted?

Article 32(1) of the SCC Arbitration Rules regulates hearings. This article differs in one respect from section 24 of the SAA. Article 32(1) of the SCC Arbitration Rules reads as follows:

> A hearing shall be held if requested by a party, or if the Arbitral Tribunal deems it appropriate.

Unlike section 24 of the SAA which uses the wording 'oral hearing', the SCC Arbitration Rules merely use the word 'hearing', but these rules are silent as to the form of such hearing. The wording of Article 32(1) is the same in the previous version of the Arbitration Rules from 2010.

In a commentary to the Arbitration Rules from 2010, it is pointed out that even if the parties, by agreeing to settle disputes through arbitration, may have opted out of the

51. Arbitration Institute of the Stockholm Chamber of Commerce, *SCC Virtual Hearing Survey*, October 2020, https://sccinstitute.com/media/1773182/scc-rapport_virtual_hearing-2.pdf (accessed 19 April 2021).
52. *See* section 15.03 above.
53. *See* section 15.03 above; Lindskog, *supra* n. 4, at 691-692 and 697.

right to settle their disputes before the courts, a party still has an absolute right to an oral hearing if so requested.[54] However, this absolute right to an oral hearing has its limits since the parties can agree that no oral hearing shall be held. In other words, the parties are free to agree that no oral hearing shall be held.[55] It may be noted that in international arbitration, it is considered widely accepted that the requirement of an oral hearing can be waived without breaching Article 6 of the ECHR.[56]

Under the SCC Arbitration Rules for Expedited Arbitrations from 2017 (hereinafter the 'Expedited Rules'), a party has the right to an oral hearing *only* at the request of the party *and* if the sole arbitrator considers the reasons for the request to be compelling.[57] Considering the risk for challenge of the award based on arguments of due process, it may be questioned how common it is for an arbitrator to deny a party an oral hearing if so requested. Furthermore, the validity of rules such as Article 33 of the Expedited Rules is questioned based on the opinion that parties cannot in advance agree to sacrifice their right to present their case.[58]

Moreover, Article 23, first paragraph of the SCC Arbitration Rules, affords the arbitrators considerable freedom in terms of how to conduct the arbitration:

> The Arbitral Tribunal may conduct the arbitration in such manner as it considers appropriate, subject to these Rules and any agreement between the parties.

Nothing in the SCC Arbitration Rules requires that a hearing in the traditional sense is held.

The SCC has published information and guidance relating to COVID-19 and encourages tribunals to 'to use alternative means such as audio- and visual meeting facilities'. Moreover, the SCC states that 'arbitral tribunals are expected to manage the proceedings in accordance with timetables previously established, or otherwise in accordance with Article 23 of the SCC Arbitration Rules'. In addition, pursuant to Article 2 of the SCC Arbitration Rules, the parties are 'expected to act in an efficient and expeditious manner throughout the proceedings and act in the spirit of the rules in all matters not expressly provided for therein'. The parties are, despite the outbreak of COVID-19, 'expected to live up to their obligations under the SCC Arbitration Rules and make efforts to keep established timetables by, when necessary and deemed possible, for example, transferring the arbitration to a fully digital environment, including using audio- and visual meeting facilities in the proceedings going forward'. The SCC also emphasizes that each party's contribution to the efficiency and expeditiousness of the arbitral procedure is assessed in light of the costs of the arbitration.[59]

---

54. Öhrström, *supra* n. 5, at 198; *See* also Ragnwaldh et. al., 106 with regard to Article 32(1) of the 2017 Arbitration Rules, *A Guide to the SCC Arbitration Rules* (Kluwer Law International B.V., 2020).
55. Cf. Lindskog's statement that the parties cannot in advance decide that no oral hearing shall be held; Lindskog, *supra* n. 4, at 691-692 and 695-696.
56. Georios Petrochilos, *Procedural Law in International Arbitration*, 150, para 4.92 (Oxford University Press 2004).
57. Article 33(1) in the SCC Rules for Expedited Arbitrations.
58. Lindskog, *supra* n. 4, at 691-692; Heuman, *supra* n. 6, at 274.
59. *See* the statement from the SCC dated 27 March 2020, Arbitration Institute of the Stockholm Chamber of Commerce, *Covid-19: Information and Guidelines in SCC Arbitration*, News 2020,

Arbitration institutes around the world have encouraged the use of audiovisual hearings in light of the pandemic. On 16 April 2020, the major international arbitration institutes issued a joint statement titled 'Arbitration and COVID-19: Institutions speak with one voice'.[60] It states that:

> [C]ollaboration is particularly important as each of our institutions looks to ensure that we make the best use of digital technologies for working remotely. We encourage parties and arbitrators to discuss any impact of the pandemic and potential ways to address it in an open and constructive manner. Arbitral tribunals and parties are asked to mitigate the effects of any impediments to the largest extent possible while ensuring the fairness and efficiency of arbitral proceedings. In so doing, they are invited to use the full extent of our respective institutional rules and any case management techniques that may permit arbitrations to substantially progress without undue delay despite such impediments. [61]

As emphasized by the SCC in the above-cited statement, the arbitral procedure shall be conducted expeditiously. The arbitrators must adhere to section 21 of the SAA which states that the 'arbitrators shall handle the dispute in an impartial, practical, and speedy manner'. The same follows from Article 21 of the SCC Arbitration Rules which stipulates that 'the Arbitral Tribunal and the parties shall act in an efficient and expeditious manner'. Should it prove impossible to hold a traditional hearing without causing significant delay to the arbitration, this gives rise to a conflict between the parties' right to fully present their case, on the one hand, and the right to an award within reasonable time, on the other. In this situation, the arbitrators need to balance the two conflicting interests, thus taking into account the potential delay of the case. However, the requirement concerning speed – in many instances one of the main reasons for selecting arbitration as a means for settling disputes – may not infringe on the principle of due process. It would appear sensible that a virtual hearing and the use of videoconferencing is acceptable since such a procedure is compatible with the adversarial principle which is an element in the right to a fair trial and due process according to Article 6 of the ECHR.

To sum up, considering the requirement of speed in arbitration and that there are no obstacles in the SCC Arbitration Rules, it seems that a reference to the SCC Arbitration Rules in the arbitration agreement does not affect the possibility to conduct a virtual hearing against the will of one party.

§15.09 VIRTUAL HEARINGS INTERNATIONALLY

It can be noted that internationally it is widely accepted to conduct a hearing virtual through the means of videoconferencing.

---

https://sccinstitute.com/about-the-scc/news/2020/covid-19-information-and-guidance-in-scc-arbitrations/ (accessed 19 April 2021).

60. The statement is signed by the CRCICA, DIS, ICC, ICDR/AAA, ICSD, KCAB, LCIA, MCA, HKIAC, SCC, CIAC, VIAC and the IFCAI.

61. Arbitration Institute of the Stockholm Chamber of Commerce, *Arbitration and Covid-19: Institutions Speak with One Voice*, News 2020, https://sccinstitute.com/about-the-scc/news/2020/arbitration-and-covid-19-institutions-speak-with-one-voice/ (accessed 19 April 2021).

Article 26 of the International Chamber of Commerce (hereinafter the ICC) Rules of Arbitration, which entered into force on 1 January 2021, concerns hearings and has recently been amended to explicitly deal with the subject of videoconferencing. The article states, *inter alia*, that '[t]he arbitral tribunal may decide, after consulting the parties, and on the basis of the relevant facts and circumstances of the case, that any hearing will be conducted by physical attendance or remotely by videoconference, telephone or other appropriate means of communication. 2) If any of the parties, although duly summoned, fails to appear without valid excuse, the arbitral tribunal shall have the power to proceed with the hearing'. The arbitral tribunal has thus been given explicit powers to decide if the hearing should be conducted virtually or not.

Further, the London Court of International Arbitration (hereinafter the LCIA) Arbitration Rules, which entered into effect on 1 October 2020, have been amended and now explicitly give the tribunal the power to decide whether the hearing should be conducted through means of videoconferencing. Article 19 of the LCIA Arbitration Rules states, *inter alia*, that 'the Arbitral Tribunal shall have the fullest authority under the Arbitration Agreement to establish the conduct of a hearing, including its date, duration, form, content, procedure, time-limits and geographical place (if applicable). As to form, a hearing may take place in person, or virtually by conference call, videoconference or using other communications technology with participants in one or more geographical places (or in a combined form)'.

The topic is also addressed in the IBA Rules on the Taking of Evidence in International Arbitration (both in the old version dated 2010 and in the new version dated 2020) which define an Evidentiary Hearing to also include a hearing held by videoconference. '"Evidentiary Hearing" means any hearing, whether or not held on consecutive days, at which the Arbitral Tribunal, whether in person, by teleconference, videoconference or other method, receives oral or other evidence.' The IBA Rules dated 2020 also state in Article 8.1, regarding an Evidentiary Hearing, that 'At the request of a Party or on its own motion, the Arbitral Tribunal may, after consultation with the Parties, order that the Evidentiary Hearing be conducted as a Remote Hearing.' According to the definitions, a '"Remote Hearing" means a hearing conducted, for the entire hearing or parts thereof, or only with respect to certain participants, using teleconference, videoconference or other communication technology by which persons in more than one location simultaneously participate.'

A case from the Austrian Supreme Court published on 28 September 2020 concerned the issue of whether a hearing held through videoconference against the objection of one party in an arbitration violated due process. The case is said to be the first case in the world from a national supreme court which addresses the issue of COVID-19 and videoconferencing.[62] The Austrian Supreme Court concluded that it lies

62. Maxi Scherer, Franz Schwarz, Helmut Ortner & J. Ole Jensen, *'In a "First" Worldwide, Austrian Supreme Court Confirms Arbitral Tribunal's Power to Hold Remote Hearings Over One Party's Objection and Rejects Due Process Concerns'* Kluwer Arbitration Blog, 24 October 2020 http://arbitrationblog.kluwerarbitration.com/2020/10/24/in-a-first-worldwide-austrian-supreme-court-confirms-arbitral-tribunals-power-to-hold-remote-hearings-over-one-partys-objection-and-rejects-due-process-concerns/ (accessed 19 April 2021).

within the arbitral tribunal's discretion to decide whether or not a hearing should be held by videoconference and that holding a hearing remotely over the objection of one of the parties does not constitute a violation of due process.[63]

§15.10 DIFFERENT WAYS TO CONDUCT VIRTUAL HEARINGS

The increased use of virtual hearings, whether in full or partial, has stirred up a debate as to whether or not such hearings are in line with due process. So, based on the above, can and does a virtual hearing live up to the requirements of due process in the same way that a traditional hearing does? And in terms of due process arguments, what are the differences between a traditional hearing and a virtual hearing?

A virtual hearing can be conducted in different ways and either fully virtually or virtually in part. At the far end of the spectrum, we have a scenario where all the participants, including the tribunal members, attend the hearing through means of videoconferencing. Another scenario is a hearing where the tribunal is physically present together with the parties in the hearing room, whereas witnesses and experts attend through videoconferencing. It may be desirable for the tribunal members to be together as this facilitates the handling of procedural matters as well as continuous discussion and deliberations throughout the hearing.

During a traditional hearing, the tribunal, parties, witnesses and experts are all physically present in the same room. The parties and the tribunal are thus afforded the opportunity to observe all persons in the room which provides a sense of intimacy at all times.[64] It is difficult to argue that such intimacy is not important when assessing, e.g., the behaviour of a witness, or the reactions of the tribunal in different situations. But is this impossible to achieve through the use of audiovisual equipment?

With modern-day technology, it is hard to imagine that a virtual hearing could not be just as good as a traditional hearing. A virtual hearing can include all elements of a traditional physical hearing, such as opening and closing statements, examination of multiple fact and expert witnesses, and matters of procedural nature. Can these elements of a hearing not be performed just as effectively through advanced audiovisual equipment as through a physical meeting?

The sense of intimacy connected with a traditional hearing where it is possible to observe the participants, their reactions and body language can be achieved also if the hearing is conducted virtually. The quality of the audiovisual equipment can pick up on subtle details such as the trembling hand of a nervous witness. However, one could argue that it may be less intimidating for a witness to be examined virtually than for the witness to physically sit face to face with the person in charge of the examination and the observing tribunal, thus making it more difficult for counsel to throw a witness off balance in cross-examination. Nonetheless, it should be recalled that even the examination of witnesses in criminal cases is considered to be in line with due process by the

63. Scherer, Schwarz, Ortner & Jensen, *supra* n. 62.
64. Lindskog, *supra* n. 20, at 293.

ECtHR.[65] As a result of the technological developments, it would appear that a virtual hearing can be just as good as a traditional hearing, allowing for a live adversarial exchange and thus meeting the standards of due process.[66]

If virtual hearings basically accord with the SAA, it may be asked if that includes asymmetrical virtual hearings, e.g., where one of the parties is physically present through counsel but the other party only virtually present. Or would this not be consistent with the principle of procedural equality and the equal treatment of the parties? As mentioned, the principle of equal treatment of the parties is fundamental in Swedish arbitration law and is expressed in section 21 of the SAA which states, *inter alia*, that the arbitrators shall handle the dispute in an impartial manner. The principle does entail not only that the arbitrators must be impartial but also that the parties must have equal access to procedural benefits.[67] Defining the contours of procedural equality could indeed prove difficult, as is the question of how the principle of procedural equality affects the possibilities of conducting a virtual hearing.

As elaborated above, a virtual hearing can be conducted in many different ways. There are few rules in the SAA regarding the procedure. If the parties are not in agreement as to procedural matters, it is an issue for the arbitrators to decide how to manage the proceedings.[68] Any such decision is, however, subject to the principle of equal treatment of the parties. This principle is, however, not absolute as the arbitrators may deviate from it when, e.g., adhering to the requirement of an appropriate management of the case.[69]

To be on the safe side and avoid the risk of a challenged award, tribunals should ensure that any virtual element of a hearing should be equally provided to both parties. For example, if claimant's witnesses are to be heard by videoconference, the same should be the case for respondent's witnesses. The aforementioned cases from ECtHR where the court assessed videoconferencing and its compliance with the ECHR seem to suggest that due process is not violated even though only one of the parties or one of the parties' witnesses attended the hearing audio visually, provided there was a good reason for this. However, such a procedure appears hazardous and exposes the award to challenge. Still, in order to save time and costs, it is sometimes necessary for certain witnesses or experts to be heard audio visually to facilitate the hearing. This should not automatically amount to a ground for challenge of the award on the basis that the parties have not been treated equally. The question is whether conducting witness examinations through videoconference is a procedural benefit. Even though the ECtHR has stated that physical presence is not an end in itself but serves the greater goal of

65. *Schatschaschwili v. Germany*, case no. 9154/10, https://hudoc.echr.coe.int/eng#{%22itemid%22:[%22001-159566%22]} (accessed 19 April 2021).
66. Erica Stein, 'Chapter 9: Challenges to Remote Arbitration Awards in Setting Aside and Enforcement Proceedings', 173, in Maxi Scherer, Niuscha Bassiri, et al. (eds), *International Arbitration and the COVID-19 Revolution*, (Kluwer Law International 2020).
67. Heuman, *supra* n. 6, at 277.
68. Heuman, *supra* n. 6, at 279.
69. Heuman, *supra* n. 6, at 280.

securing the fairness of the proceedings,[70] it is difficult to see that physical presence is not an advantage compared to presence via videoconference.

Both section 21 of the SAA and Article 23 of the SCC Arbitration Rules contain provisions that require the arbitrators to handle the dispute in an expeditious manner. For obvious reasons, virtual hearings offer an easy way of satisfying this requirement, while also being cost-efficient as a bonus. Irrespective of this, there are views that the pandemic and the delays it has caused and is causing for arbitral proceedings do not constitute a valid reason to conduct an arbitration hearing virtually.[71] However, it has been expressed in Swedish arbitration law that witness examinations may be conducted by phone or videoconference[72] and that witness examination via videoconference may be allowed but must be considered an exception from the requirement for an otherwise physical hearing.[73]

This view may be questioned as the element of a hearing which would reasonably benefit the most from being conducted physically is indeed the witness examinations. Allowing virtual witness examinations as part of an otherwise physical hearing while not allowing a full virtual hearing is a view which seems to stem from an overly rigid interpretation of section 24 of the SAA. A more sensible approach could be inspired by the Swedish Code of Judicial Procedure pursuant to which the *general rule* is that the parties shall be physically present at the hearings, but the court is afforded the opportunity to decide to hold the hearing, when appropriate – fully or in part – through videoconferencing.

While this chapter might not provide any definite answers regarding virtual hearings in arbitrations seated in Sweden, a case pending before the Svea Court of Appeal at the time of writing will hopefully shed some light on the issue.[74] An arbitration award was challenged on grounds that the hearing was conducted virtually. The hearing took place with all counsel and witnesses present by means of videoconferencing. The challenge is based on, *inter alia*, the ground that the claimant had been deprived of its right to an oral hearing in accordance with both section 24 of the SAA and Article 32 of the SCC Arbitration Rules. If the Svea Court of Appeal were to come to the conclusion that virtual hearings fall outside the scope of section 24 of the SAA (and also Article 32 of the SCC Arbitration Rules), this would be somewhat of a surprise in light of recent international best practice. Internationally, the use of virtual hearings is less controversial than what appears to be the case in Sweden.

§15.11 CONCLUDING REMARKS

On the basis of the above and, *inter alia*, case law from the ECtHR, it would appear reasonable to assume that the parties may agree in advance to hold a virtual hearing

70. *Golubev v. Russia*, case no. 26260/02, http://hudoc.echr.coe.int/eng?i=001-78357 (accessed 19 April 2021).
71. Lindskog, *supra* n. 20, at 8.
72. Lindskog, *supra* n. 4, at 727.
73. Lindskog, *supra* n. 20, at 6.
74. Case no. T 7158-20.

and that section 24 of the SAA permits this. Considering that the Swedish Code of Judicial Procedure explicitly permits remote hearings and the use of videoconferencing, it is difficult to regard virtual hearings in arbitration as denying the parties the right to a fair trial.

In order for a virtual hearing to comply with the fundamental principle of due process, it appears important that the virtual hearing, to the extent possible, mimics a traditional physical hearing. To facilitate this, it would be prudent that the hearing participants at a virtual hearing have access to several different video monitors, thus allowing them to view and observe all of the other participants at all times during the hearing without technical impediments. In this regard, it may be noted that, for example, the 'ICC guidance note on possible measures aimed at mitigating the effects of the pandemic'[75] contains a protocol on virtual hearings which may be helpful in meeting the requirements of due process.

The issue of whether a virtual hearing can be held against the objection of a party is yet to be tried under Swedish law in the case currently pending before the Svea Court of Appeal. Consequently, time will tell if a virtual hearing under such circumstances is compatible with section 24 of the SAA, or if it constitutes a ground for a successful challenge of the arbitration award.

75. International Court of Arbitration, *ICC Guidance Note on Possible Measures Aimed at Mitigating the Effects of the COVID-19 Pandemic*, 9 April 2020, https://iccwbo.org/content/uploads/sites/3/2020/04/guidance-note-possible-measures-mitigating-effects-covid-19-english.pdf (accessed 19 April 2021).

STOCKHOLM ARBITRATION YEARBOOK

1. Axel Calissendorff & Patrik Schöldström (eds), *Stockholm Arbitration Yearbook 2019*, 2019 (ISBN 978-94-035-0692-0).
2. Axel Calissendorff & Patrik Schöldström (eds), *Stockholm Arbitration Yearbook 2020*, 2020 (ISBN 978-94-035-2410-8).
3. Axel Calissendorff & Patrik Schöldström (eds), *Stockholm Arbitration Yearbook 2021*, 2021 (ISBN 978-94-035-3524-1).